Xamarin.Forms Projects
Second Edition

Build multiplatform mobile apps and a game from scratch
using C# and Visual Studio 2019

Daniel Hindrikes
Johan Karlsson

BIRMINGHAM - MUMBAI

Xamarin.Forms Projects
Second Edition

Commissioning Editor: Pavan Ramchandani
Acquisition Editor: Heramb Bhavsar
Content Development Editor: Keagan Carneiro
Senior Editor: Sofi Rogers
Technical Editor: Shubham Sharma
Copy Editor: Safis Editing
Project Coordinator: Kinjal Bari
Proofreader: Safis Editing
Indexer: Manju Arasan
Production Designer: Jyoti Chauhan

First published: December 2018

Second edition: June 2020

Production reference: 1180620

Published by Packt Publishing Ltd.
Livery Place
35 Livery Street
Birmingham
B3 2PB, UK.

ISBN 978-1-83921-005-1

www.packt.com

I dedicate this book to all the people I met during my years as a Xamarin developer that never believed in Xamarin. If you read this book, you will hopefully understand how great Xamarin is!

– Daniel Hindrikes

This book is dedicated to the spider in my basement that motivated me to write a book thick enough to finally kill him with.

– Johan Karlsson

Packt.com

Subscribe to our online digital library for full access to over 7,000 books and videos, as well as industry leading tools to help you plan your personal development and advance your career. For more information, please visit our website.

Why subscribe?

- Spend less time learning and more time coding with practical eBooks and Videos from over 4,000 industry professionals

- Improve your learning with Skill Plans built especially for you

- Get a free eBook or video every month

- Fully searchable for easy access to vital information

- Copy and paste, print, and bookmark content

Did you know that Packt offers eBook versions of every book published, with PDF and ePub files available? You can upgrade to the eBook version at www.packt.com and as a print book customer, you are entitled to a discount on the eBook copy. Get in touch with us at customercare@packtpub.com for more details.

At www.packt.com, you can also read a collection of free technical articles, sign up for a range of free newsletters, and receive exclusive discounts and offers on Packt books and eBooks.

Foreword

Sometimes I scratch my head and wonder why Xamarin.Forms continues to rise in developer satisfaction ratings, winning more fans than ever before in its 6-year history. A developer recently said to me, "It's like you listened to our complaints and requests, and just fixed them." While that's an over-simplified summary, I get what they meant. Our program managers and engineers constantly feed their curiosity to figure out how we can delight those using our software. This has led to a faster build and deploy loop, Hot Reload for instant XAML changes in your running app, and Hot Restart for developing on your iOS device directly from Visual Studio on Windows.

Today, Xamarin.Forms ships with more controls "in the box" than ever before, largely thanks to an ever-expanding community of faithful contributors. And what about tomorrow? As I write this, we have just finished Microsoft Build 2020, where we announced our long-term plans for Xamarin.Forms and .NET 6, taking our roadmap all the way into 2022. What a great time to be a Xamarin.Forms and .NET developer! Your investment in .NET for building multi-platform apps will continue to pay off for years to come.

In my role at Microsoft on the .NET team, I'm frequently asked by developers where to find guidance to build Xamarin apps just like those presented in this book. I completely understand why! I love to learn by doing, playing, fiddling, and hopefully not banging my head too hard on the keyboard. Daniel and Johan bring many years of experience to this formula, to lead us down the path of success. I recommend this book to you, whether you are new to Xamarin.Forms or a grizzled .NET veteran. You'll find some lessons that are worth your while.

David Ortinau

Principal Program Manager, .NET

Microsoft

Contributors

About the authors

Daniel Hindrikes is a developer and architect with a passion for developing mobile apps powered by the cloud. Daniel fell in love with Xamarin in the early days of Xamarin when he realized that he could use C# even for iOS and Android apps, and that he could share code with the Windows apps he was also building. But Daniel started to build mobile apps long before that, working on Android apps with Java and even Java ME apps (a long, long time ago).

Daniel enjoys sharing his knowledge and can be found speaking at conferences, blogging, or recording the podcast, *The Code Behind*. Daniel works at the company tretton37 in Sweden and has experience working with both local and global customers.

I want to say a special thanks to my family, my wife, Anna-Karin, and our twins, Ella and Willner, all of whom have supported me during the writing process.

I also would like to say thanks to the fantastic team at Packt and our technical reviewers, Jimmy and Geoff, who helped us to write this book and make us look better than we really are.

Johan Karlsson has been working with Xamarin since the days of MonoTouch and Mono for Android, and it all started with writing a game. He is a full-stack developer, currently focusing on mobile applications using Xamarin, but has in the past worked a lot with ASP.NET MVC, Visual Basic.NET (not proud), and C# in general. Also, he's created a whole bunch of databases in SQL Server over the years.

Johan works at tretton37 in Sweden and has about 20 years' experience in the trade of assembling ones and zeros.

I want to send a special thanks to my partner in life, Elin. Thanks for being there during this special period of time including (but not limited to) moving together, a pandemic, writing a book, and selling a house. And of course to my children, Ville and Lisa, for being an inspiration in life!

Also thanks to Packt and our tech reviewers, Jimmy and Geoff, who nitpicked our applications apart, making us spend late nights correcting our code.

About the reviewers

Jimmy Engstrom wrote his first line of code when he was 7 years old, and it has since that day been his greatest passion. It is a passion that has made him the developer he is today and that has taken him around the world, spreading his knowledge. It has earned him awards such as second place in Dice's worldwide game developer competition, a place in the top-ten best developers in Sweden, six Microsoft MVP awards in Windows development, not to mention becoming Geek of the Year. When he is not out spreading his knowledge, he is working as a web developer, trying out the latest tech, or reading up on the latest framework.

Jimmy also runs his own company called Azm Dev with his wife, where they focus on "future tech" such as Blazor and holographic computing, but also teaching UX and presentation skills. He is the co-host of a podcast called *Coding After Work* and also a Twitch channel with the same name.

> *A big thank you to my wife, Jessica, who has been picking up my slack while reviewing this book.*

Geoff Webber-Cross has over 16 years' software development experience, working in a variety of sectors on Windows, web, and mobile applications. He has worked on XAML/MVVM applications since the days of Silverlight and Windows Phone 7 and has been building Xamarin apps commercially for a number of years. Geoff is also the author of two books for Packt: *Learning Microsoft Azure* and *Learning Windows Azure Mobile Services for Windows 8 and Windows Phone 8*.

Packt is searching for authors like you

If you're interested in becoming an author for Packt, please visit `authors.packtpub.com` and apply today. We have worked with thousands of developers and tech professionals, just like you, to help them share their insight with the global tech community. You can make a general application, apply for a specific hot topic that we are recruiting an author for, or submit your own idea.

Table of Contents

Preface

Xamarin.Forms Projects is a hands-on book in which you get to create nine applications from the ground up. You will gain the fundamental skills you need in order to set up your environment, and we will explain what Xamarin is before we transition into Xamarin.Forms to really take advantage of truly native cross-platform code.

After reading this book, you will have a real-life understanding of what it takes to create an app that you can build on and that stands the test of time.

We will cover, among other things, animations, augmented reality, consuming REST interfaces, real-time chat using SignalR, and location tracking using a device's GPS. There is also room for machine learning and the must-have to-do list.

Happy coding!

Who this book is for

This book is for developers who know their way around C# and Visual Studio. You don't have to be a professional programmer, but you should have basic knowledge of object-oriented programming using .NET and C#. The typical reader would be someone who wants to explore how you can use Xamarin, and specifically Xamarin.Forms, to create applications using .NET and C#.

No knowledge of Xamarin is required in advance, but it would be a great help if you've worked in traditional Xamarin and want to take the step toward Xamarin.Forms.

What this book covers

Chapter 1, *Introduction to Xamarin*, explains the basic concepts of Xamarin and Xamarin.Forms. It helps you understand the building blocks of how to create a true cross-platform app. It's the only theoretical chapter of the book and will help you get started and set up your development environment.

Chapter 2, *Building Our First Xamarin.Forms App*, guides you through the concepts of Model-View-ViewModel and explains how to use the Inversion of Control pattern to simplify the creation of Views and ViewModels. We will create a to-do app that supports navigation, filtering, and the adding of to-do items to a list, and will also render a user interface that takes advantage of the powerful data-binding mechanisms in Xamarin.Forms.

Chapter 3, *Building a News App Using Xamarin.Forms Shell*, explores one of the biggest pieces of news in Xamarin.Forms 4 –Shell, a new way to define the structure of Xamarin.Forms apps. There is also a new navigation system. In this chapter, you will learn all you have to know to use Shell in a Xamarin.Forms app.

Chapter 4, *A Matchmaking App with a Rich UX Using Animations*, lets you dive deeper into how to define a richer user interface with animations and content placement. It also covers the concept of custom controls to encapsulate the user interface into components that are self-contained.

Chapter 5, *Building a Photo Gallery App Using CollectionView and CarouselView*, details how Xamarin.Forms 4 introduces CollectionView and CarouselView. In this chapter, we will use them to build a photo gallery app to learn how to master the controls.

Chapter 6, *Building a Location Tracking App Using GPS and Maps*, taps into the use of geolocation data from the device's GPS and how to plot this data on a layer on a map. It also explains how to use background services to keep tracking the location over a long period of time to create a heat map of where you spend your time.

Chapter 7, *Building a Weather App for Multiple Form Factors*, is all about consuming a third-party REST interface and displaying the data in a user-friendly way. We will hook up to a weather service to get the forecast for the current location you are in and display the results in a list.

Chapter 8, *Setting Up a Backend for a Chat App Using Azure Services*, is the first of a two-part chapter in which we'll set up a chat app. This chapter explains how to use Azure Services to create a backend that exposes functionality through SignalR to set up a real-time communication channel between apps.

Chapter 9, *Building a Real-Time Chat Application*, follows on from the previous chapter and covers the frontend of the app, in this case, a Xamarin.Forms app that connects to the backend and that relays messages between users. The chapter focuses on setting up SignalR on the client side and explains how to create a service model that abstracts this communication through messages and events.

Chapter 10, *Creating an Augmented Reality Game*, ties the two different AR APIs into a single UrhoSharp solution. Android uses ARCore to handle augmented reality, and iOS uses ARKit to do the same. We will drop down into platform-specific APIs through custom renderers and expose the result as a common API for the Xamarin.Forms app to consume.

Chapter 11, *Hot Dog or Not Hot Dog Using Machine Learning*, covers the creation of an app that uses machine learning to identify whether an image contains a hot dog or not.

To get the most out of this book

We recommend that you read the first chapter to make sure that you are up to speed with the basic concepts of Xamarin in general. After that, you could pretty much pick any chapter you would like to learn more about. Each chapter is standalone but the chapters are ordered by complexity; the further you are into the book, the more complex the app will be.

The apps are adapted for real-world use but some parts are left out, such as proper error handling and analytics, since they are out of the scope of the book. You should, however, get a good grasp of the building blocks of how to create an app.

Having said that, it does help if you have been a C# and .NET developer for a while, since many of the concepts are not really app-specific but are good practice in general, such as Model-View-ViewModel and Inversion of Control.

But, most of all, it's a book you can use to kick-start your Xamarin.Forms development learning curve by focusing on what chapters interest you the most.

Software/Hardware covered in the book	OS Requirements
Visual Studio Community Edition. A computer capable of running Windows 10 or later for UWP and Android. A mac that is capable of running macOS Mojave 10.14 to use the iOS simulator	Windows 10 or later, macOS Sierra 10.12 or later
Xcode. A mac that is capable of running macOS Sierra 10.14	macOS Mojave 10.14

If you are using the digital version of this book, we advise you to type the code yourself or access the code via the GitHub repository (link available in the next section). Doing so will help you avoid any potential errors related to the copying and pasting of code.

Download the example code files

You can download the example code files for this book from your account at
www.packt.com. If you purchased this book elsewhere, you can visit
www.packtpub.com/support and register to have the files emailed directly to you.

You can download the code files by following these steps:

1. Log in or register at www.packt.com.
2. Select the **Support** tab.
3. Click on **Code Downloads**.
4. Enter the name of the book in the **Search** box and follow the onscreen
   instructions.

Once the file is downloaded, please make sure that you unzip or extract the folder using the
latest version of:

- WinRAR/7-Zip for Windows
- Zipeg/iZip/UnRarX for Mac
- 7-Zip/PeaZip for Linux

The code bundle for the book is also hosted on GitHub at https://github.com/
PacktPublishing/Xamarin.Forms-4-Projects. In case there's an update to the code, it will
be updated on the existing GitHub repository.

We also have other code bundles from our rich catalog of books and videos available
at https://github.com/PacktPublishing/. Check them out!

Download the color images

We also provide a PDF file that has color images of the screenshots/diagrams used in this
book. You can download it here: https://static.packt-cdn.com/downloads/
9781839210051_ColorImages.pdf.

Conventions used

There are a number of text conventions used throughout this book.

`CodeInText`: Indicates code words in text, database table names, folder names, filenames, file extensions, pathnames, dummy URLs, user input, and Twitter handles. Here is an example: "Mount the downloaded `WebStorm-10*.dmg` disk image file as another disk in your system."

A block of code is set as follows:

```
html, body, #map {
  height: 100%;
  margin: 0;
  padding: 0
}
```

When we wish to draw your attention to a particular part of a code block, the relevant lines or items are set in bold:

```
[default]
exten => s,1,Dial(Zap/1|30)
exten => s,2,Voicemail(u100)
exten => s,102,Voicemail(b100)
exten => i,1,Voicemail(s0)
```

Any command-line input or output is written as follows:

```
$ mkdir css
$ cd css
```

Bold: Indicates a new term, an important word, or words that you see onscreen. For example, words in menus or dialog boxes appear in the text like this. Here is an example: "Select **System info** from the **Administration** panel."

Warnings or important notes appear like this.

Tips and tricks appear like this.

Get in touch

Feedback from our readers is always welcome.

General feedback: If you have questions about any aspect of this book, mention the book title in the subject of your message and email us at customercare@packtpub.com.

Errata: Although we have taken every care to ensure the accuracy of our content, mistakes do happen. If you have found a mistake in this book, we would be grateful if you would report this to us. Please visit www.packtpub.com/support/errata, selecting your book, clicking on the Errata Submission Form link, and entering the details.

Piracy: If you come across any illegal copies of our works in any form on the Internet, we would be grateful if you would provide us with the location address or website name. Please contact us at copyright@packt.com with a link to the material.

If you are interested in becoming an author: If there is a topic that you have expertise in and you are interested in either writing or contributing to a book, please visit authors.packtpub.com.

Reviews

Please leave a review. Once you have read and used this book, why not leave a review on the site that you purchased it from? Potential readers can then see and use your unbiased opinion to make purchase decisions, we at Packt can understand what you think about our products, and our authors can see your feedback on their book. Thank you!

For more information about Packt, please visit packt.com.

Introduction to Xamarin

1

This chapter is all about getting to know Xamarin and what to expect from it. It is the only chapter that is pure theory; all the others cover hands-on projects. You are not expected to write any code at this point, but instead, simply read through this chapter to develop a high-level understanding of what Xamarin is and how Xamarin.Forms relates to Xamarin and how to set up a development machine.

We will start by defining what a native app is and what .NET as a technology brings to the table. After that, we will look at how Xamarin.Forms fits into the bigger picture and learn when it is appropriate to use the traditional Xamarin and Xamarin.Forms apps. We often use the term **traditional Xamarin** to describe apps that don't use Xamarin.Forms, even though Xamarin.Forms apps are bootstrapped through a traditional Xamarin app.

In this chapter, we will cover the following topics:

- Native applications
- Xamarin and Mono
- Xamarin.Forms
- Setting up a development machine

Let's get started!

Native applications

The term **native application** means different things to different people. For some people, it is an app that is developed using the tools specified by the creator of the platform, such as an app developed for iOS with Objective-C or Swift, an Android app developed with Java or Kotlin, or a Windows app developed with .NET. Others use the term native application to refer to apps that are compiled into machine code that is native. In this book, we will define a native application as one that has a native UI, performance, and API access. The following list explains these three concepts in greater detail:

- **Native UI**: Apps built with Xamarin use the standard controls for each platform. This means, for example, that an iOS app built with Xamarin will look and behave as an iOS user would expect and an Android app built with Xamarin will look and behave as an Android user would expect.

- **Native performance**: Apps built with Xamarin are compiled for native performance and can use platform-specific hardware acceleration.

- **Native API access:** Native API access means that apps built with Xamarin can use everything that the target platforms and devices offer to developers.

Xamarin and Mono

Xamarin is a developer platform that is used to develop native applications for iOS (Xamarin.iOS), Android (Xamarin.Android), and macOS (Xamarin.Mac). It is technically a binding layer on top of these platforms. Binding to platform APIs enables .NET developers to use C# (and F#) to develop native applications with the full capacity of each platform. The C# APIs we use when we develop apps with Xamarin are more or less identical to the platform APIs, but they are **.NETified**. For example, APIs are often customized to follow .NET naming conventions and the Android `set` and `get` methods are often replaced by properties. The reason for this is that APIs should be easier to use for .NET developers.

Mono (`https://www.mono-project.com`) is an open source implementation of the Microsoft .NET framework, which is based on the **European Computer Manufacturers Association (ECMA)** standards for C# and the **Common Language Runtime (CLR)**. Mono was created to bring the .NET framework to platforms other than Windows. It is part of the .NET Foundation (`http://www.dotnetfoundation.org`), an independent organization that supports open development and collaboration involving the .NET ecosystem.

With a combination of the Xamarin platforms and Mono, we can use both the platform-specific APIs and the platform-independent parts of .NET, including namespaces, systems, System.Linq, System.IO, System.Net, and System.Threading.Tasks.

There are several reasons for using Xamarin for mobile app development, which we will cover in the following sections.

> When .NET 5 is released, it will partly replace Mono. We will get one unified **Base Class Library** (**BCL**) for all the .NET platforms. Xamarin.iOS will still run on the Mono runtime because iOS apps need to be **Ahead Of Time** (**AOT**) compiled. The .NET runtime (currently called .NET Core Runtime) will not support AOT.

Code sharing

If we use one common programming language for multiple mobile platforms (and even server platforms), then we can share a lot of code between our target platforms, as illustrated in the following diagram. All code that isn't related to the target platform can be shared with other .NET platforms. Code that is typically shared in this way includes business logic, network calls, and data models:

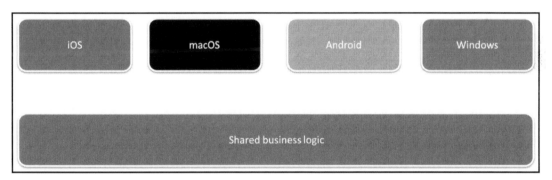

There is also a large community based around the .NET platforms, as well as a wide range of third-party libraries and components that can be downloaded from NuGet (https://nuget.org) and used across the .NET platforms.

Code sharing across platforms leads to shorter development times. It also produces apps of a higher quality because, for example, we only need to write the code for business logic once. There is a lower risk of bugs and are also be able to guarantee that a calculation returns the same result, regardless of what platform our users use.

Using existing knowledge

For .NET developers who want to start building native mobile apps, it is easier to just learn the APIs for the new platforms than it is to learn programming languages and APIs for both old and new platforms.

Similarly, organizations that want to build native mobile apps can use existing developers with their knowledge of .NET to develop apps. Because there are more .NET developers than Objective-C and Swift developers, it's easier to find new developers for mobile app development projects.

Xamarin platforms

The different Xamarin platforms available are Xamarin.iOS, Xamarin.Android, and Xamarin.Mac. In this section, we will take a look at each of them.

Xamarin.iOS

Xamarin.iOS is used to build apps for iOS with .NET and contains the bindings to the iOS APIs mentioned previously. Xamarin.iOS uses AOT compiling to compile the C# code into **Advanced RISC Machine (ARM)** assembly language. The Mono runtime runs alongside the Objective-C runtime. Code that uses .NET namespaces, such as `System.Linq` or `System.Net`, are executed by the Mono runtime, while code that uses iOS-specific namespaces are executed by the Objective-C runtime. Both the Mono runtime and the Objective-C runtime run on top of the **X is Not Unix (XNU)** Unix-like kernel (`https://github.com/apple/darwin-xnu`), which was developed by Apple. The following diagram shows an overview of the iOS architecture:

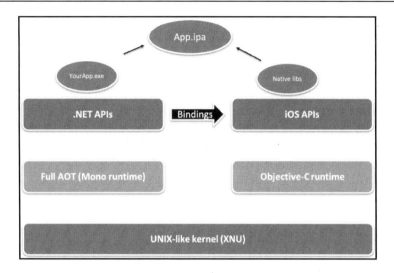

Xamarin.Android

Xamarin.Android is used to build apps for Android with .NET and contains bindings to the Android APIs. The Mono runtime and the **Android Runtime** (**ART**) run side by side on top of a Linux kernel. Xamarin.Android apps could either be **Just-In-Time** (**JIT**)-compiled or AOT-compiled, but to AOT-compile them, we need to use Visual Studio Enterprise.

Communication between the Mono runtime and ART occurs via a **Java Native Interface** (**JNI**) bridge. There are two types of JNI bridges—**Manage Callable Wrapper** (**MCW**) and **Android Callable Wrapper** (**ACW**). An MCW is used when code needs to run in ART and an ACW is used when ART needs to run code in the Mono runtime, as shown:

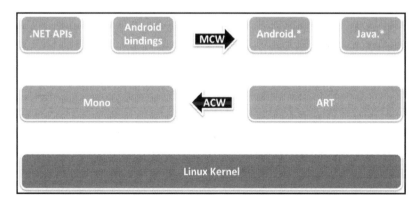

Xamarin.Mac

Xamarin.Mac is used to build apps for macOS with .NET and contains the bindings to the macOS APIs. Xamarin.Mac has the same architecture as Xamarin.iOS—the only difference is that Xamarin.Mac apps are JIT-compiled, unlike Xamarin.iOS apps, which are AOT-compiled. This is shown in the following diagram:

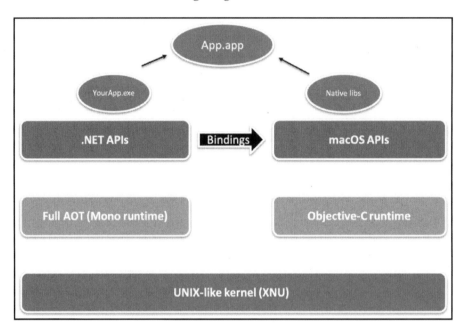

Xamarin.Forms

Xamarin.Forms is a UI framework that is built on top of Xamarin (for iOS and Android) and the **Universal Windows Platform** (**UWP**). Xamarin.Forms allows developers to create a UI for iOS, Android, and UWP with one shared code base, as illustrated in the following diagram. If we build an app with Xamarin.Forms, we can use XAML, C#, or a combination of both to create the UI:

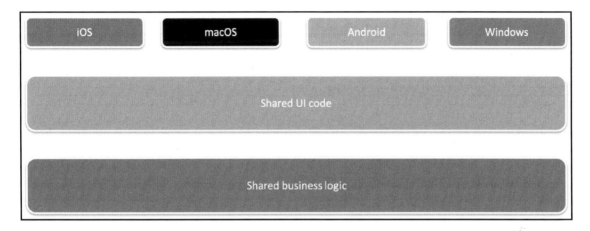

The architecture of Xamarin.Forms

Xamarin.Forms is more or less just an abstract layer on top of each platform. Xamarin.Forms has a shared layer that is used by all platforms, as well as a platform-specific layer. The platform-specific layer contains renderers. A renderer is a class that maps a Xamarin.Forms control to a platform-specific native control. Each Xamarin.Forms control has a platform-specific renderer.

The following diagram illustrates how entry control in Xamarin.Forms is rendered to a `UITextField` control from the `UIKit` namespace when the shared Xamarin.Forms code is used in an iOS app. The same code in Android renders an `EditText` control from the `Android.Widget` namespace:

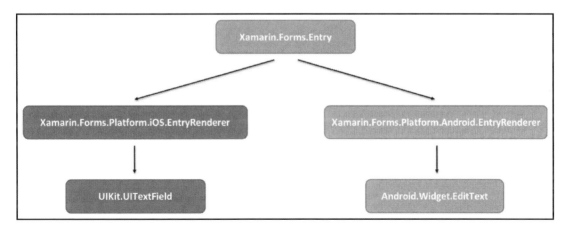

Defining a UI using XAML

The most common way to declare our UI in Xamarin.Forms is by defining it in a XAML document. It is also possible to create the GUI in C#, since XAML is really only a markup language for instantiating objects. We could, in theory, use XAML to create any type of object, as long as it has a parameterless constructor. A XAML document is an **Extensible Markup Language** (**XML**) document with a specific schema.

Defining a Label control

As a simple example, let's look at the following snippet of a XAML document:

```
<Label Text="Hello World!" />
```

When the XAML parser encounters this snippet, it creates an instance of a Label object and then sets the properties of the object that correspond to the attributes in the XAML. This means that if we set a Text property in XAML, it sets the Text property on the instance of the Label object that is created. The XAML in the preceding example has the same effect as the following:

```
var obj = new Label()
{
    Text = "Hello World!"
};
```

XAML exists to make it easier to view the object hierarchy that we need to create in order to make a GUI. An object model for a GUI is also hierarchical by design, so XAML supports adding child objects. We can simply add them as child nodes, as follows:

```
<StackLayout>
    <Label Text="Hello World" />
    <Entry Text="Ducks are us" />
</StackLayout>
```

StackLayout is a container control that organizes the children vertically or horizontally within a container. Vertical organization is the default value and is used unless we specify otherwise. There are also a number of other containers, such as Grid and FlexLayout. These will be used in many of the projects in the following chapters.

Creating a page in XAML

A single control is no use unless it has a container that hosts it. Let's see what an entire page would look like. A fully valid `ContentPage` object defined in XAML is an XML document. This means that we must start with an XML declaration. After that, we must have one—and only one—root node, as shown:

```
<?xml version="1.0" encoding="UTF-8"?>
<ContentPage
    xmlns="http://xamarin.com/schemas/2014/forms"
    xmlns:x="http://schemas.microsoft.com/winfx/2009/xaml"
    x:Class="MyApp.MainPage">

    <StackLayout>
        <Label Text="Hello world!" />
    </StackLayout>
</ContentPage>
```

In the preceding example, we defined a `ContentPage` object that translates into a single view on each platform. In order to make it a valid XAML, we need to specify a default namespace (`xmlns="http://xamarin.com/schemas/2014/forms"`) and then add the x namespace (`xmlns:x="http://schemas.microsoft.com/winfx/2009/xaml"`).

The default namespace lets us create objects without prefixing them, such as the `StackLayout` object. The x namespace lets us access properties such as `x:Class`, which tells the XAML parser which class to instantiate to control the page when the `ContentPage` object is created.

A `ContentPage` object can have only one child. In this case, it's a `StackLayout` control. Unless we specify otherwise, the default layout orientation is vertical. A `StackLayout` object can, therefore, have multiple children. Later on, we will touch on more advanced layout controls, such as the `Grid` and `FlexLayout` controls.

In this specific example, we will create a `Label` control as the first child of `StackLayout`.

Creating a page in C#

For clarity, the following code shows you how the previous example would look in C#:

```
public class MainPage : ContentPage
{
}
```

page is a class that inherits from Xamarin.Forms.ContentPage. This class is automatically generated for us if we create an XAML page, but if we just use code, we will need to define it ourself.

Let's create the same control hierarchy as the XAML page we defined earlier using the following code:

```
var page = new MainPage();

var stacklayout = new StackLayout();
stacklayout.Children.Add(
    new Label()
    {
        Text = "Welcome to Xamarin.Forms"
    });

page.Content = stacklayout;
```

The first statement creates a page object. We could, in theory, create a new ContentPage page directly, but this would prohibit us from writing any code behind it. For this reason, it's good practice to subclass each page that we plan to create.

The block following this first statement creates the StackLayout control, which contains the Label control that is added to the Children collection.

Finally, we need to assign StackLayout to the Content property of the page.

XAML or C#?

Generally, using XAML provides a much better overview, since the page is a hierarchical structure of objects and XAML is a very nice way of defining that structure. In code, the structure is flipped around as we need to define the innermost object first, making it harder to read the structure of our page. This was demonstrated in the *Creating a page in XAML* section of this chapter. Having said that, it is generally a matter of preference as to how we decide to define the GUI. This book will use XAML rather than C# in the projects to come.

Xamarin.Forms versus traditional Xamarin

While this book is about Xamarin.Forms, we will also highlight the differences between using traditional Xamarin and Xamarin.Forms. Traditional Xamarin is used when developing apps that use iOS and an Android **Software Development Kit** (**SDK**) without any means of abstraction. For example, we can create an iOS app that defines its UI in a storyboard or in the code directly. This code would not be reusable for other platforms, such as Android. Apps built using this approach can still share non-platform-specific code by simply referencing a .NET standard library. This relationship is shown in the following diagram:

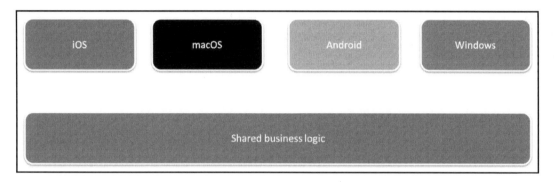

Xamarin.Forms, on the other hand, is an abstraction of the GUI, which allows us to define UIs in a platform-agnostic way. It still builds on top of Xamarin.iOS, Xamarin.Android, and all the other supported platforms. The Xamarin.Forms app can be created as a .NET standard library or as a shared code project, where the source files are linked as copies and built within the same project as the platform we are currently building for. This relationship is shown in the following diagram:

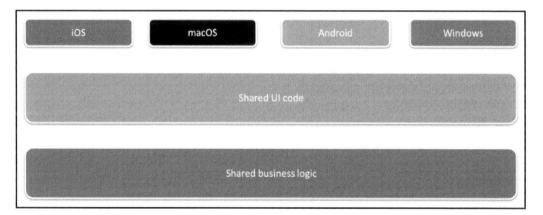

Having said that, Xamarin.Forms cannot exist without traditional Xamarin since it's bootstrapped through an app for each platform. This gives us the ability to extend Xamarin.Forms on each platform using custom renderers and platform-specific code that can be exposed to our shared code base through interfaces. We'll look at these concepts in more detail later on in this chapter.

When to use Xamarin.Forms

We can use Xamarin.Forms in most cases and for most types of apps. If we need to use controls that not are available in Xamarin.Forms, we can always use the platform-specific APIs. There are, however, cases where Xamarin.Forms is not useful. The most common situation where we might want to avoid using Xamarin.Forms is if we build an app that should look very different across our different target platforms.

Setting up a development machine

Developing an app for multiple platforms imposes higher demands on our development machine. One reason for this is that we often want to run one or multiple simulators or emulators on our development machine. Different platforms also have different requirements with regard to what is needed to begin development. Regardless of whether we use macOS or Windows, Visual Studio will be our **integrated development environment (IDE)**. There are several versions of Visual Studio, including the free community edition. Go to `https://visualstudio.microsoft.com/` to compare the available versions. The following list is a summary of what we need to begin development for each platform:

- **iOS**: To develop an app for iOS, we need a **Macintosh (Mac)** device. This could either be the machine that we are developing on or a machine on our network, if we are using one. The reason we need to connect to a Mac is that we need to use Xcode to compile and debug an app. Xcode also provides an iOS simulator. It is possible to do some iOS development on Windows without a connected Mac; you can read more about this in the *Xamarin Hot Restart* section of this chapter.
- **Android**: Android apps can be developed on either macOS or Windows. Everything we need, including SDKs and simulators, are installed with Visual Studio.
- **UWP**: UWP apps can only be developed in Visual Studio on a Windows machine.

Setting up a Mac

There are two main tools that are required to develop apps for iOS and Android with Xamarin on a Mac. These are Visual Studio for Mac (if we are only developing Android apps, this is the only tool we need) and Xcode. In the following sections, we will take a look at how to set up a Mac for app development.

Installing Xcode

Before we install Visual Studio, we need to download and install Xcode. Xcode is the official development IDE from Apple and contains all the tools available for iOS development, including SDKs for iOS, macOS, tvOS, and watchOS.

We can download Xcode from the Apple developer portal (`https://developer.apple.com`) or from the Apple App Store. I recommend that you download it from the App Store because this guarantees you have the latest stable version. The only reason to download Xcode from the developer portal is if you want to use a prerelease version of Xcode to develop it for a prerelease of iOS.

After the first installation, and after each update of Xcode, it is important that you open it. Xcode often needs to install additional components after an installation or an update. We also need to open Xcode to accept the license agreement with Apple.

Installing Visual Studio

To install Visual Studio, we first need to download it from `https://visualstudio.microsoft.com`.

When we start the Visual Studio installer via the file we downloaded, it will start to check what we already have installed on our machine. When the check is finished, we can select which platforms and tools we would like to install.

Once we have selected the platforms that we want to install, Visual Studio downloads and installs everything that we need to get started with app development using Xamarin, as shown:

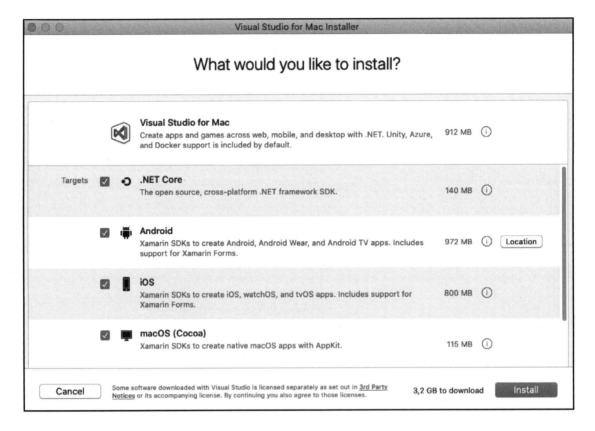

Configuring the Android emulator

Visual Studio uses the Android emulators provided by Google. If we want our emulator to be fast, then we need to ensure that it is hardware-accelerated. To hardware-accelerate the Android emulator, we need to install the **Intel Hardware Accelerated Execution Manager (HAXM)**, which can be downloaded from `https://software.intel.com/en-us/articles/intel-hardware-accelerated-execution-manager-intel-haxm`.

The next step is to create the Android emulator. First, we need to ensure that the Android emulator and the Android OS images are installed. To do this, take the following steps:

1. Go to the **Tools** tab to install the Android emulator:

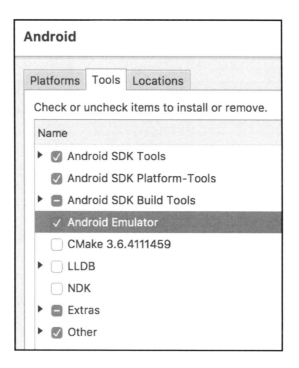

2. We also need to install one or multiple images to use with the emulator. We can install multiple images if, for example, we want to run our app on different versions of Android. We can select emulators with Google Play (as in the following screenshot) so that we can use Google Play services in our app, even when we are running it in an emulator. This is required if, for example, we want to use Google Maps in our app:

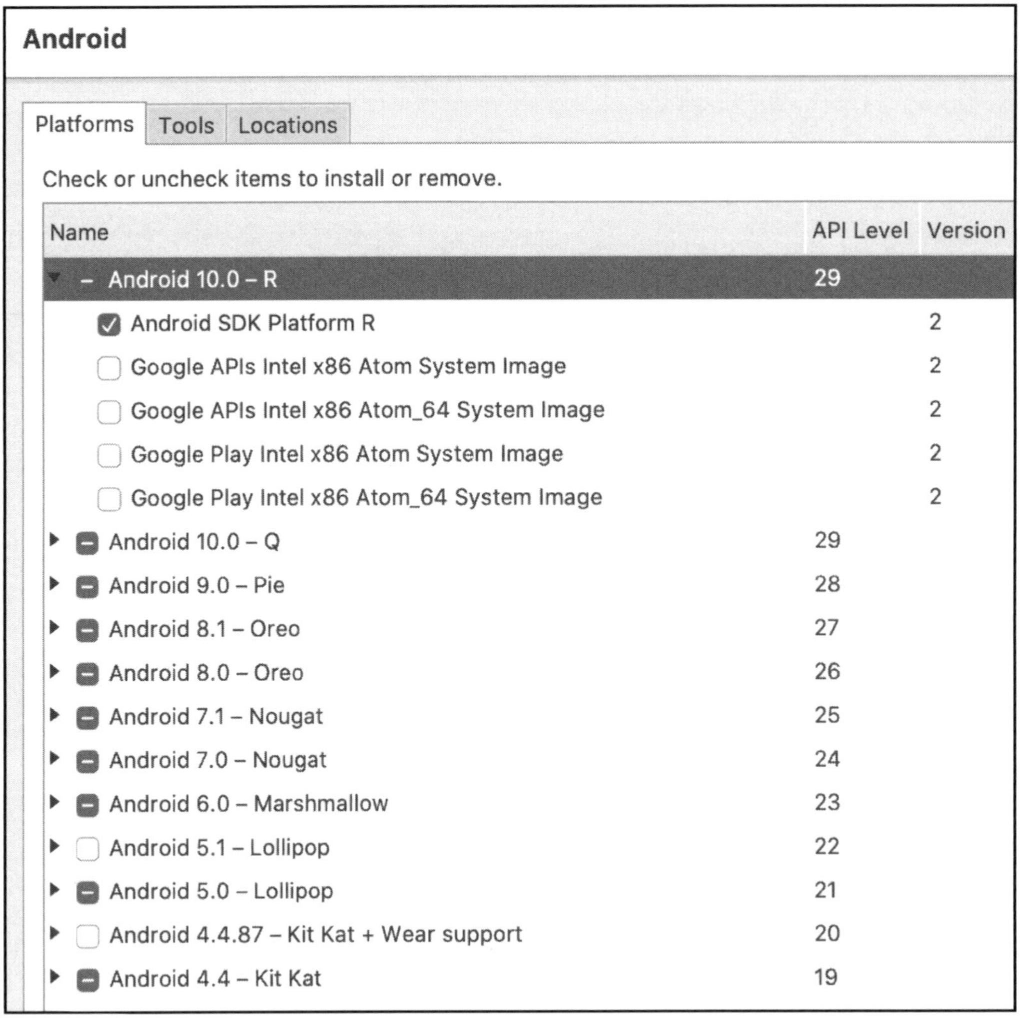

Android

| Platforms | Tools | Locations |

Check or uncheck items to install or remove.

Name	API Level	Version
▼ – Android 10.0 – R	29	
☑ Android SDK Platform R		2
☐ Google APIs Intel x86 Atom System Image		2
☐ Google APIs Intel x86 Atom_64 System Image		2
☐ Google Play Intel x86 Atom System Image		2
☐ Google Play Intel x86 Atom_64 System Image		2
▶ ⊖ Android 10.0 – Q	29	
▶ ⊖ Android 9.0 – Pie	28	
▶ ⊖ Android 8.1 – Oreo	27	
▶ ⊖ Android 8.0 – Oreo	26	
▶ ⊖ Android 7.1 – Nougat	25	
▶ ⊖ Android 7.0 – Nougat	24	
▶ ⊖ Android 6.0 – Marshmallow	23	
▶ ☐ Android 5.1 – Lollipop	22	
▶ ⊖ Android 5.0 – Lollipop	21	
▶ ☐ Android 4.4.87 – Kit Kat + Wear support	20	
▶ ⊖ Android 4.4 – Kit Kat	19	

3. Then, to create and configure an emulator, go to **Device Manager** in the **Android** section of the **Tools** tab in Visual Studio. From **Android Device Manager**, we can start an emulator if we already have one created; or, we can create new emulators, as shown:

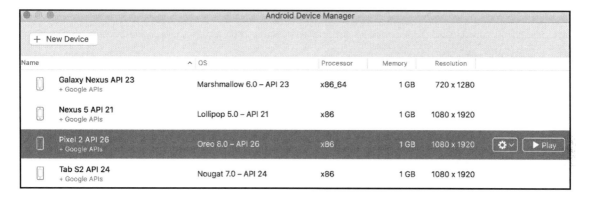

4. If we click on the **New Device** button, we can create a new emulator with the specifications that we need. The easiest way to create a new emulator here is to select a base device that matches our needs. These base devices are preconfigured, which is often enough. However, it is also possible to edit the properties of the device so that we have an emulator that matches our specific needs.

Because we will not run the emulator on a device with an ARM processor, we have to select either an **x86** processor or an **x64** processor, as in the following screenshot. If we try to use an ARM processor, the emulator will be very slow:

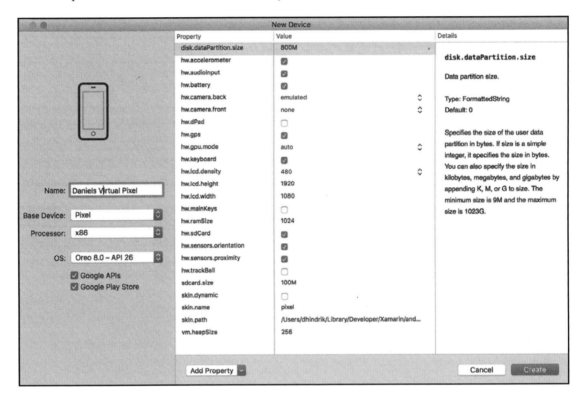

Setting up a Windows machine

We can use either a virtual or physical Windows machine for development with Xamarin. We can, for example, run a virtual Windows machine on our Mac. The only tool we need for app development on our Windows machine is Visual Studio.

Installing Xamarin for Visual Studio

If we already have Visual Studio installed, we first need to open **Visual Studio Installer**; otherwise, we need to go to `https://visualstudio.microsoft.com` to download the installation files.

Before the installation starts, we need to select which workloads we want to install.

If we want to develop apps for Windows, we need to select the **Universal Windows Platform development** workload, as shown:

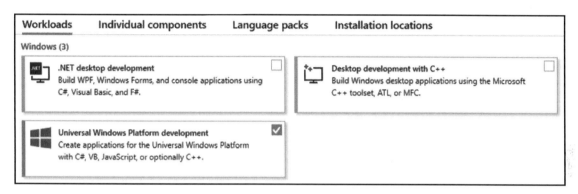

For Xamarin development, we need to install **Mobile development with .NET**. If you want to use Hyper-V for hardware acceleration, you can deselect the checkbox for Intel HAXM in the detailed description of the **Mobile development with .NET** workload on the left-hand side, as in the following screenshot. When you deselect Intel HAXM, the Android emulator is also deselected, but you can reinstall it later:

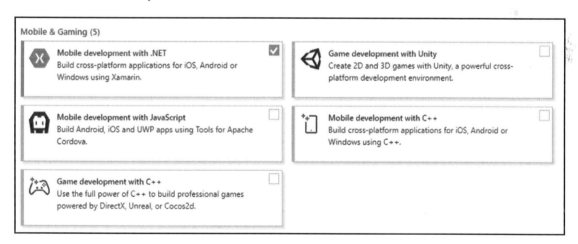

When we first start Visual Studio, we will be asked whether we want to sign in. It is not necessary for us to sign in unless we want to use Visual Studio Profession or Enterprise, in which case we will need to sign in so that our license can be verified.

Pairing Visual Studio with a Mac

If we want to run, debug, and compile our iOS app, then we need to connect it to a Mac. We can set up our Mac manually, as described earlier in this chapter, or we can use **Automatic Mac Provisioning**. This installs Mono and Xamarin.iOS on the Mac that we are connecting to. It will not install the Visual Studio IDE, but this isn't necessary if we just want to use it as a build machine. We do, however, need to install Xcode manually.

To be able to connect to a Mac—either manually or using **Automatic Mac Provisioning**—we need to be able to access the Mac via our network, and we need to enable **Remote Login** on the Mac. To do this, go to **Settings** | **Sharing** and select the checkbox for **Remote Login**. To the left of the window, we can select which users are allowed to connect with **Remote Login**, as shown:

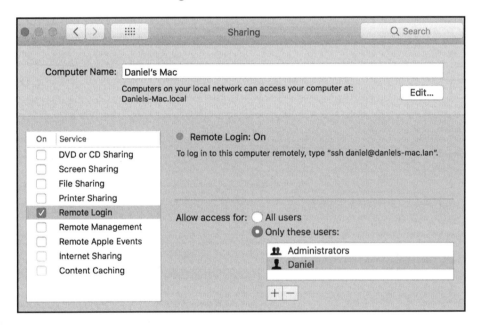

To connect to the Mac from Visual Studio, use the **Pair to Mac** button in the toolbar (as in the following screenshot); or, in the top menu, go to **Tools** | **iOS** | **Pair to Mac**:

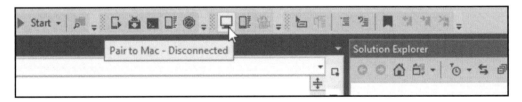

A dialog box will appear showing all the Macs that can be found on the network. If your Mac doesn't appear in the list of available Macs, we can use the **Add Mac...** button at the bottom-left corner of the window to enter an IP address, as shown:

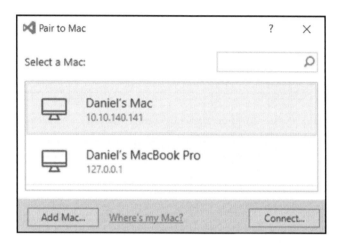

If everything that we need is installed on the Mac, then Visual Studio will connect and we can start building and debugging our iOS app. If Mono is missing on the Mac, a warning will appear. This warning will also give us the option to install it, as shown:

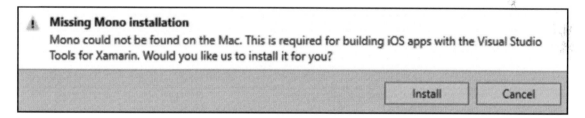

Configuring an Android emulator and hardware acceleration

If we want a fast Android emulator that works smoothly, we need to enable hardware acceleration. This can be done using either Intel HAXM or Hyper-V. The disadvantage of Intel HAXM is that it can't be used on machines with an **Advanced Micro Devices** (**AMD**) processor; we have to use a machine with an Intel processor. We can't use Intel HAXM in parallel with Hyper-V.

Because of this, Hyper-V is the preferred way to hardware-accelerate an Android emulator on a Windows machine. To use Hyper-V with our Android emulator, we need to have the April 2018 update (or later) for Windows and Visual Studio version 15.8 (or later) installed. To enable Hyper-V, we need to take the following steps:

1. Open the Start menu and type in **Turn Windows features on or off**. Click the option that appears to open it, as shown:

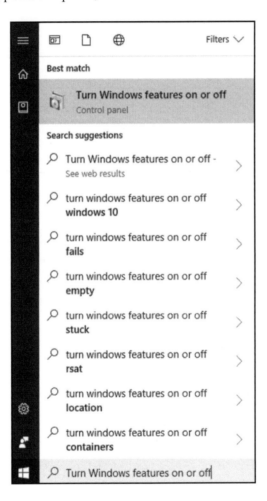

2. To enable Hyper-V, select the **Hyper-V** checkbox. Also, expand the **Hyper-V** option and check the **Hyper-V Platform** checkbox. We also need to select the **Windows Hypervisor Platform** checkbox, as shown:

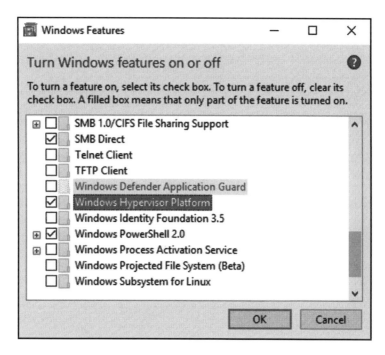

3. Restart the machine when Windows prompts you to.

Because we didn't install an Android emulator during the installation of Visual Studio, we need to install it now. Go to the **Tools** menu in Visual Studio, then click on **Android** and then **Android SDK Manager**.

Under **Tools** in **Android SDK Manager**, we can install the emulator by selecting **Android Emulator**, as in the following screenshot. Also, we should ensure that the latest version of **Android SDK Build Tools** is installed:

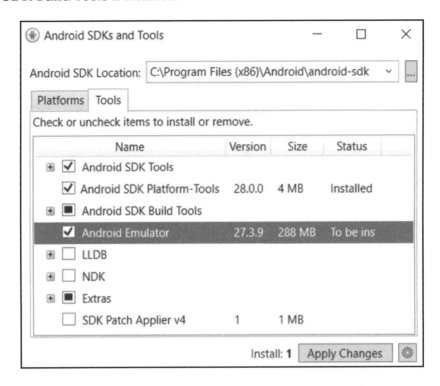

We also recommend installing the Native Development Kit (NDK). The NDK makes it possible to import libraries that are written in C or C++. An NDK is also required if we want to AOT-compile an app.

The Android SDK allows multiple emulator images to be installed simultaneously. We can install multiple images if, for example, we want to run our app on different versions of Android. Select emulators with **Google Play** (as in the following screenshot) so that we can use Google Play services in our app, even when we are running it in an emulator.

This is required if, for example, we want to use Google Maps in our app:

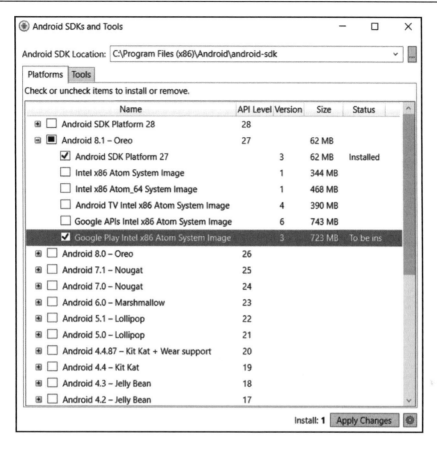

The next step is to create a virtual device to use the emulator image. To create and configure an emulator, go to **Android Device Manager**, which we can open from the **Tools** tab in Visual Studio. From the device manager, we can either start an emulator—if we already have one created—or we can create new emulators, as shown:

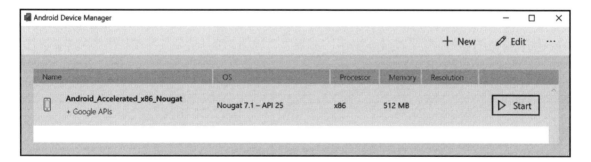

If we click on the **New Device** button, we can create a new emulator with the specifications that we need. The easiest way to create a new emulator here is to select a base device that matches our needs. These base devices are preconfigured, which is often enough. However, it is possible to edit the properties of the device so that we have an emulator that matches our specific needs.

We have to select either an **x86** processor (as in the following screenshot) or an **x64** processor since we are not running the emulator on a device with an ARM processor. If we try to use an ARM processor, the emulator will be very slow:

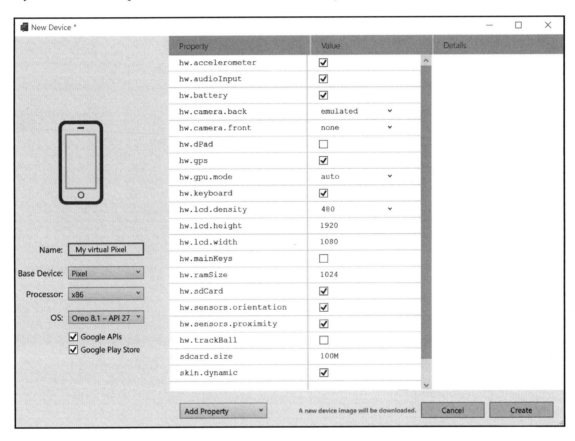

Configuring UWP developer mode

If we want to develop UWP apps, we need to activate developer mode on our development machine. To do this, go to **Settings** | **Update & Security** | **For developers**. Then, click on **Developer Mode**, as in the following screenshot. This makes it possible for us to sideload and debug apps via Visual Studio:

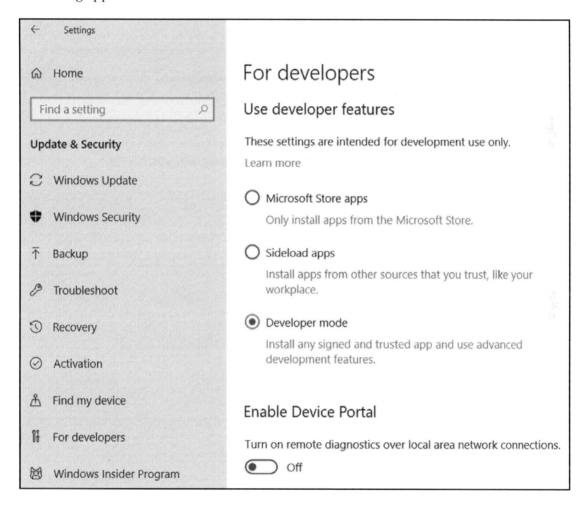

If we select **Sideload apps** instead of **Developer mode**, we will only be able to install apps without going to Microsoft Store. If we have a machine to test, rather than debug our apps on, we can just select **Sideload apps**.

Xamarin productivity tooling

Xamarin Hot Restart and Xamarin Hot Reload are two tools that increase productivity for Xamarin developers.

Xamarin Hot Restart

Hot Restart is a Visual Studio feature, which is currently in preview, to make developers more productive. It also gives us a way of running and debugging iOS apps on an iPhone without having to use a Mac connected to Visual Studio. Microsoft describes Hot Restart as follows:

"Xamarin Hot Restart enables you to quickly test changes to your app during development, including multi-file code edits, resources, and references. It pushes the new changes to the existing app bundle on the debug target which results in a much faster build and deploy cycle."

To use Hot Restart, you need the following:

- Visual Studio 2019 version 16.5 or later
- iTunes (64 bit)
- An Apple Developer account and paid Apple Developer Program (https://developer.apple.com/programs/) enrollment

Hot Restart can currently only be used with Xamarin.Forms apps.

To activate Hot Restart, go to **Tools** | **Options** | **Environment** | **Preview Features** | **Enable Xamarin Hot Restart**.

Read more about the current state of Hot Restart at https://docs.microsoft.com/en-us/xamarin/xamarin-forms/deploy-test/hot-restart.

Xamarin XAML Hot Reload

Xamarin XAML Hot Reload allows us to make changes to our XAML without having to redeploy our app. When we have carried out changes to the XAML, we just save the file and it updates the page on the simulator/emulator or on a device. XAML Hot Reload is currently only supported by iOS and Android.

To enable XAML Hot Reload for Visual Studio on Windows, go to **Visual Studio** | **Preferences** | **Tools for Xamarin** | **XAML Hot Reload**.

To enable XAML Hot Reload for Visual Studio on Mac, go
to **Tools** | **Options** | **Xamarin** | **Hot Reload**.

To use XAML Hot Reload, we have to use Xamarin.Forms 4.1+ with Visual Studio 2019
16.4+ (or Visual Studio for Mac 8.4+).

Summary

You should now feel a bit more comfortable about what Xamarin is and how
Xamarin.Forms relates to Xamarin itself.

In this chapter, we established a definition of what a native app is and saw how it has a
native UI, native performance, and native API access. We talked about how Xamarin is
based on Mono, which is an open source implementation of the .NET framework, and
discussed how, at its core, Xamarin is a set of bindings to platform-specific APIs. We then
looked at how Xamarin.iOS and Xamarin.Android work under the hood.

After that, we began to touch on the core topic of this book, which is Xamarin.Forms. We
started off with an overview of how platform-agnostic controls are rendered to platform-
specific controls and how to use XAML to define a hierarchy of controls to assemble a page.
We then spent some time looking at the difference between a Xamarin.Forms app and a
traditional Xamarin app.

A traditional Xamarin app uses platform-specific APIs directly, without any abstraction,
other than what .NET adds as a platform. Xamarin.Forms is an API that is built on top of
the traditional Xamarin APIs and allows us to define platform-agnostic GUIs in XAML or in
code that is rendered to platform-specific controls. There's more to Xamarin.Forms than
this, but this is what it does at its core.

In the last part of this chapter, we discussed how to set up a development machine on
Windows or macOS.

Now, it's time to put our newly acquired knowledge to use! We will start off by creating a
to-do app from the ground up in the next chapter. We will look at concepts such
as **Model–View–ViewModel** (**MVVM**) for a clean separation between business logic and
the UI, and SQLite.NET to persist data to a local database on our device. We will do this for
three platforms at the same time—so, read on!

2
Building Our First Xamarin.Forms App

In this chapter, we will create a to-do list app and, in doing so, explore all the bits and pieces of what makes up an app. We will look at creating pages, adding content to pages, navigating between pages, and creating a stunning layout. Well, *stunning* might be a bit of a stretch, but we will be sure to design the app so that you can tweak it to your needs once it is complete!

The following topics will be covered in this chapter:

- Setting up the project
- Persisting data locally on a device
- Using the repository pattern
- What MVVM is and why it's a great fit for Xamarin.Forms
- Using Xamarin.Forms pages (as views) and navigating between them
- Using Xamarin.Forms controls in XAML
- Using data binding
- Using styling in Xamarin.Forms

Technical requirements

To complete this project, you need to have Visual Studio installed to your **Macintosh** (**Mac**) or PC, as well as the Xamarin components. Refer to `Chapter 1`, *Introduction to Xamarin*, for more details on how to set up your environment.

An overview of the project

Everyone needs a way of keeping track of things. To kick-start our Xamarin.Forms development learning curve, we've decided that a to-do list app is the best way to get started and to help you keep track of things. A simple, classic win-win scenario.

We will start by creating a project and defining a repository to store the items of a to-do list. We will render these items in list form and allow the user to edit them using a detailed user interface. We will also look at how to store the to-do list items locally on a device through **SQLite.NET** so that they don't get lost when we exit the app.

The build time for this project is about 2 hours.

Beginning the project

It's time to start coding! Before starting, however, make sure you have your development environment set up as described in `Chapter 1`, *Introduction to Xamarin*.

This chapter will be a classic **File** | **New** | **Project** chapter, guiding you step by step through the process of creating your first to-do list app. There will be no downloads required whatsoever.

Setting up the project

A Xamarin app can essentially be created by using one of two code-sharing strategies:

- As a shared project
- The .NET Standard library

The first choice, a **shared project**, creates a project that is essentially a linked copy of each file in it. The files exist in one common place and are linked in at build time. This means that we cannot determine the runtime when writing the code and we can only access the APIs that are available on each target platform. It does allow us to use conditional compilations, which can be useful in certain circumstances, but can also be confusing to someone who reads the code later on. Going for the shared project option may also be a bad choice as it locks our code to specific platforms.

We will use the second choice, the **.NET Standard library**. This is, of course, a matter of choice and both ways will work. With a little imagination, you can still follow along with this chapter, even if you select the shared project option.

Let's get started!

Creating the new project

The first step is to create a new Xamarin.Forms project. Open Visual Studio 2019 and go to **File** | **New** | **Project**:

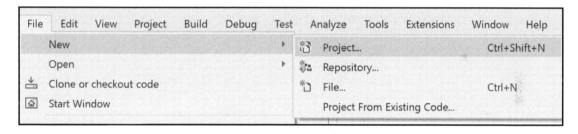

This will open the **Create a new project** wizard. In the top-middle section of the wizard, there is a search field. Type in xamarin and select the **Mobile App (Xamarin.Forms)** item from the list:

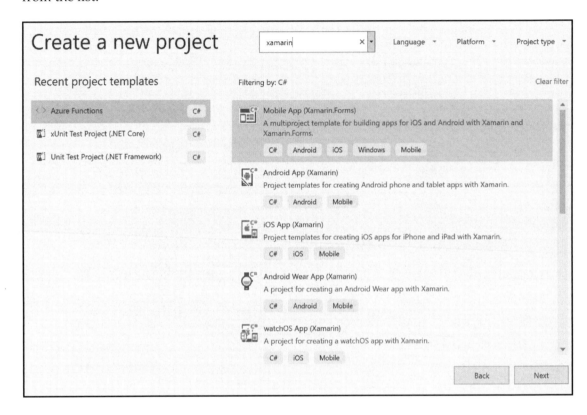

Complete the next page of the wizard by naming your project, and then click **Create.** Make sure you name the project `DoToo` to avoid any namespace issues:

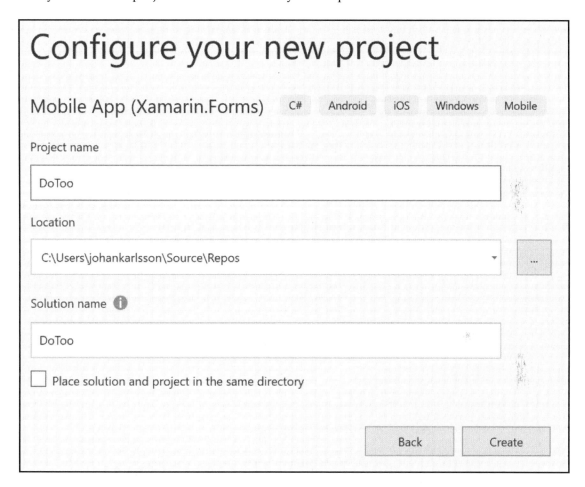

Configure your new project

Mobile App (Xamarin.Forms)   C#   Android   iOS   Windows   Mobile

Project name

DoToo

Location

C:\Users\johankarlsson\Source\Repos

Solution name ⓘ

DoToo

☐ Place solution and project in the same directory

Back   Create

The next step is to select a project template and a code-sharing strategy to use. Select **Blank** to create a bare Xamarin.Forms app. In versions of Visual Studio earlier than 2019, you will also need to change the **Code Sharing Strategy** option to **.NET Standard**. In the 2019 version, the blank Xamarin.Forms template app will create a .NET Standard library for you and you will not have the choice to select a shared project. Finalize the setup by clicking **OK** and wait for Visual Studio to create the necessary projects:

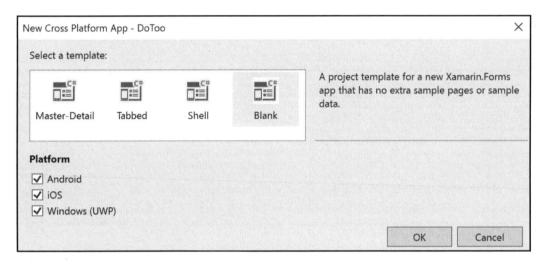

Congratulations! We've just created our first Xamarin.Forms app.

Examining the files

The selected template has now created four projects:

- `DoToo`: This is a .NET Standard library targeting .NET Standard 2.0. It can be imported by any runtime that supports this version of .NET Standard.
- `DoToo.Android`: This is an Android app for bootstrapping Xamarin.Forms on Android.
- `DoToo.iOS`: This is an iOS app for bootstrapping Xamarin.Forms on iOS.
- `DoToo.UWP`: This is a **Universal Windows Platform** (**UWP**) app for bootstrapping Xamarin.Forms on UWP. The UWP option is only available on Windows.

These three platform-specific libraries reference the .NET Standard library. Most of our code will be written in the .NET Standard library and only a small portion of platform-specific code will be added to each target platform.

The project should now look as follows:

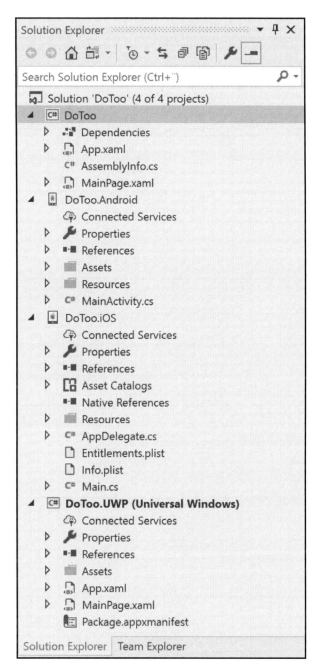

We will highlight a few important files in each project so that we have a basic understanding of what they are. We'll go through these project by project.

DoToo

This is the .NET Standard library that all the platform-specific projects reference and the location that most of our code will be added to. The following screenshot displays the structure of the .NET Standard library:

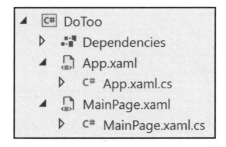

Under **Dependencies**, we will find references to any external dependencies, such as Xamarin.Forms. We will update the Xamarin.Forms package version in the *Updating Xamarin.Forms packages* section of this chapter and add more dependencies as we progress through the chapter.

The App.xaml file is an XAML file that represents the app. This is a good place to put application-wide resources, which we will do later on. We can also see the App.xaml.cs file, which contains the start up code and some application lifetime events that we can add custom code to, such as OnStart or OnSleep.

If we open up App.xaml.cs, we can see the starting point for our Xamarin.Forms application:

```
public partial class App : Application
{
    public App()
    {
        InitializeComponent();
        MainPage = new DoToo.MainPage();
    }

    protected override void OnStart()
    {
        // Handle when your app starts
    }
```

```
    // code omitted for brevity
}
```

The `MainPage` property is assigned to a page, which is particularly important as this is what determines which page is first shown to the user. In this template, this is the `DoToo.MainPage()` class.

The last two files are the `MainPage.xaml` file, which contains the first page of the application, and the code-behind file, which is called `MainPage.xaml.cs`. These files are removed in order to comply with the **Model–View–View–Model** (**MVVM**) naming standards.

DoToo.Android

This is the Android app. It only has one file:

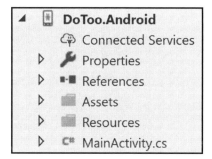

The important file here is `MainActivity.cs`. This contains the entry point for our application if we run the app on an Android device. The entry point method for an Android app is `OnCreate(...)`.

If you open `MainActivity.cs` and examine the `OnCreate(...)` method, it should look something as follows:

```
protected override void OnCreate(Bundle savedInstanceState)
{
    TabLayoutResource = Resource.Layout.Tabbar;
    ToolbarResource = Resource.Layout.Toolbar;

    base.OnCreate(bundle);

    Xamarin.Essentials.Platform.Init(this, savedInstanceState);
    global::Xamarin.Forms.Forms.Init(this, savedInstanceState);
    LoadApplication(new App());
}
```

The first two lines assign resources for `Tabbar` and `Toolbar`. We then call the `base` method, followed by the mandatory initialization of Xamarin.Essentials and Xamarin.Forms. Finally, we have the call to load the Xamarin.Forms application that we defined in the .NET Standard library.

You don't need to understand these files in detail; just remember that they are important for the initialization of our app.

 Xamarin.Essentials is a library that offers a lot of cross-platform APIs to commonly used resources on your phone, such as the accelerometer or the compass. Check it out at `https://docs.microsoft.com/en-us/xamarin/essentials/`.

DoToo.iOS

This is the iOS app. It contains a few more files than its Android counterpart:

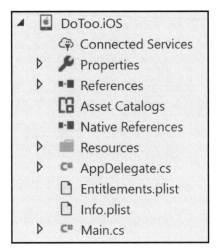

The `AppDelegate.cs` file is the entry point for an iOS app. This file contains a method called `FinishedLaunching(...)`, which is where we start writing code:

```
public override bool FinishedLaunching(UIApplication app, NSDictionary
options)
{
    global::Xamarin.Forms.Forms.Init();
    LoadApplication(new App());
    return base.FinishedLaunching(app, options);
}
```

The code starts off by initializing Xamarin.Forms and then loads the application from the .NET Standard library. After that, it returns the control to iOS. It must do this within 17 seconds or the app is terminated by the OS.

The `info.plist` file is an iOS-specific file that contains information about the app, such as the bundle ID and its provisioning profiles. It has a graphical editor but can also be edited in any text editor since it's a standard XML file.

The `Entitlements.plist` file is also an iOS-specific file that configures the entitlements that we want our app to take advantage of, such as **in-app purchases** or **push notifications**.

As with the Android app's start up code, we don't need to understand what is going on here in detail, other than that it's important for the initialization of our app.

DoToo.UWP

The last project to examine is the UWP app. The file structure of the project appears as in the following screenshot:

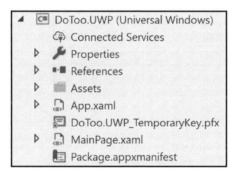

It has an `App.xaml` file, which is similar to the one in the .NET Standard library but specific to the UWP app. It also has a related file called `App.xaml.cs`. This contains a method called `OnLaunched(...)`, which is the entry point for a UWP app. This file is quite large, so we won't print it here, but do open it up and see whether you can locate the Xamarin.Forms initialization code in it.

Updating the Xamarin.Forms packages

After creating the project, you should always update your Xamarin.Forms packages to the latest version. To do this, follow these steps:

1. Right-click on your solution in **Solution Explorer.**
2. Click on **Manage NuGet Packages for Solution...**:

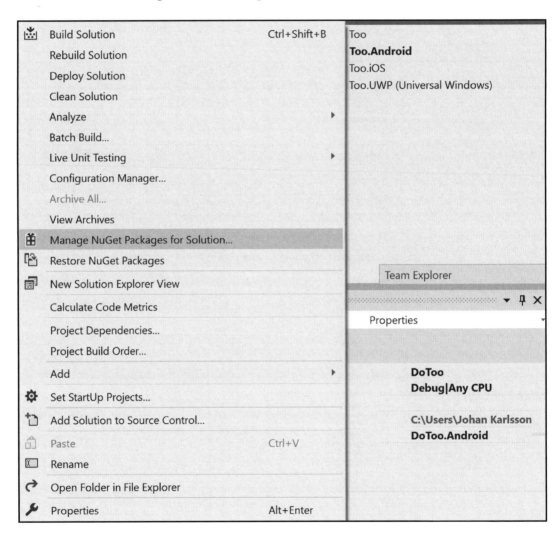

3. This brings up the NuGet package manager in Visual Studio:

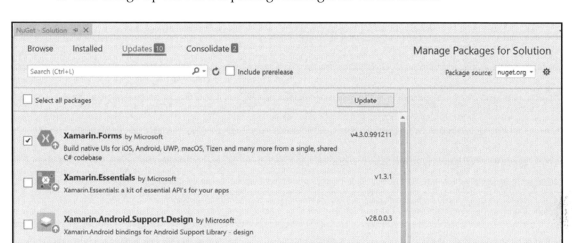

To update Xamarin.Forms to the latest version, perform the following steps:

1. Click on the **Updates** tab.
2. Check **Xamarin.Forms** and click **Update**.
3. Accept any license agreements.

Keep an eye on the output pane and wait for all the packages to update. However, ensure that you don't update any Android packages manually as this might break your application.

Removing the MainPage file

In Xamarin.Forms, we have the concept of pages. This is not the case, however, for the MVVM architectural pattern, which instead uses views. Views (in this version of MVVM) are the same thing as pages, but they are not suffixed with -Page, so we will need to delete the MainPage class generated by the template. We will go into more detail about MVVM shortly, but for the time being, we will need to remove the MainPage.cs class from the solution. This can be done as follows:

1. Right-click on the MainPage.xaml file in the DoToo project (the .NET Standard library).
2. Click **Delete** and confirm the delete action.

Some MVVM-frameworks do, however, use the concept of pages instead of views, such as Prism. It doesn't really matter, as long as you stick to one convention.

Creating a repository and a TodoItem model

Any good architecture always involves abstraction. In this app, we need something to store and retrieve the items of our to-do list. These will later be stored in an SQLite database, but adding a reference to the database directly in the code that is responsible for the GUI is generally a bad idea.

What we need, instead, is something to abstract our database from the GUI. For this app, we've chosen to use a simple repository pattern. This repository is simply a class that sits between the SQLite database and our upcoming `ViewModels` class. This is the class that handles the interaction with the view, which in turn handles the GUI.

The repository will expose methods for getting, adding, and updating items, as well as events that allow other parts of the app to react to changes in the repository. It will be hidden behind an interface so that we can replace the entire implementation later on without modifying anything but a line of code in the initialization of the app. This is made possible by **Autofac**.

Defining a to-do list item

We will start off by creating a `TodoItem` class, which represents a single item on the list. This is a simple **Plain Old CLR Object (POCO)** class, where **CLR** stands for **Common Language Runtime**. In other words, this is a .NET class without any dependencies on third-party assemblies. To create the class, follow these steps:

1. In the .NET Standard library project, create a folder called `Models`.
2. Add a class called `TodoItem.cs` to that folder and enter the following code:

```
using System;

namespace DoToo.Models
{
    public class TodoItem
    {
        public int Id { get; set; }
        public string Title { get; set; }
        public bool Completed { get; set; }
```

```
                public DateTime Due { get; set; }
        }
    }
```

This code is pretty self-explanatory; it's a simple POCO class that only contains properties and no logic. We have a `Title` property that describes what we want to be done, a flag (`Completed`) that determines whether the to-do list item is completed, a `Due` date for when we expect it to be done, and a unique `id` class that we will need later on for the database.

Creating a repository and its interface

Now that we have the `TodoItem` class, let's define an interface that describes a repository to store our to-do list items:

1. In the .NET Standard library project, create a folder called `Repositories`.
2. Create an interface called `ITodoItemRepository.cs` in the `Repositories` folder and write the following code:

```
using System;
using System.Collections.Generic;
using System.Threading.Tasks;
using DoToo.Models;

namespace DoToo.Repositories
{
    public interface ITodoItemRepository
    {
        event EventHandler<TodoItem> OnItemAdded;
        event EventHandler<TodoItem> OnItemUpdated;

        Task<List<TodoItem>> GetItems();
        Task AddItem(TodoItem item);
        Task UpdateItem(TodoItem item);
        Task AddOrUpdate(TodoItem item);
    }
}
```

The eagle-eyed among you might notice that we are not defining a `Delete` method in this interface. This is definitely something that should be there in a real-world app. While the app that we are creating in this chapter does not support deleting items, we are quite sure that you could add this yourself if you want to!

This interface defines everything we need for our app. It is there to create logical insulation between your implementation of a repository and the user of that repository. If any other parts of your application want an instance of `TodoItemRepository`, we can pass it an object that implements `ITodoItemRepository`, regardless of how it's implemented.

Having that said, let's implement `ITodoItemRepository`:

1. Create a class called `TodoItemRepository.cs`.
2. Enter the following code:

```csharp
using DoToo.Models;
using System;
using System.Collections.Generic;
using System.IO;
using System.Threading.Tasks;

namespace DoToo.Repositories
{
    public class TodoItemRepository : ITodoItemRepository
    {
        public event EventHandler<TodoItem> OnItemAdded;
        public event EventHandler<TodoItem> OnItemUpdated;

        public async Task<List<TodoItem>> GetItems()
        {
            return null; // Just to make it build
        }

        public async Task AddItem(TodoItem item)
        {
        }

        public async Task UpdateItem(TodoItem item)
        {
        }

        public async Task AddOrUpdate(TodoItem item)
        {
            if (item.Id == 0)
            {
                await AddItem(item);
            }
            else
            {
                await UpdateItem(item);
            }
        }
```

```
        }
    }
```

This code is the bare-bones implementation of the interface, except for the `AddOrUpdate(...)` method. This handles a small piece of logic that states that if the ID of an item is 0, it's a new item. Any item with an ID value greater than 0 is stored in the database. This is because the database assigns a value larger than 0 when we create rows in a table.

There are also two events defined in the preceding code. They will be used to notify subscribers of a list that items have been updated or added.

Connecting SQLite to persist data

We now have an interface, as well as a skeleton to implement that interface. The last thing we need to do to finish this section is to connect SQLite in the implementation of the repository.

Adding the SQLite NuGet package

To access SQLite in this project, we need to add a NuGet package called `sqlite-net-pcl` to the .NET Standard library project. To do this, right-click on the **Dependencies** item under the **DoToo** project node of the solution and click **Manage NuGet Packages...**:

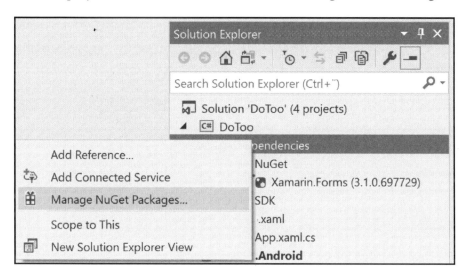

You might notice that the NuGet package is suffixed with -pcl. This is an example of what happens when naming conventions go wrong. This package actually supports .NET Standard 1.0, even though the name says **Portable Class Library** (**PCL**), which was the predecessor to .NET Standard.

This brings up the **NuGet Package Manager** window:

To install the SQLite NuGet package:

1. Click **Browse** and enter `sqlite-net-pcl` in the search box.
2. Select the package by **Frank A. Krueger** and click **Install.**

Wait for the installation to complete. We'll then add some code to the `TodoItem` class and the repository.

Updating the TodoItem class

Since SQLite is a relational database, it needs to know some basic information about how to create the tables that will store our objects. This is done using attributes, which are defined in the SQLite namespace:

1. Open up `Models/TodoItem`.
2. Add a `using SQLite` statement at the start of the file right below the existing `using` statements, as in the following code:

   ```
   using System;
   using SQLite;
   ```

3. Add the `PrimaryKey` and `AutoIncrement` attributes right before the `Id` property, as in the following code:

   ```
   [PrimaryKey, AutoIncrement]
   public int Id { get; set; }
   ```

The `PrimaryKey` attribute instructs SQLite that the `Id` property is the primary key of the table. The `AutoIncrement` attribute makes sure that the value of `Id` is increased by 1 for each new `TodoItem` class that is added to the table.

Creating a connection to the SQLite database

We will now add all the code needed to communicate with the database. The first thing we need to do is define a connection field that will hold the connection to the database:

1. Open up the `Repositories/TodoItemRepository` file.
2. Add a `using SQLite` statement at the start of the file right below the existing `using` statements, as in the following code:

   ```
   using DoToo.Models;
   using System.Collections.Generic;
   using System.IO;
   using System.Threading.Tasks;
   using SQLite;
   ```

3. Add the following field right below the class declaration:

   ```
   private SQLiteAsyncConnection connection;
   ```

The connection needs to be initialized. Once it is initialized, it can be reused throughout the life span of the repository. Since the method is asynchronous, it cannot be called from the constructor without introducing a locking strategy. To keep things simple, we will simply call it from each of the methods that are defined by the interface:

1. Add the following code to the `TodoItemRepository` class.
2. Add a `using System.IO` statement at the start of the file so that we can use `Path.Combine(...)`:

```
private async Task CreateConnection()
{
    if (connection != null)
    {
        return;
    }
    var documentPath = Environment.GetFolderPath(
                       Environment.SpecialFolder.MyDocuments);
    var databasePath = Path.Combine(documentPath, "TodoItems.db");

    connection = new SQLiteAsyncConnection(databasePath);
    await connection.CreateTableAsync<TodoItem>();

    if (await connection.Table<TodoItem>().CountAsync() == 0)
    {
        await connection.InsertAsync(new TodoItem()
        {
            Title = "Welcome to DoToo",
            Due = DateTime.Now
        });
    }
}
```

The method begins by checking whether we already have a connection. If we do, we can simply `return`. If we don't have a connection set up, we define a path on the disk to indicate where we want the database file to be located. In this case, we will choose the `MyDocuments` folder. Xamarin will find the closest match to this on each platform that we target.

We then create the connection and store the reference to that connection in the `connection` field. We need to make sure that SQLite has created a table that mirrors the schema of the `TodoItem` table. To make the development of the app easier, we add a default to-do list item if the `TodoItem` table is empty.

Implementing the GetItems(), AddItems(), and UpdateItems() methods

The only thing left to do in the repository is to implement the methods for getting, adding, and updating items:

1. Locate the `GetItems()` method in the `TodoItemRepository` class.
2. Update the `GetItems()` method with the following code:

```
public async Task<List<TodoItem>> GetItems()
{
    await CreateConnection();
    return await connection.Table<TodoItem>().ToListAsync();
}
```

To ensure that the connection to the database is valid, we call the `CreateConnection()` method we created in the previous section. When this method returns, we can make sure that it is initialized and that the `TodoItem` table has been created.

We then use the connection to access the `TodoItem` table and return a `List<TodoItem>` item that contains all the to-do list items in the database.

SQLite supports querying data using **Language Integrated Query** (**LINQ**). You can play around with this after the project is complete to get a better understanding of how to work it with databases in your app.

The code for adding items is even simpler:

1. Locate the `AddItem()` method in the `TodoItemRepository` class.
2. Update the `AddItem()` method with the following code:

```
public async Task AddItem(TodoItem item)
{
    await CreateConnection();
    await connection.InsertAsync(item);
    OnItemAdded?.Invoke(this, item);
}
```

The call to `CreateConnection()` makes sure that we have a connection in the same way as we did for the `GetItems()` method. After this, we insert it into the database using the `InsertAsync(...)` method on the `connection` object. After an item has been inserted into the table, we invoke the `OnItemAdded` event to notify any subscribers.

The code to update an item is basically the same as the `AddItem()` method, but also includes calls to `UpdateAsync` and `OnItemUpdated`. Let's finish up by updating the `UpdateItem()` method with the following code:

1. Locate the `UpdateItem()` method in the `TodoItemRepository` class.
2. Update the `UpdateItem()` method with the following code:

```
public async Task UpdateItem(TodoItem item)
{
    await CreateConnection();
    await connection.UpdateAsync(item);
    OnItemUpdated?.Invoke(this, item);
}
```

In the next section, we'll get started with MVVM. Grab a cup of coffee and let's get started!

Using MVVM – creating views and ViewModel

MVVM is all about the separation of concerns. Each part has a specific meaning:

- **Model**: This relates to anything that represents data and that can be referenced with `ViewModel`.
- **View**: This is the visual component. In Xamarin.Forms, this is represented by a page.
- `ViewModel`: This is the class that acts as the glue between the model and the view.

In our app, we could say that the model is the repository and the to-do list items it returns. `ViewModel` refers to this repository and exposes properties that the view can bind to. The ground rule is that any logic should reside in `ViewModel` and no logic should reside in the view. The view should know how to present data, such as converting a Boolean value into `Yes` or `No`.

MVVM can be implemented in many ways and there are quite a few frameworks that we can use to do so, such as **Prism**, **MVVMCross**, or even **TinyMvvm**. In this chapter, we have chosen to keep things simple and implement MVVM in a vanilla way, without any framework at all.

The main benefits of using MVVM as an architectural pattern are a clear separation of concerns, cleaner code, and great testability of `ViewModel`.

Well, enough of that—let's write some code instead!

Defining a ViewModel base class

`ViewModel` is the mediator between the view and the model. We can benefit from it greatly by creating a common base class for all our `ViewModel` classes to inherit from. To do this, follow these steps:

1. Create a folder called `ViewModels` in the `DoToo` .NET Standard project.
2. Create a class called `ViewModel` in the `ViewModels` folder.
3. Resolve references to `System.ComponentModel` and `Xamarin.Forms` and add the following code:

```
public abstract class ViewModel : INotifyPropertyChanged
{
    public event PropertyChangedEventHandler PropertyChanged;

    public void RaisePropertyChanged(params string[] propertyNames)
    {
        foreach (var propertyName in propertyNames)
        {
            PropertyChanged?.Invoke(this, new
            PropertyChangedEventArgs(propertyName));
        }
    }

    public INavigation Navigation { get; set; }
}
```

The `ViewModel` class is a base class for all `ViewModel` objects. It is not meant to be instantiated on its own, so we mark it as abstract. It implements `INotifyPropertyChanged`, which is an interface defined in `System.ComponentModel` in the .NET base class libraries. This interface only defines one thing—the `PropertyChanged` event. Our `ViewModel` class must raise this event whenever we want the GUI to be aware of any changes to a property. This can be done manually by adding code to a setter in a property or by using an **Intermediate Language** (**IL**) weaver, such as `PropertyChanged.Fody`. We will talk about this in more detail in the next section.

We will also take a little shortcut here by adding an `INavigation` property to `ViewModel`. This will help us with navigation later on. This is also something that can (and should) be abstracted since we don't want `ViewModel` to be dependent on `Xamarin.Forms` in order to be able to reuse the `ViewModel` classes on any platform.

Introducing PropertyChanged.Fody

The traditional way of implementing a `ViewModel` class is to inherit it from a base class (such as the `ViewModel` class that we defined previously) and then add code that might look as follows:

```
public class MyTestViewModel : ViewModel
{
    private string name;
    public string Name
    {
        get { return name; }
        set
        {
            if (name != value)
            {
                name = value;
                RaisePropertyChanged(nameof(Name));
            }
        }
    }
}
```

Each property that we want to add to a `ViewModel` class yields 13 lines of code. Not too bad, you might think. However, considering that a `ViewModel` class could potentially contain 10 to 20 properties, this rapidly turns into a lot of code. We can do better than this.

In just a few simple steps, we can use a tool called `PropertyChanged.Fody` to automatically inject almost all the code during the build process:

1. In the .NET Standard library, install the `PropertyChanged.Fody` NuGet package.
2. Create a file called `FodyWeavers.xml` in the root of the .NET Standard library and add the following XML to it:

```
<?xml version="1.0" encoding="utf-8" ?>
<Weavers>
    <PropertyChanged />
</Weavers>
```

`PropertyChanged.Fody` scans the assembly for any class that implements the `INotifyPropertyChanged` interface and adds the code needed to raise the `PropertyChanged` event. It also takes care of dependencies between properties, meaning if you have a property that returns values based on two other properties, it is raised if either of those two values changes.

The result is that the `test` class we had previously is reduced to a single line of code per property. This makes the code base more readable because everything happens behind the scenes:

```
public class MyTestViewModel : ViewModel
{
    public string Name { get; set; }
}
```

 It is worth noting that there are a lot of different plugins that can be used to make `Fody` automate tasks, such as logging or method decoration. Check out `https://github.com/Fody/Fody` for more info.

Creating the MainViewModel

Up to this point, we have mainly prepared to write the code that will make up the app itself. `MainViewModel` is the `ViewModel` class for the first view that is displayed to the user. It is responsible for providing data and logic to a list of to-do list items. We will create the bare-bones `ViewModel` classes and add code to them as we progress through this chapter:

1. Create a class called `MainViewModel` in the `ViewModels` folder.

2. Add the following template code and resolve the references:

```
public class MainViewModel : ViewModel
{
    private readonly TodoItemRepository repository;

    public MainViewModel(TodoItemRepository repository)
    {
        this.repository = repository;
        Task.Run(async () => await LoadData());
    }

    private async Task LoadData()
    {
```

```
        }
    }
```

The structure of this class is something that we will reuse for all the ViewModel classes to come.

Let's summarize the important features we want the ViewModel class to have:

- We inherit from the ViewModel class to gain access to shared logic, such as the INotifyPropertyChanged interface and common navigation code.
- All dependencies to other classes, such as repositories and services, are passed through the constructor of ViewModel. This is handled by the **dependency injection** pattern and, more specifically for our case, by Autofac, which is the implementation of the dependency injection we are using.
- We use an asynchronous call to LoadData() as an entry point to initialize the ViewModel class. Different MVVM libraries might do this in different ways, but the basic functionally is the same.

Creating the TodoItemViewModel

TodoItemViewModel is the ViewModel class that represents each item in the to-do list on MainView. It does not have an entire view of its own (although it could have), but is instead rendered by a template in ListView. We will get back to this when we create the controls for MainView.

The important thing here is that this ViewModel object represents a single item, regardless of where we choose to render it.

Let's create the TodoItemViewModel class:

1. Create a class called TodoItemViewModel in the ViewModels folder.
2. Add the following template code and resolve the references:

```
public class TodoItemViewModel : ViewModel
{
    public TodoItemViewModel(TodoItem item) => Item = item;

    public event EventHandler ItemStatusChanged;
    public TodoItem Item { get; private set; }
    public string StatusText => Item.Completed ? "Reactivate" :
    "Completed";
}
```

As with any other `ViewModel` class, we inherit the `TodoItemViewModel` class from `ViewModel`. We conform to the pattern of injecting all the dependencies into the constructor. In this case, we pass an instance of the `TodoItem` class to the constructor that the `ViewModel` object will use to expose to the view.

The `ItemStatusChanged` event handler will be used later when we want to signal to the view that the state of the `TodoItem` class has changed. The `Item` property allows us to access the item that we passed in.

The `StatusText` property is used to make the status of the to-do item human-readable in the view.

Creating the ItemViewModel class

`ItemViewModel` represents the to-do list item in a view that can be used to create new items and to edit existing items:

1. In the `ViewModels` folder, create a class called `ItemViewModel`.
2. Add the following code:

```
using DoToo.Models;
using DoToo.Repositories;
using System;
using System.Windows.Input;
using Xamarin.Forms;

namespace DoToo.ViewModels
{
    public class ItemViewModel : ViewModel
    {
        private readonly TodoItemRepository repository;

        public ItemViewModel(TodoItemRepository repository)
        {
            this.repository = repository;
        }
    }
}
```

The pattern is the same as for the previous two `ViewModel` classes:

- We use dependency injection to pass the `TodoItemRepository` class to the `ViewModel` object.
- We use inheritance from the `ViewModel` base class to add the common features defined by the base class

Creating the MainView view

Now that we are done with the `ViewModel` classes, let's create the skeleton code and the XAML required for the views. The first view that we are going to create is `MainView`, which is the view that will be loaded first:

1. Create a folder called `Views` in the .NET Standard library.
2. Right-click on the `Views` folder, select **Add**, and then click **New Item...**.
3. Select **Xamarin.Forms** under the **Visual C# Items** node on the left.
4. Select **Content Page** and name it `MainView`.
5. Click **Add** to create the page:

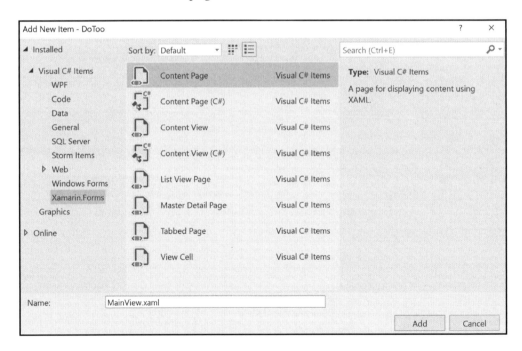

Let's add some content to the newly created view:

1. Open `MainView.xaml`.

2. Remove all the template code below the `ContentPage` root node and add the XAML code marked in bold in the following code:

```xml
<?xml version="1.0" encoding="utf-8"?>
<ContentPage xmlns="http://xamarin.com/schemas/2014/forms"
             xmlns:x="http://schemas.microsoft.com/winfx/2009/xaml"
             xmlns:local="clr-namespace:DoToo"
             x:Class="DoToo.Views.MainView"
             Title="Do Too!">

    <ContentPage.ToolbarItems>
        <ToolbarItem Text="Add" />
    </ContentPage.ToolbarItems>

    <Grid>
        <Grid.RowDefinitions>
            <RowDefinition Height="auto" />
            <RowDefinition Height="*" />
        </Grid.RowDefinitions>

        <Button Text="Toggle filter" />

        <ListView Grid.Row="1">
        </ListView>
    </Grid>
</ContentPage>
```

To be able to access custom converters, we need to add a reference to a local namespace. The `xmlns:local="clr-namespace:DoToo"` line defines this namespace for us. We will not use it directly in this case, but it's a good idea to have a local namespace defined. If we create custom controls, we can then access them by writing something such as `<local:MyControl />`.

The `Title` property on the `ContentPage` page gives the page a title. Depending on the platform we are running on, the title is displayed differently. If we use a standard navigation bar, it will be displayed at the top, for example, in both iOS and Android. A page should always have a title.

The `ContentPage.Toolbar` node defines a toolbar item for adding new to-do items. It will also be rendered differently based on the platform, but it always follows the platform-specific UI guidelines.

A page in Xamarin.Forms (and also in an XML document, in general) can only have one root node. The root node in a Xamarin.Forms page populates the `Content` property of the page itself. Since we want our `MainView` view to contain a list of items and a button at the top to toggle a filter (to switch between all items and only active items), we need to add a `Layout` control to position them on the page. `Grid` is a control that allows you to split up the available space based on rows and columns.

For our `MainView` view, we want to add two rows. The first row is a space calculated by the height of the button (`Height="auto"`) and the second row takes up all of the remaining space for the `ListView` (`Height="*"`). Elements such as `ListView` are positioned in the grid using the `Grid.Row` and `Grid.Column` attributes. Both of these properties default to `0` if they are not specified, just like the button.

`ListView` is a control that presents items in a list, which is coincidently exactly what our app will do. It's worth noting though that in Xamarin.Forms 4, a new control called `CollectionView` has been introduced. Subsequent chapters will use this control, but we wanted to introduce you to the good old `ListView` control as well.

 If you are interested in how `Grid` works, you can search for more information about Xamarin.Forms grids on the internet or check out the official documentation at `https://docs.microsoft.com/en-us/xamarin/xamarin-forms/user-interface/layouts/grid`.

We also need to wire up `ViewModel` to the view. This can be done by passing the `ViewModel` class in the constructor of the view:

1. Open up the code-behind file of `MainView` by expanding the `MainView.xaml` file in **Solution Explorer**. The code-behind file is named `MainView.xaml.cs`.
2. Add a `using DoToo.ViewModels` statement to the top of the file, adjacent to the existing `using` statements.
3. Modify the constructor of the class to look as in the following code by adding the code marked in bold:

```
public MainView(MainViewModel viewModel)
{
    InitializeComponent();
    viewModel.Navigation = Navigation;
    BindingContext = viewModel;
}
```

We follow the same pattern as we did with the ViewModel classes by passing any dependencies through the constructor. A view is always dependent on a ViewModel class. To simplify the project, we also assign the Navigation property of the page directly to the Navigation property defined in the ViewModel base class. In a larger project, we might want to abstract this property as well to make sure that we separate the ViewModel classes completely from Xamarin.Forms. For the sake of this app, however, it is OK to reference it directly.

Lastly, we assign ViewModel to the BindingContext class of the page. This tells the Xamarin.Forms binding engine to use our ViewModel object for the bindings that we will create later on.

Creating the ItemView view

Next up is the second view. We will use this to add and edit the to-do list items:

1. Create a new content page (in the same way that we created the MainView view) and name it ItemView.
2. Edit the XAML file so that it appears as in the following code:

```xml
<?xml version="1.0" encoding="UTF-8"?>
<ContentPage xmlns="http://xamarin.com/schemas/2014/forms"

  xmlns:x="http://schemas.microsoft.com/winfx/2009/xaml"
             x:Class="DoToo.Views.ItemView"
             Title="New todo item">

    <ContentPage.ToolbarItems>
        <ToolbarItem Text="Save" />
    </ContentPage.ToolbarItems>

    <StackLayout Padding="14">
        <Label Text="Title" />
        <Entry />
        <Label Text="Due" />
        <DatePicker />
        <StackLayout Orientation="Horizontal">
            <Switch />
            <Label Text="Completed" />
        </StackLayout>
    </StackLayout>
</ContentPage>
```

As with `MainView`, we need a title. We will give it a default title of `New todo item` for now, but we will change this to `Edit todo item` when we reuse this view for editing later on. The user must be able to save a new or edited item, so we have added a **toolbar save button**. The content of the page uses `StackLayout` to structure the controls. `StackLayout` adds an element vertically (the default option) or horizontally based on the space it calculates that the element takes up. This is a CPU-intensive process, so we should only use it on small portions of our layout. In `StackLayout`, we add a `Label` control that is a line of text over the `Entry` control that comes underneath it. The `Entry` control is a text input control that contains the name of the to-do list item. We then have a section for `DatePicker`, where the user can select a due date for the to-do list item. The final control is a `Switch` control, which renders a toggle button to control when an item is complete, as well as a heading next to it. Since we want these to be displayed next to each other horizontally, we use a horizontal `StackLayout` control to do this.

The last step for the views is to wire up the `ItemViewModel` model to `ItemView`:

1. Open up the code-behind file of `ItemView` by expanding the `ItemView.xaml` file in **Solution Explorer.**

2. Modify the constructor of the class to appear as in the following code. Add the code that is marked in bold:

```
public ItemView (ItemViewModel viewmodel)
{
    InitializeComponent ();
    viewmodel.Navigation = Navigation;
    BindingContext = viewmodel;
}
```

3. Add a `using DoToo.ViewModels` statement at the top of the file, adjacent to the existing `using` statements:

```
using DoToo.ViewModels;
```

This code is identical to the code that we added for `MainView`, except for the type of `ViewModel` class.

Wiring up a dependency injection through Autofac

Earlier, we discussed the dependency injection pattern, which states that all dependencies, such as the repositories and view models, must be passed through the constructor of the class. This has several benefits:

- It increases the readability of the code since we can quickly determine all the external dependencies.
- It makes dependency injection possible.
- It makes unit testing possible by mocking classes.
- We can control the life time of an object by specifying whether it should be a singleton or a new instance for each resolution.

Dependency injection is a pattern that lets us determine, at runtime, which instance of an object should be passed to a constructor when an object is created. We do this by defining a container where we register all the types of a class. We let the framework that we are using resolve any dependencies between them. Let's say that we ask the container for a `MainView` class. The container takes care of resolving `MainViewModel` and any dependencies that the class has.

To set this up, we need to reference a library called Autofac. There are other options out there, so feel free to switch to one that better fits your needs. We also need an entry point to resolve the types into instances. To do this, we will define a bare-bones `Resolver` class. To wrap it all up, we need a bootstrapper that we will call to initialize the dependency injection configuration.

Adding a reference to Autofac

We need a reference to Autofac to get started. We will use NuGet to install the packages needed:

1. Open up the NuGet manager by right-clicking on the **Solution** node and clicking on **Manage NuGet packages for solution...**.
2. Click on **Browse** and type `autofac` in the search box.

3. Tick all the checkboxes under **Project**, scroll down, and click **Install**:

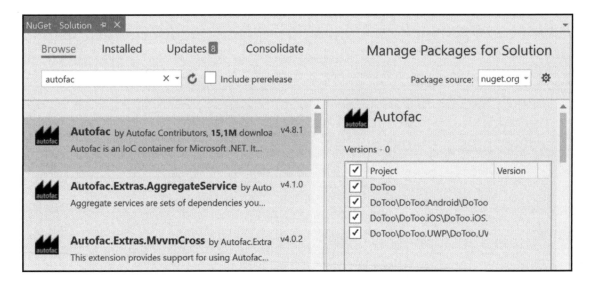

Creating the resolver

The resolver is responsible for creating objects for us based on the type that we request. Let's create the resolver:

1. In the root of the .NET Standard library project, create a new file called `Resolver.cs`.
2. Add the following code to the file:

```
using Autofac;

namespace DoToo
{
    public static class Resolver
    {
        private static IContainer container;

        public static void Initialize(IContainer container)
        {
            Resolver.container = container;
        }

        public static T Resolve<T>()
        {
            return container.Resolve<T>();
```

```
            }
        }
    }
```

The `container` property of the `IContainer` type is defined in `Autofac` and represents a container that holds the configuration on how to resolve types. The `Initialize` method takes an instance of an object that implements the `IContainer` interface and assigns it to the `container` property. The `Resolve` method uses the `container` property to resolve a type to an instance of an object. While it might seem strange to use this at first, it will become much easier with experience.

Creating the bootstrapper

The bootstrapper's responsibility is to initialize Autofac. It is called at the startup of the application. We can create it as follows:

1. In the root of the .NET Standard library project, create a new file called `Bootstrapper.cs`.

2. Enter the following code:

```
using Autofac;
using System.Linq;
using System.Reflection;
using Xamarin.Forms;
using DoToo.Views;
using DoToo.Repositories;
using DoToo.ViewModels;

namespace DoToo
{
    public abstract class Bootstrapper
    {
        protected ContainerBuilder ContainerBuilder { get; private
        set; }

        public Bootstrapper()
        {
            Initialize();
            FinishInitialization();
        }

        protected virtual void Initialize()
        {
            var currentAssembly = Assembly.GetExecutingAssembly();
            ContainerBuilder = new ContainerBuilder();
```

```
                    foreach (var type in currentAssembly.DefinedTypes
                        .Where(e =>
                                e.IsSubclassOf(typeof(Page)) ||
                                e.IsSubclassOf(typeof(ViewModel))))
                    {
                        ContainerBuilder.RegisterType(type.AsType());
                    }


            ContainerBuilder.RegisterType<TodoItemRepository>().SingleInstance(
                );
                }

                private void FinishInitialization()
                {
                    var container = ContainerBuilder.Build();
                    Resolver.Initialize(container);
                }
            }
        }
```

The Bootstrapper class is implemented by each platform since this is where the execution of the app begins. This also gives us the option to add platform-specific configurations. To ensure that we inherit from the class, we define it as abstract.

ContainerBuilder is a class defined in Autofac that takes care of creating the container property for us after we finish the configuration. The building of the container property happens in the FinishInitialization method defined at the end and is called by the constructor right after we call the virtual Initialize method. We can override the Initialize method to add custom registrations to each platform.

The Initialize method scans the assembly using reflection for any types that inherit from Page or ViewModel and adds them to the container property. It also adds the TodoItemRepository property as a singleton to the container property. This means that each time we ask for TodoItemRepository, we get the same instance. The default behavior for Autofac (this may vary between libraries) is to give a new instance for each resolution.

Adding a bootstrapper on iOS

The bootstrapper for iOS is a simple wrapper for the common bootstrapper defined in the .NET Standard library, but with the addition of an `Init` method that is called at startup:

1. In the root of the iOS project, create a new class called `Bootstrapper.cs`.
2. Add the following code to it:

```
public class Bootstrapper : DoToo.Bootstrapper
{
    public static void Init()
    {
        var instance = new Bootstrapper();
    }
}
```

The `Init` method may look strange since we don't retain a reference to the instance we create. Keep in mind, however, that we do keep a reference to a `Resolver` instance in the `Resolver` class, which is itself a singleton.

The final step for iOS is to call this `Init` method in the right place:

1. Open up `AppDelegate.cs`.
2. Locate the `FinishedLaunching` method and add the code in bold from the following code block:

```
public override bool FinishedLaunching(UIApplication app,
NSDictionary options)
{
    global::Xamarin.Forms.Forms.Init();
    Bootstrapper.Init();
    LoadApplication(new App());

    return base.FinishedLaunching(app, options);
}
```

Adding a bootstrapper in Android

Just as for iOS, the bootstrapper for Android is a simple wrapper for the common bootstrapper defined in the .NET Standard library, but with the addition of an `Init` method that is called at startup:

1. In the root of the Android project, create a new class called `Bootstrapper.cs`.
2. Add the following code to it:

```
public class Bootstrapper : DoToo.Bootstrapper
{
    public static void Init()
    {
        var instance = new Bootstrapper();
    }
}
```

We then need to call this `Init` method. A good place to do this is right before the `LoadApplication` call in `OnCreate`:

1. Open up `MainActivity.cs`.
2. Locate the `OnCreate` method and add the code in bold from the following code block:

```
protected override void OnCreate(Bundle savedInstanceState)
{
    TabLayoutResource = Resource.Layout.Tabbar;
    ToolbarResource = Resource.Layout.Toolbar;

    base.OnCreate(savedInstanceState);
    Xamarin.Essentials.Platform.Init(this, savedInstanceState);
    global::Xamarin.Forms.Forms.Init(this, savedInstanceState);
    Bootstrapper.Init();
    LoadApplication(new App());
}
```

Adding a bootstrapper in UWP

The bootstrapper for UWP is identical to the other platforms:

1. In the root of the UWP project, create a new class called `Bootstrapper.cs`.
2. Add the following code to it:

```
public class Bootstrapper : DoToo.Bootstrapper
{
    public static void Init()
```

```
        {
            var instance = new Bootstrapper();
        }
    }
```

As with the other platforms, we need to call the `Init` method in a good place:

1. In the UWP project, open up the `App.xaml.cs` file.
2. Locate the call to the `Xamarin.Forms.Forms.Init()` method and add the code in bold from the following code block:

```
Xamarin.Forms.Forms.Init(e);
Bootstrapper.Init();
```

Making the app run

We can start the app for the first time as follows:

1. Open up `App.xaml.cs` by expanding the `App.xaml` node in the .NET Standard library.
2. Locate the constructor.
3. Add a `using` statement for `DoToo.Views` and add the following code line in bold:

```
public App ()
{
    InitializeComponent();
    MainPage = new NavigationPage(Resolver.Resolve<MainView>());
}
```

The line we have just added resolves the `MainView` class (and all its dependencies, including `MainViewModel` and `TodoItemRepository`) and wraps it in `NavigationPage`. `NavigationPage` is a page defined in Xamarin.Forms that adds a navigation bar and enables the user to navigate to other views.

 In Xamarin.Forms 4, a brand new way of declaring the structure of an app has been added. It's called **Shell** and we have a whole chapter about it in this book. However, to become a good Xamarin developer, you need to know the basics, and the basics of navigating in Xamarin.Forms uses the good old `NavigationPage` control.

That's it! Now, your project should start. Depending on the platform you are using, it might look as in the following screenshot:

Adding data bindings

Data binding is the heart and soul of MVVM. This is the way that the views and ViewModel communicate with each other. In Xamarin.Forms, we need two things to make data binding happen:

1. We need an object to implement INotifyPropertyChanged.
2. We need to set the BindingContext class of the page to that object. We already do this on both ItemView andMainView.

A really useful feature of data binding is that it allows us to use two-way communication. For example, when data binding text to an Entry control, the property on the data-bound object is updated directly. Consider the following XAML:

```
<Entry Text="{Binding Title}" />
```

To make this work, we need a property named `Title` on the string object. We have to look at the documentation, define an object, and let **Intellisense** provide us with a hint to find out what type our property should be.

Controls that perform some kind of action, such as `Button`, usually expose a property called `Command`. This property is of the `ICommand` type and we can either return `Xamarin.Forms.Command` or an implementation of our own. The `Command` property is explained in the next section, where we will use it to navigate to `ItemView`.

> It's also worth noting that Xamarin.Forms supports one-way binding, which comes in handy when you want to display data in a view but don't allow it to update `ViewModel`. From a performance perspective, it's a good idea to mark those bindings as one-way bindings.

Navigating from MainView to ItemView to add a new item

We have an **Add** toolbar button in `MainView`. When the user taps this button, we want it to take them to `ItemView`. The MVVM way to do this is to define a command and then bind that command to the button. Let's add the code:

1. Open `ViewModels/MainViewModel.cs`.
2. Add `using` statements for `System.Windows.Input`, `DoToo.Views`, and `Xamarin.Forms`.
3. Add the following property to the class:

```
public ICommand AddItem => new Command(async () =>
{
    var itemView = Resolver.Resolve<ItemView>();
    await Navigation.PushAsync(itemView);
});
```

All commands should be exposed as a generic `ICommand` type. This abstracts the actual command implementation, which is good general practice to follow. The command must be a property; in our case, we are creating a new `Command` object that we assign to this property. The property is read-only, which is usually fine for a `Command` object. The action of the command (the code that we want to run when the command is executed) is passed to the constructor of the `Command` object.

The action of the command creates a new `ItemView` view through `Resolver`, and Autofac builds the necessary dependencies. Once the new `ItemView` view has been created, we simply tell the `Navigation` service to push it to the stack for us.

After that, we just have to wire up the `AddItem` command from `ViewModel` to the **Add** button in the view:

1. Open `Views/MainView.xaml`.
2. Add the `Command` attribute to `ToolbarItem`:

```
<ContentPage.ToolbarItems>
    <ToolbarItem Text="Add" Command="{Binding AddItem}" />
</ContentPage.ToolbarItems>
```

Run the app and tap the **Add** button to navigate to the new `ItemView` view. Notice that the back button appears automatically.

Adding new items to the list

We have now finished adding navigation to a new item. Let's now add the code needed to create a new item and save it to the database:

1. Open `ViewModels/ItemViewModel.cs`.
2. Add the following code in bold.
3. Resolve the reference to `System.Windows.Input`:

```
public class ItemViewModel : ViewModel
{
    private TodoItemRepository repository;

    public TodoItem Item { get; set; }

    public ItemViewModel(TodoItemRepository repository)
    {
        this.repository = repository;
        Item = new TodoItem() { Due = DateTime.Now.AddDays(1) };
    }
    public ICommand Save => new Command(async () =>
    {
        await repository.AddOrUpdate(Item);
        await Navigation.PopAsync();
    });
}
```

The `Item` property holds a reference to the current item that we want to add or edit. A new item is created in the constructor and when we want to edit an item, we can simply assign our own item to this property. The new item is not added to the database unless we execute the `Save` command defined at the end. After the item is added or updated, we remove the view from the navigation stack and return to `MainView` again.

 Since the navigation keeps pages in a stack, the framework declares methods that reflect operations that you can perform on a stack. The operation of removing the topmost item in a stack is known as **popping the stack**, so instead of `RemoveAsync()`, we have `PopAsync()`. To add a page to the navigation stack, we push it, so the method is called `PushAsync()`.

Now that we have extended `ItemViewModel` with the necessary commands and properties, it's time to data-bind them in the XAML:

1. Open `Views/ItemView.xaml`.
2. Add the code marked in bold:

```xml
<?xml version="1.0" encoding="UTF-8"?>
<ContentPage xmlns="http://xamarin.com/schemas/2014/forms"
             xmlns:x="http://schemas.microsoft.com/winfx/2009/xaml"
             x:Class="DoToo.Views.ItemView">
    <ContentPage.ToolbarItems>
        <ToolbarItem Text="Save" Command="{Binding Save}" />
    </ContentPage.ToolbarItems>
    <StackLayout Padding="14">
        <Label Text="Title" />
        <Entry Text="{Binding Item.Title}" />
        <Label Text="Due" />
        <DatePicker Date="{Binding Item.Due}" />
        <StackLayout Orientation="Horizontal">
            <Switch IsToggled="{Binding Item.Completed}" />
            <Label Text="Completed" />
        </StackLayout>
    </StackLayout>
</ContentPage>
```

The binding to the `ToolbarItems` command attribute triggers the `Save` command exposed by `ItemViewModel` when a user taps the `Save` link. It's worth noting again that any attribute called `Command` indicates that an action will take place and we must bind it to an instance of an object implementing the `ICommand` interface.

The `Entry` control that represents the title is data-bound to the `Item.Title` property of `ItemViewModel`, and the `Datepicker` and `Switch` controls bind in a similar way to their respective properties.

We could have exposed `Title`, `Due`, and `Complete` as properties directly on `ItemViewModel`, but we instead chose to reuse the already-existing `TodoItem` object as a reference. This is fine, as long as the properties of the `TodoItem` object implement the `INotifyPropertyChange` interface.

Binding ListView in MainView

A to-do list is not much use without a list of items. Let's extend `MainViewModel` with a list of items:

1. Open `ViewModels/MainViewModel.cs`.
2. Add `using` statements for `System.Collections.ObjectModel` and `System.Linq`.
3. Add a property for the to-do list items:

   ```
   public ObservableCollection<TodoItemViewModel> Items { get; set; }
   ```

`ObservableCollection` is like an ordinary collection, but it has a useful superpower. It can notify listeners about changes in the list, such as when items are added or deleted. The **ListView** control listens to changes in the list and updates itself automatically based on these. It's important, however, to be aware that a change to an item in the list will not trigger an update. Changing the title of an item will not cause the list to re-render. Let's move on to implementing the rest of `MainViewModel`.

We now need some data:

1. Open `ViewModels/MainViewModel.cs`.
2. Replace (or complete) the `LoadData` method and create the `CreateTodoItemViewModel` and `ItemStatusChanged` methods.
3. Resolve the reference to `DoToo.Models` by adding a `using` statement:

   ```
   private async Task LoadData()
   {
       var items = await repository.GetItems();
       var itemViewModels = items.Select(i =>
       CreateTodoItemViewModel(i));
       Items = new ObservableCollection<TodoItemViewModel>
       (itemViewModels);
   ```

```
    }

    private TodoItemViewModel CreateTodoItemViewModel(TodoItem item)
    {
        var itemViewModel = new TodoItemViewModel(item);
        itemViewModel.ItemStatusChanged += ItemStatusChanged;
        return itemViewModel;
    }

    private void ItemStatusChanged(object sender, EventArgs e)
    {
    }
```

The `LoadData` method calls the repository to fetch all items. We then wrap each to-do list item in `TodoItemViewModel`. This contains more information that is specific to the view that we don't want to add to the `TodoItem` class. It is good practice to wrap plain objects in `ViewModel`; this makes it simpler to add actions or extra properties to it. `ItemStatusChanged` is a stub that is called when we change the status of the to-do list item from `active` to `completed` and vice versa.

We also need to hook up some events from the repository to know when data changes:

1. Open `ViewModels/MainViewModel.cs`.
2. Add the following code in bold:

```
    public MainViewModel(TodoItemRepository repository)
    {
        repository.OnItemAdded += (sender, item) =>
            Items.Add(CreateTodoItemViewModel(item));
        repository.OnItemUpdated += (sender, item) =>
            Task.Run(async () => await LoadData());

        this.repository = repository;
        Task.Run(async () => await LoadData());
    }
```

When an item is added to the repository, no matter who added it, MainView will add it to the items list. Since the items collection is an observable collection, the list updates. If an item is updated, we simply reload the list.

Let's data-bind our items to ListView:

1. Open up MainView.xaml and locate the ListView element.
2. Modify it to reflect the following code:

```
<ListView Grid.Row="1"
          RowHeight="70"
          ItemsSource="{Binding Items}">
    <ListView.ItemTemplate>
        <DataTemplate>
            <ViewCell>
                <Grid Padding="15,10">
                    <Grid.ColumnDefinitions>
                        <ColumnDefinition Width="10" />
                        <ColumnDefinition Width="*" />
                    </Grid.ColumnDefinitions>

                    <BoxView Grid.RowSpan="2" />
                    <Label Grid.Column="1"
                           Text="{Binding Item.Title}"
                           FontSize="Large" />
                    <Label Grid.Column="1"
                           Grid.Row="1"
                           Text="{Binding Item.Due}"
                           FontSize="Micro" />
                    <Label Grid.Column="1"
                           Grid.Row="1"
                           HorizontalTextAlignment="End"
                           Text="Completed"
                           IsVisible="{Binding Item.Completed}"
                           FontSize="Micro" />
                </Grid>
            </ViewCell>
        </DataTemplate>
    </ListView.ItemTemplate>
</ListView>
```

The `ItemsSource` binding tells `ListView` where to find the collection to iterate over and is local to `ViewModel`. Any bindings in the `ViewCell` node, however, are local to each item that we iterate in the list. In this case, we are binding to the `TodoItemViewModel`, which contains a property named `Item`. This, in turn, has properties such as `Title`, `Due`, and `Completed`. We can navigate down the hierarchy of objects without any problem when defining a binding.

The `DataTemplate` element defines what each row will look like. We use a grid to partition the space, just as we did earlier.

Creating a ValueConverter object for the item status

Sometimes, we want to bind to objects that are a representation of the original value. This could be a piece of text that is based on a Boolean value. Instead of `true` and `false`, for example, we might want to write `Yes` and `No`, or return a color. This is where `ValueConverter` comes in handy. It can be used to convert a value to and from another value. We are going to write a `ValueConverter` object that converts the status of a to-do list item to a color:

1. In the root of the .NET Standard library project, create a folder called `Converters`.

2. Create a class called `StatusColorConverter.cs` and add the following code:

```
using System;
using System.Globalization;
using Xamarin.Forms;

namespace DoToo.Converters
{
    public class StatusColorConverter : IValueConverter
    {
        public object Convert(object value, Type targetType,
                              object parameter, CultureInfo
                              culture)
        {
            return (bool)value ?
            (Color)Application.Current.Resources[
            "CompletedColor"]:

            (Color)Application.Current.Resources[
            "ActiveColor"];
        }

        public object ConvertBack(object value, Type
```

```
                        targetType,
                        object parameter, CultureInfo culture)
                    {
                        return null;
                    }
            }
        }
```

A `ValueConverter` object is a class that implements `IValueConverter`. This, in turn, only has two methods defined. The `Convert` method is called when the view reads data from `ViewModel` and the `ConvertBack` method is used when `ViewModel`, gets data from the view. The `ConvertBack` method is only used for controls that return data from plain text, such as the `Entry` control.

If we look at the implementation of the `Convert` method, we notice that any value passed to the method is of the object type. This is because we don't know what type the user has bound to the property that we are adding this `ValueConverter` class to. We may also notice that we fetch colors from a resource file. We could have defined the colors in the code, but this is not recommended. So, instead, we went the extra mile and added them as a global resource to the `App.xaml` file. Resources are a good thing to take another look at once you have finished this chapter:

1. Open `App.xaml` in the .NET Standard library project.
2. Add the following `ResourceDictionary` element:

```xml
<Application ...>
    <Application.Resources>
        <ResourceDictionary>
            <Color x:Key="CompletedColor">#1C8859</Color>
            <Color x:Key="ActiveColor">#D3D3D3</Color>
        </ResourceDictionary>
    </Application.Resources>
</Application>
```

`ResourceDictionary` can define a wide range of different objects. We settle for the two colors that we want to access from `ValueConverter`. Notice that these can be accessed by the key given to them and from any other XAML file using a static resource binding. `ValueConverter` itself is referenced as a static resource, but from a local scope.

Using ValueConverter

We want to use our brand new `StatusColorConverter` object in `MainView`. Unfortunately, we have to jump through some hoops to make this happen. We need to do three things:

- Define a namespace in XAML
- Define a local resource that represents an instance of the converter
- Declare in the binding that we want to use the converter

Let's start with the namespace:

1. Open `Views/MainView.xaml.`
2. Add the following namespace to the page:

```
<ContentPage xmlns="http://xamarin.com/schemas/2014/forms"
             xmlns:x="http://schemas.microsoft.com/winfx/2009/xaml"
             xmlns:converters="clr-namespace:DoToo.Converters"
             x:Class="DoToo.Views.MainView"
             Title="Do Too!>
```

Add a `Resource` node to the `MainView.xaml` file:

1. Open `Views/MainView.xaml.`
2. Add the following `ResourceDictionary` element, shown in bold under the root element of the XAML file:

```
<ContentPage ...>
    <ContentPage.Resources>
        <ResourceDictionary>
            <converters:StatusColorConverter
            x:Key="statusColorConverter" />
        </ResourceDictionary>
    </ContentPage.Resources>
    <ContentPage.ToolBarItems>
        <ToolbarItem Text="Add" Command="{Binding AddItem}" />
    </ContentPage.ToolbarItems>
    <Grid ...>
    </Grid>
</ContentPage>
```

This has the same form as the global resource dictionary, but since this one is defined in `MainView`, it can only be accessed from there. We could have defined this in the global resource dictionary, but it's usually more efficient to define objects that you only consume in one place as close to that place as possible.

The last step is to add the converter:

1. Locate the `BoxView` node in the XAML file.
2. Add the `BackgroundColor` XAML, which is marked in bold:

```
<BoxView Grid.RowSpan="2"
    BackgroundColor="{Binding Item.Completed,
                Converter={StaticResource
                statusColorConverter}}" />
```

What we have done here is bind a Boolean value to a property that takes a `Color` object. Right before the data binding takes place, however, `ValueConverter` converts the Boolean value into a color. This is just one of the many cases where `ValueConverter` comes in handy. Keep this in mind when you define the GUI.

Navigating to an item using a command

We want to be able to see the details for a selected to-do list item. When we tap a row, we should navigate to the item in that row.

To do this, we need to add the following code:

1. Open `ViewModels/MainViewModel.cs`.
2. Add the `SelectedItem` property and the `NavigateToItem` method to the class:

```
public TodoItemViewModel SelectedItem
{
    get { return null; }
    set
    {
        Device.BeginInvokeOnMainThread(async () => await
        NavigateToItem(value));
        RaisePropertyChanged(nameof(SelectedItem));
    }
}

private async Task NavigateToItem(TodoItemViewModel item)
{
    if (item == null)
    {
        return;
    }

    var itemView = Resolver.Resolve<ItemView>();
    var vm = itemView.BindingContext as ItemViewModel;
```

```
        vm.Item = item.Item;

        await Navigation.PushAsync(itemView);
    }
```

The `SelectedItem` property is a property that we will data-bind to `ListView`. When we select a row in `ListView`, this property is set to the `TodoItemViewModel` object that represents that row. Since we can't really use Fody here to carry out its `PropertyChanged` magic (because of the need for a method call in the setter), we need to go old school and manually add a getter and a setter.

The setter then calls `NavigateToItem`, which creates a new `ItemView` view using `Resolver`. We extract `ViewModel` from the newly created `ItemView` view and assign the current `TodoItem` object that `TodoItemViewModel` contains. Confused? Remember that `TodoItemViewModel` actually wraps a `TodoItem` object and it is that item that we want to pass to `ItemView`.

We are not done yet. We now need to data-bind the new `SelectedItem` property to the right place in the view:

1. Open `Views/MainView.xaml`.
2. Locate `ListView` and add the attributes in bold:

```
<ListView x:Name="ItemsListView"
          Grid.Row="1"
          RowHeight="70"
          ItemsSource="{Binding Items}"
          SelectedItem="{Binding SelectedItem}">
```

The `SelectedItem` attribute binds the `SelectedItem` property's `ListView` view to the `ViewModel` property. When the selection of an item in `ListView` changes, the `ViewModel` property's `SelectedItem` property is called and we navigate to the new and exciting views.

The x:Name attribute is for naming ListView because we do need to make a small and ugly hack to make this work. ListView actually stays selected after the navigation is done. When we navigate back, it cannot be selected again until we select another row. To mitigate this, we need to hook up to the ItemSelected event of ListView and reset the selected item directly on ListView. This is not recommended because we shouldn't really have any logic in our views, but sometimes we have no other choice:

1. Open Views/MainView.xaml.cs.
2. Add the following code in bold:

```
public MainView(MainViewModel viewmodel)
{
    InitializeComponent();
    viewmodel.Navigation = Navigation;
    BindingContext = viewmodel;

    ItemsListView.ItemSelected += (s, e) =>
    ItemsListView.SelectedItem = null;
}
```

We should now be able to navigate to an item in the list.

Marking an item as complete using a command

We need to add a functionality that allows us to toggle items between complete and active. It is possible to navigate to the detailed view of the to-do list item, but this is too much work for a user. Instead, we'll add a ContextAction item to ListView. In iOS, for example, this is accessed by swiping left on a row:

1. Open ViewModel/TodoItemViewModel.cs.
2. Add a using statement for System.Windows.Input and Xamarin.Forms.
3. Add a command to toggle the status of the item and a piece of text that describes the status:

```
public ICommand ToggleCompleted => new Command((arg) =>
{
    Item.Completed = !Item.Completed;
    ItemStatusChanged?.Invoke(this, new EventArgs());
});
```

Here, we have added a command for toggling the state of an item. When executed, it inverses the current state and raises the `ItemStatusChanged` event so that subscribers are notified. To change the text of the context action button depending on the status, we added a `StatusText` property. This is not recommended practice because we are adding code that only exists because of a specific UI case to `ViewModel`. Ideally, this would be handled by the view, perhaps by using `ValueConverter`. To save us from having to implement these steps, however, we have left it as a string property:

1. Open `Views/MainView.xaml`.
2. Locate the `ListView.ItemTemplate` node and add the following `ViewCell.ContextActions` node:

```
<ListView.ItemTemplate>
    <DataTemplate>
        <ViewCell>
            <ViewCell.ContextActions>
                <MenuItem Text="{Binding StatusText}"
                          Command="{Binding ToggleCompleted}" />
            </ViewCell.ContextActions>
            <Grid Padding="15,10">
            ...
            </Grid>
        </DataTemplate>
</ListView.ItemTemplate>
```

Creating the filter toggle function using a command

We want to be able to toggle between viewing active items only and all the items. We will create a simple mechanism to do this.

Hook up the changes in `MainViewModel` as follows:

1. Open `ViewModels/MainViewModel.cs` and locate `ItemStatusChangeMethod`.
2. Add the implementation to the `ItemStatusChanged` method and a property called `ShowAll` to control the filtering:

```
private void ItemStatusChanged(object sender, EventArgs e)
{
    if (sender is TodoItemViewModel item)
    {
        if (!ShowAll && item.Item.Completed)
        {
            Items.Remove(item);
        }
```

```
                    Task.Run(async () => await
                    repository.UpdateItem(item.Item));
            }
    }

    public bool ShowAll { get; set; }
```

The `ItemStatusChanged` event handler is triggered when we use the context action from the last section. Since the sender is always an object, we try to cast it to `TodoItemViewModel`. If this is successful, we check whether we can remove it from the list if `ShowAll` is not true. This is a small optimization; we could have called `LoadData` and reloaded the entire list, but since the `Items` list is set to `ObservableCollection`, it communicates to `ListView` that one item has been removed from the list. We also call the repository to update the item to persist the change of status.

The `ShowAll` property is what controls which state our filter is in. We need to adjust the `LoadData` method to reflect this:

1. Locate the `Load` method in `MainViewModel`.
2. Add the following lines of code marked in bold:

```
    private async Task LoadData()
    {
        var items = await repository.GetItems();

        if (!ShowAll)
        {
            items = items.Where(x => x.Completed == false).ToList();
        }

        var itemViewModels = items.Select(i =>
        CreateTodoItemViewModel(i));
        Items = new ObservableCollection<TodoItemViewModel>
        (itemViewModels);
    }
```

If `ShowAll` is false, we limit the content of the list to the items that have not been completed. We can do this either by having two methods, `GetAllItems()` and `GetActiveItems()`, or by using a filter argument that can pass to `GetItems()`. Take a minute to think about how we could implement this.

Let's add the code that toggles the filter:

1. Open `ViewModels/MainViewModel.cs`.
2. Add the `FilterText` and `ToggleFilter` properties:

```
public string FilterText => ShowAll ? "All" : "Active";

public ICommand ToggleFilter => new Command(async () =>
{
    ShowAll = !ShowAll;
    await LoadData();
});
```

The `FilterText` property is a read-only property used to display the status as a string in a human-readable form. We could have used `ValueConverter` for this, but to save some time, we simply expose it as a property. The logic for the `ToggleFilter` command is a simple inversion of the state and then a call to `LoadData`. This, in turn, causes a reload of the list.

Before we can filter the items, we need to hook up the filter button:

1. Open `Views/MainView.xaml`.
2. Locate the button that controls the filter (the only button in the file).
3. Adjust your code to reflect the following code:

```
<Button Text="{Binding FilterText, StringFormat='Filter: {0}'}"
        Command="{Binding ToggleFilter}" />
```

We have now finished with this feature! However, our app isn't very attractive; we'll deal with this in the following section.

Laying out the contents

This last section is about making the app look a bit nicer. We will just scratch the surface of the possibilities here, but this should give you some ideas about how styling works.

Setting an application-wide background color

Styles are a great way of applying styling to elements. They can be applied either to all elements of a type or to the elements referenced by a key if you add an x:Key attribute:

1. Open App.xaml in the .NET Standard project.
2. Add the following XAML, which is in bold, to the file:

```
<ResourceDictionary>
    <Style TargetType="NavigationPage">
        <Setter Property="BarBackgroundColor" Value="#A25EBB" />
        <Setter Property="BarTextColor" Value="#FFFFFF" />
    </Style>
    <Style x:Key="FilterButton" TargetType="Button">
        <Setter Property="Margin" Value="15" />
        <Setter Property="BorderWidth" Value="1" />
        <Setter Property="BorderRadius" Value="6" />
        <Setter Property="BorderColor" Value="Silver" />
        <Setter Property="TextColor" Value="Black" />
    </Style>
    <Color x:Key="CompletedColor">#1C8859</Color>
    <Color x:Key="ActiveColor">#D3D3D3</Color>
</ResourceDictionary>
```

The first style we will apply is a new background color and text color to the navigation bar. The second style will be applied to the filter button. We can define a style by setting TargetType, which instructs Xamarin.Forms which type of object this style can be applied to. We can then add one or more properties that we want to set. The result will be the same as if we had added these properties directly to the element in the XAML code.

Styles that lack the x:Key attribute are applied to all instances of the type defined in TargetType. Styles that have a key must be explicitly assigned in the XAML of the user interface. We will see examples of this when we define the filter button in the next section.

Laying out the MainView and ListView items

In this section, we will improve the appearance of MainView and ListView. Open up Views/MainView.xaml and apply the changes in bold in the XAML code in each of the following sections.

The filter button

The filter button allows us to toggle the state of the list to show only the active to-do items or all the to-do items. Let's style it to make it stand out a bit in the layout:

1. Find the filter button.
2. Make the following changes:

```
<Button Style="{StaticResource FilterButton}"
        Text="{Binding FilterText, StringFormat='Filter: {0}'}"
        BackgroundColor="{Binding ShowAll,
        Converter={StaticResource statusColorConverter}}"
        TextColor="Black"
        Command="{Binding ToggleFilter}">
  <Button.Triggers>
    <DataTrigger TargetType="Button" Binding="{Binding ShowAll}"
        Value="True">
      <Setter Property="TextColor" Value="White" />
    </DataTrigger>
  </Button.Triggers>
</Button>
```

The style is applied using `StaticResource`. Anything defined in a resource dictionary, either in the `App.xaml` file or in the local XAML file, is accessible through it. We then set `BackgroundColor`, based on the `ShowAll` property of `MainViewModel`, and set `TextColor` to `Black`.

The `Button.Triggers` node is a useful feature. We can define a number of types of triggers that fire when certain criteria are met. In this case, we use a data trigger that checks whether the value of `ShowAll` changes to `true`. If it does, we set `TextColor` to white. The coolest part is that when `ShowAll` becomes `false` again, it switches back to whichever color it was before.

Touching up ListView

`ListView` could use a couple of minor changes. The first change is formatting the due date string to a more human-readable format and the second is changing the color of the `Completed` label to a nice green tint:

1. Open up `Views/MainView.xaml`.
2. Locate the labels that bind `Item.Due` and `Item.Completed` in `ListView`:

```
<Label Grid.Column="1"
       Grid.Row="1"
       Text="{Binding Item.Due, StringFormat='{0:MMMM d, yyyy}'}"
```

```
                        FontSize="Micro" />
        <Label Grid.Column="1"
               Grid.Row="1"
               HorizontalTextAlignment="End"
               Text="Completed"
               IsVisible="{Binding Item.Completed}"
               FontSize="Micro"
               TextColor="{StaticResource CompletedColor}" />
```

We added a formatting string to the binding to format the date using a specific format. In this case, we used the 0:MMMM d, yyyy format, which will display the date as a string in the format of, for example, May 5, 2020.

We also added a text color to the Completed label that is only visible if an item is completed. We do this by referencing our dictionary in App.xaml.

Summary

You should now have a good grasp of all the steps involved in creating a Xamarin.Forms app from scratch. We learned about the project structure and the important files in a newly created project. We talked about dependency injection using Autofac and learned the basics of MVVM by creating all the views and the ViewModel classes needed. We also covered data storage in SQLite to persist data on our device in a fast and secure way. Using the knowledge gained from this chapter, you should now be able to create the backbone of any app you like.

The next chapter will focus on creating a richer user experience by creating a match-making application that displays images that you can pan around the screen. We will take a closer look at XAML and how to create custom controls.

3
Building a News App Using Xamarin.Forms Shell

In this chapter, we will create a news app that leverages the new Shell navigation functionality provided to us by the Xamarin team at Microsoft. The old way still works—no worries, but we are sure that you will enjoy the new way of defining the structure of your app. Also, you can mix and match old and new as well.

By the end of this chapter, you will have learned how to define an app structure using Shell, consume data from a REST API and configure navigation and passing data between views using query style routes.

So what is Shell, then? In Shell, you define the structure of your app using **Extensible Application Markup Language (XAML)** instead of hiding it in spread-out pieces of code in your app. You can also navigate using routes, just like those fancy web developers are doing.

The following topics will be covered in this chapter:

- Defining a Shell navigation page
- Creating a flyout
- Creating a navigation bar
- Navigating using routes and passing data in query strings
- Consuming data from a public **representational state transfer (REST) application programming interface (API)**
- Adding content in the form of a `CollectionView` control

Technical requirements

To be able to complete this project, you will need to have Visual Studio for Mac or Windows installed, as well as the necessary Xamarin components. See `Chapter 1`, *Introduction to Xamarin*, for more details on how to set up your environment.

Project overview

We will create a Xamarin.Forms project using a .NET Standard library as the code-sharing strategy. It will contain two parts, detailed as follows:

- In the first part, we will create views and make them navigable using Shell.
- In the second part, we will add some content by consuming a REST API of news.

The second part is not needed in order to learn about Shell, but it will take you a bit further down the road to a complete app. This project will target iOS and Android only since at the time of writing, there was no good support for the **Universal Windows Platform** (**UWP**).

Getting started

Let's get started! Make sure that you have a working Xamarin development environment before you start, though. You can read all about that in `Chapter 1`, *Introduction to Xamarin*.

Building the news app

This chapter will be all about building a news app from the beginning. It will guide you through every step, but it will not go down into every detail. For that, we recommend `Chapter 2`, *Building Our First Xamarin.Forms App*, which goes into more detail.

Happy coding!

Setting up the project

This project, like all the rest, is a **File** I **New** I **Project...**-style project. That means that we will not be importing any code at all. So, this first section is all about creating the project and setting up the basic project structure.

Creating the new project

Open Visual Studio and click on **File | New | Project...**, as illustrated in the following screenshot:

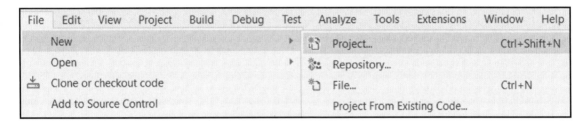

This will open the **Create a new project dialog** wizard. Follow these next steps:

1. Search for `xamarin forms` as per screenshot.
2. Select the **Mobile App (Xamarin.Forms)** project template, and click **Next**, as illustrated in the following screenshot:

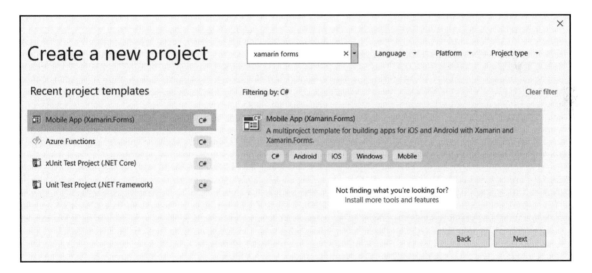

3. Enter **News** as the name of the app, as shown in the following screenshot:

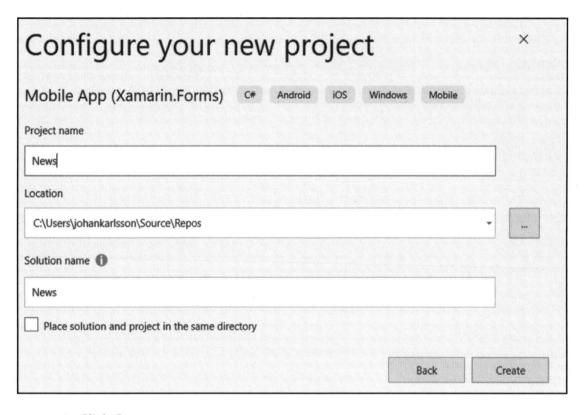

4. Click **Create**.

5. Select the **Blank** template and select **Android** and **iOS** under **Platform**, as illustrated in the following screenshot (At the time of writing, the `CollectionView` control that we will be using was not fully supported by **UWP**. If you need it to work in **UWP**, give it a try.):

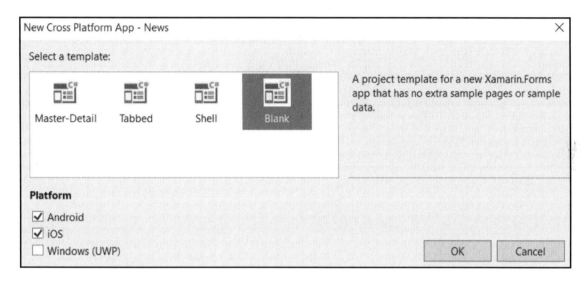

6. Click **OK**.

That's it for project creation. We just need to do some package updating to make sure that we are using the latest and greatest version of Xamarin.Forms.

Updating Xamarin.Forms packages

After creating the project, we should always update our Xamarin.Forms packages to the latest version. To do this, follow these steps:

1. In the **Solution Explorer**, right-click on our **Solution**.
2. Click on **Manage NuGet Packages for Solution...**, as illustrated in the following screenshot:

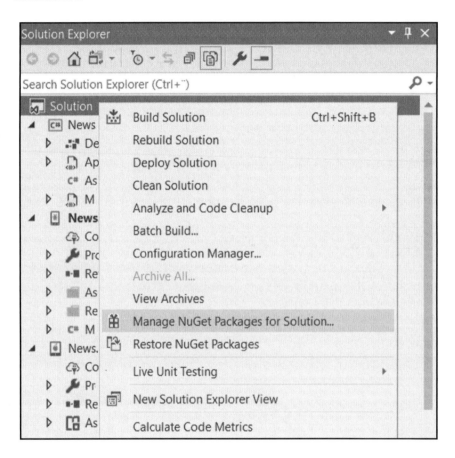

3. This brings up the **NuGet** package manager in Visual Studio, as can be seen in the following screenshot:

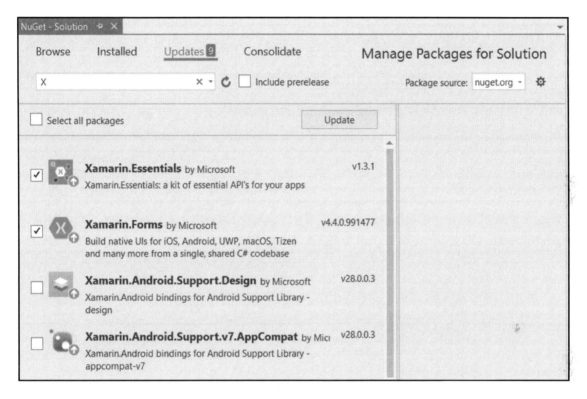

4. Click on the **Updates** tab and check **Xamarin.Essentials** and **Xamarin.Forms** (and only those).
5. Click **Update**, and accept any license dialog boxes that might pop up.

Great job! We've got our project set up and have updated all Xamarin.Forms-related packages to the latest version.

Let's continue by setting up the structure of the app.

Don't update any Android packages manually except for the Xamarin.Forms package. Doing so might lead to version confusion and headaches.

Creating the structure of the app

In this section, we will start to build the **Views** and **ViewModels** of the app. Chapter 2, *Building Our First Xamarin.Forms, App* has a section on **Model-View-ViewModel (MVVM)** as a design pattern. It's recommended that you read that first if you don't know what MVVM is and what PropertyChanged.Fody brings to the table.

Creating the ViewModel base class

The ViewModel is the mediator between the View and the Model. Let's create a base class for ViewModels with common functionality that we can reuse. In practice, the ViewModel must implement an interface called INotifyPropertyChanged in order for MVVM to function. We will do so in the base class, and will also add a little handy helper tool called PropertyChanged.Fody that will save us a lot of time. Again, please check out Chapter 2, *Building Our First Xamarin. Forms App,* if you are feeling unsure about MVVM.

The first step is to create a base class. Proceed as follows:

1. In the **News** project, create a folder called ViewModels.
2. In the ViewModels folder, create a class called ViewModel.
3. Add using statements to System.ComponentModel and change the existing class to look like the following code:

```
using System.ComponentModel;

namespace News.ViewModels
{
    public abstract class ViewModel
    {
    }
}
```

Excellent! Let's implement INotifyPropertyChanged in the base ViewModel class.

Recapping on Quick PropertyChanged.Fody

PropertyChanged.Fody is an **Intermediate Language** (IL) weaver that will automatically add code to your model properties at build time. It will—more specifically—inject a call that will raise the PropertyChanged event whenever a setter is called. It also takes care of property dependencies—if I change the FirstName property, the FullName read-only property will also get a PropertyChanged event. Before PropertyChanged.Fody, you would have had to write this code manually.

It's all explained in more detail in Chapter 2, *Building Our First Xamarin. Forms App*. Have you read it yet?

Implementing INotifyPropertyChanged

The ViewModel sits between the View and the Model. When a change in the ViewModel occurs, the View must be notified. The mechanism for this is the INotifyPropertyChanged interface that defines an event that the controls in the View subscribe to. There is really no magic going on here at all—every ViewModel must implement this interface and the best place to do it would be in the ViewModel base class. Follow these steps:

1. In the **News** project, open up ViewModels.cs.
2. Add the following code in bold:

```
public abstract class ViewModel : INotifyPropertyChanged
{
    public event PropertyChangedEventHandler PropertyChanged;
}
```

This implements the INotifyPropertyChanged interface. The next step is all about reducing the number of lines of code that we will have to write. Normally, you would have to manually raise the PropertyChanged event from your own code, but thanks to IL weavers that inject code at build time, we simply have to create normal properties and let PropertyChanged.Fody do the magic.

 PropertyChanged.Fody reduces the amount of code per property from seven lines to one, not only saving your fingers from typing but also making code readability higher.

Adding a reference to PropertyChanged.Fody

`PropertyChanged.Fody` and its dependencies are installed using NuGet. So let's install the NuGet package as follows:

1. In the **News** project, install the `PropertyChanged.Fody` NuGet package.
2. Accept any license dialog boxes.

This will install the relevant NuGet packages. If you are using Visual Studio for Mac, you also need to create a `FodyWeaver` file. It's nothing complex, just a simple **Extensible Markup Language** (**XML**) file that describes which weavers you have installed. The next section explains how to add this file to the project if it's missing.

Creating a FodyWeaver file

First, check if you have a file called `FodyWeavers.xml` at the root of the .NET Standard library project. If you do, make sure it looks like the XML code shown next. If you can't find it, follow these two simple steps to create it:

1. In the root of the **News** project, create a new file called `FodyWeavers.xml`.
2. Add the following code to the file:

```xml
<?xml version="1.0" encoding="utf-8"?>
<Weavers xmlns:xsi="http://www.w3.org/2001/XMLSchema-instance"
         xsi:noNamespaceSchemaLocation="FodyWeavers.xsd">
  <PropertyChanged />
</Weavers>
```

Fody will read this file during the build process and execute the plugins that you have specified in this file. Since we only have one line (`PropertyChanged`), it will execute that plugin and magically implement `INotifyPropertyChanged` for us.

Let's move on and create our first `ViewModel`.

Creating the HeadlinesViewModel class

We will now start to create some `Views` and `ViewModel` placeholders that we will expand on during this chapter. We will not directly implement all graphical features but, rather, keep it simple and think of all these pages as placeholders for what's to come next.

The first one is the `HeadLinesViewModel` class that will serve as the `ViewModel` for the `HeadlinesView`. Proceed as follows:

1. In the **News** project, create a new class called `HeadlinesViewModel`.
2. Edit the class to inherit from the `ViewModel` base class, as shown in bold in the following code snippet:

```
public class HeadlinesViewModel : ViewModel
{
    public HeadlinesViewModel()
    {
    }
}
```

OK—not bad. It doesn't do much yet, but we'll just leave it for now. Let's create the matching **view**.

Creating the HeadlinesView

This **view** will eventually show a list of news, but in the first section of this chapter, it will be kept simple. Follow these steps to create the page:

1. In the **News** project, create a folder named `Views`.
2. Right-click the `Views` folder, select **Add**, and then click **New Item...** .
3. Under the **Visual C# Items** node on the left, select **Xamarin.Forms**.
4. Select **Content Page** and name it `HeadlinesView`.
5. Click **Add** to create the page.

Refer to the following screenshot to view the preceding information:

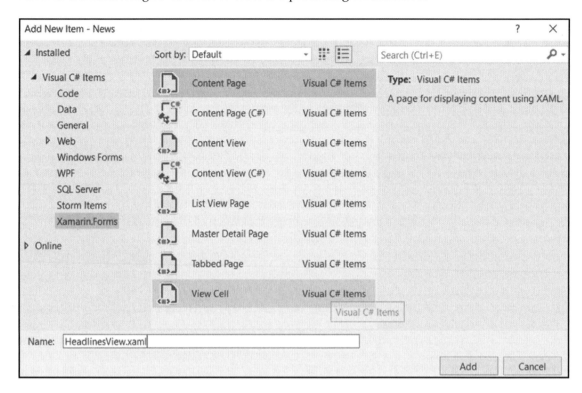

Let's add some placeholder code to the `HeadlinesView`, just to have something to navigate to and from. We will replace it with something hotter later on in the chapter, but to keep things simple, let's add a label. To do so, proceed as follows:

1. In the **News** project, open `HeadlinesView.xaml` .
2. Edit the XAML code by adding the following code marked in bold:

```xml
<?xml version="1.0" encoding="UTF-8"?>
<ContentPage xmlns="http://xamarin.com/schemas/2014/forms"
             xmlns:x="http://schemas.microsoft.com/winfx/2009/xaml"
             Title="Home"
             x:Class="News.Views.HeadlinesView">
    <ContentPage.Content>
        <Label VerticalOptions="Center"
               HorizontalOptions="Center"
               Text="HeadlinesView!" />
    </ContentPage.Content>
</ContentPage>
```

This will set the title of the page and add a label with the text `HeadlinesView` centered in the middle of the page. Let's move on and create some additional **view** placeholders.

Creating the ArticleItem

The app will eventually display a list of articles where each article will be rendered using a reusable component. We will call this reusable component `ArticleItem`. In Xamarin.Forms, a reusable component is called a `ContentView`. Please don't confuse this with an MVVM View, which is represented by a page in Xamarin.Forms. We know that this is confusing, but the rule is that a Xamarin.Forms page is an MVVM View and a Xamarin.Forms Content View is essentially a reusable control.

That said, let's create the `ArticleItem` class, as follows:

1. In the **News** project, right-click the `Views` folder, select **Add**, and then click **New Item...** .
2. Under the **Visual C# Items** node on the left, select **Xamarin.Forms**.
3. **IMPORTANT:** Make sure that you select the **Content View** template in the next step and **NOT** the **Content Page** template.
4. Select **Content View** (important, remember?) and name it `ArticleItem`.
5. Click **Add** to create the view.

Refer to the following screenshot to view the preceding information:

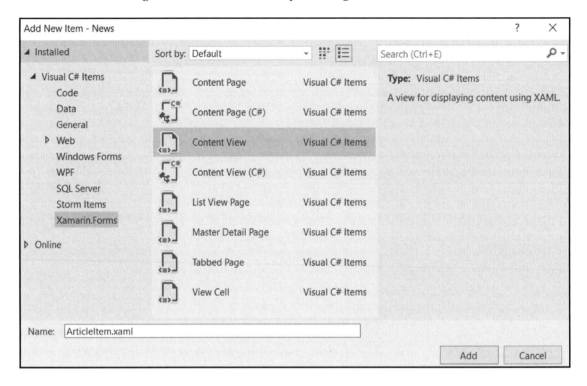

We don't need to alter the XAML code generated at this point, so we'll simply leave it as is.

Creating the ArticleView

In the last section, we created the `ArticleItem` content view. This view (the `ArticleView`) will contain a ListView where each cell will render one `ArticleItem`. But for the moment, let's just add the `ArticleView` as a placeholder. Follow these steps to do so:

1. In the **News** project, right-click the `Views` folder, select **Add**, and then click **New Item...** .
2. Select **Xamarin.Forms** under the **Visual C# Items** node on the left.
3. Select **Content Page** and name it `ArticleView`.
4. Click **Add** to create the page.

Since this view is also a placeholder view at the moment, we'll just add a label to indicate the type of page. Edit the content as shown by the following few steps:

1. In the **News** project, open `Article.xaml`.
2. Edit the XAML code by adding the following code marked in bold:

```xml
<?xml version="1.0" encoding="UTF-8"?>
<ContentPage xmlns="http://xamarin.com/schemas/2014/forms"
             xmlns:x="http://schemas.microsoft.com/winfx/2009/xaml"
             x:Class="News.Views.ArticleView">
    <ContentPage.Content>
        <Label VerticalOptions="Center"
               HorizontalOptions="Center"
               Text="Article view!" />
    </ContentPage.Content>
</ContentPage>
```

Alright—just one more view to mock before we start to wire things up.

Creating the AboutView

The last view will be created in the same way as all the others. Proceed as follows:

1. In the **News** project, right-click the `Views` folder, select **Add**, and then click **New Item...** .
2. Under the **Visual C# Items** node on the left, select **Xamarin.Forms**.
3. Select **Content Page** and name it `AboutView`.
4. Click **Add** to create the page.

This view is the only view that will actually stay a placeholder view. It's up to you to do something with it if you choose to build something cool out of this project later on. So, we will only add a label that states that this is the `AboutView`.

1. In the **News** project, open `About.xaml` .
2. Edit the XAML code by adding the following code marked in bold:

```xml
<?xml version="1.0" encoding="UTF-8"?>
<ContentPage xmlns="http://xamarin.com/schemas/2014/forms"
             xmlns:x="http://schemas.microsoft.com/winfx/2009/xaml"
             x:Class="News.Views.AboutView">
    <ContentPage.Content>
        <Label VerticalOptions="Center"
               HorizontalOptions="Center"
               Text="About view!" />
```

```
        </ContentPage.Content>
    </ContentPage>
```

Now, we have all the views we need to start wiring the app up. The first step is to configure dependency injection through Autofac.

Wiring up dependency injection through Autofac

Using dependency injection as a pattern, we can keep our code cleaner and more testable. This app will use constructor injection, which means that all dependencies that a class has must be passed through its constructor. Autofac then helps out with constructing objects for you so you don't have to care too much about the dependency chain. Let's dive into installing Autofac.

 Confused over dependency injection?

Check out the *Wiring up a dependency injection through Autofac* section in `Chapter 2`, *Building Our First Xamarin.Forms App*, for more details on dependency injection.

Adding a reference to Autofac

Autofac lives in a NuGet package that we need to install, and we need to reference it in our project files. Proceed as follows:

1. Open up the **NuGet** package manager by right-clicking on the **Solution** node and clicking on **Manage NuGet Packages for Solution...** .
2. Click on **Browse**, and type `Autofac` in the search box.
3. Tick all the checkboxes under **Project**, scroll down, and click **Install**.

Refer to the following screenshot to view the preceding information:

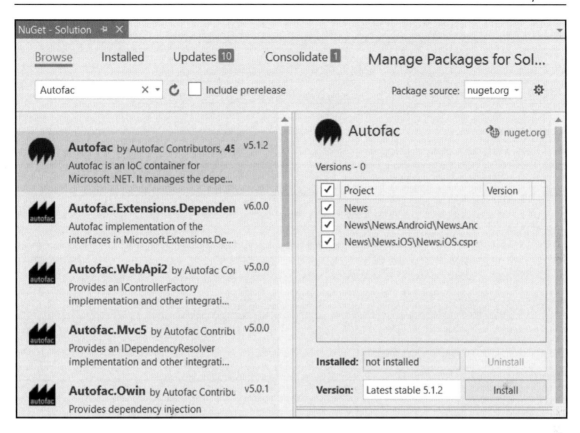

This will download and install Autofac into all your projects. The next step is to add some code that will allow us to use Autofac.

Creating the resolver

The resolver will be responsible for creating our objects for us, based on the type that we have in the request. It wraps the specific functionality of Autofac, making it easy to replace Autofac if needed. Let's create the resolver, as follows:

1. In the root folder of the **News** project, create a new file called `Resolver.cs`.
2. Add the following code to the file:

```
using Autofac;

namespace News
{
    public static class Resolver
```

```
        {
            private static IContainer container;

            public static void Initialize(IContainer container)
            {
                Resolver.container = container;
            }

            public static T Resolve<T>()
            {
                return container.Resolve<T>();
            }
        }
    }
```

The `container` property of the `IContainer` type is defined in **Autofac** and represents a container that holds the configuration on how to resolve types. The `Initialize` method takes an instance of an object that implements the `IContainer` interface and assigns it to the `container` property. The `Resolve` method uses the `container` property to resolve a type to an instance of an object. It might seem like a strange way of instantiating objects, but just hang in there—it will make sense.

Creating the bootstrapper

The bootstrapper is responsible for initializing Autofac. It will be called at the startup of the application and run once. Let's create the bootstrapper, as shown in the following steps:

1. In the root of the **News** project, create a new file called `Bootstrapper.cs`.
2. Enter the following code:

```
using Autofac;
using News.ViewModels;

namespace News
{
    public static class Bootstrapper
    {
        public static void Initialize()
        {
            var containerBuilder = new ContainerBuilder();
containerBuilder.RegisterAssemblyTypes(typeof(App).Assembly)
                           .Where(x =>
x.IsSubclassOf(typeof(ViewModel))));
            var container = containerBuilder.Build();
            Resolver.Initialize(container);
        }
```

```
        }
    }
```

Autofac uses the `ContainerBuilder` class to configure and finally build the container that we will pass to our resolver. Think of a builder as something that collects a lot of information on what needs to be done, and then finally builds the object we need. It's a very useful pattern on its own, by the way.

We only use the builder for one thing at the moment. Later on, we will use it to register any class in the assembly that inherits from our abstract `ViewModel` class. Autofac is now prepared for us to ask for these types.

 The very keen-eyed might notice that this bootstrapper is simpler than the one in `Chapter 2`, *Building Our First Xamarin.Forms App*. That's correct, and the reason for that is that this bootstrapper will not be called by the individual platform projects since there is no need for that in this app. However, as soon as you need to create platform-specific implementations of interfaces, you will need to fall back to the slightly more complicated bootstrapper approach.

Initializing the bootstrapper

Now, we need to wire up the bootstrapper into the app. This should be done as early as possible in the life cycle. Proceed as follows:

1. In the **News** project, open `App.Xaml.cs` by expanding the `App.Xaml` node in the **Solution Explorer**.

2. Locate the constructor, and add the following line of code marked in bold:

```
public App()
{
    InitializeComponent();
    Bootstrapper.Initialize();
    MainPage = new MainPage();
}
```

Not much to say—it's a single line of code to a static method that initializes the bootstrapper. Well done! Now, we need some graphical touches on our app and we rely on **Font Awesome** to do the magic.

Downloading and configuring Font Awesome

Font Awesome is a free collection of images packaged into a font. Xamarin.Forms has excellent support for using Font Awesome in toolbars, navigation bars, and all over the place. It's not strictly needed to make this app, but we think that it's worth the extra round trip since you are most likely going to need something like this in your new killer app.

The first step is to download the font.

Downloading Font Awesome

Downloading the font is straightforward. Please note the renaming of the file—not really needed but it's easier to edit configuration files and such if it has a simpler name. Follow these steps to acquire and copy the font to each project:

1. Browse to `https://fontawesome.com/download`.
2. Click the **Free for Desktop** button to download Font Awesome.
3. Unzip the downloaded file, then locate the `otfs` folder.
4. Rename the `Font Awesome 5 Free-Solid-900.otf` file to `FontAwesome.otf` (you can keep the original name, but it's just less to type if you rename it).
5. Copy `FontAwesome.otf` to the `Resources` folder in the iOS project.
6. Copy `FontAwesome.otf` to the `Assets` folder in the Android project.

Alright—now, we need to configure iOS to accept FontAwesome. It's only iOS that needs this extra configuration. For Android, you are good to go.

Adding Font Awesome to Info.plist on iOS

On iOS, we have a file called `info.plist`. This file is a standard XML file with a funny internal format. For this operation, we strongly suggest that you open this file using a standard text editor and not the built-in editor in your **integrated development environment** (**IDE**). The reason for this is that most IDEs have a graphical **user interface** (**UI**) built on top of this file that just gets in the way of adding the small amount of XML that we want to add.

That said, let's edit the `info.plist` file, as follows:

1. In the **iOS** project, open `info.plist` with a standard text editor.
2. Add the tags marked in bold in the following code block:

```xml
<?xml version="1.0" encoding="UTF-8"?>
<!DOCTYPE plist PUBLIC "-//Apple//DTD PLIST 1.0//EN"
"http://www.apple.com/DTDs/PropertyList-1.0.dtd">
<plist version="1.0">
    <dict>
        <key>UIDeviceFamily</key>
        <array>
            <integer>1</integer>
            <integer>2</integer>
        </array>

        <!-- Tags removed for brevity, don't remove any tags -->

        <key>XSAppIconAssets</key>
        <string>Assets.xcassets/AppIcon.appiconset</string>
        <key>UIAppFonts</key>
        <array>
            <string>FontAwesome.otf</string>
        </array>
    </dict>
</plist>
```

That's it for platform-specific hoop-jumping. The next step is to make Xamarin.Forms aware of the FontAwesome.

Adding the font to a static resource

In a Xamarin.Forms app, we can define application-wide resources that we can use anywhere in our app. They are added in the same way as page-/view-specific resources but to the `App.xaml` file instead. Let's add a reference to FontAwesome that will be unified under one name in our Xamarin.Forms app, as follows:

1. In the **News** project, open `App.xaml`.
2. Add the following code marked in bold:

```xml
<?xml version="1.0" encoding="utf-8"?>
<Application xmlns="http://xamarin.com/schemas/2014/forms"
             xmlns:x="http://schemas.microsoft.com/winfx/2009/xaml"
             xmlns:d="http://xamarin.com/schemas/2014/forms/design"
             xmlns:mc="http://schemas.openxmlformats.org/
              markup-compatibility/2006"
```

```
                            mc:Ignorable="d"
                            x:Class="News.App">
            <Application.Resources>
                <ResourceDictionary>
                    <OnPlatform x:Key="IconFont"
                        x:TypeArguments="x:String">
                        <On Platform="iOS" Value="Font Awesome 5 Free" />
                        <On Platform="Android" Value="FontAwesome.otf#" />
                    </OnPlatform>
                </ResourceDictionary>
            </Application.Resources>
        </Application>
```

The `ResourceDictionary` tag defines that we need a dictionary of resources. Additional resources will, later on, be added within this tag. In the preceding example, we only have one resource, but it's wrapped inside an `OnPlatform` tag. The `OnPlatform` tag is a cool feature of Xamarin.Forms that enables instantiation of different resources based on the runtime platform.

What we are saying here is that we need a resource named `IconFont` (`x:Key="IconFont"`) and that it will be a string (`x:TypeArguments="x:String"`). For iOS, this string will be `Font Awesome 5 Free`, and for Android, this string will be `FontAwesome.otf#`.

What's the reason why we need a different string anyway? It has to do with what each platform expects in the way of identifying a loaded font.

Defining some icons in the resource dictionary

Now that we have defined the font, we will put that to use and define five icons to use in our app. Let's add the XAML first and we'll then examine one of the `FontImage` tags. Proceed as follows:

1. In the **News** project, open `App.xaml`.
2. Add the following code marked in bold under the `OnPlatform` tag that we just added:

```
        <ResourceDictionary>
            <OnPlatform x:Key="IconFont" x:TypeArguments="x:String">
                <On Platform="iOS" Value="Font Awesome 5 Free" />
                <On Platform="Android" Value="FontAwesome.otf#" />
            </OnPlatform>

            <FontImage x:Key="HomeIcon"
                    FontFamily="{StaticResource IconFont}"
```

```
                          Glyph='& #xf015;' Size="22" Color="Black" />

          <FontImage x:Key="HeadlinesIcon"
                     FontFamily="{StaticResource IconFont}"
                     Glyph="& #xf70e;" Size="22" />

          <FontImage x:Key="NewsIcon"
                     FontFamily="{StaticResource IconFont}"
                     Glyph="& #xf1ea;" Size="22" />

          <FontImage x:Key="SettingsIcon"
                     FontFamily="{StaticResource IconFont}"
                     Glyph="& #xf013;" Size="22"
                     Color="Black" />

          <FontImage x:Key="AboutIcon"
                     FontFamily="{StaticResource IconFont}"
                     Glyph="& #xf05a;"
                     Size="22" Color="Black" />
      </ResourceDictionary>
```

A `FontImage` is a class that can be used anywhere in Xamarin.Forms expect an **ImageSource** object. It's designed to render one character (or glyph) into an image. The `FontImage` class needs a few attributes to work, detailed as follows:

- A key for reference used by other views in the application.
- A `FontFamily` resource that uses a `StaticResource` reference back to the `IconFont` resource that we defined in the preceding section.
- The `Glyph` object representing the image to be shown. To find which image these cryptic values refer to, check out `fontawesome.com`, click on **Icons**, select **Free**, and start browsing.
- `Size` and `Color`. Not strictly needed but nice to define.

FontAwesome is now installed and configured. We've done a lot of work to get to the actual topic of the chapter. It's time to define the **shell!**

Defining the shell

As stated earlier, Xamarin.Forms Shell is the newest way of defining the structure of your app. The different projects in the book use alternate ways of defining the overall structure of the app, but Xamarin.Forms Shell is, in our opinion, the best way of defining the UI structure. We hope you find it as exciting as we do!

We are going to start by creating a `MainShell` file that describes the structure of the app.

Creating the MainShell file

We'll add the `MainShell` file directly to the root of the .NET Standard Library. There is no template for a shell available, so we need to add a regular **content page** file and make some minor changes to it. No worries—it's quickly done, as detailed here:

1. In the **News** project, right-click the project node, select **Add**, and then click **New Item...** .
2. Under the **Visual C# Items** node on the left, select **Xamarin.Forms**.
3. Select **Content Page** and name it `MainShell`.
4. Click **Add** to create the page.

Excellent! Now, we need to modify the XAML and change the root node to Shell and remove some unnecessary tags.

1. In the **News** project, open the `MainShell.xaml` file.
2. Replace the root node and remove the content of the root node so that the file looks like the code in the following snippet:

```
<?xml version="1.0" encoding="UTF-8"?>
<Shell xmlns="http://xamarin.com/schemas/2014/forms"
       xmlns:x="http://schemas.microsoft.com/winfx/2009/xaml"
       x:Class="News.MainShell">
</Shell>
```

To make the code-behind file match the XAML, we need to let it inherit from Shell by doing the following:

1. Open the `MainShell.xaml.cs` file.
2. Change the base class to `Shell` (or remove it, since it's a partial class declaration), as illustrated in the following code snippet:

```
public partial class MainShell : Shell
{
    public MainShell()
    {
        InitializeComponent();
    }
}
```

That's it. The next section will focus on setting up the main structure of the app.

Defining the basic structure

We're going to start by defining a basic structure for the app without really adding any of our defined views to it. After that, we'll add the actual views one by one. But let's start by adding some content and creating `ContentPage` objects using XAML directly. Follow these two steps to do so:

1. In the **News** project, open the `MainShell.xaml` file.
2. Alter the file so that it looks like the following code:

```xml
<?xml version="1.0" encoding="UTF-8"?>
<Shell xmlns="http://xamarin.com/schemas/2014/forms"
       xmlns:x="http://schemas.microsoft.com/winfx/2009/xaml"
       xmlns:views="clr-namespace:News.Views"
       x:Class="News.MainShell">
   <FlyoutItem Title="Home"
               Icon="{StaticResource HomeIcon}">
     <ShellContent Title="Headlines" Icon="{StaticResource
       HeadlinesIcon}" >
         <ContentPage Title="Headlines" />
     </ShellContent>
     <Tab Title="News" Icon="{StaticResource NewsIcon}">
         <ContentPage Title="Local" />
         <ContentPage Title="Global" />
     </Tab>
   </FlyoutItem>

   <FlyoutItem Title="Settings" Icon="{StaticResource
     SettingsIcon}">
         <ContentPage Title="Settings" />
   </FlyoutItem>

    <ShellContent Title="About" Icon="{StaticResource AboutIcon}">
         <ContentPage Title="About"/>
    </ShellContent>
</Shell>
```

Let's break this down. The direct children of the **shell** itself are two FlyoutItem objects and one ShellContent object. All three of these have a **Title** and an **Icon** defined as shown in the screenshot below. The icons are referenced to the Font Awesome resources we created earlier. This will render a flyout, as shown in the following screenshot:

The flyout is accessible by swiping in from the left. The Flyout objects can have multiple children, while the ShellContent element can only have a single child.

The **Home** flyout item is the most complex example. It has two children; a ShellContent with a page with the title **Headlines** and a tab that defines two child pages on its own. The first level of children will render the **Tab bar** at the bottom of the app, as shown in the following screenshot. The second level of children, under the Tab element with the title **News** will be rendered as a tab bar directly under the title of the **Navigation bar** at the top:

The **Settings** and **About** flyouts will simply render the pages that they define.

Adding the MainShell type to the container

We now need to register the `MainShell` that we created into our container so that we can instantiate it and show it off to the world. Proceed as follows:

1. In the **News** project, open the `Bootstrapper.cs` file.

2. Locate the `Initialize()` method and add the following code shown in bold:

```
public static void Initialize()
{
    var containerBuilder = new ContainerBuilder();
    containerBuilder.RegisterType<MainShell>();
    // code omitted for brevity
}
```

This makes the Autofac container aware of which instances it should return when asking for a class or an interface.

Making the app run

We are getting closer to the first moment of truth. It's time to try the app out and see if it looks like the screenshots shown throughout the chapter. We only have one last thing to do, and that is to instantiate the `MainShell` and assign it to the `MainPage` property of the app. Proceed as follows:

1. In the **News** project, open the `App.xaml.cs` file.
2. Replace the assignment of the main page with a call to the `Resolver` with the following code marked in bold:

```
public App()
{
    InitializeComponent();
    Bootstrapper.Initialize();
    MainPage = Resolver.Resolve<MainShell>();
}
```

The app should now run. If not, calm down and simply go through the code again. After you are done with navigating around the app, let's create a news service to fetch news from, and extend all those views that we've created.

Creating the news service

In order to find cool content, we'll consume an already existing news API provided by `newsapi.org`. To do so, you must register for an API key that we can use to request the news. If you aren't comfortable with doing so, you can mock the news service if you would like, instead of using the API.

The first thing is to obtain an API key.

Obtaining an API key

The process of registering is pretty straightforward. But since this is a book, be aware that the UI of `newsapi.org` might have changed by the time you read this.

OK—let's get that key, as follows:

1. Browse to `https://newsapi.org/`.
2. Click **Get API key**.
3. Fill out the form, as illustrated in the following screenshot:

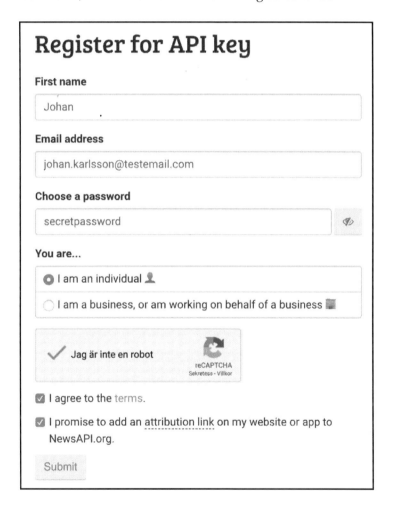

4. Copy the API key provided on the next page, as illustrated in the following screenshot:

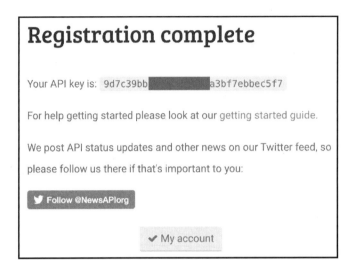

Now, we need a place to store the key for easy access. We'll create a static class that will hold the key for us. Proceed as follows:

1. In the **News** project, create a new class called `Settings` in the root folder.
2. Add the code as shown in the following snippet, to insert the API key obtained in the preceding section:

```
namespace News
{
    public static class Settings
    {
        public static string NewsApiKey
        {
            get
            {
                return "<Your APIKey here>";
            }
        }
    }
}
```

The important thing here is that you actually copy and paste the key into the file. Now, we need models.

Creating the models

The data returned from the API needs to go somewhere, and the most convenient way of accessing it would be to deserialize the data into **POCO** objects (**Plain Old CLR Objects**, also known as regular C# classes). These POCO objects we usually call models, and they usually like to live in a folder called `Models`. Let's create our models:

1. In the **News** project, create a new folder called `Models`.
2. In the `Models` folder, add a new class called `NewsApiModels`.
3. Add the following code to the class:

```csharp
using System;
using System.Collections.Generic;

namespace News.Models
{
    public class Source
    {
        public string Id { get; set; }
        public string Name { get; set; }
    }

    public class Article
    {
        public Source Source { get; set; }
        public string Author { get; set; }
        public string Title { get; set; }
        public string Description { get; set; }
        public string Url { get; set; }
        public string UrlToImage { get; set; }
        public DateTime PublishedAt { get; set; }
        public string Content { get; set; }
    }

    public class NewsResult
    {
        public string Status { get; set; }
        public int TotalResults { get; set; }
        public List<Article> Articles { get; set; }
    }
}
```

When we call the API it will return a `NewsResult` object that will, in turn, contain a list of articles. The next step is to create a service that will wrap the API and allow us to access the latest news.

> If you ever need to create a class model out of a bunch of **JavaScript Object Notation (JSON)**, you can use the Paste JSON as Classes tool in Visual Studio for Windows (**Edit | Paste Special | Paste JSON as Classes**).

Creating a service class

The service class will wrap the API so that we can access it in a nice .NET-ish kind of way. We'll also use a cool C# 8 feature called **switch expressions** to increase the readability of the code.

But we'll start with defining an enum that will define the scope of the news that we request.

Creating the NewsScope enum

The `NewsScope` enum defines the different kinds of news that our service supports. Let's add it by following these few steps:

1. In the **News** project, create a new folder called **Services**.
2. In the **Services** folder, add a new file called `NewsScope.cs`.
3. Add the following code to that file:

```
namespace News.Services
{
    public enum NewsScope
    {
        Headlines,
        Local,
        Global
    }
}
```

To be able to use this enum in a `switch` expression, we'll need to enable C# 8 for the project.

Enabling C# 8

C# 8 features are usually not enabled by default when creating new projects in Visual Studio. However, it's fairly simple to enable, but it does involve editing the project file manually. Follow these few steps to do so:

1. Right-click the **News** project node and click **Edit Project File**, as illustrated in the following screenshot:

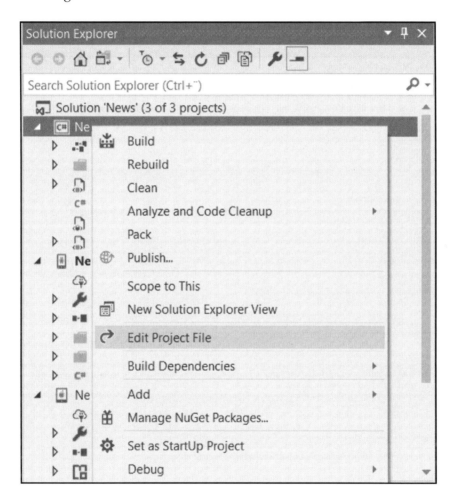

2. Add the following line marked in bold to the project file:

```
<Project Sdk="Microsoft.NET.Sdk">
    <PropertyGroup>
        <TargetFramework>netstandard2.0</TargetFramework>
```

```
        <ProduceReferenceAssembly>true</ProduceReferenceAssembly>
        <LangVersion>8.0</LangVersion>
    </PropertyGroup>

    <!-- xml removed for brevity -->
</Project>
```

That's it. We've now specified that we want to use C# 8. You could also specify `latest` as the value of the `LangVersion` tag. The next step is to create the `NewsService` class that will wrap the call to the **News API**.

Creating the NewsService class

The purpose of the `NewsService` class is to wrap the HTTP calls to the news REST API and make them easily accessible to our code in the form of regular .NET method calls. It also acts as an abstraction, making it easier to replace the source of the news if you would like to do so.

Creating the `NewsService` class is quite straightforward. Follow these steps:

1. In the **News** project, install the `Newtonsoft.Json` NuGet package in the same way that we added the **Autofac** package earlier.
2. In the **Services** folder, create a new class called `NewsService`.
3. Edit the class so that it looks like the following code:

```
using System;
using System.Net;
using System.Threading.Tasks;
using News.Models;
using Newtonsoft.Json;

namespace News.Services
{
    public class NewsService
    {
        public async Task<NewsResult> GetNews(NewsScope scope)
        {
            string url = GetUrl(scope);

            var webclient = new WebClient();
            var json = await
             webclient.DownloadStringTaskAsync(url);
            return JsonConvert.DeserializeObject<NewsResult>(json);
        }
        private string GetUrl(NewsScope scope)
```

```
        {
            return scope switch
            {
                NewsScope.Headlines => Headlines,
                NewsScope.Global => Global,
                NewsScope.Local => Local,
                _ => throw new Exception("Undefined scope")
            };
        }
        private string Headlines =>
            "https://newsapi.org/v2/top-headlines?" +
            "country=us&" +
            $"apiKey={Settings.NewsApiKey}";

        private string Local =>
            "https://newsapi.org/v2/everything?q=local&" +
            $"apiKey={Settings.NewsApiKey}";

        private string Global =>
            "https://newsapi.org/v2/everything?q=global&" +
            $"apiKey={Settings.NewsApiKey}";
    }
}
```

The `NewsService` class is composed of five methods;

The first method, `GetNews`, is the method that we will eventually call from our app. It takes one parameter, `scope`, which is the enum that we created earlier. Depending on the value of this parameter, we will get different types of news. The first thing this method does is to resolve the **Uniform Resource Locator (URL)** to call, and it does so by calling the `GetUrl` method with the scope.

The `GetUrl` method uses a switch expression to resolve the URL and, depending on the value of the scope parameter passed, it returns one of three URLs. The URL points to the REST API of **NewsAPI** with some predefined query parameters and the API key that we registered for.

When we've resolved the correct URL, we are ready to make the HTTP request and download the news in the form of JSON. The built-in `WebClient` class in .NET does a fine job of fetching the JSON for us. All that is left after acquiring the data is to deserialize it into the news models that we defined earlier.

The next step is to wire up the `NewsService` class.

Wiring up the NewsService class

We are now ready to wire up the `NewsService` class in our app and integrate it with a real news source. We will extend all the existing ViewModels that we have and also define the UI elements to be able to render the news in the Views.

Extending the HeadlinesViewModel class

In MVVM, the `ViewModel` is the place to handle the logic of the app. The model is the news data that we will get from our `NewsService` class. We will now extend the `HeadlinesViewModel` class to use the `NewsService` to fetch news by following these two steps:

1. In the **News** project, expand the `ViewModels` folder and open the `HeadlinesViewModel.cs` file.
2. Add the following code marked in bold and resolve references:

```
using System;
using System.Threading.Tasks;
using System.Web;
using System.Windows.Input;
using News.Models;
using News.Services;
using Xamarin.Forms;

namespace News.ViewModels
{

public class HeadlinesViewModel : ViewModel
{
    private readonly NewsService newsService;
    public NewsResult CurrentNews { get; set; }

    public HeadlinesViewModel(NewsService newsService)
    {
        this.newsService = newsService;
    }

    public async Task Initialize(string scope)
    {
        var resolvedScope = scope.ToLower() switch
        {
            "local" => NewsScope.Local,
            "global" => NewsScope.Global,
            "headlines" => NewsScope.Headlines,
```

```
                    _ => NewsScope.Headlines
        };

        await Initialize(resolvedScope);
    }

    public async Task Initialize(NewsScope scope)
    {
        CurrentNews = await newsService.GetNews(scope);
    }

    public ICommand ItemSelected =>
        new Command(async (selectedItem) =>
        {
            var selectedArticle = selectedItem as Article;
            var url = HttpUtility.UrlEncode(selectedArticle.Url);
            // Placeholder for more code later on
        });
    }
    }
    }
```

Since we are using (constructor) dependency injection, we need to inject our dependencies in the constructor. The only dependency this ViewModel has is the `NewsService`, and we store it internally in the class as a field.

The `CurrentNews` property is defined in order to get something to bind the UI to.

We then have two `Initialize` methods, one that takes `scope` as an enum and one that takes `scope` as a string. The string overload of the `Initialize` method will be used in XAML, and it simply translates the string into the enum representation of the `scope` and then calls the other `Initialize` method, which in turn calls the `GetNews(...)` method on the news service.

The property at the end, `ItemSelected`, returns a Xamarin.Forms command that we will wire up to respond to when the user of the app selects an item. Half of the method is implemented from the start. The selected item will be passed into the method and then we encode the URL to the article since we will be passing it as a query parameter when we navigate within the app. We will get back to the navigation part in a while.

So, now we have the code needed to fetch the data, and we'll move on to defining the UI to display it.

Extending the HeadlinesView

The HeadlinesView is a shared view that will be used in several places in the app. The purpose of the view is to display a list of articles and to allow for navigation from one article into a web browser that will display the entire article.

Extending the HeadlinesView comes in two steps; first, we edit the XAML and define the UI, then we need to add some code to initialize it. Proceed as follows:

1. In the **News** project, expand the Views folder and open the HeadlinesView.xaml file.

2. Edit the XAML, as shown in the following code block:

```xml
<?xml version="1.0" encoding="UTF-8"?>
<ContentPage xmlns="http://xamarin.com/schemas/2014/forms"
             xmlns:x="http://schemas.microsoft.com/winfx/2009/xaml"
             xmlns:views="clr-namespace:News.Views"
             x:Name="headlinesview"
             Title="Home"
             x:Class="News.Views.HeadlinesView">
    <ContentPage.Content>
        <StackLayout Padding="14">
            <CollectionView ItemsSource="{Binding
              CurrentNews.Articles}">
              <CollectionView.EmptyView>
                 <Label Text="Loading" />
              </CollectionView.EmptyView>
              <CollectionView.ItemTemplate>
                 <DataTemplate>
                    <ContentView>
                       <ContentView.GestureRecognizers>
                          <TapGestureRecognizer
                             Command="{Binding
                             BindingContext.ItemSelected,
                             Source={x:Reference headlinesview}}"
                             CommandParameter="{Binding .}" />
                       </ContentView.GestureRecognizers>
                       <views:ArticleItem />
                    </ContentView>
                 </DataTemplate>
              </CollectionView.ItemTemplate>
            </CollectionView>
        </StackLayout>
    </ContentPage.Content>
</ContentPage>
```

The `HeadlinesView` uses a `CollectionView` to display the list of articles. The `ItemsSource` property is set to the `CurrentNews.Articles` property of the `ViewModel`, which, after loading news, should contain a list of news. While the list is empty or loading, we display a loading label, defined within the `CollectionView.EmptyView` element. You could, of course, create any valid UI inside of that tag to create a cooler loading screen.

Each article in the `CurrentNews.Articles` list will be rendered using whatever is inside the `CollectionView.ItemTemplate` element, and it's what's inside of the `ContentView` element that will represent the actual item. The article will be rendered using an `ArticleItem` view, which is basically a custom control that we defined earlier. We will define this view right after we are done with this view.

To enable navigation from the view, we need to detect when a user clicks on the specific article. We do so by adding a `TapGestureRecognizer` and bind it to the `ItemSelected` command of the root `ViewModel`. The `Source={x:Reference headlinesview}}` snippet is what references the current context back to the root of the page, and not the current article in the list that we are iterating. If we didn't specify the source, the binding engine would try to bind the `ItemSelected` command to a property defined in the current article of the `CurrentNews.Articles` property.

That's all for the GUI part. Now, we need to alter the code-behind to enable initialization based on data that we will pass from the XAML itself. Follow these steps to make it happen:

1. In the **News** project, open the `HeadlinesView.xaml.cs` code-behind file.
2. Add the following code marked in bold to the file:

```
using System.Threading.Tasks;
using News.Services;
using News.ViewModels;
using Xamarin.Forms;

namespace News.Views
{
    public partial class HeadlinesView : ContentPage
    {
        public HeadlinesView()
        {
            InitializeComponent();
            Task.Run(async () => await Initialize("Headlines"));
        }

        public HeadlinesView(string scope)
        {
```

```
                          InitializeComponent();
                          Title = $"{scope} news";
                          Task.Run(async () => await Initialize(scope));
                      }

                      private async Task Initialize(string scope)
                      {
                          var viewModel = Resolver.Resolve<HeadlinesViewModel>();
                          BindingContext = viewModel;
                          await viewModel.Initialize(scope);
                      }
                  }
              }
```

Usually, we don't want to add code to the code-behind of a view directly, but we need to make an exception to enable the passing of arguments from XAML to our `ViewModel`.

Depending on the format of the XAML, one of the two preceding constructors will be called during the initialization of the page. If we don't specify any arguments at all in the XAML, the first constructor will be called. If we specify arguments, then the second constructor will be called. Both constructors call a private method that creates an instance of the `HeadlinesViewModel` for us, sets it as the binding context of the view, and calls the `Initialize()` method on the ViewModel that makes the REST call to the news API. We will make use of the two constructors in a while when we edit the shell file.

But first, we need to extend the `ContentView` of the `ArticleItem` to display a single-row item in the news lists.

Extending the ContentView of the ArticleItem

The `ContentView` of the `ArticleItem` represents one item in a list of news, as the following screenshot illustrates:

Tesla Cybertruck with laser blade
lights shows up at esports Dota 2
February 22, 2020

To create this layout, we will use a `Grid` control. Follow these steps to create the layout needed:

1. In the **News** project, expand the `Views` folder and open the `ArticleItem.xaml` file.
2. Edit the XAML code, as shown in the following code block:

```xml
<?xml version="1.0" encoding="UTF-8"?>
<ContentView xmlns="http://xamarin.com/schemas/2014/forms"
             xmlns:x="http://schemas.microsoft.com/winfx/2009/xaml"
             x:Class="News.Views.ArticleItem">
  <Grid Margin="0">
    <Grid.RowDefinitions>
      <RowDefinition Height="10" />
      <RowDefinition Height="40" />
      <RowDefinition Height="15" />
      <RowDefinition Height="10" />
      <RowDefinition Height="1" />
    </Grid.RowDefinitions>
    <Grid.ColumnDefinitions>
      <ColumnDefinition Width="65" />
      <ColumnDefinition Width="*" />
    </Grid.ColumnDefinitions>

    <Label Text="{Binding Title}"
           Padding="10,0"
           Grid.Row="1"
           Grid.Column="1"
           FontSize="Medium"
           FontAttributes="Bold" />

    <Label Text="{Binding PublishedAt, StringFormat='{0:MMMM d,
    yyyy}'}"
           Padding="10"
           Grid.Column="1"
           Grid.Row="2"
           FontSize="Small" />

    <Frame Grid.Row="1"
           Grid.RowSpan="2"
           CornerRadius="15"
           Padding="0"
           BackgroundColor="#667788"
           IsClippedToBounds="True">

      <Image Source="{Binding UrlToImage}"
             HorizontalOptions="Center"
```

```
                    VerticalOptions="Center" />
        </Frame>
        <BoxView BackgroundColor="LightGray"
                Grid.Row="4"
                Grid.ColumnSpan="2" />
    </Grid>
</ContentView>
```

The preceding XAML code defines a grid layout with two columns and five rows. The `Grid.Row` and `Grid.Column` attributes position child elements into the grid and the `Grid.ColumnSpan` attribute allows for a control to span multiple columns.

A rounded image can be achieved using a `Frame` element with a `CornerRadius` specified in conjunction with `IsClippedToBounds` set to `True`.

Strings in labels can be formatted directly in the binding statement. Check out the `Text="{Binding PublishedAt, StringFormat='{0:MMMM d, yyyy}'}"` line of code that formats a date into a specific string format.

Lastly, the gray divider line is the `BoxView` at the end of the XAML code.

Now that we have the `NewsService` created and all related views fixed, it's time to make use of them.

Adding to the bootstrapper

Since the `HeadlinesViewModel` depends on the `NewsService`, we need to register it into our **inversion of control (IoC)** container. Follow these steps to do so:

1. In the **News** project, open the `Bootstrapper.cs` file.
2. Locate the `Initialize()` method, add the following line marked in bold, and resolve using references:

```
public static void Initialize()
{
    var containerBuilder = new ContainerBuilder();
    containerBuilder.RegisterType<NewsService>();
    containerBuilder.RegisterType<MainShell>();

containerBuilder.RegisterAssemblyTypes(typeof(App).Assembly).Where(
x => x.IsSubclassOf(typeof(ViewModel)));
    var container = containerBuilder.Build();
    Resolver.Initialize(container);
  }
```

This will allow for the dependency injection of the `NewsService`.

Adding a ContentTemplate attribute

Up to this point, we only have placeholder code in our `MainShell` file. Let's replace this with actual content, as follows:

1. In the **News** project, open `MainShell.xaml`.
2. Locate the `FlyoutItem` element with the title set to **Home**.
3. Edit the XAML so that the `ShellContent` element becomes self-closing, add the following `ContentTemplate` attribute marked in bold, and replace the contents of the `Tab` element:

```xml
<FlyoutItem Title="Home"
            Icon="{StaticResource HomeIcon}">
  <ShellContent Title="Headlines"
                Icon="{StaticResource HeadlinesIcon}"
                ContentTemplate="{DataTemplate
                  views:HeadlinesView}" />

  <Tab Title="News" Route="news" Icon="{StaticResource NewsIcon}">
    <ShellContent Title="Local" Route="local" >
      <ShellContent.ContentTemplate>
        <DataTemplate>
          <views:HeadlinesView>
            <x:Arguments>
              <x:String>Local</x:String>
            </x:Arguments>
          </views:HeadlinesView>
        </DataTemplate>
      </ShellContent.ContentTemplate>
    </ShellContent>
    <ShellContent Title="Global" Route="global">
      <ShellContent.ContentTemplate>
        <DataTemplate>
          <views:HeadlinesView>
            <x:Arguments>
              <x:String>Global</x:String>
            </x:Arguments>
          </views:HeadlinesView>
        </DataTemplate>
      </ShellContent.ContentTemplate>
    </ShellContent>
  </Tab>
</FlyoutItem>
```

Two things are going on here. The first is that we specify the content of a `ShellContent` using the `ContentTemplate` attribute. This means that we point to the type of view that we want to have created when it becomes visible. Usually, you want to defer the creation of a view until right before it is going to be displayed, and the `ContentTemplate` attribute gives you that.

The second thing is that we have the same thing going on below for the `Local` and `Global` news, but we specify that when these views get created, we want to call the constructor that takes a string argument. As you can see, the XAML for passing a single argument to the constructor is quite verbose, but it gets the job done.

If you run the app at this point, you should end up with something that looks like the following screenshot:

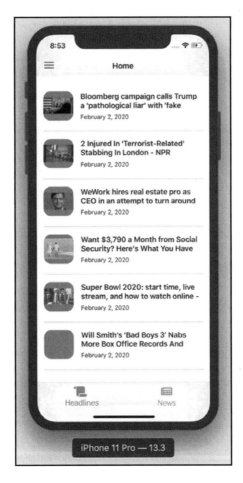

The last thing we need to implement is to view the articles when we tap on the item in the list.

Handling navigation

We are on the home stretch now for this app. The only thing we have left is to implement navigation to the article view that will display the entire article in a web view. Since we are using Shell, we will be navigating using routes. Routes can be registered directly in the Shell markup—for example, in the `MainShell.xaml` file—and this is done by using `Route` attributes on the `ShellContent` elements.

In the following code, we will add a route programmatically and register a view to handle it for us. We will also create a navigation service to abstract the concept of navigation a bit.

So, buckle up and let's finish this app!

Creating the navigation service

The first step is to define an interface that will wrap Xamarin.Forms navigation. Why do we do this? Well, it's a good practice to separate the interfaces from the implementation; it makes unit testing easier; and so on.

Creating the INavigation interface

The `INavigation` interface is simple, and we will overshoot the target a little bit. We are really only interested in the `NavigateTo` method, but we will add the `PushModal()` and `PopModal()` methods since it is likely that you will use them if you continue extending the app.

Adding the navigation interface is simple, as the following steps illustrate:

1. In the **News** project, expand the `ViewModels` folder and add a new file called `INavigate.cs`.
2. Add the following code to the file:

   ```
   using System.Threading.Tasks;
   using Xamarin.Forms;

   namespace News.ViewModels
   {
       public interface INavigate
   ```

```
            {
                Task NavigateTo(string route);
                Task PushModal(Page page);
                Task PopModal();
            }
        }
```

The `NavigateTo()` method declaration takes the route we want to navigate to. This is the method that we will be calling. The `PushModal()` method adds a new page on top of the navigation stack as a modal page, forcing the user only to interact with this specific page. The `PopModal()` method removes it from the navigation stack. So, if you use the `PushModal()` method, make sure that you give the user a way to pop it off the stack. Otherwise, you will be stuck viewing the modal page forever.

That's all for the interface. Let's create an implementation using Xamarin.Forms Shell.

Implementing the INavigation interface using Shell

The implementation is very straightforward since each method is only calling Xamarin.Forms static methods provided by the Shell API.

Create the `Navigator` class, as shown in the following steps:

1. In the **News** project, add a new class called `Navigator`.
2. Add the following code to the class:

```
using System.Threading.Tasks;
using News.ViewModels;
using Xamarin.Forms;

namespace News
{
    public class Navigator : INavigate
    {
        public async Task NavigateTo(string route)
        {
            await Shell.Current.GoToAsync(route);
        }

        public async Task PushModal(Page page)
        {
            await Shell.Current.Navigation.PushModalAsync(page);
        }

        public async Task PopModal()
        {
```

```
                    await Shell.Current.Navigation.PopModalAsync();
            }
        }
    }
```

This is simply pass-through code that calls already existing methods.

Adding the INavigation interface to the ViewModel class

To be able to access the navigator we extend the `ViewModel` base class, making it available to all ViewModels. Proceed as follows:

1. In the **News** project, open the `ViewModels` folder, and then open the `ViewModel.cs` file.
2. Add the following code marked in bold to the class:

```
public abstract class ViewModel : INotifyPropertyChanged
{
    public event PropertyChangedEventHandler PropertyChanged;
    public INavigate Navigation { get; set; } = new Navigator();
}
```

The `ViewModel` now exposes the `Navigator` property through the `INavigate` interface, and we are ready to wire up the navigation to our `Article` view.

Navigating using routes

Routes are a very handy way to navigate since they abstract the creation of the page away. All we need to know is the route to the view we want to navigate to and Xamarin.Forms Shell takes care of the rest for us. If you are familiar with how web navigation works, you might recognize the way that we pass arguments in routes. They are passed as query parameters.

Finalizing the ItemSelected command

We previously defined the `ItemSelected` command in the `HeadlinesViewModel` class. It's now time to add code that will perform the navigation to the `ArticleView` by following these two steps:

1. In the **News** project, expand the `ViewModels` folder and open `HeadlinesViewModel.cs`.
2. Locate the `ItemSelected` property and add the following line marked in bold:

```
public ICommand ItemSelected =>
    new Command(async (selectedItem) =>
    {
        var selectedArticle = selectedItem as Article;
        var url = HttpUtility.UrlEncode(selectedArticle.Url);
        await Navigation.NavigateTo($"articleview?url={url}");
    });
```

We will define a route called `articleview` that takes a query-line parameter called `url` that points the URL of the article itself, and it will look something like this: `articleview?url=www.mypage.com`. Only the data passed after the `url=` argument must be **UrlEncoded**, meaning that we need to encode it to replace characters that would interfere with the route itself. The **URL encoding** is done through the `HttpUtility.UrlEncode()` method, which is defined in `System.Web` for us.

The preceding `NavigateTo()` method call uses this encoded data in the query parameter.

On the recipient side of the navigation call, we need to handle the incoming `url` parameter.

Extending the ArticleView to receive query data

The `ArticleView` is responsible for rendering the article for us. To keep things simple (and also illustrate that you don't always need a `ViewModel`), we will not define a `ViewModel` for this class, but rather define the `BindingContext` as an instance of the `UrlWebViewSource` class.

Add the following code to the `ArticleView.xaml.cs` file:

1. In the **News** project, expand the `Views` folder and open the `ArticleView.xaml.cs` file.
2. Add the following code marked in bold to the file:

```
using System.Web;
using Xamarin.Forms;

namespace News.Views
{
    [QueryProperty("Url", "url")]
    public partial class ArticleView : ContentPage
    {
        public string Url
        {
            set
            {
                BindingContext = new UrlWebViewSource
                {
                    Url = HttpUtility.UrlDecode(value)
                };
            }
        }

        public ArticleView()
        {
            InitializeComponent();
        }
    }
}
```

The `ArticleView` is dependent on a URL being set, and we do so by defining a set-only property called `Url`. When this property is set, it creates a new instance of a `UrlWebViewSource` with the value of the property and assigns it to the `BindingContext` of the page. This setter is called by the Shell framework since we added an attribute called `QueryProperty` to the class itself. It takes two arguments—the first is which property to set, and the second is the name of the `url` query parameter.

Since the data comes URL encoded, we need to decode it using the `HttpUtility.UrlDecode()` method.

Now, we have a binding context that points to the web page we want to display. We just need now to define the `WebView` in the XAML.

Extending the ArticleView with a WebView

This page only has one purpose, and that is to display the web page from the URL that we passed to it. Let's add a `WebView` control to the page, as follows:

1. In the **News** project, expand the `Views` folder and open `ArticleView.xaml`.
2. Add the following XAML marked in bold:

```xml
<?xml version="1.0" encoding="UTF-8"?>
<ContentPage xmlns="http://xamarin.com/schemas/2014/forms"
             xmlns:x="http://schemas.microsoft.com/winfx/2009/xaml"
             x:Class="News.Views.ArticleView">
    <ContentPage.Content>
        <WebView Source="{Binding .}" />
    </ContentPage.Content>
</ContentPage>
```

The `WebView` control will take up all available space in the view and the source will be set to ".", meaning that it will be the same as the `BindingContext` property of the `ViewModel`. The `BindingContext` property, in this case, is a `UrlWebViewSource` instance, exactly what the `WebView` needs to navigate and display the content.

One step left. Our app needs to now about the `articleview` route and what to do with it.

Registering the route

As mentioned before, routes can be added declaratively in the XAML (`Route="MyDucks"`) or in code, as shown here next:

1. In the **News** project, open the `MainShell.xaml.cs` file.
2. Add the following lines of code marked in bold:

```csharp
1. using News.Views;
   using Xamarin.Forms;

   namespace News
   {
       public partial class MainShell
       {
           public MainShell()
           {
               InitializeComponent();
               Routing.RegisterRoute("articleview",
                typeof(ArticleView));
           }
```

```
        }
    }
```

The `RegisterRoute()` method takes two arguments; the first is the route we want to use, and it's the one that we specify in the `NavigateTo()` calls. The second is the type of the page (view) that we want to create, and in our case, we want to create an `ArticleView`.

Cool! That wraps it up. The app should now run, and you should be able to navigate to the article from any of the `CollectionViews`. Good work!

Summary

We learned how to define a navigation structure using Xamarin.Forms Shell, how to navigate to views using routes, and how to pass arguments between views in the form of a query string. There is a lot more to Shell, but this should get you started and confident enough to start exploring the Shell APIs. Also keep in mind that the Shell APIs are constantly evolving so make sure to check out the latest features available.

We also learned how to create an API client to an arbitrary REST API, which always comes in handy since most of the apps you will write need to communicate with a server at some point. There is a very good chance that the server will expose its data and functionality through a REST API.

The next project will be about creating a match-making app, and how to create your own swiping enabled Yes/No image selector app, using nothing but Xamarin Forms to render and animate cross-platform UI controls.

4

A Matchmaking App with a Rich UX Using Animations

In this chapter, we will create the base functionality for a matchmaking app. We won't be rating people, however, because of privacy issues. Instead, we will download images from a random source on the internet. This project is for anyone who wants an introduction to how to write reusable controls. We will also look at using animations to make our application feel nicer to use. This app will not be a **Model-View-ViewModel** (**MVVM**) application since we want to isolate the creation and usage of a control from the slight overhead of MVVM.

The following topics will be covered in this chapter:

- Creating a custom control
- Styling the app to look like a photo, with descriptive text beneath it
- Animations using Xamarin.Forms
- Subscribing to custom events
- Reusing the custom control over and over again
- Handling pan gestures

Technical requirements

To be able to complete this project, you will need to have Visual Studio for Mac or Windows installed, as well as the necessary Xamarin components. See Chapter 1, *Introduction to Xamarin*, for more details on how to set up your environment.

Project overview

Many of us have been there, faced with the conundrum of whether to swipe left or right. All of a sudden, you may find yourself wondering: *How does this work? How does the swipe magic happen?* Well, in this project, we're going to learn all about it. We will start by defining a MainPage file in which the images of our application will reside. After that, we will create the image control, and gradually add the **graphical user interface (GUI)** and functionality to it until we have nailed the perfect swiping experience.

The build time for this project is about 90 minutes.

Creating the matchmaking app

In this project, we will learn more about creating reusable controls that can be added to an **Extensible Application Markup Language (XAML)** page. To keep things simple, we will not be using MVVM, but bare-metal Xamarin.Forms without any data binding. What we aim to create is an app that allows the user to swipe images, either to the right or the left, just as most popular matchmaking applications do.

Well, let's get started by creating the project!

Creating the project

Just as with the to-do list app in Chapter 2, *Building Our First Xamarin.Forms App*, this chapter will start with a clean **File** | **New** |**Project** approach.

Let's get started!

Creating the new project

So, let's begin, as follows:

1. Open up Visual Studio and click on **File** | **New** | **Project**, as illustrated in the following screenshot:

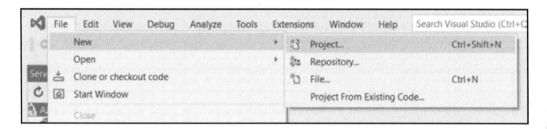

2. Enter **Xamarin.Forms** in the search field and select the **Mobile App (Xamarin.Forms)** template, as illustrated in the following screenshot:

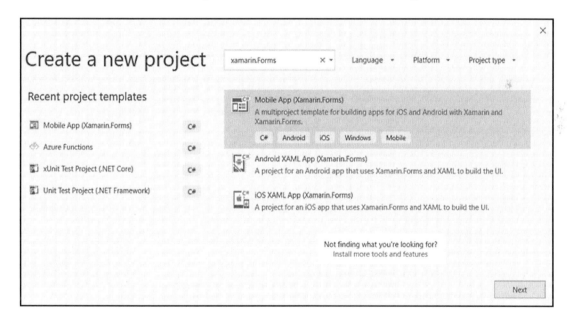

3. Complete the next step of the wizard by naming your project. We will be calling our application `Swiper` in this case. Move on to the next dialog box by clicking **Create**, as illustrated in the following screenshot:

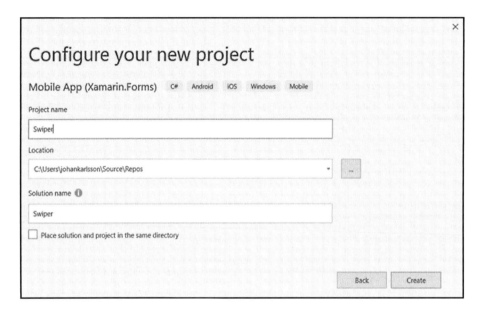

4. We will now select a project template. Select **Blank** to create a bare minimum Xamarin.Forms app. Make sure that all platforms are checked. Please note that **Windows (UWP)** will only be available if you are using Windows.
5. Finish the setup wizard by clicking **OK**, and let Visual Studio scaffold the project for you. This might take a couple of minutes.

Refer to the following screenshot to view the preceding information:

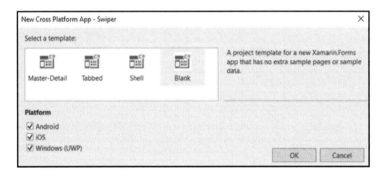

Just like that, the app is created. Let's move on to updating Xamarin.Forms to the latest version.

Updating the Xamarin.Forms NuGet packages

Currently, the Xamarin.Forms version that your project will be created with is most likely a bit old. To rectify this, we need to update the **NuGet packages**. Please note that you should only update the Xamarin.Forms packages and not the Android packages; doing the latter might cause your packages to get out of sync with each other, resulting in the app not building at all. To update the NuGet packages, perform the following steps:

1. Right-click on our **solution** in the **Solution Explorer**.
2. Click **Manage NuGet Packages for Solution...**, as illustrated in the following screenshot:

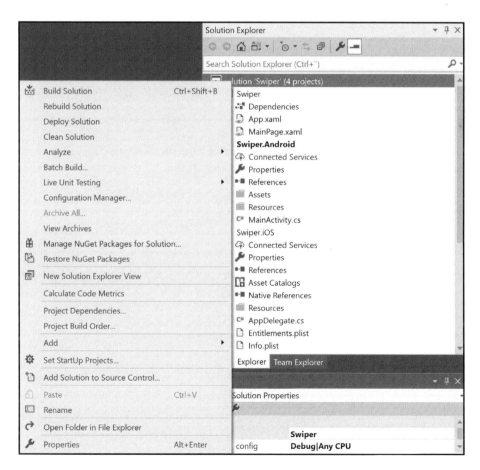

This will open the **NuGet** package manager in Visual Studio, illustrated in the following screenshot:

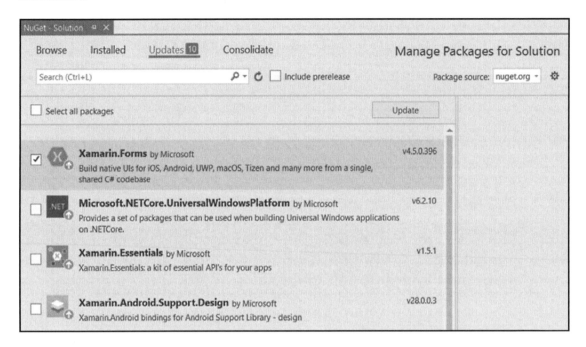

To update Xamarin.Forms to the latest version, perform the following steps:

1. Click the **Updates** tab.
2. Check **Xamarin.Forms** and click **Update.**
3. Accept any license agreements.

The update takes, at most, a few minutes. Check the output pane to find information about the update. At this point, we can run the app to make sure it works. We should see the text **Welcome to Xamarin.Forms!** in the middle of the screen, as illustrated in the following screenshot:

Designing the MainPage file

A brand new blank Xamarin.Forms app named `Swiper` is created, with a single page called `MainPage.xaml`. This is located in the .NET Standard project that is referenced by all platform-specific projects. We will need to replace the XAML template with a new layout that will contain our `Swiper` control.

Let's edit the already existing `MainPage.xaml` file by replacing the default content with what we need, as follows:

1. Open the `MainPage.xaml` file.
2. Replace the content of the page with the following XAML code marked in bold:

```xml
<?xml version="1.0" encoding="utf-8"?>
<ContentPage xmlns="http://xamarin.com/schemas/2014/forms"
             xmlns:x="http://schemas.microsoft.com/winfx/2009/xaml"
             xmlns:local="clr-namespace:Swiper"
             x:Class="Swiper.MainPage">
    <Grid Padding="0,40" x:Name="MainGrid">
```

```
            <Grid.RowDefinitions>
                <RowDefinition Height="400" />
                <RowDefinition Height="*" />
            </Grid.RowDefinitions>
            <Grid Grid.Row="1" Padding="30">
                <!-- Placeholder for later -->
            </Grid>
        </Grid>
    </Grid>
</ContentPage>
```

The XAML code within the `ContentPage` node defines two grids in the application. A grid is simply a container for other controls. It positions those controls based on rows and columns. The outer grid, in this case, defines two rows that will cover the entire available area of the screen. The first row is `400` units high and the second row, with `Height="*"`, uses the rest of the available space.

The inner grid, which is defined within the first grid, is assigned to the second row with the attribute `Grid.Row="1"`. The row and column indexes are zero-based, so `"1"` actually refers to the second row. We will add some content to this grid later on in the chapter, but we'll leave it empty for now.

Both grids define their padding. You could enter a single number, meaning that all sides will have the same padding, or—as in this case—enter two numbers. We have entered `0, 40`, which means that the left and right sides should have `0` units of padding and the top and bottom should have `40` units of padding. There is also a third option with four digits, which sets the padding of the *left* side, the *top*, the *right* side, and the *bottom*, in that specific order.

The last thing to notice is that we give the outer grid a name, `x:Name="MainGrid"`. This will make it directly accessible from the code-behind defined in the `MainPage.xaml.cs` file. Since we are not using MVVM in this example, we will need a way to access the grid without data binding.

Creating the Swiper control

The main part of this project involves creating the `Swiper` control. A control is a self-contained **user interface** (**UI**) with a code-behind to go with it. It can be added to any XAML page as an element, or in code in the code-behind file. We will be adding the control from code in this project.

Creating the control

Creating the `Swiper` control is a straightforward process. We just need to make sure that we select the correct item template, which is the **Content View**, by doing the following:

1. In the .NET Standard library project, create a folder called `Controls`.
2. Right-click on the `Controls` folder, select **Add**, and then click **New item...** .
3. Select **Visual C# Items** and then **Xamarin.Forms** in the left pane of the **Add New Item** dialog box.
4. Select the **Content View** item. Make sure you don't select the **Content View (C#)** option; this only creates a C# file and not a XAML file.
5. Name the control `SwiperControl.xaml`.
6. Click **Add.**

Refer to the following screenshot to view the preceding information:

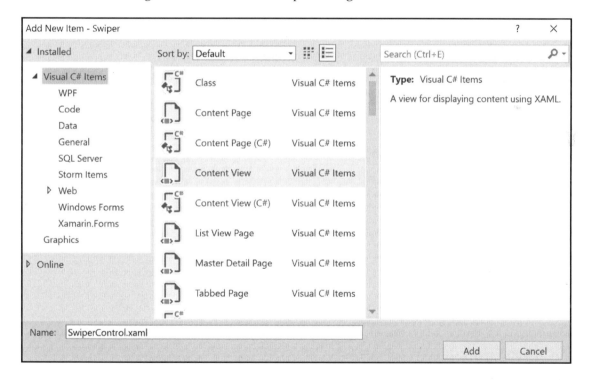

This adds a XAML file for the UI and a C# code-behind file. It should look like the following screenshot:

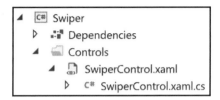

Defining the main grid

Let's set the basic structure of the `Swiper` control, as follows:

1. Open the `SwiperControl.xaml` file.
2. Replace the content with the code marked in bold in the following code block:

```xml
<?xml version="1.0" encoding="UTF-8"?>
<ContentView xmlns="http://xamarin.com/schemas/2014/forms"
             xmlns:x="http://schemas.microsoft.com/winfx/2009/xaml"
             x:Class="Swiper.Controls.SwiperControl">
    <ContentView.Content>
        <Grid>
            <Grid.ColumnDefinitions>
                <ColumnDefinition Width="100" />
                <ColumnDefinition Width="*" />
                <ColumnDefinition Width="100" />
            </Grid.ColumnDefinitions>

            <!-- ContentView for photo here -->

            <!-- StackLayout for like here -->

            <!-- StackLayout for deny here -->
        </Grid>
    </ContentView.Content>
</ContentView>
```

This defines a grid with three columns. The leftmost and the rightmost columns will take up 100 units of space, and the center will occupy the rest of the available space. The spaces on the sides will be areas in which we will add labels to highlight the choice that the user has made. We've also added three comments that act as placeholders for the XAML code to come.

Adding a content view for the photo

We will now extend the `SwiperControl.xaml` file by adding a definition of what we want the photo to look like. Our final result will look like the following photo. Since we are going to pull images off the internet, we'll display a loading text to make sure that the user gets feedback on what's going on. To make it look like an instantly printed photo, we add some handwritten text under the photo, as can be seen in the following screenshot:

A horrible picture of grandpa

The preceding photo is what we would like the photo to look like. To make it a reality, we need to add some XAML code to the `SwiperControl` file by doing the following:

1. Open up `SwiperControl.xaml`.
2. Add the XAML code in bold to the following comment: `<!-- ContentView for photo here -->`. Make sure that you do not replace the entire `ContentView` control for the page; just add this under the comment, as illustrated in the following code block. The rest of the page should be untouched:

```
<!-- ContentView for photo here -->
<ContentView x:Name="photo" Padding="40" Grid.ColumnSpan="3" >
    <Grid x:Name="photoGrid" BackgroundColor="Black" Padding="1" >
        <Grid.RowDefinitions>
            <RowDefinition Height="*" />
            <RowDefinition Height="40" />
        </Grid.RowDefinitions>

        <BoxView BackgroundColor="White" Grid.RowSpan="2" />
```

```
<Image x:Name="image" Margin="10"
       BackgroundColor="#AAAAAA"
       Aspect="AspectFill" />

<Label x:Name="loadingLabel"
       Text="Loading..."
       TextColor="White"
       FontSize="Large"
       FontAttributes="Bold"
       HorizontalOptions="Center"
       VerticalOptions="Center" />

<Label x:Name="descriptionLabel"
       Margin="10,0"
       Text="A picture of grandpa"
       Grid.Row="1"
       FontFamily="Bradley Hand" />
    </Grid>
</ContentView>
```

A `ContentView` control defines a new area where we can add other controls. One very important feature of a `ContentView` control is that it only takes one child control. Most of the time, we would add one of the layout controls that are available. In this case, we'll use a `Grid` control to lay out the control, as shown in the preceding code.

The grid defines two rows, as follows:

- A row for the photo itself, which takes up all the available space when the other rows have been allocated space
- A row for the comment, which will be exactly `40` units in height

The `Grid` control itself is set to use a black background and a padding of `1`. This, in combination with a `BoxView` control, which has a white background, creates the frame that we see around the control. The `BoxView` control is also set to span both rows of the grid (`Grid.RowSpan="2"`), taking up the entire area of the grid, minus the padding.

The `Image` control comes next. It has a background color set to a nice gray tone (`#AAAAAA`) and a margin of `40`, which will separate it a bit from the frame around it. It also has a hardcoded name (`x:Name="image"`), which will allow us to interact with it from the code-behind. The last attribute, called `Aspect`, determines what we should do if the image control isn't of the same ratio as the source image. In this case, we want to fill the entire image area, but not show any blank areas. This effectively crops the image either in height or in width.

We finish off by adding two labels, which also have hardcoded names for later reference.

Creating the DescriptionGenerator class

At the bottom of the image, we see a description. Since we don't have any general descriptions of the images from our upcoming image source, we need to create a generator that makes up descriptions. Here's how we would do it:

1. Create a folder called Utils in the .NET Standard project.
2. Create a new class called DescriptionGenerator in that folder.
3. Add a using statement for System.Linq (using System.Linq;).
4. Add the following code to the class:

```
public class DescriptionGenerator
{
    private string[] _adjectives = { "nice", "horrible", "great",
    "terribly old", "brand new" };
    private string[] _other = { "picture of grandpa", "car", "photo
    of a forest", "duck" };
    private static Random random = new Random();

    public string Generate()
    {
        var a = _adjectives[random.Next(_adjectives.Count())];
        var b = _other[random.Next(_other.Count())];
        return $"A {a} {b}";
    }
}
```

This class only has one purpose. It takes one random word from the _adjectives array and combines it with a random word from the _other array. By calling the Generate() method, we get a fresh new combination. Feel free to enter your own words in the arrays. Note that the Random instance is a static field. This is because if we create new instances of the Random class that are too close to each other in time, they get seeded with the same value and return the same sequence of random numbers.

Creating a picture class

To abstract all the information about the image we want to display, we'll create a class that encapsulates this information. There isn't much information in our `Picture` class, but it is good coding practice to do this. Proceed as follows:

1. Create a new class called `Picture` in the `Utils` folder.

2. Add the following code to the class:

```
public class Picture
{
 public Uri Uri { get; set; }
  public string Description { get; set; }

 public Picture()
 {
 Uri = new Uri($"https://picsum.photos/400/400/?random&ts=
 {DateTime.Now.Ticks}");

 var generator = new DescriptionGenerator();
 Description = generator.Generate();
 }
}
```

The `Picture` class has the following two public properties:

- The **Uniform Resource Identifier** (**URI**) of an image exposed as the `Uri` property, which points to its location on the internet
- A description of that image exposed as the `Description` property.

In the constructor, we create a new **URI**, which points to a public source of test photos that we can use. The width and height are specified in the query string part of the URI. We also append a random timestamp to avoid the images being cached by Xamarin.Forms. This generates a unique URI each time we request an image.

We then use the `DescriptionGenerator` class that we created to generate a random description for the image.

Binding the picture to the control

Let's begin to wire up the `Swiper` control so that it starts displaying images. We need to set the source of an image, and then control the visibility of the loading label based on the status of the image. Since we are using an image fetched from the internet, it might take a couple of seconds to download. This has to be communicated to the user to avoid confusion about what is going on.

Setting the source

We begin by setting the source of the image. The `image` control (referred to as `image` in the code) has a `source` property. This property is of the `ImageSource` abstract type. There are a few different types of image sources that you can use. The one we are interested in is the `UriImageSource` type, which takes a URI, downloads the image, and allows the image control to display it.

Let's extend the `Swiper` control to set the source and description, by doing the following:

1. Open the `Controls/Swiper.Xaml.cs` file (the code-behind for the `Swiper` control).
2. Add a `using` statement for `Swiper.Utils` (`using Swiper.Utils;`).
3. Add the following code marked in bold to the constructor:

```
public SwiperControl()
{
    InitializeComponent();
    var picture = new Picture();
    descriptionLabel.Text = picture.Description;
    image.Source = new UriImageSource() { Uri = picture.Uri };
}
```

We create a new instance of a `Picture` class and assign the description to the `descriptionLabel` control in the GUI by setting the text property of that control. We then set the source of the image to a new instance of the `UriImageSource` class, and assign the URI from the `picture` instance. This will start the download of the image from the internet, and display it as soon as it is downloaded.

Controlling the loading label

While the image is downloading, we want to show a loading text centered over the image. This is already in the XAML file that we created earlier, so what we really need to do is hide it once the image is downloaded. We will do this by controlling the IsVisibleProperty property (the property is actually named IsVisibleProperty) of the loadingLabel control by setting a binding to the IsLoading property of the image. Any time the IsLoading property is changed on the image, the binding changes the IsVisible property on the label. This is a nice fire-and-forget approach.

Let's add the code needed to control the loadingLabel control, as follows:

1. Open the Swiper.xaml.cs code-behind file.
2. Add the following code marked in bold to the constructor:

```
public SwiperControl()
{
    InitializeComponent();
    var picture = new Picture();
    descriptionLabel.Text = picture.Description;
    image.Source = new  UriImageSource() { Uri = picture.Uri };

    loadingLabel.SetBinding(IsVisibleProperty, "IsLoading");
    loadingLabel.BindingContext = image;
}
```

In the preceding code, the loadingLabel control sets a binding to the IsVisibleProperty property, which actually belongs to the VisualElement class that all controls inherit from. It tells the loadingLabel to listen to changes in the IsLoading property of whichever object is assigned to the binding context. In this case, this is the image control.

Handling pan gestures

A core feature of this app is the pan gesture. A pan gesture is when a user presses on the control and moves it around the screen. We will also add a random rotation to the Swiper control to make it look like there are photos in a stack when we add multiple images.

We start by adding some fields to the `SwiperControl` class, as follows:

1. Open the `SwiperControl.xaml.cs` file.
2. Add the following fields in the code to the class:

```
private readonly double _initialRotation;
private static readonly Random _random = new Random();
```

The first field, `_initialRotation`, stores the initial rotation of the image. We will set this in the constructor. The second field is a `static` field containing a `Random` object. As you might remember, it's better to create one static random object to make sure multiple random objects don't get created with the same seed. The seed is based on time, so if we create objects too close in time to each other, they get the same random sequence generated, so it wouldn't actually be that random at all.

The next thing we have to do is create an event handler for the `PanUpdated` event that we will bind to at the end of this section, as follows:

1. Open the `SwiperControl.xaml.cs` code-behind file.
2. Add the `OnPanUpdated` method to the class, like this:

```
private void OnPanUpdated(object sender, PanUpdatedEventArgs e)
{
    switch (e.StatusType)
    {
        case GestureStatus.Started:
            PanStarted();
            break;

        case GestureStatus.Running:
            PanRunning(e);
            break;

        case GestureStatus.Completed:
            PanCompleted();
            break;
    }
}
```

The code is really straightforward. We handle an event that takes a `PanUpdatedEventArgs` object as the second argument. This is a standard method of handling events. We then have a `switch` clause that checks which status the event refers to.

A pan gesture can have the following three states:

- GestureStatus.Started: The event is raised once with this state when the panning begins.
- GestureStatus.Running: The event is then raised multiple times, once for each time you move your finger.
- GestureStatus.Completed: The event is raised one last time when you let go.

For each of these states, we call specific methods that handle the different states. We'll continue with adding those methods now, as follows:

1. Open the SwiperControl.xaml.cs code-behind file.
2. Add the following three methods to the class, like this:

```
private void PanStarted()
{
    photo.ScaleTo(1.1, 100);
}

private void PanRunning(PanUpdatedEventArgs e)
{
    photo.TranslationX = e.TotalX;
    photo.TranslationY = e.TotalY;
    photo.Rotation = _initialRotation + (photo.TranslationX / 25);
}

private void PanCompleted()
{
    photo.TranslateTo(0, 0, 250, Easing.SpringOut);
    photo.RotateTo(_initialRotation, 250, Easing.SpringOut);
    photo.ScaleTo(1, 250);
}
```

Let's start by looking at PanStarted(). When the user starts dragging the image, we want to add the effect of it raising up a little bit over the surface. This is done by scaling the image by 10%. Xamarin.Forms has a set of excellent functions to do this. In this case, we call the ScaleTo() method on the image control (named Photo) and tell it to scale to 1.1, which corresponds to 10% of its original size. We also tell it to do this in a duration of 100 **milliseconds (ms)**. This call is also awaitable, which means we can wait for the control to finish animating before executing the next call. In this case, we are going to use a fire-and-forget approach.

Next, we have `PanRunning()`, which is called multiple times during the pan operation. This takes an argument, which is the `PanUpdatedEventArgs` argument, from the event handler that `PanRunning()` is called from. We could also just pass in an X and a Y value as arguments to reduce the coupling of the code. This is something that you can experiment with. The method extracts the X and Y components from the `TotalX`/`TotalY` properties of the event and assigns them to the `TranslationX`/`TranslationY` properties of the image control. We also adjust the rotation slightly, based on how far the image has been moved.

The last thing to do is to restore everything to its initial state when the image is released. This can be done in `PanCompleted()`. First, we translate (or move) the image back to its original local coordinates (0, 0) in 250 ms. We also add an easing function to make it overshoot the target a bit and then animate back. We can play around with the different predefined easing functions; these are really useful for creating nice animations. We do the same to move the image back to its initial rotation. Finally, we scale it back to its original size in 250 ms.

It's now time to add the code in the constructor that will wire up the pan gesture and set some initial rotation values. Proceed as follows:

1. Open the `SwiperControl.xaml.cs` code-behind file.
2. Add the code in bold to the constructor. Note that there is more code in the constructor, so don't copy and paste the whole method; just add the bold text shown in the following code block:

```
public SwiperControl()
{
    InitializeComponent();

    var panGesture = new PanGestureRecognizer();
    panGesture.PanUpdated += OnPanUpdated;
    this.GestureRecognizers.Add(panGesture);

    _initialRotation = _random.Next(-10, 10);
    photo.RotateTo(_initialRotation, 100, Easing.SinOut);

    <!-- other code omitted for brevity -->
}
```

All Xamarin.Forms controls have a property called `GestureRecognizers`. There are different types of gesture recognizers, such as `TapGestureRecognizer` or `SwipeGestureRecognizer`. In our case, we are interested in the `PanGestureRecognizer` type. We create a new `PanGestureRecognizer` instance and subscribe to the `PanUpdated` event by hooking it up to the `OnPanUpdated()` method we created earlier. We then add it to the `Swiper` controls `GestureRecognizers` collection.

We then set an initial rotation of the image and make sure we store it so that we can modify the rotation, and then rotate it back to the original state.

Testing the control

We now have all the code written to take the control for a test run. Proceed as follows:

1. Open `MainPage.xaml.cs`.
2. Add a `using` statement for the `Swiper.Controls` (using `Swiper.Controls;`).
3. Add the following code marked in bold to the constructor:

```
public MainPage()
{
    InitializeComponent();
    MainGrid.Children.Add(new SwiperControl());
}
```

If all goes well with the build, we should end up with an photo like the one shown in the following screenshot:

A great duck

We can also drag the photo around (pan it). Notice the slight lift effect when you begin dragging, and the rotation of the photo based on the amount of translation, which is the total movement. If you let go of the photo, it animates back into place.

Creating decision zones

A matchmaking app is nothing without those special drop-zones on each side of the screen. We want to do a few things here, as follows:

- When a user drags an image to either side, text should appear that says *LIKE* or *DENY* (the decision zones).
- When a user drops an image on a decision zone, the app should remove the image from the page.

We will create the zones by adding some XAML code to the `SwiperControl.xaml` file and then move on to adding the necessary code to make this happen. It is worth noting here that the zones are not actually hotspots for dropping the image, but rather for displaying labels on top of the control surface. The actual drop-zones are calculated and determined based on how far you drag the image.

Extending the grid

The `Swiper` control has three columns (left, right, and centre) defined. We want to add some kind of visual feedback to the user if the image is dragged to either side of the page. We will do this by adding a `StackLayout` control with a `Label` control on each side.

Adding the StackLayout for liking photos

The first thing to do is to add the `StackLayout` control for liking photos on the right-hand side of the control, as follows:

1. Open `Controls/SwiperControl.xaml`.
2. Add the following code under the comment `<!-- StackLayout for like here -->`:

```
<StackLayout x:Name="likeStackLayout" Grid.Column="2"
             Opacity="0" Padding="0, 100">
    <Label Text="LIKE"
           TextColor="Lime"
           FontSize="30"
           Rotation="30"
```

```
                    FontAttributes="Bold" />
        </StackLayout>
```

The `StackLayout` control is the container of child elements that we want to display. It has a name and is assigned to be rendered in the third column (it says `Grid.Column="2"` in the code, due to the zero indexing). The `Opacity` property is set to 0, making it completely invisible, and the `Padding` property is adjusted to make it move down a bit from the top.

Inside the `StackLayout` control, we'll add the `Label` control.

Adding the StackLayout for denying photos

The next step is to add the `StackLayout` for denying photos on the left-hand side of the control, as follows:

1. Open `Controls/SwiperControl.xaml`.
2. Add the following code under the comment `<!-- StackLayout for deny here -->`:

```
<StackLayout x:Name="denyStackLayout" Opacity="0"
            Padding="0, 100" HorizontalOptions="End">
    <Label Text="DENY"
            TextColor="Red"
            FontSize="30"
            Rotation="-20"
            FontAttributes="Bold" />
</StackLayout>
```

The setup for the left-hand side `StackLayout` is the same, except that it should be in the first column, which is the default, so there is no need to add a `Grid.Column` attribute. We have also specified `HorizontalOptions="End"`, which means that the content should be right-justified.

Determining the screen size

To be able to calculate a percentage of how far the user has dragged the image, we need to know the size of the control. This is not determined until the control is laid out by Xamarin.Forms.

We will override the `OnSizeAllocated()` method and add a `_screenWidth` field in the class to keep track of the current width of the window, by following these few steps:

1. Open `SwiperControl.xaml.cs`.
2. Add the following code to the file, putting the field at the beginning of the class and the `OnSizeAllocated()` method below the constructor:

```
private double _screenWidth = -1;

protected override void OnSizeAllocated(double width, double
height)
{
    base.OnSizeAllocated(width, height);

    if (Application.Current.MainPage == null)
    {
        return;
    }

    _screenWidth = Application.Current.MainPage.Width;
}
```

The `_screenWidth` field is used to store the width as soon as we have resolved it. We do this by overriding the `OnSizeAllocated()` method that is called by Xamarin.Forms when the size of the control is allocated. This is called multiple times. The first time it's called is actually before the width and height have been set and before the `MainPage` property of the current app is set. At this time, the width and height are set to `-1`, and the `Application.Current.MainPage` property is null. We look for this state by null checking `Application.Current.MainPage` and returning if it is null. We could also have checked for `-1` values on the width. Either method would work. If it does have a value, however, we want to store it in our `_screenWidth` field for later use.

Xamarin.Forms will call the `OnSizeAllocated()` method any time the frame of the app changes. This is most relevant for **Universal Windows Platform** (**UWP**) apps since they are in a window that a user can easily change. Android and iOS apps are less likely to get a call to this method a second time since the app will take up the entire screen's real estate.

Adding a clamp function

To be able to calculate the state, we need to clamp a value later on. At the time of writing, this function is already in Xamarin.Forms, but it's marked as an internal function, meaning that we shouldn't really be using it. According to the rumors, it will soon be made public in later versions of Xamarin.Forms, but for now, we need to redefine it ourselves, as follows:

1. Open `SwiperControl.xaml.cs`.
2. Add the following `static` method to the class:

```
private static double Clamp(double value, double min, double max)
{
    return (value < min) ? min : (value > max) ? max : value;
}
```

The method takes a value to clamp, a minimum boundary, and a maximum boundary. It returns either the value itself or the edge value if it's greater or larger than the set boundaries.

Adding code to calculate the state

To calculate the state of the image, we need to define what our zones are, and then create a function that takes the current amount of movement and updates the opacity of the GUI decision zones based on how far we panned the image.

Defining a method for calculating the state

Let's add the `CalculatePanState()` method to calculate how far we have panned the image, and if it should start to affect the GUI, by following these few steps:

1. Open `Controls/SwiperControl.xaml.cs`.
2. Add the properties at the top and the `CalculatePanState()` method anywhere in the class, as shown in the following code block:

```
private const double DeadZone = 0.4d;
private const double DecisionThreshold = 0.4d;

private void CalculatePanState(double panX)
{
    var halfScreenWidth = _screenWidth / 2;
    var deadZoneEnd = DeadZone * halfScreenWidth;

    if (Math.Abs(panX) < deadZoneEnd)
    {
```

```
        return;
    }

    var passedDeadzone = panX < 0 ? panX + deadZoneEnd : panX -
    deadZoneEnd;
    var decisionZoneEnd = DecisionThreshold * halfScreenWidth;
    var opacity = passedDeadzone / decisionZoneEnd;

    opacity = Clamp(opacity, -1, 1);

    likeStackLayout.Opacity = opacity;
    denyStackLayout.Opacity = -opacity;
}
```

We define the following two values as constants:

- The DeadZone, which defines that 40% (0.4) of the available space on either side of the center point is a dead zone when panning an image. If we release the image in this zone, it simply returns to the center of the screen without any action being taken.
- The next constant is the DecisionThreshold constant, which defines another 40% (0.4) of the available space. This is used for interpolating the opacity of the StackLayout on either side of the layout.

We then use these values to check the state of the panning action whenever the panning changes. If the absolute panning value of X (panX) is less than the dead zone, we return without any action being taken. If not, we calculate how far over the dead zone we have passed and how far into the decision zone we are. We calculate the opacity values based on this interpolation and clamp the value between -1 and 1.

Finally, we set the opacity to this value for both likeStackLayout and denyStackLayout.

Wiring up the pan state check

While the image is being panned, we want to update the state, as follows:

1. Open Controls/SwiperControl.xaml.cs.
2. Add the following code in bold to the PanRunning() method:

```
private void PanRunning(PanUpdatedEventArgs e)
{
    photo.TranslationX = e.TotalX;
    photo.TranslationY = e.TotalY;
```

```
photo.Rotation = _initialRotation + (photo.TranslationX / 25);

CalculatePanState(e.TotalX);
}
```

This addition to the `PanRunning()` method passes the total amount of movement on the *x* axis to the `CalculatePanState()` method, to determine if we need to adjust the opacity of either the `StackLayout` on the right or the left of the control.

Adding exit logic

So far, all is good, except for the fact that if we drag an image to the edge and let go, the text stays. We need to determine when the user stops dragging the image, and, if so, whether or not the image is in a decision zone.

Checking if the image should exit

We want a simple function that determines if an image has panned far enough for it to count as an exit of that image. To create such a function, proceed as follows:

1. Open `Controls/SwiperControl.xaml.cs`.
2. Add the `CheckForExitCriteria()` method to the class, as shown in the following code snippet:

```
private bool CheckForExitCriteria()
{
    var halfScreenWidth = _screenWidth / 2;
    var decisionBreakpoint = DeadZone * halfScreenWidth;
    return (Math.Abs(photo.TranslationX) > decisionBreakpoint);
}
```

This function calculates whether we have passed over the dead zone and into the decision zone. We need to use the `Math.Abs()` method to get the total absolute value to compare it against. We could have used a < and a > operator as well, but we are using this approach as it is more readable. This is a matter of code style and taste—feel free to do it your own way.

Removing the image

If we determine that an image has panned far enough for it to exit, we want to animate it off the screen and then remove the image from the page. To do this, proceed as follows:

1. Open `Controls/SwiperControl.xaml.cs`.
2. Add the `Exit()` method to the class, as shown in the following code block:

```
private void Exit()
{
    Device.BeginInvokeOnMainThread(async () =>
    {
        var direction = photo.TranslationX < 0 ? -1 : 1;

        await photo.TranslateTo(photo.TranslationX +
        (_screenWidth * direction),
        photo.TranslationY, 200, Easing.CubicIn);
        var parent = Parent as Layout<View>;
        parent?.Children.Remove(this);
    });
}
```

Let's break down the preceding code block to understand what the `Exit()` method does, as follows:

1. We begin by making sure that this call is done on the UI thread, which is also known as the `MainThread` thread. This is because only the UI thread can do animations.
2. We also need to run this thread asynchronously, so that we can kill two birds with one stone. Since this method is all about animating the image to either side of the screen, we need to determine in which direction to animate it.
3. We do this by determining if the total translation of the image is positive or negative.
4. We then use this value to await a translation through the `photo.TranslateTo()` call.
5. We await this call since we don't want the code execution to continue until it's done. Once it has finished, we remove the control from the parent's collection of children, causing it to disappear from existence forever.

Updating PanCompleted

The decision on whether the image should disappear or simply return to its original state is triggered in the `PanCompleted()` method. Here, we wire up the two methods that we created in the previous two sections. Proceed as follows:

1. Open `Controls/SwiperControl.xaml.cs`.
2. Add the following code in bold to the `PanCompleted()` method:

```
private void PanCompleted()
{
    if (CheckForExitCriteria())
    {
        Exit();
    }

    likeStackLayout.Opacity = 0;
    denyStackLayout.Opacity = 0;

    photo.TranslateTo(0, 0, 250, Easing.SpringOut);
    photo.RotateTo(_initialRotation, 250, Easing.SpringOut);
    photo.ScaleTo(1, 250);
}
```

The last step in this section is to use the `CheckForExitCriteria()` method, and the `Exit()` method if those criteria are met. If the exit criteria are not met, we need to reset the state and the opacity of the `StackLayout` to make everything go back to normal.

Adding events to the control

The last thing we have left to do in the control itself is to add some events that indicate whether the image has been *liked* or *denied*. We are going to use a clean interface, allowing for simple use of the control while hiding all the implementation details.

Declaring two events

To make the control easier to interact with from the application itself, we'll need to add events for `Like` and `Deny`, as follows:

1. Open `Controls/SwiperControl.xaml.cs`.
2. Add two event declarations at the beginning of the class, as shown in the following code snippet:

```
public event EventHandler OnLike;
public event EventHandler OnDeny;
```

These are two standard event declarations with out-of-the-box event handlers.

Raising the events

We need to add code in the `Exit()` method to raise the events we created earlier, as follows:

1. Open `Controls/SwiperControl.xaml.cs`.
2. Add the following code in bold to the `Exit()` method:

```
private void Exit()
{
    Device.BeginInvokeOnMainThread(async () =>
    {
        var direction = photo.TranslationX < 0 ? -1 : 1;

        if (direction > 0)
        {
            OnLike?.Invoke(this, new EventArgs());
        }

        if (direction < 0)
        {
            OnDeny?.Invoke(this, new EventArgs());
        }

        await photo.TranslateTo(photo.TranslationX + (_screenWidth
        * direction),
        photo.TranslationY, 200, Easing.CubicIn);
        var parent = Parent as Layout<View>;
        parent?.Children.Remove(this);
    });
}
```

Here, we inject the code to check whether we are liking or denying an image. We then raise the correct event based on this information.

Wiring up the Swiper control

We have now reached the final part of the chapter. In this section, we are going to wire up the images and make our app a closed-loop app that can be used forever. We will add 10 images that we will download from the internet when the app starts up. Each time an image is removed, we'll simply add another one.

Adding images

Let's start by creating some code that will be adding the images to the `MainView` class. We will first add the initial images, and then create a logic model for adding a new image to the bottom of the stack each time an image is liked or denied.

Adding initial photos

To make the photos look like they are stacked, we need at least 10 of them. Proceed as follows:

1. Open `MainPage.xaml.cs`.
2. Add the `AddInitalPhotos()` method and the `InsertPhotoMethod()` to the class, as illustrated in the following code block:

```
private void AddInitialPhotos()
{
    for (int i = 0; i < 10; i++)
    {
        InsertPhoto();
    }
}

private void InsertPhoto()
{
    var photo = new SwiperControl();
    this.MainGrid.Children.Insert(0, photo);
}
```

First, we create a method called `AddInitialPhotos()` that will be called upon startup. This method simply calls the `InsertPhoto()` method 10 times and adds a new `SwiperControl` to the `MainGrid` each time. It inserts the control at the first position in the stack, effectively putting it at the bottom of the pile since the collection of controls is rendered from the beginning to the end.

Making the call from the constructor

We need to call this method in order for the magic to happen, so follow these steps to do so:

1. Open `MainPage.xaml.cs`.
2. Add the following code in bold to the constructor:

```
public MainPage()
{
    InitializeComponent();
    AddInitialPhotos();
}
```

There isn't much to say here. After the `MainPage` object is initialized, we call the method to add 10 random photos that we will download from the internet.

Adding count labels

We want to add some values to the app as well. We can do this by adding two labels below the collection of `Swiper` controls. Each time a user rates an image, we will increment one of two counters and display the result.

So, let's add the XAML code needed to display the labels, as follows:

1. Open `MainPage.xaml`.
2. Replace the comment `<!-- Placeholder for later -->` with the following code marked in bold:

```
<Grid Grid.Row="1" Padding="30">
    <Grid.RowDefinitions>
        <RowDefinition Height="auto" />
        <RowDefinition Height="auto" />
        <RowDefinition Height="auto" />
        <RowDefinition Height="auto" />
    </Grid.RowDefinitions>
    <Label Text="LIKES" />
    <Label x:Name="likeLabel"
            Grid.Row="1"
```

```
                    Text="0"
                    FontSize="Large"
                    FontAttributes="Bold" />
        <Label Grid.Row="2"
                    Text="DENIED" />
        <Label x:Name="denyLabel"
                    Grid.Row="3"
                    Text="0"
                    FontSize="Large"
                    FontAttributes="Bold" />
    </Grid>
```

This code adds a new `Grid` control with four auto-height rows. This means that we calculate the height of the content of each row and use this for the layout. It is basically the same thing as a `StackLayout`, but we wanted to demonstrate a better way of doing this.

We add a `Label` control in each row and name two of them as `likeLabel` and `denyLabel`. The two named labels will hold information on how many images have been liked and how many have been denied.

Subscribing to events

The last step is to wire up the `OnLike` and `OnDeny` events and display the total count to the user.

Adding methods to update the GUI and respond to events

We need some code to update the GUI and to keep track of the count. Proceed as follows:

1. Open `MainPage.xaml.cs`.
2. Add the following code to the class:

```
private int _likeCount;
private int _denyCount;

private void UpdateGui()
{
    likeLabel.Text = _likeCount.ToString();
    denyLabel.Text = _denyCount.ToString();
}

private void Handle_OnLike(object sender, EventArgs e)
{
    _likeCount++;
    InsertPhoto();
```

```
        UpdateGui();
    }

    private void Handle_OnDeny(object sender, EventArgs e)
    {
        _denyCount++;
        InsertPhoto();
        UpdateGui();
    }
```

The two fields at the top of the preceding code block keep track of the number of likes and denies. Since they are value-type variables, they default to zero.

To make the changes of these labels show up in the UI, we've created a method called `UpdateGui()`. This takes the value of the two aforementioned fields and assigns it to the `Text` properties of both labels.

The two methods that follow are the event handlers that will be handling the `OnLike` and `OnDeny` events. They increase the appropriate field, add a new photo, and then update the GUI to reflect the change.

Wiring up events

Each time a new `SwiperControl` instance is created, we need to wire up the events, as follows:

1. Open `MainPage.xaml.cs`.
2. Add the following code in bold to the `InsertPhoto()` method:

```
    private void InsertPhoto()
    {
        var photo = new SwiperControl();
        photo.OnDeny += Handle_OnDeny;
        photo.OnLike += Handle_OnLike;

        this.MainGrid.Children.Insert(0, photo);
    }
```

The added code wires up the event handlers that we defined earlier. The events make it really easy to interact with our new control. Try it for yourself and have a play around with the app that you have created.

Summary

Good job! In this chapter, we have learned how to create a reusable, good-looking control that can be used in any Xamarin.Forms app. To enhance the **user experience (UX)** of the app, we used some animations that give the user more visual feedback. We also got creative with the use of XAML to define a GUI of the control that looks like a photo, with a hand-written description.

After that, we used events to expose the behavior of the control back to the `MainPage` page to limit the contact surface between your app and the control. Most importantly of all, we touched on the subject of **GestureRecognizers**, which can make our life much easier when dealing with common gestures.

In the next chapter, we will take a look at how to use track the location of a user in the background on an iOS and Android device. To visualize what we are tracking, we will use the **map** component in Xamarin.Forms.

5
Building a Photo Gallery App Using CollectionView and CarouselView

In this chapter, we will build an app that shows photos from the camera roll (photo gallery) of a user's device. The user will also be able to select photos as favorites. We will then look at the different ways to display photos—in carousels and in a multi-column grid control. If we learn how to use these controls, we can then use them in a lot of other cases when we build real-world apps.

The following topics will be covered in this chapter:

- How to import photos from the iOS photo gallery
- How to import photos from the Android photo gallery
- How to use `CarouselView` in Xamarin.Forms
- How to use `CollectionView` in Xamarin.Forms

Technical requirements

To complete this project, you need to have Visual Studio for Mac or your Visual Studio 2019 on PC installed, as well as the Xamarin components. See `Chapter 1`, *Introduction to Xamarin*, for more details on how to set up your environment. To build an iOS app using Visual Studio for your PC, you have to have a Macintosh (Mac) device connected. If you don't have access to a Mac at all, you can just follow the Android part of this project.

Project overview

Almost all apps visualize collections of data, and in this chapter, we will focus on two of the Xamarin.Forms controls that can be used to display data collections—`CollectionView` and `CarouselView`. Our app will show the photos that users have on their devices; to do that, we need to create a photo importer for each platform—one for iOS and one for Android.

Building the photo gallery app

It's time to start building the app using the following steps:

1. Use the **Mobile App (Xamarin.Forms)** template. The easiest way to find the template is to search for `Xamarin.Forms` in the search bar at the top of the dialog that appears when we start Visual Studio:

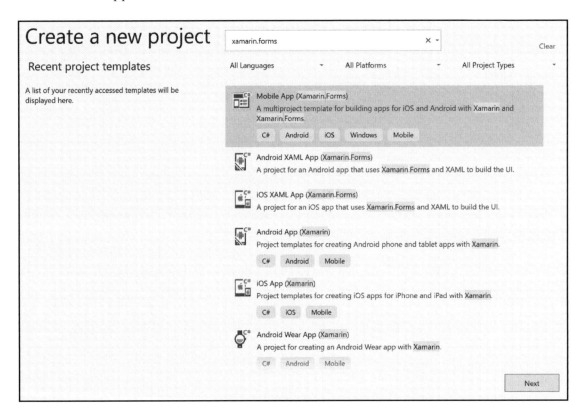

2. Name the app `GalleryApp`:

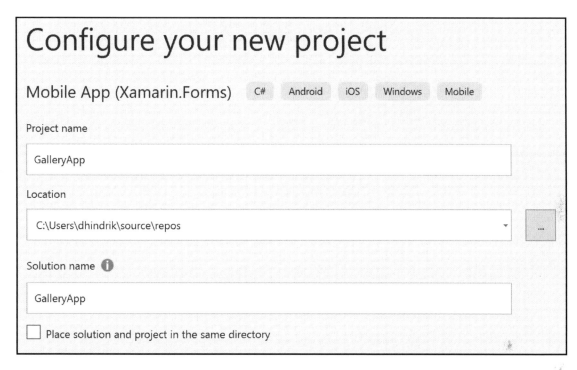

3. Select the **Blank** template, and **Android** and **iOS** as the platforms:

4. Update the NuGet packages that are added by the template to make sure that we use the latest versions. We will do so by right-clicking on the solution file and selecting **Manage NuGet Packages for solution**. Then, select the **Update** tab, select all the packages, and click **Update**.

In this project, we will use some C# 8 features. At the time of writing this book, C# 8 is not the default language version. To use it, you need to add `<LangVersion>8.0</LangVersion>` to each project file.

Importing photos

Importing photos is something that is carried out for both the platforms, so we will create a photo importer interface. The interface will have two `get` methods—one that supports paging and one that gets photos with specified filenames. Both methods will also take a quality argument, but we will only use the one in the iOS photo importer. The quality argument will be an enum with two options—`High` and `Low`. However, before we create the interface, we will create a model class that should represent an imported photo using the following steps:

1. Create a new folder named `Models` in the `GalleryApp` project.
2. Create a new class named `Photo` in the recently created folder:

```
public class Photo
{
    public string Filename { get; set; }
    public byte[] Bytes { get; set; }
}
```

Now that we have created the model class, we can continue to create the interface. The interface will have two `get` methods—one for getting photos in a specific range and one for getting photos with specific filenames:

1. Create a new interface named `IPhotoImporter` in the `GalleryApp` project.
2. In the same file (but outside the interface), create an enum named `Quality` with two members—`Low` and `High`:

```
public interface IPhotoImporter
{
    Task<ObservableCollection<Photo>> Get(int start, int count,
    Quality quality = Quality.Low);
    Task<ObservableCollection<Photo>> Get(List<string> filenames,
    Quality quality = Quality.Low);
}
```

```
public enum Quality
{
    Low,
    High
}
```

Now that we have the interface, we can start with the platform implementations.

Importing photos from the iOS photo gallery

First, we will write the iOS code. To access photos, we need permission from the user, so we need a way of asking users for permission. To do that, we need to add text that explains why we need permission to the info.plist file. This text will be displayed when we ask the users for permission. To open the info.plist file, right-click on the file and click **Open With**, then select **XML (Text) Editor**:

```
<key>NSPhotoLibraryUsageDescription</key>
<string>We want to show your photos in this app</string>
```

The first thing we will do is create a private Import method that reads what photos can be loaded:

1. In the GalleryApp.iOS project, create a new class called PhotoImporter.
2. Implement the IPhotoImporter interface.
3. Resolve all the references.
4. Create a private field with a PHAsset type array named results. This will be used to store photo information.
5. Create a new private method named Import.
6. Request authorization using the PHPhotoLibrary.RequestAuthorizationAsync method.
7. If the users authorize us to use photos, fetch all the image assets by using PHAsset.FetchAssets:

```
public class PhotoImporter : IPhotoImporter
{
    private PHAsset[] results;

    private async Task<bool> Import()
    {
        var status = await
        PHPhotoLibrary.RequestAuthorizationAsync();

        if (status != PHAuthorizationStatus.Authorized)
```

```
        {
            return false;
        }

        results = PHAsset.FetchAssets(PHAssetMediaType.Image,
         null).Select(x => (PHAsset)x).ToArray();

        return true;
    }

    Task<ObservableCollection<Photo>> Get(int startIndex, int
     count, Quality quality = Quality.Low)
    {
        throw new NotImplementedException();
    }
    Task<ObservableCollection<Photo>> Get(List<string> filenames,
     Quality quality = Quality.Low)
    {
        throw new NotImplementedException();
    }
}
```

Now, we have fetched PHAssets for all the photos; but to show the photo, we need to get the actual photo. To do that, we need to request the image for the asset. This is something that is carried out asynchronously; to handle that, we will use ObservableCollection:

```
private void RequestImage(ObservableCollection<Photo> photos, PHAsset
asset, string filename, PHImageRequestOptions options)
{
    PHImageManager.DefaultManager.RequestImageForAsset(asset,
    PHImageManager.MaximumSize, PHImageContentMode.AspectFill,
    options, (image, info) =>
    {
        using (NSData imageData = image.AsPNG())
        {
            var bytes = new byte[imageData.Length];
            System.Runtime.InteropServices.Marshal.Copy
            (imageData.Bytes, bytes, 0, Convert.ToInt32(
             imageData.Length));
            var photo = new Photo()
            {
                Bytes = bytes,
                Filename = filename
            };
            photos.Add(photo);
        }
    });
}
```

Now, we have what we need to start implementing the two methods from the interface. We will start with the `Task<ObservableCollection<Photo>> Get(int start, int count, Quality quality = Quality.Low)` method, which will be used to get photos from a `CollectionView` view that loads photos incrementally:

```
public async Task<ObservableCollection<Photo>> Get(int start, int count,
Quality quality = Quality.Low)
{
    if (results == null)
    {
        var succeded = await Import();
        if (!succeded)
        {
            return new ObservableCollection<Photo>();
        }
    }
    var photos = new ObservableCollection<Photo>();
    var options = new PHImageRequestOptions()
    {
        NetworkAccessAllowed = true,
        DeliveryMode = quality == Quality.Low ?
        PHImageRequestOptionsDeliveryMode.FastFormat :
         PHImageRequestOptionsDeliveryMode.HighQualityFormat
    };

    Index startIndex = start;
    Index endIndex = start + count;

    if (endIndex.Value >= results.Length)
    {
        endIndex = results.Length - 1;
    }

    if (startIndex.Value > endIndex.Value)
    {
        return new ObservableCollection<Photo>();
    }

    foreach (PHAsset asset in results[startIndex..endIndex])
    {
        var filename =
        (NSString)asset.ValueForKey((NSString)"filename");RequestImage(
         photos, asset, filename, options);
    }
    return photos;
}
```

To use Index, we need to set the language version of the project to C# 8. To do so, see the instructions provided in the *Building the photo gallery app* section earlier in this chapter.

The other method from the IPhotoImporter interface,
Task<ObservableCollection<Photo>> Get(List<string> filenames, Quality quality = Quality.Low), is very similar to
the Task<ObservableCollection<Photo>> Get(int start, int count, Quality quality = Quality.Low) method. The only difference is that there is no code to handle indexes and the foreach loop that loops through the result's array contains an if statement that checks whether the filename is the same as the current PHAsset object, and if it is, it calls the RequestImage method:

```
public async Task<ObservableCollection<Photo>> Get(List<string> filenames,
Quality quality = Quality.Low)
{
    if (results == null)
    {
        var succeded = await Import();
        if (!succeded)
        {
            return new ObservableCollection<Photo>();
        }
    }

    var photos = new ObservableCollection<Photo>();

    var options = new PHImageRequestOptions()
    {
        NetworkAccessAllowed = true,
        DeliveryMode = quality == Quality.Low ?
PHImageRequestOptionsDeliveryMode.FastFormat :
PHImageRequestOptionsDeliveryMode.HighQualityFormat
    };

    foreach (PHAsset asset in results)
    {
        var filename = (NSString)asset.ValueForKey((NSString)"filename");
        if (filenames.Contains(filename))
        {
            RequestImage(photos, asset, filename, options);
        }
    }
    return photos;
}
```

In the preceding code, we set `NetworkAccessAllowed = true`. We do this to make it possible to download photos from iCloud.

Now, one of the two photo importers of our project is complete.

Importing photos from the Android photo gallery

Now that we have created an implementation for iOS, we will do the same for Android:

1. Create a new interface named `PhotoImporter` in the `GalleryApp.Android` project.
2. Import all the members from the `IPhotoImporter` interface.
3. Resolve all the references.
4. Create a new method named `ContinueWithPermission`, which we will call when we get permission from the user to get photos from the photo gallery.
5. Use `ContentResolver` to get the photos (as in the following code block).
6. Loop through the result and add it to a class-level field with a `string[]` type named `result`:

```
public class PhotoImporter : IPhotoImporter
{
    private bool hasCheckedPermission;
    private string[] result;

    public bool ContinueWithPermission(bool granted)
    {
        if (!granted)
        {
            return false;
        }

        Android.Net.Uri imageUri =
         MediaStore.Images.Media.ExternalContentUri;
        var cursor =
         MainActivity.Current.ContentResolver.Query(imageUri, null,
         MediaStore.Images.ImageColumns.MimeType + "=? or " +
         MediaStore.Images.ImageColumns.MimeType + "=?",
         new string[] { "image/jpeg", "image/png" },
         MediaStore.Images.ImageColumns.DateModified);

        var paths = new List<string>();

        while (cursor.MoveToNext())
        {
```

```
                        string path = cursor.GetString(cursor.GetColumnIndex(
                            MediaStore.Images.ImageColumns.Data));
                    paths.Add(path);
                    }

                    result = paths.ToArray();

                    hasCheckedPermission = true;
                    return true;
                }

                Task<ObservableCollection<Photo>> Get(int startIndex,
                int count, Quality quality = Quality.Low)
                {
                    throw new NotImplementedException();
                }
                Task<ObservableCollection<Photo>> Get(List<string> filenames,
                 Quality quality = Quality.Low)
                {
                    throw new NotImplementedException();
                }
        }
```

The next thing to do is to write an `Import` method that will carry out the first step of the import, including a check for user permissions, before the preceding method runs. In the call to `RequestPermissions`, we will set an identifier/code so that we know what to do when the user responds to a permission request. The method should look as in the following code:

```
private async Task<bool> Import()
{
    string[] permissions = { Manifest.Permission.ReadExternalStorage };

    if
(MainActivity.Current.CheckSelfPermission(Manifest.Permission.ReadExternalS
torage) == Permission.Granted)
    {
        ContinueWithPermission(true);
        return true;
    }

    MainActivity.Current.RequestPermissions(permissions, 33);

    while (hasCheckedPermission)
    {
        await Task.Delay(100);
    }
```

```
        return
MainActivity.Current.CheckSelfPermission(Manifest.Permission.ReadExternalSt
orage) == Permission.Granted;
}
```

The last step for the Android import, before we add the `Get` methods from the
`IPhotoImporter` interface, is to add code to handle what happens when the user answers
a request for permissions. We will do that in `MainActivity` of the `Gallery.Android`
project:

```
public static MainActivity Current { get; private set; }

public override void OnRequestPermissionsResult(int requestCode, string[]
permissions, [GeneratedEnum] Android.Content.PM.Permission[] grantResults)
{
    Xamarin.Essentials.Platform.OnRequestPermissionsResult(requestCode,
    permissions, grantResults);

    if (requestCode == 33)
    {
        var importer = (PhotoImporter)Resolver.Resolve<IPhotoImporter>();
        importer.ContinueWithPermission(grantResults[0] ==
        Permission.Granted);
    }

    base.OnRequestPermissionsResult(requestCode, permissions,
     grantResults);
}
```

We will then start editing the `Task<ObservableCollection<Photo>> Get(int start,`
`int count, Quality quality = Quality.Low)` method. If the import succeeds or if
the `results` variable already has a value, we will continue to write the code that handles
what photos should be imported in this loading of images. Conditions are specified with
the `start` and `count` parameters. Take the following steps to calculate what end index we
should use:

```
public async Task<ObservableCollection<Photo>> Get(int start, int count,
Quality quality = Quality.Low)
{
    if (result == null)
    {
        var succeded = await Import();
        if (!succeded)
        {
            return new ObservableCollection<Photo>();
        }
    }
```

```
    if (result.Length == 0)
    {
        return new ObservableCollection<Photo>();
    }

    Index startIndex = start;
    Index endIndex = start + count;

    if (endIndex.Value >= result.Length)
    {
        endIndex = result.Length - 1;
    }
    if (startIndex.Value > endIndex.Value)
    {
        return new ObservableCollection<Photo>();
    }

    var photos = new ObservableCollection<Photo>();
    foreach (var path in result[startIndex..endIndex])
    {
        var filename = Path.GetFileName(path);
        var stream = new FileStream(path, FileMode.Open, FileAccess.Read);
        var memoryStream = new MemoryStream();
        stream.CopyTo(memoryStream);
        var photo = new Photo()
        {
            Bytes = memoryStream.ToArray(),
            Filename = filename
        };
        photos.Add(photo);
    }

    return photos;
}
```

Now, we will continue with the other `Task<ObservableCollection<Photo>>`
`Get(List<string> filenames, Quality quality = Quality.Low)` method:

1. Create a `foreach` loop to loop through all the photos and to check whether each
   photo is specified in the `filenames` parameter. If this is the case, read the photo
   from the path, as in the first `Get` method:

```
public async Task<ObservableCollection<Photo>> Get(List<string>
filenames, Quality quality = Quality.Low)
{
    if (result == null)
    {
```

```
    var succeded = await Import();

    if (!succeded)
    {
        return new ObservableCollection<Photo>();
    }
}

if (result.Length == 0)
{
    return new ObservableCollection<Photo>();
}

var photos = new ObservableCollection<Photo>();

foreach (var path in result)
{
    var filename = Path.GetFileName(path);

    if (!filenames.Contains(filename))
    {
        continue;
    }

    var stream = new FileStream(path, FileMode.Open,
     FileAccess.Read);
    var memoryStream = new MemoryStream();
    stream.CopyTo(memoryStream);

    var photo = new Photo()
    {
        Bytes = memoryStream.ToArray(),
        Filename = filename
    };
        photos.Add(photo);
}

return photos;
}
```

The photo importers are now finished and we are ready to write the rest of the app, which will mostly involve adding code that is shared between the platforms.

Writing the app-initializing code

We have now written the code that we will use to get data to the app. Let's continue to build the app, starting with initializing the core parts of the app.

Creating a shell

The main navigation for this app will be tabs at the bottom of the screen. The app will have a fly-out menu with two options—**Home** and **Gallery**:

1. In the `Views` folder in the `GalleryApp` project, create two new `ContentPage` files with XAML—one named `MainView` and one named `GalleryView`.

2. At the root of the `GalleryApp` project, create a new `ContentPage` file named `MainShell`.

3. Change the base class of `MainShell` to `Shell` instead of `ContentPage`. We need to do this in both `MainShell.xaml` and `MainShell.xaml.cs`.

4. Add `MainView` to the `Shell` object wrapped in a `ShellContent` object.

5. Add `GalleryView` to the `Shell` object using the `ContentTemplate` property of `ShellContent`. Use the `DataTemplate` mark-up extension. This will load `GalleryView` when the user taps the tab, instead of when `Shell` is loading, as is the case with `MainView`:

```
<Shell xmlns="http://xamarin.com/schemas/2014/forms"
  xmlns:x="http://schemas.microsoft.com/winfx/2009/xaml"
  xmlns:views="clr-namespace:GalleryApp.Views"
  x:Class="GalleryApp.MainShell">
    <ShellContent Title="Home">
        <views:MainView />
    </ShellContent>
    <ShellContent Title="Gallery" ContentTemplate="{DataTemplate
views:GalleryView}" />
</Shell>
```

When we have defined the shell, we can navigate to `App.xaml.cs` and set `MainPage` to `MainShell`:

```
public App()
{
    InitializeComponent();
    MainPage = new MainShell();
}
```

Now that we have created a shell, let's continue with some other base code before we start to create the views.

Creating a base view model

Before we create an actual view model, we will create an abstract base view model that all view models can inherit from. The idea behind this base view model is that we can write common code in it. In this case, we will implement the INotifyPropertyChanged interface by going through the following steps:

1. In the GalleryApp project, create a folder named ViewModels.

2. Create a new abstract class named ViewModel:

```
public abstract class ViewModel : INotifyPropertyChanged
{
    public event PropertyChangedEventHandler PropertyChanged;

    protected void Set<T>(ref T field, T newValue,
[CallerMemberName]
      string propertyName = null)
    {
        if (!EqualityComparer<T>.Default.Equals(field, newValue))
        {
            field = newValue;
            RaisePropertyChanged(propertyName);
        }
    }

    protected void RaisePropertyChanged([CallerMemberName] string
     propertyName = null)
    {
        PropertyChanged?.Invoke(this, new
          PropertyChangedEventArgs(propertyName));
    }

    private bool isBusy;
    public bool IsBusy
    {
        get => isBusy;
        set
        {
            Set(ref isBusy, value);
            RaisePropertyChanged(nameof(IsNotBusy));
        }
    }
```

```
public bool IsNotBusy => !IsBusy;
}
```

 The `CallerMemberName` attribute is used so that we don't have to specify the property name when calling it; it will use the name of the property that we called it from.

Now, we have a `ViewModel` base that we can use for all `ViewModel` instances that we will create later in this project.

Creating a bootstrapper and a resolver

We will be using dependency injection in this project with a library called Autofac. Autofac is an open source **inversion of control** (**IoC**) container. We will create a `Resolver` class in order to easily resolve the types that we will add to the container later in this chapter. To do so, we will go through the following steps:

1. Install Autofac from NuGet in the `GalleryApp`, `GalleryApp.Android`, and `GalleryApp.iOS` projects.
2. In the `GalleryApp` project, create a new class called `Resolver` in the root of the project.
3. Create a `private static IContainer` field called `container`.
4. Create a `static` method called `Initialized` that has an `IContainer` argument and set the value of the `container` field, as in the following code:

```
using Autofac;
using System;
using System.Collections.Generic;
using System.Text;

namespace GalleryApp
{
    public class Resolver
    {
        private static IContainer container;

        public static void Initialize(IContainer container)
        {
            Resolver.container = container;
        }
    }
}
```

The `Initialize` method will be called after the configuration of Autofac is complete, which we will do when we create the bootstrapper. This method simply takes the `container` field that it gets as an argument and stores it in the `static` container field.

Now, we need a method to access it from. Create one more `static` method called `Resolve`. This method will be generic and when we use it, we will specify its type as the type that will be resolved. Use the `container` field to resolve the type, as in the following code:

```
public static T Resolve<T>()
{
    return container.Resolve<T>();
}
```

The `Resolve<T>` method takes a type as an argument and looks in the container to see whether there is any information on how to construct this type. If there is, then we return it.

So, now that we have the resolver that we will use to resolve instances of types of objects, we need to configure it. That's the job of the bootstrapper.

Creating the bootstrapper

To configure the dependency injection and initialize the resolver, we will create a bootstrapper. We will have one shared bootstrapper and other bootstrappers for each platform to meet their specific configurations. The reason that we need them to be platform-specific is that we will have different implementations of `IPhotoImporter` on iOS and Android. To create a bootstrapper, we take the following steps:

1. Create a new class in the `GalleryApp` project and name it `Bootstrapper`.
2. Add the following code to the new class:

```
using System.Linq;
using System.Reflection;
using Autofac;
using GalleryApp.ViewModels;
using Xamarin.Forms;

namespace GalleryApp
{
    public class Bootstrapper
    {
        protected ContainerBuilder ContainerBuilder { get;
         private set; }
        public Bootstrapper()
        {
```

```
        Initialize();
        FinishInitialization();
    }

    protected virtual void Initialize()
    {
        ContainerBuilder = new ContainerBuilder();

        ContainerBuilder.RegisterType<MainShell>();

        var currentAssembly = Assembly.GetExecutingAssembly();

        foreach (var type in
        currentAssembly.DefinedTypes.Where(e =>
         e.IsSubclassOf(typeof(ContentPage))))
        {
            ContainerBuilder.RegisterType(type.AsType());
        }

        foreach (var type in
        currentAssembly.DefinedTypes.Where(e =>
         e.IsSubclassOf(typeof(ViewModel))))
        {
            ContainerBuilder.RegisterType(type.AsType());
        }
    }
    private void FinishInitialization()
    {
        var container = ContainerBuilder.Build();

        Resolver.Initialize(container);
    }
    }
    }
}
```

Creating the iOS bootstrapper

In the iOS bootstrapper, we have configurations that are specific to iOS apps. To create an iOS app, we go through the following steps:

1. In the iOS project, create a new class and name it Bootstrapper.
2. Make the new class inherit from GalleryApp.Bootstrapper.
3. Add the following code:

```
using System;
using Autofac;
```

```
namespace GalleryApp.iOS
{
    public class Bootstrapper : GalleryApp.Bootstrapper
    {
        protected override void Initialize()
        {
            base.Initialize();

ContainerBuilder.RegisterType<PhotoImporter>().As<IPhotoImporter>()
.SingleInstance();
        }
    }
}
```

4. Go to `AppDelegate.cs` in the iOS project.

5. Before the call to `LoadApplication`, in the `FinishedLaunching` method, create a new instance of the `Bootstrapper`, as in the following code:

```
public override bool FinishedLaunching(UIApplication app,
NSDictionary options)
{
    _ = new Bootstrapper();
    global::Xamarin.Forms.Forms.Init();

    LoadApplication(new App());

    return base.FinishedLaunching(app, options);
}
```

Creating the Android bootstrapper

In the Android bootstrapper, we have configurations that are specific to
the Android app. To create the bootstrapper in Android, we go through the following steps:

1. In the Android project, create a new class and name it `Bootstrapper`.

2. Make the new class inherit from `GalleryApp.Bootstrapper`.

3. Add the following code:

```
using System;
using Autofac;

namespace GalleryApp.Droid
{
    public class Bootstrapper : GalleryApp.Bootstrapper
    {
        protected override void Initialize()
        {
```

```
            base.Initialize();
ContainerBuilder.RegisterType<PhotoImporter>().As<IPhotoImporter>()
.SingleInstance();
            }
        }
    }
```

4. Go to the `MainActivity.cs` file in the Android project.

5. Before the call to `LoadApplication`, in the `FinishedLaunching` method, create a new instance of `Bootstrapper`, as in the following code:

```
protected override void OnCreate(Bundle savedInstanceState)
{
    TabLayoutResource = Resource.Layout.Tabbar;
    ToolbarResource = Resource.Layout.Toolbar;

    base.OnCreate(savedInstanceState);

    _ = new Bootstrapper();
    Xamarin.Essentials.Platform.Init(this, savedInstanceState);

    global::Xamarin.Forms.Forms.Init(this, savedInstanceState);

    LoadApplication(new App());
}
```

 Discards are "dummy variables" that are used when, for example, a method has a return value—but we will never use them. To mark a discard, we will use an underscore (_). For example, in the preceding case, we have `_ = new Bootstrapper();`. You can read more about discards at `https://docs.microsoft.com/en-us/dotnet/csharp/discards`.

Now, we have created the code for importing for both iOS and Android, as well as the initializing part of the app. So now, are we ready to start to create the views.

Creating the gallery view

Now, we will start to build the views. We will start with the gallery view, which will show the photos as a grid.

Creating the ViewModel

`ViewModel` is the class that will be responsible for fetching the data and handling the view logic. Because photos will be added asynchronously to the photos collection, we don't want to set `IsBusy` to `false` immediately after we call the `Get` method of `PhotoImporter`. We will instead wait 3 seconds, first. However, we will also add an event listener to the collection so that we can listen for changes. If the collection changes and there are items in it, we will set `IsBusy` to `false`. Add the following code to implement this:

```
public class GalleryViewModel : ViewModel
{
    private readonly IPhotoImporter photoImporter;
    private readonly ILocalStorage localStorage;

    public GalleryViewModel(IPhotoImporter photoImporter, ILocalStorage
localStorage)
    {
        this.photoImporter = photoImporter;
        this.localStorage = localStorage;
        Task.Run(Initialize);
    }

    public ObservableCollection<Photo> Photos { get; set; }
    private async Task Initialize()
    {
        IsBusy = true;
        Photos = await photoImporter.Get(0,20);
        RaisePropertyChanged(nameof(Photos));

        Photos.CollectionChanged += Photos_CollectionChanged;
        await Task.Delay(3000);
        IsBusy = false;
    }

    private void Photos_CollectionChanged(object sender,
    System.Collections.Specialized.NotifyCollectionChangedEventArgs e)
    {
        if(e.NewItems != null && e.NewItems.Count > 0)
        {
            IsBusy = false;
            Photos.CollectionChanged -= Photos_CollectionChanged;
        }
    }
}
```

Now, `ViewModel` is ready, so we can start to create the view.

Creating the view

First, we will create a converter that will convert a `byte[]`
to `Xamarin.Forms.ImageSource`. In the `GalleryApp` project, create a new folder
named `Converters`, and inside the folder, create a new class
named `BytesToImageConverter`:

```
public class BytesToImageConverter : IValueConverter
{
    public object Convert(object value, Type targetType, object parameter,
CultureInfo culture)
    {
        if (value != null)
        {
            var bytes = (byte[])value;
            var stream = new MemoryStream(bytes);
            return ImageSource.FromStream(() => stream);
        }
        return null;
    }

    public object ConvertBack(object value, Type targetType, object
parameter, CultureInfo culture)
    {
        throw new NotImplementedException();
    }
}
```

To use the converter, we need to add it as a resource. We will do this by adding it to a
`ResourceDictionary` object in the `Resources` property of `GalleryView`:

1. Open `GalleryView.xaml`.
2. Add the following bold-styled code to the view:

```
<ContentPage xmlns="http://xamarin.com/schemas/2014/forms"
xmlns:x="http://schemas.microsoft.com/winfx/2009/xaml"
xmlns:converters="clr-namespace:GalleryApp.Converters"
x:Class="GalleryApp.Views.GalleryView" Title="Photos">
    <ContentPage.Resources>
        <ResourceDictionary>
            <converters:BytesToImageConverter x:Key="ToImage" />
        </ResourceDictionary>
    <ContentPage.Resources>
</ContentPage>
```

To be able to bind to `ViewModel`, we will set `BindingContext` to `GalleryViewModel`.
Use the resolver in `GalleryView.xaml.cs` to create an instance of `GalleryViewModel`:

1. Open `GalleryView.xaml.cs`.
2. Add the following code marked in bold to the class:

```
public GalleryView()
{
    InitializeComponent();
    BindingContext = Resolver.Resolve<GalleryViewModel>();
}
```

What we will show in this view is a grid with three columns. To build this with
Xamarin.Forms, we will use the `CollectionView` control. To specify what layout
`CollectionView` should have, add a `GridItemsLayout` element to
the `ItemsLayout` property of `CollectionView`.

Follow these steps to build this view:

1. Navigate to `GalleryView.xaml`.
2. Import the namespaces for `GalleryApp.ViewModels` and
   `GalleryApp.Models`.
3. On `ContentPage`, set `x:DataType` to `vm:GalleryViewModel`. This makes the
   bindings compile, which will make our view faster to render:

```
<CollectionView x:Name="Photos" ItemsSource="{Binding Photos}">
    <CollectionView.ItemsLayout>
        <GridItemsLayout Orientation="Vertical" Span="3"
HorizontalItemSpacing="0" />
    </CollectionView.ItemsLayout>
</CollectionView><CollectionView.ItemTemplate>

<DataTemplate x:DataType="models:Photo">
    <Grid>
        <Image Aspect="AspectFill" Source="{Binding Bytes,
Converter={StaticResource ToImage}}" HeightRequest="120" />
    </Grid>
</DataTemplate>
</CollectionView.ItemTemplate>
```

Now, we can see the photos in the view. However, we will also need to create the content that will be shown when we don't have any photos to show as they not have been loaded yet, or if there are no photos available. Follow these steps to create a `DataTemplate` object to show when `CollectionView` doesn't have any data:

```
<CollectionView EmptyView="{Binding}">

<CollectionView.EmptyViewTemplate>
    <DataTemplate x:DataType="vm:GalleryViewModel">
        <Grid>
            <ActivityIndicator IsVisible="{Binding IsBusy}" />
            <Label Text="No photos to import could be found"
IsVisible="{Binding IsNotBusy}" HorizontalOptions="Center"
VerticalOptions="Center" HorizontalTextAlignment="Center" />
        </Grid>
    </DataTemplate>
</CollectionView.EmptyViewTemplate>
```

Now, we can run the app. The next step is to load more photos when a user reaches the end of the view.

Loading photos incrementally

To load more than the first 20 items, we will load photos incrementally so that when users scroll to the end of `CollectionView`, it will start to load more items. `CollectionView` has built-in support for loading data incrementally. Because we get an `ObeservableCollection` object back from the photo importer and data is added asynchronously to it, we need to create an event listener to handle when items are added to the photo importer so that we can add it to the `ObservableCollection` instance that we bound to `CollectionView`. Create the event listener by following these steps:

1. Navigate to `GalleryViewModel.cs`.
2. Add the following code:

```
private int itemsAdded;
private void Collection_CollectionChanged(object sender,
System.Collections.Specialized.NotifyCollectionChangedEventArgs
args)
{
    foreach(Photo photo in args.NewItems)
    {
        itemsAdded++;
        Photos.Add(photo);
    }
```

```
        if(itemsAdded == 20)
        {
            var collection = (ObservableCollection<Photo>)sender;
            collection.CollectionChanged -=
Collection_CollectionChanged;
        }
    }

    private int currentStartIndex = 0;
    public ICommand LoadMore => new Command(async() =>
    {
        currentStartIndex += 20;
        itemsAdded = 0;
        var collection = await photoImporter.Get(currentStartIndex,
20);
        collection.CollectionChanged += Collection_CollectionChanged;
    });
```

The only thing we have left to do to get the incremental load to work is to bind
`CollectionView` to the code we created in `ViewModel`. The following code will trigger the
loading of more photos when the user has just five items left:

```
<CollectionView x:Name="Photos" EmptyView="{Binding}" ItemsSource="{Binding
Photos}" RemainingItemsThreshold="5"
RemainingItemsThresholdReachedCommand="{Binding LoadMore}">
```

Now that we have a view that shows photos and loads them incrementally, we can make it
possible to add photos as favorites.

Saving favorites

In `GalleryView`, we want to be able to select favorites that we can show in `MainView`. To
do that, we need to store the photos that we have selected so that it remembers our
selection. Create a new interface in the `GalleryApp` project named `ILocalStorage`:

```
public interface ILocalStorage
{
    Task Store(string filename);
    Task<List<string>> Get();
}
```

The easiest way to store/persist data in Xamarin.Forms is to use the built-in property store. `Properties` is a property of the `Application` class, the base class of our `App` class. Follow these steps to use it:

1. Install the `Newtonsoft.Json` NuGet package for the `GalleryApp` project.
2. Create a new class named `FormsLocalStorage` in the `GalleryApp` project.
3. Implement the `ILocalStorage` interface:

```
public class FormsLocalStorage : ILocalStorage
{
    public const string FavoritePhotosKey = "FavoritePhotos";

    public async Task<List<string>> Get()
    {
        if
(Application.Current.Properties.ContainsKey(FavoritePhotosKey))
        {
            var filenames =
(string)Application.Current.Properties[FavoritePhotosKey];
            return
JsonConvert.DeserializeObject<List<string>>(filenames);
        }
        return new List<string>();
    }

    public async Task Store(string filename)
    {
        var filenames = await Get();
        filenames.Add(filename);

        var json = JsonConvert.SerializeObject(filenames);

        Application.Current.Properties[FavoritePhotosKey] = json;
        await Application.Current.SavePropertiesAsync();
    }
}
```

To be able to use `ILocalStorage` with constructor injection, we need to register it to the container:

1. Navigate to the `Bootstrapper` class in the `GalleryApp` project.
2. Add the following code at the end of the `Initialize` method:

```
ContainerBuilder.RegisterType<FormsLocalStorage>().As<ILocalStorage
>();
```

Now, we are ready to use the local storage:

1. Navigate to the `GalleryViewModel` class in the `GalleryApp` project.
2. Add the `ILocalStorage` interface to the constructor and assign it to a field:

```
private readonly IPhotoImporter photoImporter;
private readonly ILocalStorage localStorage;

public GalleryViewModel(IPhotoImporter photoImporter, ILocalStorage
localStorage)
{
    this.photoImporter = photoImporter;
    this.localStorage = localStorage;
}
```

The next step is to create a command that we can bind to from the view when we select photos. The command will monitor what photos we have selected and notify others that we have added favorite photos:

1. Navigate to `GalleryViewModel` in the `GalleryApp` project.
2. Create a new property of the `ICommand` type named `AddFavorites`.
3. Add the following code:

```
public ICommand AddFavorites => new Command<List<Photo>>((photos)
=>
{
    foreach (var photo in photos)
    {
        localStorage.Store(photo.Filename);
    }
    MessagingCenter.Send(this, "FavoritesAdded");
});
```

Now, we are ready to start working with the view. The first thing we will do is make it possible to select photos. Follow these steps to do that:

1. Navigate to `GalleryView.xaml` in the `GalleryApp` project.
2. Set the `SelectionMode` mode of `CollectionView` to `Multiple` to make it possible to select multiple items:

```
<CollectionView x:Name="Photos" EmptyView="{Binding}"
ItemsSource="{Binding Photos}" SelectionMode="Multiple"
RemainingItemsThreshold="5"
RemainingItemsThresholdReachedCommand="{Binding LoadMore}">
```

When a user selects a photo, we want it to be clear what photos have been selected. To achieve this, we will use VisualStateManager. We will do this by creating a style for Grid and setting Opacity to 0.5, as in the following code. Add the code to Resources of the page:

```
<ContentPage.Resources>
    <ResourceDinctionary>
        <Style TargetType="Grid">
            <Setter Property="VisualStateManager.VisualStateGroups">
                <VisualStateGroupList>
                    <VisualStateGroup x:Name="CommonStates">
                        <VisualState x:Name="Normal" />
                        <VisualState x:Name="Selected">
                            <VisualState.Setters>
                                <Setter Property="Opacity" Value="0.5" />
                            </VisualState.Setters>
                        </VisualState>
                    </VisualStateGroup>
                </VisualStateGroupList>
            </Setter>
        </Style>
    </ResourceDictionary>
</ContentPage.Resources>
```

To save the selected photos, we will create a toolbar item that the user can tap:

1. Add ToolbarItem with the Text property set to Select.

2. Add an event handler named SelectToolBarItem_Clicked:

```
<ContentPage.ToolbarItems>
    <ToolbarItem Text="Select" Clicked="SelectToolBarItem_Clicked"
/>
</ContentPage.ToolbarItems>
```

3. Navigate to the code behind the GalleryView.xaml.cs file.

4. Create an event handler named SelectToolBarItem_Clicked:

```
private void SelectToolBarItem_Clicked(object sender, EventArgs e)
{
    if (!Photos.SelectedItems.Any())
    {
        DisplayAlert("No photos", "No photos selected", "OK");
        return;
    }
    var viewModel = (GalleryViewModel)BindingContext;
    viewModel.AddFavorites.Execute(Photos.SelectedItems.Select(x =>
(Photo)x).ToList());
```

```
        DisplayAlert("Added", "Selected photos has been added to
    favorites", "OK");
    }
```

Now that we are done with `GalleryView`, we will continue with the main view, which should view the latest photos and the favorite photos in two carousels.

Creating the carousels

The last view in this app is `MainView`, the view that is visible when users start the app. This view will show two carousel views—one with recent photos and one with the favorite photos.

Creating the view model for the favorite photos

We will start by creating a `ViewModel` model that we will use for the view. In the `ViewModel` folder in the `GalleryApp` project, create a new class named `MainViewModel`:

```
public class MainViewModel : ViewModel
{
    private readonly IPhotoImporter photoImporter;
    private readonly ILocalStorage localStorage;

    public ObservableCollection<Photo> Recent { get; set; }
    public ObservableCollection<Photo> Favorites { get; set; }

    public MainViewModel(IPhotoImporter photoImporter, ILocalStorage
localStorage)
    {
        this.photoImporter = photoImporter;
        this.localStorage = localStorage;
    }

    public async Task Initialize()
    {
        var photos = await photoImporter.Get(0, 20, Quality.Low);

        Recent = photos;
        RaisePropertyChanged(nameof(Recent));

        await LoadFavorites();

        MessagingCenter.Subscribe<GalleryViewModel>(this, "FavoritesAdded",
    (sender) =>
```

```
        {
            MainThread.BeginInvokeOnMainThread(async () =>
            {
                await LoadFavorites();
            });
        });
    }

    private async Task LoadFavorites()
    {
      var filenames = await localStorage.Get();
      var favorites = await photoImporter.Get(filenames, Quality.Low);

      Favorites = favorites;
      RaisePropertyChanged(nameof(Favorites));
    }
}
```

Now that we have created a `ViewModel` model for the favorite photos, we will continue with the latest photos.

Creating the view model for the latest photos

We are now ready to set up the carousel views. We have already created the view model, so we can start to add content to it.

 `CarouselView` and `IndicatorView` (which we will use later) are in preview in Xamarin.Forms. To use them, we have to add the following code to the `FinishLaunching` method in `AppDelegate.cs` for iOS and in the `OnCreated` method in the `MainActivity.cs` for Android:

```
global::Xamarin.Forms.Forms.SetFlags("CarouselView_Experi
mental", "IndicatorView_Experimental");
```

Let's look at the steps to create the view:

1. In the contractor of the code, behind the `MainView.xaml.cs` file, set `ViewModel` to `BindingContext`:

```
public MainView()
{
    InitializeComponent();
    BindingContext = Resolver.Resolve<MainViewModel>();
}
```

2. Navigate to `MainView.xaml`.

3. Add the following code:

```xml
<ContentPage xmlns="http://xamarin.com/schemas/2014/forms"
    xmlns:x="http://schemas.microsoft.com/winfx/2009/xaml"
    xmlns:converters="clr-namespace:GalleryApp.Converters"
    x:Class="GalleryApp.Views.MainView" Title="My photos">
    <ContentPage.Resources>
        <ResourceDictionary>
            <converters:BytesToImageConverter x:Key="ToImage" />
        </ResourceDictionary>
    </ContentPage.Resources>

    <Grid>
        <Grid.RowDefinitions>
            <RowDefinition Height="*" />
            <RowDefinition Height="*" />
        </Grid.RowDefinitions>
    </Grid>

    <CarouselView ItemsSource="{Binding Recent}">
        <CarouselView.ItemsLayout>
            <LinearItemsLayout Orientation="Horizontal"
SnapPointsAlignment="Start" SnapPointsType="Mandatory" />
        </CarouselView.ItemsLayout>
        <CarouselView.ItemTemplate>
            <DataTemplate>
                <Image Source="{Binding Bytes,
Converter={StaticResource ToImage}}" Aspect="AspectFill" />
            </DataTemplate>
        </CarouselView.ItemTemplate>
    </CarouselView>
</ContentPage>
```

Now that we have shown the latest photos in a carousel, the next (and the last) step is to show the favorite photos in another carousel.

Showing the favorites photos

The last thing we will do in this app is add a carousel to show the favorite photos. Add the following code to do so:

```xml
<StackLayout Grid.Row="1">
    <Label Margin="10" Text="Favorites" FontSize="Subtitle"
FontAttributes="Bold" />
    <CarouselView ItemsSource="{Binding Favorites}"
```

```
PeekAreaInsets="0,0,40,0" IndicatorView="Indicator">
        <CarouselView.ItemsLayout>
            <LinearItemsLayout Orientation="Horizontal"
SnapPointsAlignment="Start" SnapPointsType="MandatorySingle" />
        </CarouselView.ItemsLayout>
        <CarouselView.EmptyViewTemplate>
            <DataTemplate>
                <Label Text="No favorites selected" />
            </DataTemplate>
        </CarouselView.EmptyViewTemplate>
        <CarouselView.ItemTemplate>
            <DataTemplate>
                <Image Source="{Binding Bytes,
Converter={StaticResource ToImage}}" Aspect="AspectFill" />
            </DataTemplate>
        </CarouselView.ItemTemplate>
    </CarouselView>
    <IndicatorView x:Name="Indicator" HorizontalOptions="Center"
SelectedIndicatorColor="Red" IndicatorColor="LightGray" />
</StackLayout>
```

That is all—now, we can run the app and see both the most recent photos and the photos that have been marked as favorites.

Summary

In this chapter, we focused on photos. We learned how to import photos from the iOS and Android photo galleries and how we can display them as a grid using `CollectionView` and in carousels using `CarouselView`. This makes it possible for us to build other apps and provides multiple options for presenting data to users. We can, therefore, pick the best method for the situation.

In the next chapter, we will take a look at how we can build an app using location services and how to visualize location data on a map.

6
Building a Location Tracking App Using GPS and Maps

In this chapter, we will create a location tracking app that saves the location of the user and displays it as a heat map. We will learn how to run tasks in the background on iOS and Android devices and how to use custom renderers to extend the functionality of Xamarin.Forms maps.

The following topics will be covered in this chapter:

- Tracking the location of a user in the background on an iOS device
- Tracking the location of a user in the background on an Android device
- How to show maps in a Xamarin.Forms app
- How to extend the functionality of Xamarin.Forms maps with custom renderers

Let's get started!

Technical requirements

To be able to complete this project, you'll need to have Visual Studio for Mac or PC installed, as well as the Xamarin components. See Chapter 1, *Introduction to Xamarin*, for more details on how to set up your environment. To build an iOS app using Visual Studio for PC, you have to have a Mac connected. If you don't have access to a Mac at all, you can just complete the Android part of this project.

Project overview

Many apps can be made richer by adding a map and location services. In this project, we will build a location tracking app that we will call **MeTracker**. This app will track the position of the user and save it to a SQLite database so that we can visualize the result in the form of a heat map. To build this app, we will learn how to set up processes in the background on both iOS and Android since we cannot share code between iOS and Android. For the map, we will use the `Xamarin.Forms.Maps` component and extend its functionality in order to build a heat map. To do this, we will use a custom renderer for iOS and a custom renderer for Android so that we can use the platform's APIs.

The estimated build time for this project is 180 minutes.

Building the MeTracker app

It's time to start building the app. Use the **Mobile App (Xamarin.Forms)** template. The easiest way to find this template is to search for `xamarin.forms` in the search bar at the top of the dialog that appears when you start Visual Studio:

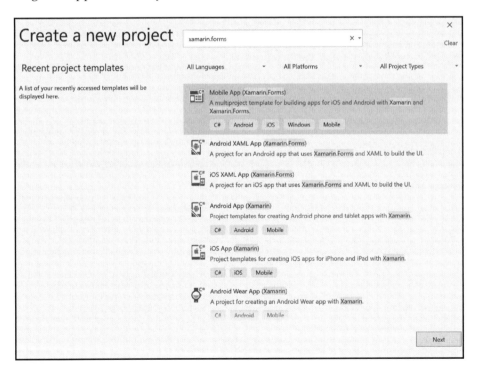

We will name the project **MeTracker**:

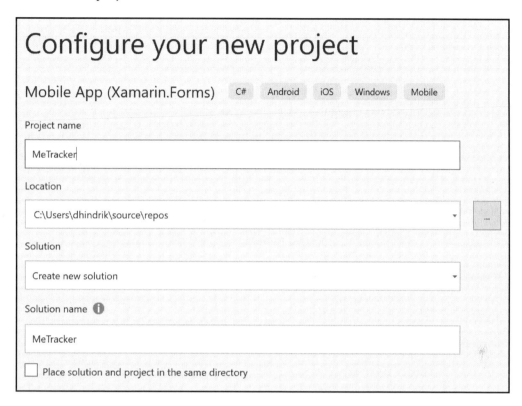

We will use the **Blank** template and build for the **Android** and **iOS** platforms:

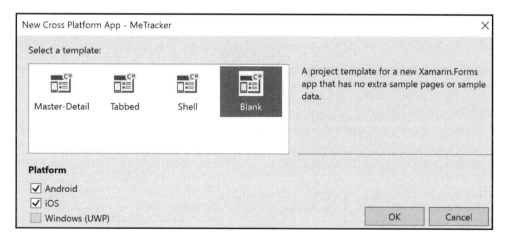

Make sure that you are compiling using Android version Oreo (API level 26) or higher. We can set this in the project's **Properties**, under the **Application** tab.

Update the NuGet packages that were added by the template to make sure that we're using the latest versions.

Creating a repository to save the locations of our users

The first thing we will do is create a repository that we can use to save the locations of our users.

Creating a model for the location data

Before we create the repository, we will create a model class that will represent a user location. Follow these steps to do so:

1. Create a new folder that we can use for this and other models called `Models`.
2. Create a class called `Location` in the `Models` folder and add properties for `Id`, `Latitude`, and `Longitude`.
3. Create two constructors – one that's empty and one that takes `latitude` and `longitude` as arguments. Use the following code to do so:

```
using System;

namespace MeTracker.Models
{
    public class Location
    {
        public Location() {}

        public Location(double latitude, double longitude)
        {
            Latitude = latitude;
            Longitude = longitude;
        }

        public int Id { get; set; }
        public double Latitude { get; set; }
        public double Longitude { get; set; }
    }
}
```

Creating the repository

Now that we have created a model, we can start creating the repository. First, we will create an interface for the repository. Follow these steps to do so:

1. In the `MeTracker` project, create a new folder called `Repositories`.
2. In our new folder, create an interface called `ILocationRepository`.
3. Write the following code in the new file that we created for the `interface`:

```
using MeTracker.Models;
using System;
using System.Threading.Tasks;

namespace MeTracker.Repositories
{
    public interface ILocationRepository
    {
        Task Save(Location location);
    }
}
```

4. Add a `using` directive for `MeTracker.Models` and `System.Threading.Tasks` to resolve the references for `Location` and `Task`.

Now that we have an `interface`, we need to create an implementation of it. Follow these steps to do so:

1. In the `MeTracker` project, create a new class called `LocationRepository`.
2. Implement the `ILocationRepository` interface and add the `async` keyword to the `Save` method using the following code:

```
using System;
using System.Threading.Tasks;
using MeTracker.Models;

namespace MeTracker.Repositories
{
    public class LocationRepository : ILocationRepository
    {
        public async Task Save(Location location)
        {
        }
    }
}
```

To store the data, we will use a SQLite database and the **object-relational mapper (ORM)** known as SQLite-net so that we can write code against a domain model instead of using SQL to perform operations against the database. This is an open source library that was created by Frank A. Krueger. Let's set this up by going through the following steps:

1. Install the NuGet package, `sqlite-net-pcl`, for the `MeTracker` project.

2. Go to the `Location` model class and add the `PrimaryKeyAttribute` and `AutoIncrementAttribute` attributes to the `Id` property. When we add these attributes, the `Id` property will be a primary key in the database, and a value for it will be automatically created.

3. Write the following code in the `LocationRepository` class to create a connection to the SQLite database. The `if` statement is used to check whether we have already created a connection. If we have, we won't create a new one; instead, we will use the connection that we've already created:

```
private SQLiteAsyncConnection connection;
private async Task CreateConnection()
{
    if (connection != null)
    {
        return;
    }

    var databasePath =
    Path.Combine(Environment.GetFolderPath
    (Environment.SpecialFolder .MyDocuments), "Locations.db");

    connection = new SQLiteAsyncConnection(databasePath);
    await connection.CreateTableAsync<Location>();
}
```

Now, it's time to implement the `Save` method, which will take a location object as a parameter and store it in the database.

We will now use the `CreateConnection` method in the `Save` method to ensure that a connection is created when we try to save data to the database. When we know that we have an active connection, we can just use the `InsertAsync` method and pass the `location` parameter of the `Save` method as an argument.

Edit the `Save` method in the `LocationRepository` class so that it looks as follows:

```
public async Task Save(Location location)
{
    await CreateConnection();
    await connection.InsertAsync(location);
}
```

Xamarin.Essentials

Xamarin.Essentials is a library that was created by Microsoft and Xamarin so that developers can use platform-specific APIs from shared code. Xamarin.Essentials targets Xamarin.iOS, Xamarin.Android, and UWP. In this project, we will use Xamarin.Essentials for various tasks, including getting a location and executing code on the main thread.

Creating a service for location tracking

To track a user's location, we need to write the code according to the platform. Xamarin.Essentials has methods for getting the location of a user in shared code, but it cannot be used in the background. To be able to use the code that we will write for each platform, we need to create an interface. For the `ILocationRepository` interface, there will be just one implementation that will be used on both platforms, whereas for the location tracking service, we will have one implementation for the iOS platform and one for the Android platform.

Go through the following steps to create the `ILocationRepository` interface:

1. In the `MeTracker` project, create a new folder called `Services`.
2. Create a new interface in the `Services` folder called `ILocationTrackingService`.
3. In the interface, add a method called `StartTracking`, as shown in the following code:

```
public interface ILocationTrackingService
{
    void StartTracking();
}
```

For the moment, we will just create an empty implementation of the interface in both the iOS and the Android projects by going through the following steps. We will come back to each implementation later in this chapter:

1. Create a folder called `Services` in both the iOS and Android projects.
2. Create an empty implementation in a class called `LocationTrackingService` in the new `Service` folder in both the iOS and Android projects, as shown in the following:

```
public class LocationTrackingService : ILocationTrackingService
{
    public void StartTracking()
    {
    }
}
```

Setting up the app logic

Now that we have created the interfaces, we need to track the location of the user and save it locally on the device. It's time to write some code so that we can start tracking a user. We still don't have any code that actually tracks the location of the user, but it will be easier to write this if we have already written the code that starts the tracking process.

Creating a view with a map

To start with, we will create a view with a simple map that is centered on the position of the user. Let's set this up by going through the following steps:

1. In the `MeTracker` project, create a new folder called `Views`.
2. In the `Views` folder, create a XAML-based `ContentPage` and name it `MainView`:

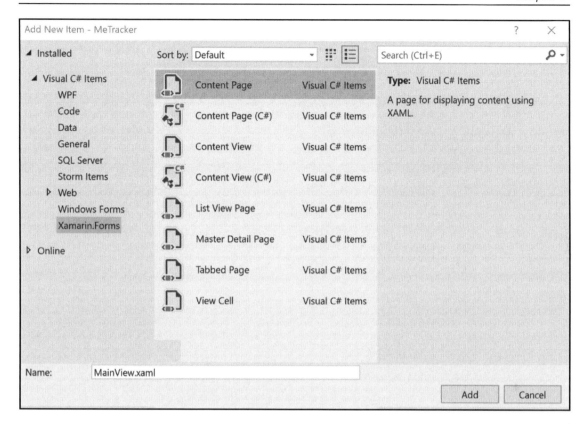

The Xamarin.Forms package has no map controls, but there is an official package from Microsoft and Xamarin that can be used to show maps in a Xamarin.Forms app. This package is called `Xamarin.Forms.Maps`, and we can install it from NuGet by following these steps:

1. Install `Xamarin.Forms.Maps` in the `MeTracker`, `MeTracker.Android`, and `MeTracker.iOS` projects.

2. Add the namespace for `Xamarin.Forms.Maps` to `MainView` using the following code:

```
<ContentPage xmlns="http://xamarin.com/schemas/2014/forms"

xmlns:x="http://schemas.microsoft.com/winfx/2009/xaml"
             xmlns:map="clr-
             namespace:Xamarin.Forms.Maps;assembly
             =Xamarin.Forms.Maps"
             x:Class="MeTracker.Views.MainView">
```

Now, we can use the map in our view. Because we want Map to cover the whole page, we can add it to the root of ContentPage. Let's set this up by going through the following steps:

1. Add Map to ContentPage.
2. Give the map a name so we can access it from the code-behind file. Name it Map, as shown in the following code:

```
<ContentPage xmlns="http://xamarin.com/schemas/2014/forms"
xmlns:x="http://schemas.microsoft.com/winfx/2009/xaml"
            xmlns:map="clr-
namespace:Xamarin.Forms.Maps;assembly=Xamarin.Forms.Maps"
            x:Class="MeTracker.Views.MainView">
    <map:Map x:Name="Map" />
</ContentPage>
```

To use the map control, we need to run code on each platform to initialize it. Follow these steps to do so:

1. In the iOS project, go to AppDelegate.cs.
2. In the FinishedLaunching method, after the Init part of Xamarin.Forms, add global::Xamarin.FormsMaps.Init() to initialize the map control for the iOS app using the following code:

```
public override bool FinishedLaunching(UIApplication app,
NSDictionary options)
{
    global::Xamarin.Forms.Forms.Init();
    global::Xamarin.FormsMaps.Init();

    LoadApplication(new App());

    return base.FinishedLaunching(app, options);
}
```

Perform the same initialization for Android:

1. In the Android project, go to MainActivity.cs.
2. In the OnCreate method, after the Init part of Xamarin.Forms, add global::Xamarin.FormsMaps.Init(this, savedInstanceState) to initialize the map control for Android.

3. Initialize Xamarin.Essentials by
   using `Xamarin.Essentials.Platform.Init(this, savedInstanceState)`
   , as shown in the following code:

```
protected override void OnCreate(Bundle savedInstanceState)
{
    TabLayoutResource = Resource.Layout.Tabbar;
    ToolbarResource = Resource.Layout.Toolbar;

    base.OnCreate(savedInstanceState);
    global::Xamarin.Forms.Forms.Init(this, savedInstanceState);
    global::Xamarin.FormsMaps.Init(this, savedInstanceState);

    Xamarin.Essentials.Platform.Init(this, savedInstanceState);

    LoadApplication(new App());
}
```

For Android, we also need to decide what happens when a user has answered a request for
permission dialog and send the result to Xamarin.Essentials. We will do that by adding the
following code to `MainActivity.cs`:

```
public override void OnRequestPermissionsResult(int requestCode,
            string[] permissions,
            [GeneratedEnum] Android.Content.PM.Permission[]
            grantResults)
{       Xamarin.Essentials.Platform.OnRequestPermissionsResult(requestCode,
            permissions, grantResults);
            base.OnRequestPermissionsResult(requestCode,
            permissions, grantResults);
}
```

For Android, we will need an **API key** for Google Maps in order to get the maps to work.
The Microsoft documentation regarding how to obtain an API key can be found at `https:/`
`/docs.microsoft.com/en-us/xamarin/android/platform/maps-and-location/maps/`
`obtaining-a-google-maps-api-key`. Here's how we go about obtaining the API key:

1. Open `AndroidMainfest.xml`, which is located in the `Properties` folder in the
   Android project.
2. Insert a metadata element as a child of the application element, as shown in the
   following code:

```
<application android:label="MeTracker.Android">
    <meta-data android:name="com.google.android.maps.v2.API_KEY"
    android:value="{YourKeyHere}" />
</application>
```

We also want the map to be centered on the position of the user. We will do this in the constructor of `MainView.xaml.cs`. Because we want to fetch the user's location asynchronously and this needs to be executed on the main thread, we will wrap it in `MainThread.BeginInvokeOnMainThread`. To get the current location of the user, we will use Xamarin.Essentials. When we have the location, we can use the `MoveToRegion` method of `Map`. We can set this up by going through the following steps:

1. In the `MeTracker` project, open `MainView.xaml.cs`.
2. Add the code shown in bold in the following code snippet to the constructor of the `MainView.xaml.cs` class:

```
public MainView ()
{
    InitializeComponent ();
    MainThread.BeginInvokeOnMainThread(async() =>
    {
        var location = await
Geolocation.GetLastKnownLocationAsync();

        if(location == null)
        {
            location = await Geolocation.GetLocationAsync();
        }

        Map.MoveToRegion(MapSpan.FromCenterAndRadius(
        new Position(location.Latitude, location.Longitude),
        Distance.FromKilometers(5)));
    });
}
```

Creating a ViewModel

Before we create an actual `ViewModel`, we will create an abstract base view model that all view models can inherit from. The idea behind this base view model is that we can write common code in it. In this case, we will implement the `INotifyPropertyChanged` interface by going through the following steps:

1. Create a folder called `ViewModels` in the `MeTracker` project.
2. Create a new class called `ViewModel`.
3. Write the following code and resolve all references:

```
public abstract class ViewModel : INotifyPropertyChanged
{
    public event PropertyChangedEventHandler PropertyChanged;
```

```
public void RaisePropertyChanged(params string[] propertyNames)
{
    foreach(var propertyName in propertyNames)
    {
        PropertyChanged?.Invoke(this, new
        PropertyChangedEventArgs(propertyName));
    }
}
}
```

The next step is to create the actual view model that will use `ViewModel` as a base class. Let's set this up by going through the following steps:

1. In the `MeTracker` project, create a new class called `MainViewModel` in the `ViewModels` folder.
2. Make the `MainViewModel` inherit `ViewModel`.
3. Add a read-only field of the `ILocationTrackingService` type and name it `locationTrackingService`.
4. Add a read-only field of the `ILocationRepository` type and name it `locationRepository`.
5. Create a constructor with `ILocationTrackingService` and `ILocationRepository` as parameters.
6. Set the values of the fields that we created in *steps 3* and *4* with the values from the parameters, as shown in the following code:

```
public class MainViewModel : ViewModel
{
        private readonly ILocationRepository locationRepository;
        private readonly ILocationTrackingService
        locationTrackingService;

        public MainViewModel(ILocationTrackingService
        locationTrackingService,
        ILocationRepository locationRepository)
        {
            this.locationTrackingService =
            locationTrackingTrackingService;
            this.locationRepository = locationRepository;
        }
}
```

To make the iOS app start tracking the location of a user, we need to run the code that starts the tracking process on the main thread. Follow these steps:

1. In the constructor of the newly created `MainViewModel`, add an invocation to the main thread using `MainThread.BeginInvokeOnMainThread` from Xamarin.Essentials.

    Xamarin.Forms has a helper method for invoking code on the main thread, but if we use the one from Xamarin.Essentials, we can have a view model without any dependencies on Xamarin.Forms. If we do not have any dependencies on Xamarin.Forms in the ViewModels, we can reuse them in apps where we not using Xamarin.Forms if we want to add other platforms in the future.

2. Call `locationService.StartTracking` in the action that we pass to the `BeginInvokeOnMainThread` method. This is shown in the following code, marked in bold:

    ```
    public MainViewModel(ILocationTrackingService
                         locationTrackingService,
                         ILocationRepository locationRepository)
    {
        this.locationTrackingService = locationTrackingTrackingService;
        this.locationRepository = locationRepository;
        MainThread.BeginInvokeOnMainThread(async() =>
        {
        locationTrackingService.StartTracking();
        });
    }
    ```

Finally, we need to inject a `MainViewModel` into the constructor of `MainView` and assign the `MainViewModel` instance to the binding context of the view. This will allow what data binding we've done to be processed, and the properties of `MainViewModel` will be bound to the controls in the user interface. Follow these steps:

1. In the `MeTracker` project, go to the constructor of the `Views/MainView.xaml.cs` file.
2. Add `MainViewModel` as a parameter of the constructor and call it `viewModel`.
3. Set `BindingContext` as the instance of `MainViewModel`, as shown in the following code:

    ```
    public MainView(MainViewModel viewModel)
    {
        InitializeComponent();
    ```

```
        BindingContext = viewModel;

    MainThread.BeginInvokeOnMainThread(async () =>
    {
        var location = await
Geolocation.GetLastKnownLocationAsync();

        if(location == null)
        {
            location = await Geolocation.GetLocationAsync();
        }

        Map.MoveToRegion(MapSpan.FromCenterAndRadius(
            new Position(location.Latitude, location.Longitude),
            Distance.FromKilometers(5))); });
    }
```

Creating a resolver

We will be using dependency injection in this project. We will be using a library called Autofac to do so. Autofac is an open source **inversion of control** (**IoC**) container. We will create a Resolver class in order to easily resolve types that we will add to the container later in this chapter. To do so, go through the following steps:

1. Install Autofac from NuGet in the MeTracker, MeTracker.Android, and MeTracker.iOS projects.
2. In the MeTracker project, create a new class called Resolver in the root of the project.
3. Create a private static IContainer field called container.
4. Create a static method called Initialized that has an IContainer argument. Set the value of the container field, as follows:

```
using Autofac;
using System;
using System.Collections.Generic;
using System.Text;

namespace MeTracker
{
    public class Resolver
    {
        private static IContainer container;

        public static void Initialize(IContainer container)
```

```
        {
            Resolver.container = container;
        }
    }
}
```

The `Initialize` method will be called after the configuration of Autofac is complete, which we will do when we create the bootstrapper. This method simply takes the `container` field that it gets as an argument and stores it in the `static` container field.

Now, we need a method to access it from. Create one more `static` method called `Resolve`. This method will be generic, and when we use it, we will specify its type as the type that will be resolved. Use the `container` field to resolve the type, as shown in the following code:

```
public static T Resolve<T>()
{
    return container.Resolve<T>();
}
```

The `Resolve<T>` method takes a type as an argument and looks in the container to see whether there is any information on how to construct this type. If there is, then we return it.

So, now that we have a `Resolver`, which we will use to resolve instances of types of objects, we need to configure it. That's the job of the bootstrapper.

Creating the bootstrapper

To configure dependency injection and initialize the `Resolver`, we need to create a bootstrapper. We will have one shared bootstrapper, as well as other bootstrappers for each platform that meet their specific configurations. The reason we need them to be platform-specific is that we will have different implementations of `ILocationTrackingService` on iOS and Android. To create a bootstrapper, do the following:

1. Create a new class in the `MeTracker` project called `Bootstrapper`.
2. Write the following code in the new class:

```
using Autofac;
using MeTracker.Repositories;
using MeTracker.ViewModels;
using System;
using System.Collections.Generic;
using System.Linq;
using System.Reflection;
```

```
using System.Text;
using Xamarin.Forms;

namespace MeTracker
{
    public class Bootstrapper
    {
        protected ContainerBuilder ContainerBuilder { get; private
        set; }

        public Bootstrapper()
        {
            Initialize();
            FinishInitialization();
        }

        protected virtual void Initialize()
        {
            ContainerBuilder = new ContainerBuilder();

            var currentAssembly = Assembly.GetExecutingAssembly();

            foreach (var type in currentAssembly.DefinedTypes.
                    Where(e => e.IsSubclassOf(typeof(Page))))
            {
                ContainerBuilder.RegisterType(type.AsType());
            }

            foreach (var type in currentAssembly.DefinedTypes.
                    Where(e => e.IsSubclassOf(typeof(ViewModel))))
            {
                ContainerBuilder.RegisterType(type.AsType());
            }

            ContainerBuilder.RegisterType<LocationRepository>
            ().As<ILocationRepository>();
        }

        private void FinishInitialization()
        {
            var container = ContainerBuilder.Build();
            Resolver.Initialize(container);
        }
    }
}
```

Creating the iOS bootstrapper

In the iOS bootstrapper, we will have configurations that are specific to the iOS app. To create an iOS app, follow these steps:

1. In the iOS project, create a new class called `Bootstrapper`.
2. Make the new class inherit from `MeTracker.Bootstrapper`.
3. Write the following code:

```
using Autofac;
using MeTracker.iOS.Services;
using MeTracker.Services;

namespace MeTracker.iOS
{
    public class Bootstrapper : MeTracker.Bootstrapper
    {
        public static void Execute()
        {
            var instance = new Bootstrapper();
        }

        protected override void Initialize()
        {
            base.Initialize();


ContainerBuilder.RegisterType<LocationTrackingService>()
            .As<ILocationTrackingService>().SingleInstance();
        }
    }
}
```

4. Go to `AppDelegate.cs` in the iOS project.
5. Before the call to `LoadApplication`, in the `FinishedLaunching` method, call the `Init` method of the platform-specific bootstrapper, as shown in the following code:

```
public override bool FinishedLaunching(UIApplication app,
NSDictionary options)
{
    global::Xamarin.Forms.Forms.Init();
    global::Xamarin.FormsMaps.Init();
    Bootstrapper.Init();

    LoadApplication(new App());
```

```
            return base.FinishedLaunching(app, options);
    }
```

Creating the Android bootstrapper

In the Android bootstrapper, we will have configurations that are specific to the Android app. To create the bootstrapper in Android, follow these steps:

1. In the Android project, create a new class called `Bootstrapper`.
2. Make the new class inherit from `MeTracker.Bootstrapper`.
3. Write the following code:

```
using Autofac;
using MeTracker.Droid.Services;
using MeTracker.Services;

namespace MeTracker.Droid
{
    public class Bootstrapper : MeTracker.Bootstrapper
    {
        public static void Init()
        {
            var instance = new Bootstrapper();
        }

        protected override void Initialize()
        {
            base.Initialize();


    ContainerBuilder.RegisterType<LocationTrackingService()
            .As<ILocationTrackingService>().SingleInstance();
        }
    }
}
```

4. Go to the `MainActivity.cs` file in the Android project.
5. Before the call to `LoadApplication`, in the `OnCreate` method, call the `Init` method of the platform-specific bootstrapper, as shown in the following code:

```
protected override void OnCreate(Bundle savedInstanceState)
{
        TabLayoutResource = Resource.Layout.Tabbar;
        ToolbarResource = Resource.Layout.Toolbar;
```

```
    base.OnCreate(savedInstanceState);
    Xamarin.Essentials.Platform.Init(this, savedInstanceState);

    global::Xamarin.Forms.Forms.Init(this, savedInstanceState);
    global::Xamarin.FormsMaps.Init(this, savedInstanceState);

    Bootstrapper.Init();

    LoadApplication(new App());
}
```

Setting the MainPage

The last step before we can start the app for the first time is to set the MainPage property in the App.xaml.cs file. But first, we will delete the MainPage.xaml and MainPage.xaml.cs files that we created when we started the project since we won't be using them here:

1. Delete the MainPage.xaml and MainPage.xaml.cs files in the MeTracker project, since we will be setting our MainView as the first view that the user sees.
2. Use the Resolver to create an instance of MainView.
3. Set MainPage in the constructor to the instance of MainView, as shown in the following code:

```
public App()
{
    InitializeComponent();
    MainPage = Resolver.Resolve<MainView>();
}
```

The resolver uses Autofac to figure out all the dependencies we need in order to create a MainView instance. It looks at the constructor of MainView and decides that it requires a MainViewModel. If MainViewModel has further dependencies, then the process iterates through all those dependencies and builds all the instances we need.

Now, we will be able to run the app. It will show us a map centered around the current location of the user. Let's add some code so that we can track the user's location over time using background location tracking.

Background location tracking on iOS

The code for location tracking is something that we need to write for each platform. For iOS, we will use `CLLocationManager` from the `CoreLocation` namespace.

Enabling location updates in the background

When we want to perform tasks in the background in an iOS app, we need to declare what we want to do in the `info.plist` file. The following steps show how we go about this:

1. In the `MeTracker.iOS` project, open `info.plist`.
2. Go to the **Capabilities** tab.
3. Select **Enable Background Modes** and **Location updates**, as shown in the following screenshot:

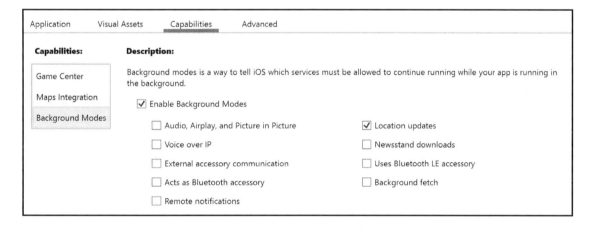

We can also enable background modes directly in the `info.plist` file if we open it with an XML editor. In this case, we will add the following XML:

```xml
<key>UIBackgroundModes</key>
<array>
    <string>location</string>
</array>
```

Getting permissions to use the location of the user

Before we can request permissions so that we can use the location of the user, we need to add a description of what we will use the location for. Since the release of iOS 11, we are no longer allowed to just ask for permission to track the location of the user all the time; the user has to be able to give us permission to only track their location while they are using the app. We can add the description to the `info.plist` file as follows:

1. Open `info.plist` with the XML (text) editor that can be found in the `MeTracker.iOS` project.
2. Add the `NSLocationWhenInUseUsageDescription` key, along with a description.
3. Add the `NSLocationAlwaysAndWhenInUsageDescription` key, along with a description, as shown in the following code:

```
<key>NSLocationWhenInUseUsageDescription</key>
<string>We will use your location to track you</string>
<key>NSLocationAlwaysAndWhenInUsageDescription</key>
<string>We will use your location to track you</string>
```

Subscribing to location updates

Now that we have prepared the `info.plist` file for location tracking, it is time to write the actual code that will track the location of the user. If we don't set `CLLocationManager` so that it doesn't pause location updates, location updates can be paused automatically by iOS when the location data is unlikely to change. In this app, we don't want that to happen because we want to save the location multiple times so that we can establish whether a user visits a particular location frequently. Let's set this up:

1. In the `MeTracker.iOS` project, open `LocationTrackingService`.
2. Add a private field for `CLLocationManager`.
3. Create an instance of `CLLocationMananger` in the `StartTracking` method.
4. Set `PausesLocationUpdatesAutomatically` to `false`.
5. Set `AllowBackgroundLocationUpdates` to `true` (as shown in the following code) so that the location updates will continue, even when the app is running in the background:

```
public void StartTracking()
{
    locationManager = new CLLocationManager
    {
```

```
        PausesLocationUpdatesAutomatically = false,
        AllowsBackgroundLocationUpdates = true
    };

    // Add code here
}
```

The next step is to ask the user for permission to track their location. We will request permission to track their location all the time, but the user has the option of only giving us permission to track their location when they are using the app. Because the user also has the option of denying us permission to track their location, we need to check this before we start to. Let's set this up:

1. Add an event listener for when authorization is changed by hooking up the AuthorizationChanged event to locationManager.

2. In the event listener, create an if statement to check whether the user is allowing us to track their location.

3. Call the RequestAlwaysAuthorization method of the instance that we recently created in CLLocationManager.

4. The code should be placed under the // Add code here comment, as shown in bold in the following code:

```
public void StartTracking()
{
    locationManager = new CLLocationManager
    {
        PausesLocationUpdatesAutomatically = false,
        AllowsBackgroundLocationUpdates = true
    };

    // Add code here
    locationManager.AuthorizationChanged += (s, args) =>
    {
        if (args.Status == CLAuthorizationStatus.Authorized)
        {
            // Next section of code goes here
        }
    };

    locationManager.RequestAlwaysAuthorization();
}
```

Before we can start tracking the location of the user, we need to set the accuracy of the data that we want to receive from CLLocationManager. We will also add an event handler to handle the location updates. Let's set this up:

1. Set DesiredAccuracy to CLLocation.AccurracyBestForNavigation. One of the constraints when running the app in the background is that DesiredAccuracy needs to be set to either AccurracyBest or AccurracyBestForNavigation.

2. Add an event handler for LocationsUpdated and, after that, call the StartUpdatingLocation method.

3. The code should be placed just after the // Next section goes here comment. It should look like the code shown in bold in the following snippet:

```
locationManager.AuthorizationChanged += (s, args) =>
    {
        if (args.Status == CLAuthorizationStatus.Authorized)
        {
            // Next section of code goes here
            locationManager.DesiredAccuracy =
            CLLocation.AccurracyBestForNavigation;
            locationManager.LocationsUpdated +=
            async (object sender, CLLocationsUpdatedEventArgs e) =>
                {
                    // Final block of code goes here
                };

            locationManager.StartUpdatingLocation();
        }
    };
```

The higher the accuracy is, the higher the battery consumption. If we only want to track where the user has been and not how popular a place is, we could also set AllowDeferredLocationUpdatesUntil. This way, we can specify that the user has to move a specific distance before the location is updated. We can also specify how often we want location to be updated using the timeout argument. The most power-efficient solution to track how long a user has been at a place is to use the StartMonitoringVisits method of CLLocationManager.

Now, it's time to handle the `LocationsUpdated` event. Let's go through the following steps:

1. Add a private field called `locationRepository` that is of the `ILocationRepository` type.
2. Add a constructor that has `ILocationRepository` as a parameter. Set the value of the parameter to the `locationRepository` field.
3. Read the latest location of the `Locations` property of `CLLocationsUpdatedEventArgs`.
4. Create an instance of `MeTracker.Models.Location` and pass the latitude and longitude of the latest location to it.
5. Save the location using the `Save` method of `ILocationRepository`.
6. The code should be placed after the `// Final block of code goes here` comment. It should look like the code shown in bold in the following fragment:

```
locationManager.LocationsUpdated +=
    async (object sender, CLLocationsUpdatedEventArgs e) =>
    {
        var lastLocation = e.Locations.Last();
        var newLocation = new
        Models.Location(lastLocation.Coordinate.Latitude,
        lastLocation.Coordinate.Longitude);

        await locationRepository.Save(newLocation);
    };
```

With that, we have completed the tracking part of the app for iOS. Now, we will implement background tracking for Android. After this, we will visualize the data.

Background location tracking with Android

The Android way to carry out background updates is very different from how we implemented this with iOS. With Android, we need to create a `JobService` and schedule it.

Adding the required permissions to use the location of the user

To track the location of the user in the background with Android, we need to request five permissions, as shown in the following table:

ACCESS_COARSE_LOCATION	To get an approximate location for the user.
ACCESS_FINE_LOCATION	To get a precise location for the user.
ACCESS_NETWORK_STATE	We need this because the location services in Android use information from a network to determine the location of the user.
ACCESS_WIFI_STATE	We need this because the location services in Android use information from a Wi-Fi network to determine the location of the user.
RECEIVE_BOOT_COMPLETED	So that the background job can start again after the device is rebooted.

Permissions can be set either from the **Android Manifest** tab in the properties of the MeTracker.Android project or via the AndroidManifest.xml file in the Properties folder. When changes are made from the **Android Manifest** tab, the changes will be written to the AndroidMainfest.xml file as well, so it doesn't matter which method you choose.

The following screenshot shows how to set the required permissions in the **Android Manifest** tab in the properties of the MeTracker.Android project:

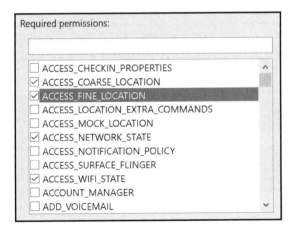

The `uses-permission` elements should be added to the `manifest` element in the `AndroidManifest.xml` file, as shown in the following code:

```
<uses-permission android:name="android.permission.ACCESS_FINE_LOCATION" />
<uses-permission android:name="android.permission.ACCESS_COARSE_LOCATION"
/>
<uses-permission android:name="android.permission.RECEIVE_BOOT_COMPLETED"
/>
<uses-permission android:name="android.permission.ACCESS_NETWORK_STATE" />
<uses-permission android:name="android.permission.ACCESS_WIFI_STATE" />
```

Creating a background job

To track the location of users in the background, we need to create a background job. Follow these steps:

1. In the Android project, create a new class called `LocationJobService` in the `Services` folder.
2. Make the class `public` and add `Android.App.Job.JobService` as a base class.
3. Implement the `OnStartJob` and `OnStopJob` abstract methods, as shown in the following code:

```
public class LocationJobService : JobService
{
    public override bool OnStopJob(JobParameters @params)
    {
        return true;
    }

    public override bool OnStartJob(JobParameters @params)
    {
        return true;
    }
}
```

All the services in the Android app need to be added to the `AndroidManifest.xml` file. We don't have to do this manually; instead, we can add an attribute to the class, which will then be generated in the `AndroidManifest.xml` file. We will use the `Name` and `Permission` properties to set the required information, as shown in the following code:

```
[Service(Name = "MeTracker.Droid.Services.LocationJobService",
        Permission = "android.permission.BIND_JOB_SERVICE")]
        public class LocationJobService : JobService
```

Scheduling a background job

When we have created a job, we can schedule it. We will do this from
`LocationTrackingService` in the `MeTracker.Android` project. To configure the job, we
will use the `JobInfo.Builder` class.

We will use the `SetPersisted` method to ensure that the job starts again after a reboot.
This is why we added the `RECEIVE_BOOT_COMPLETED` permission earlier.

To schedule a job, at least one constraint is needed. In this case, we will
use `SetOverrideDeadline`. This will specify that the job needs to run before the specified
time (in milliseconds) has elapsed.

The `SetRequiresDeviceIdle` method can be used to make sure that a job only runs when
the device is not being used by a user. We could pass `true` to the method if we wanted to
make sure that we don't slow down the device when the user is using it.

The `SetRequiresBatteryNotLow` method can be used to specify that a job should not run
when the battery level is low. We recommend that this should always be set to `true` if you
don't have a good reason to run it when the battery is low. This is because we don't want
our applications to drain the user's battery.

So, let's implement `LocationTrackingService`, which can be found in the Android
project in the `Services` folder. Follow these steps to do so:

1. Create a `JobInfo.Builder` based on an ID that we'll specify (we will use 1 here)
   and the component name (which we'll create from the application context and
   the Java class) in the `StartTracking` method. The component name is used to
   specify which code will run during the job.
2. Use the `SetOverrideDeadline` method and pass `1000` to it to make the job run
   before 1 second has elapsed from when the job was created.
3. Use the `SetPersisted` method and pass `true` to make the job persist, even after
   the device is rebooted.
4. Use the `SetRequiresDeviceIdle` method and pass `false` so that the job will
   run, even when a user is using the device.
5. Use the `SetRequiresBatteryLow` method and pass `true` to make sure that we
   don't drain the user's battery. This method was added in Android API level 26.
6. The code for `LocationTrackingService` should now look as follows:

```
using Android.App;
using Android.App.Job;
using Android.Content;
```

```
using MeTracker.Services;

namespace MeTracker.Droid.Services
{
    public class LocationTrackingService : ILocationTrackingService
    {
        var javaClass =
        Java.Lang.Class.FromType(typeof(LocationJobService));
        var componentName = new ComponentName(Application.Context,
        javaClass);
        var jobBuilder = new JobInfo.Builder(1, componentName);

        jobBuilder.SetOverrideDeadline(1000);
        jobBuilder.SetPersisted(true);
        jobBuilder.SetRequiresDeviceIdle(false);
        jobBuilder.SetRequiresBatteryNotLow(true);

        var jobInfo = jobBuilder.Build();
    }
}
```

The `JobScheduler` service is a system service. To get an instance of a system service, we will use the application context. Follow these steps to do so:

1. Use the `GetSystemService` method on `Application.Context` to get the `JobScheduler` service.
2. Cast the result to `JobScheduler`.
3. Use the `Schedule` method on the `JobScheduler` class and pass the `JobInfo` object to schedule the job, as shown in the following code:

```
var jobScheduler =
    (JobScheduler)Application.Context.GetSystemService
    (Context.JobSchedulerService);
    jobScheduler.Schedule(jobInfo);
```

Subscribing to location updates

Once we have scheduled the job, we can write the code to specify what the job should do, that is, track the location of a user. To do this, we will use `LocationManager`, which is a `SystemService`. With `LocationManager`, we can either request a single location update or we can subscribe to location updates. In this case, we want to subscribe to location updates.

We will start by creating an instance of the ILocationRepository interface. We will use this to save the locations to the SQLite database. Let's set this up:

1. Create a constructor for LocationJobService.
2. Create a private read-only field for the ILocationRepository interface called locationRepository.
3. Use Resolver in the constructor to create an instance of ILocationRepository, as shown in the following code:

```
private ILocationRepository locationRepository;
public LocationJobService()
{
      locationRepository = Resolver.Resolve<ILocationRepository>();
}
```

Before we subscribe to location updates, we will add a listener. To do this, we will use the Android.Locations.ILocationListener interface. Follow these steps:

1. Add the Android.Locations.ILocationListener interface to LocationJobService.
2. Implement the interface.
3. Remove all instances of throw new NotImplementedException();. This is added to the methods if you let Visual Studio generate the implementation of the interface.
4. In the OnLocationChanged method, map the Android.Locations.Location object to the Model.Location object.
5. Use the Save method on the LocationRepository class, as shown in the following code:

```
public void OnLocationChanged(Android.Locations.Location location)
{
    var newLocation = new Models.Location(location.Latitude,
    location.Longitude);
    locationRepository.Save(newLocation);
}
```

Now that we have created a listener, we can subscribe to location updates. Follow these steps:

1. Create a static field of the `LocationManager` type. Make sure it has the same lifetime as the app.
2. Go to the `StartJob` method in `LocationJobService`.
3. Get `LocationManager` by using `GetSystemService` on `ApplicationContext`.
4. To subscribe for location updates, use the `RequestLocationUpdates` method, as shown in the following code:

```
public override bool OnStartJob(JobParameters @params)
{
    locationManager =
    (LocationManager)ApplicationContext.GetSystemService
    (Context.LocationService);
    locationManager.RequestLocationUpdates
    (LocationManager.GpsProvider, 1000L, 0.1f, this);

    return true;
}
```

The first argument that we pass to the `RequestLocationUpdates` method ensures that we get locations from the GPS. The second ensures that at least `1000` milliseconds will elapse between location updates. The third argument ensures that the user has to move at least `0.1` meters to get a location update. The last argument specifies which listener we should use. Because the current class implements the `Android.Locations.ILocationListener` interface, we will pass `this`.

Creating a heat map

To visualize the data that we have collected, we will create a heat map. We will add lots of dots to a map and make them different colors, based on how much time a user spends in a particular place. The most popular places will have a warm color, while the least popular places will have a cold color.

Adding the GetAll method to LocationRepository

In order to visualize the data, we need to write some code so that it can be read from the database. Let's set this up:

1. In the MeTracker project, open the ILocationRepository.cs file.
2. Add a GetAll method, which returns a list of Location objects, using the following code:

```
Task<List<Location>> GetAll() ;
```

3. In the MeTracker project, open the LocationRepository.cs file, which implements ILocationRepository.
4. Implement the new GetAll method and return all the saved locations in the database, as shown in the following code:

```
public async Task<List<Location>> GetAll()
{
        await CreateConnection();
        var locations = await connection.Table<Location>
        ().ToListAsync();

        return locations;
}
```

Preparing the data for visualization

Before we can visualize the data on the map, we need to prepare the data. The first thing we will do is create a new model that we can use for the prepared data. Let's set this up:

1. In the Models folder in the MeTracker project, create a new class called Point.
2. Add properties for Location, Count, and Heat, as shown in the following code:

```
namespace MeTracker.Models
{
    public class Point
    {
        public Location Location { get; set; }
        public int Count { get; set; } = 1;
        public Xamarin.Forms.Color Heat { get; set; }
    }
}
```

`MainViewModel` will store the locations that we will find later on. Let's add a property for storing the `Points`:

1. In the `MeTracker` project, open the `MainViewModel` class.
2. Add a `private` field called `points`, which is of the `List<Point>` type.
3. Create a property called `Points`, which is of the `List<Point>` type.
4. In the `get` method, return the value of the `points` field.
5. In the `set` method, set the `points` field to the new value and call `RaisePropertyChanged` with the name of the property as an argument.
6. At the end of the `LoadData` method, assign the `pointList` variable to the `Points` property, as shown in the following code:

```
private List<Models.Point> points;
public List<Models.Point> Points
{
    get => points;
    set
    {
        points = value;
        RaisePropertyChanged(nameof(Points));
    }
}
```

Now that we have the storage for our points, we must add some code so that we can add locations. We will do this by implementing the `LoadData` method of the `MainViewModel` class and making sure that it is called on the main thread, right after location tracking has started.

The first thing we will do is group the saved locations so that all locations within 200 meters will be handled as one point. We will track how many times we have logged a position within that point so we can decide which color the point will be on the map. Let's set this up:

1. Add an `async` method called `LoadData`. This returns a `Task` to `MainViewModel`.
2. Call the `LoadData` method from the constructor after the call to the `StartTracking` method on `ILocationTrackingService`, as shown in the following code:

```
public MainViewModel(ILocationTrackingService
                     locationTrackingService,
                     ILocationRepository locationRepository)
{
    this.locationTrackingService = locationTrackingService;
```

```
        this.locationRepository = locationRepository;
        MainThread.BeginInvokeOnMainThread(async() =>
        {
            locationTrackingService.StartTracking();
            await LoadData();
        });
}
```

The first step of the LoadData method is to read all tracked locations from the SQLite database. When we have all the locations, we will loop through them and create the points. To calculate the distance between a location and a point, we will use the CalculateDistance method from Xamarin.Essentials.Location, as shown in the following code:

```
private async Task LoadData()
{
    var locations = await locationRepository.GetAll();
    var pointList = new List<Models.Point>();

    foreach (var location in locations)
    {
        //If no points exist, create a new one an continue to the next
        location in the list
        if (!pointList.Any())
        {
            pointList.Add(new Models.Point() { Location = location });
            continue;
        }

        var pointFound = false;

        //try to find a point for the current location
        foreach (var point in pointList)
        {
            var distance =
            Xamarin.Essentials.Location.CalculateDistance(
            new Xamarin.Essentials.Location(
            point.Location.Latitude, point.Location.Longitude),
            new Xamarin.Essentials.Location(location.Latitude,
            location.Longitude), DistanceUnits.Kilometers);

            if (distance < 0.2)
            {
                pointFound = true;
                point.Count++;
                break;
            }
        }
```

```
        }

        //if no point is found, add a new Point to the list of points
        if (!pointFound)
        {
            pointList.Add(new Models.Point() { Location = location });
        }

        // Next section of code goes here
    }
}
```

When we have a list of points, we can calculate the heat color for each point. We are going to use the **hue, saturation, and lightness (HSL)** representation of a color, as described here:

- **Hue**: Hue is a degree on the color wheel that goes from 0 to 360, with 0 being red and 240 being blue. Because we want our most popular places to be red (hot) and our least popular places to be blue (cold), we will calculate a value between 0 and 240 for each point, based on how many times the user has been to that point. This means that we will only use two-thirds of the scale.
- **Saturation**: Saturation is a percentage value: 0% is a shade of gray, while 100% is full color. In our app, we will always use 100% (this will be represented as 1 in the code).
- **Lightness**: Lightness is a percentage value of the amount of light: 0% is black and 100% is white. We want it to be neutral, so we will use 50% (this will be represented as 0.5 in the code).

The first thing that we need to do is find out how many times the user has been to the most popular and least popular places. Let's take a look:

1. First, check that the list of points is not empty.
2. Get the Min and Max values for the Count property in the list of points.
3. Calculate the difference between the minimum and the maximum values.
4. The code should be added after the // Next section of code goes here comment at the bottom of the LoadData method, as shown in the following code:

```
private async Task LoadData()
{
    // The rest of the method has been commented out for brevity

    // Next section of code goes here
    if (pointList == null || !pointList.Any())
    {
```

```
        return;
    }

    var pointMax = pointList.Select(x => x.Count).Max();
    var pointMin = pointList.Select(x => x.Count).Min();
    var diff = (float)(pointMax - pointMin);

    // Last section of code goes here
}
```

Now, we can calculate the heat for each point, as follows:

1. Loop through all the points.
2. The following code should be added after the `// Last section of code goes here` comment, at the bottom of the `LoadData()` method. This is shown in bold:

```
private async Task LoadData()
{
    // The rest of the method has been commented out for brevity

    // Next section of code goes here
    if (pointList == null || !pointList.Any())
    {
        return;
    }

    var pointMax = pointList.Select(x => x.Count).Max();
    var pointMin = pointList.Select(x => x.Count).Min();
    var diff = (float)(pointMax - pointMin);

    // Last section of code goes here
    foreach (var point in pointList)
    {
        var heat = (2f / 3f) - ((float)point.Count / diff);
        point.Heat = Color.FromHsla(heat, 1, 0.5);
    }

    Points = pointList;
}
```

That's all we need to do to set up location tracking in the `MeTracker` project. Now, let's turn our attention to visualizing the data we receive.

Creating custom renderers

Custom renderers are a powerful way to extend Xamarin.Forms. As we mentioned in Chapter 1, *Introduction to Xamarin*, Xamarin.Forms is built with renderers, so for each Xamarin.Forms control, there is a renderer that creates a native control. By overriding an existing renderer or creating a new one, we can extend and customize how Xamarin.Forms controls are rendered to native controls. We can also use renderers to create new Xamarin.Forms controls from scratch.

Renderers are platform-specific, so when we create custom renderers, we have to create one for each platform that we want to change or use to extend the behavior of a control. To make our renderers visible for Xamarin.Forms, we will use the ExportRenderer assembly attribute. This contains information about which control the renderer is for and which renderer will be used.

Creating a custom control for the map

To show the heat map on our map, we will create a new control. We will use a custom renderer to do this. Follow these steps:

1. In the MeTracker project, create a new folder called Controls.
2. Create a new class called CustomMap.
3. Add Xamarin.Forms.Maps.Map as a base class to the new class, as shown in the following code:

```
using System.Collections.Generic;
using Xamarin.Forms;
using Xamarin.Forms.Maps;

namespace MeTracker.Controls
{
    public class CustomMap : Map
    {
    }
}
```

If we want to have properties that we want to bind data to, we need to create a
`BindableProperty`. This should be a `public static` field in the class. We also need to
create a *regular* property. The naming of the properties is really important. The name of
`BindableProperty` needs to be `{NameOfTheProperty}Property`; for example, the name
of `BindableProperty` that we will create in the following steps will be
`PointsProperty` because the name of the property is `Points`. A `BindableProperty` is
created using the static `Create` method on the `BindableProperty` class. This requires at
least four arguments, as follows:

- `propertyName`: This is the name of the property as a string.
- `returnType`: This is the type that will be returned from the property.
- `declaringType`: This is the type of the class that `BindableProperty` is
  declared in.
- `defaultValue`: This is the default value that will be returned if no value is set.
  This is an optional argument. If it is not set, Xamarin.Forms will use `null` as a
  default value.

The `set` and `get` methods for the property will call methods in the base class to `set` or `get`
values from `BindableProperty`:

1. In the `MeTracker` project, create a `BindableProperty` called `PointsProperty`,
   as shown in the following code.
2. Create a property of the `List<Models.Point>` type called `Points`. Remember
   to cast the result of `GetValue` so that it's the same type as the property. We need
   to do this because `GetValue` will return the value as a type object:

```
public static BindableProperty PointsProperty =
  BindableProperty.Create(nameof(Points),
  typeof(List<Models.Point>), typeof(CustomMap), new
  List<Models.Point>());

public List<Models.Point> Points
{
    get => GetValue(PointsProperty) as List<Models.Point>;
    set => SetValue(PointsProperty, value);
}
```

Now that we've created a custom map control, we will use it to replace the `Map` control in `MainView`. Follow these steps:

1. In the `MainView.xaml` file, declare the namespace for the custom control.
2. Replace the `Map` control with the new control that we have created.
3. Add a binding to the `Points` property in `MainViewModel`, as shown in the following code:

```
<ContentPage xmlns="http://xamarin.com/schemas/2014/forms"
xmlns:x="http://schemas.microsoft.com/winfx/2009/xaml"
             xmlns:map="clr-namespace:MeTracker.Controls;"
             x:Class="MeTracker.Views.MainView">
    <ContentPage.Content>
    <map:CustomMap x:Name="Map" Points="{Binding Points}" />
    </ContentPage.Content>
</ContentPage>
```

Creating a custom renderer to extend the map in the iOS app

First, we will create a custom renderer for iOS by going through the following steps. Because we want to extend its functionality, we will use `MapRenderer` as a base class:

1. Create a folder called `Renderers` in the `MeTracker.iOS` project.
2. Create a new class in this folder called `CustomMapRenderer`.
3. Add `MapRenderer` as a base class.
4. Add the `ExportRenderer` attribute, as shown in the following code:

```
using System.ComponentModel;
using System.Linq;
using MapKit;
using MeTracker.Controls;
using MeTracker.iOS.Renderers;
using Xamarin.Forms;
using Xamarin.Forms.Maps.iOS;
using Xamarin.Forms.Platform.iOS;

  [assembly:ExportRenderer(typeof(CustomMap),
  typeof(CustomMapRenderer))]
  namespace MeTracker.iOS.Renderers
{
    public class CustomMapRenderer : MapRenderer
    {
    }
}
```

When a property changes for the control that we are writing a custom renderer for, the `OnElementPropertyChanged` method is called. This method is a virtual method, which means that we can override it. We want to listen to any changes to the `Points` property in our `CustomMap` control.

To do this, follow these steps:

1. Override the `OnElementPropertyChanged` method. This method will run every time a property value is changed in the element (the Xamarin.Forms control).

2. Add an `if` statement to check whether the `Points` property has changed, as shown in the following code:

```
protected override void OnElementPropertyChanged(object sender,
    PropertyChangedEventArgs e)
{
    base.OnElementPropertyChanged(sender, e);

    if (e.PropertyName == CustomMap.PointsProperty.PropertyName)
    {
        //Add code here
    }
}
```

To create the heat map, we will add circles as overlays to the map, one circle for each point. Before we do this, however, we need to add some code to specify how an overlay should be rendered. Let's set this up:

1. Create a `mapView` variable. Cast the `Control` property to `MKMapView` and assign it to the variable.

2. Create a `customMap` variable. Cast the `Element` property to `CustomMap` and assign it to the variable.

3. Create an action using an expression with the `MKMapView` and `IMKOverlay` parameters and assign it to the `OverlayRenderer` property on the map view.

4. Cast the `overlay` parameter to `MKCircle` and assign it to a new variable called `circle`.

5. Verify that the circle variable is not `null`.

6. Find the point object from the point list on the `CustomMap` object using coordinates.

7. Create a new `MKCircleRenderer` object and pass the circle variable to the constructor.

8. Set the `FillColor` property to the heat color of the point. Convert it into `UIColor` using the `ToUIColor` extension method.

9. Set the `Alpha` property to `1.0f` to make sure that the circle isn't transparent.

10. Return the `circleRenderer` variable.

11. Return `null` if the circle variable is `null`.

12. This code should look like the code shown in bold in the following snippet:

```
protected override void OnElementPropertyChanged(object sender,
    PropertyChangedEventArgs e)
{
    base.OnElementPropertyChanged(sender, e);

    if (e.PropertyName == CustomMap.PointsProperty.PropertyName)
    {
        var mapView = (MKMapView)Control;
        var customMap = (CustomMap)Element;

        mapView.OverlayRenderer = (map, overlay) =>
        {
            var circle = overlay as MKCircle;

            if (circle != null)
            {
                var point = customMap.Points.Single
                (x => x.Location.Latitude ==
                circle.Coordinate.Latitude &&
                x.Location.Longitude ==
                circle.Coordinate.Longitude);

                var circleRenderer = new MKCircleRenderer(circle)
                {
                    FillColor = point.Heat.ToUIColor(),
                    Alpha = 1.0f
                };

                return circleRenderer;
            }

            return null;
        };

        // Next section of code goes here
    }
}
```

With that, we have implemented how we want each overlay of the map to be rendered. What we need to do now is go through all the points we have gathered so far and create an `Overlay` for each one. Let's set this up:

1. Loop through all the points.
2. Create a circle overlay with the `static` method's `Circle` on the `MKCircle` class, as shown in the following code. The first argument is the position of the circle, while the second one is the radius of the circle.
3. Add the overlay to the map using the `AddOverlay` method.
4. This code should now look like the code shown in bold in the following snippet:

```
// Next section of code goes here
foreach (var point in customMap.Points)
{
        var overlay = MKCircle.Circle(
        new CoreLocation.CLLocationCoordinate2D
        (point.Location.Latitude, point.Location.Longitude), 100);

    mapView.AddOverlay(overlay);
}
```

This concludes this section on how to extend the `Maps` control for iOS. Let's do the same for Android.

Creating a custom renderer to extend the map in the Android app

Now, we will create a custom renderer for Android. The structure is the same as the one we used for iOS. We will use the `ExportRenderer` attribute in the same way and we will also add the `MapRenderer` class as the base class. This, however, is the Android-specific `MapRenderer`.

We will start by creating a custom renderer for our `CustomMap` control. The renderer will inherit from the `MapRenderer` base class so that we can extend any existing functionality. To do this, follow these steps:

1. Create a folder called `Renderers` in the `MeTracker.Android` project.
2. Create a new class in this folder called `CustomMapRenderer`.
3. Add `MapRenderer` as a base class.
4. Add the `ExportRenderer` attribute.
5. Add a constructor that has `Context` as a parameter. Pass this parameter to the constructor of the base class.

6. Resolve all the references, as shown in the following code:

```
using System.ComponentModel;
using Android.Content;
using Android.Gms.Maps;
using Android.Gms.Maps.Model;
using MeTracker.Controls;
using MeTracker.Droid.Renderers;
using Xamarin.Forms;
using Xamarin.Forms.Maps;
using Xamarin.Forms.Maps.Android;
using Xamarin.Forms.Platform.Android;

[assembly: ExportRenderer(typeof(CustomMap),
typeof(CustomMapRenderer))]
namespace MeTracker.Droid.Renderers
{
    public class CustomMapRenderer : MapRenderer
    {
        public CustomMapRenderer(Context context) : base(context)
        {
        }
    }
}
```

To get a map object to work with, we need to request one. We do this by overriding the `OnElementChanged` method that all custom renderers have. This method is called each time an element changes, such as when it's set for the first time when parsing the XAML, or when it's replaced in code. Let's set this up:

1. Override the `OnElementChanged` method.

2. If the `NewElement` property of `ElementChangedEventArgs` is not `null`, request the map object with the `GetMapAsync` method on the `Control` property, as shown in the following code:

```
protected override void OnElementChanged
                    (ElementChangedEventArgs<Map> e)
{
    base.OnElementChanged(e);

    if (e.NewElement != null)
    {
        Control.GetMapAsync(this);
    }
}
```

When we have a map to work with, the virtual `OnMapReady` method will be called. To add our own code so that we can handle this, we need to override this method:

1. Create a private field of the `GoogleMap` type called `map`.
2. Override the `OnMapReady` method.
3. Assign the new field with the parameter from the method's body, as shown in the following code:

```
protected override void OnMapReady(GoogleMap map)
{
    this.map = map;

    base.OnMapReady(map);
}
```

Just as we did with the iOS renderer, we need to handle changes in the `Points` property of our custom map. To do this, we override the `OnElementPropertyChanged` method, which is called each time a property on the control we are writing our renderer for changes. Let's do this now:

1. Override the `OnElementPropertyChanged` method. This method will run every time a property value is changed in `Element` (the Xamarin.Forms control).
2. Add an `if` statement to check that it is the `Points` property that has changed, as shown in the following code:

```
protected override void OnElementPropertyChanged(object sender,
    PropertyChangedEventArgs e)
{
    base.OnElementPropertyChanged(sender, e);

    if(e.PropertyName == CustomMap.PointsProperty.PropertyName)
    {
    }
}
```

Now, we can add the code that will handle the `Points` property being set by drawing the location out on the map. To do this, follow these steps:

1. For each point, create an instance of the `CircleOptions` class.
2. Use the `InvokeStrokeWidth` method to set the stroke width of the circle to `0`.
3. Use the `InvokeFillColor` method to set the color of the circle. Use the `ToAndroid` extension method to convert the color into an `Android.Graphics.Color`.

4. Use the `InvokeRadius` method to set the size of the circle to `200`.

5. Use the `InvokeCenter` method to set where on the map the circle should be.

6. Add the circle to `map` by using the `AddCircle` method on the `map` object.

7. This code should now look like the code shown in bold in the following snippet:

```
protected override void OnElementPropertyChanged(object sender,
    PropertyChangedEventArgs e)
{
    base.OnElementPropertyChanged(sender, e);

    if(e.PropertyName ==
CustomMap.PointsProperty.PropertyName)
    {
        var element = (CustomMap)Element;

        foreach (var point in element.Points)
        {
            var options = new CircleOptions();
            options.InvokeStrokeWidth(0);
            options.InvokeFillColor(point.Heat.ToAndroid());
            options.InvokeRadius(200);
            options.InvokeCenter(new
            LatLng(point.Location.Latitude,
            point.Location.Longitude));
            map.AddCircle(options);
        }
    }
}
```

Refreshing the map when resuming the app

The last thing we will do is make sure that the map is up to date with the latest points when the app is resumed. The easiest way to do this is to set the `MainPage` property in the `App.xaml.cs` file to a new instance of `MainView`, in the same way as the constructor, as shown in the following code:

```
protected override void OnResume()
{
    MainPage = Resolver.Resolve<MainView>();
}
```

Summary

In this chapter, we built an app for iOS and Android that tracked the location of a user. When we built the app, we learned how to use maps in Xamarin.Forms and how to use location tracking when it's running in the background. We also learned how to extend Xamarin.Forms with custom controls and custom renderers. With this knowledge, we can create applications that perform other tasks in the background. We also learned how to extend most controls in Xamarin.Forms.

The next project will be a real-time chat app. In the next chapter, we will set up a serverless backend based on services in Microsoft Azure. We will use that backend in the app that we will build in Chapter 9, *Building a Real-Time Chat Application*.

Building a Weather App for Multiple Form Factors

7

Xamarin.Forms isn't just for creating apps for phones; it can also be used to create apps for tablets and desktop computers. In this chapter, we will build an app that will work on all of these platforms. As well as using three different form factors, we are also going to be working on three different operating systems: iOS, Android, and Windows.

The following topics will be covered in this chapter:

- How to use `FlexLayout` in Xamarin.Forms
- How to use `VisualStateManager`
- How to use different views for different form factors
- How to use behaviors

Let's get started!

Technical requirements

To work on this project, we need to have Visual Studio for Mac or PC installed, as well as the Xamarin components. See Chapter 1, *Introduction to Xamarin*, for more details on how to set up your environment. To build an iOS app using Visual Studio for PC, you have to have a Mac connected. If you don't have access to a Mac at all, you can choose to just work on the Windows and Android parts of this project. Similarly, if you only have Windows, you can choose to work on only the iOS and Android parts of this project.

Project overview

Applications for iOS and Android can run on both phones and tablets. Often, apps are just optimized for phones. In this chapter, we will build an app that will work on different form factors, but we aren't going to stick to just phones and tablets – we are going to target desktop computers as well. The desktop version will be for the **Universal Windows Platform** (**UWP**).

The app that we are going to build is a weather app that displays the weather forecast based on the location of the user.

Building the weather app

It's time to start building the app. Create a new blank Xamarin.Forms app using **.NET Standard** as the **Code Sharing Strategy** and select **iOS**, **Android**, and **Windows (UWP)** as the platforms. We will name the project `Weather`.

As the data source for this app, we will use an external weather API. This project will use `OpenWeatherMap`, a service that offers a couple of free APIs. You can find this service at `https://openweathermap.org/api`. We will use the `5 day / 3 hour forecast` service in this project, which provides a 5-day forecast in 3-hour intervals. To use the `OpenWeather` API, we have to create an account to get an API key. If you don't want to create an API key, you can mock the data instead.

Creating models for the weather data

Before we write the code to fetch data from the external weather service, we will create models in order to deserialize the results from the service. We will do this so that we have a common model that we can use to return data from the service.

The easiest way to generate models to use when we are deserializing results from the service is to make a call to the service either in the browser or with a tool (such as Postman) to see the structure of the JSON. We can either create classes manually or use a tool that can generate C# classes from the JSON. One tool that can be used is **quicktype**, which can be found at `https://quicktype.io/`.

If you generate them manually, make sure to set the namespace to `Weather.Models`.

As mentioned previously, you can also create these models manually. We will describe how to do this in the next section.

Adding the weather API models manually

If you wish to add the models manually, then go through the following instructions. We will be adding a single code file called `WeatherData.cs`, which will contain multiple classes:

1. In the `Weather` project, create a folder called `Models`.
2. Add a file called `WeatherData.cs`.
3. Add the following code:

```
using System.Collections.Generic;

namespace Weather.Models
{
    public class Main
    {
        public double temp { get; set; }
        public double temp_min { get; set; }
        public double temp_max { get; set; }
        public double pressure { get; set; }
        public double sea_level { get; set; }
        public double grnd_level { get; set; }
        public int humidity { get; set; }
        public double temp_kf { get; set; }
    }

    public class Weather
    {
        public int id { get; set; }
        public string main { get; set; }
        public string description { get; set; }
        public string icon { get; set; }
    }

    public class Clouds
    {
        public int all { get; set; }
    }

    public class Wind
    {
        public double speed { get; set; }
        public double deg { get; set; }
    }

    public class Rain
    {
```

```
        }

        public class Sys
        {
            public string pod { get; set; }
        }

        public class List
        {
            public long dt { get; set; }
            public Main main { get; set; }
            public List<Weather> weather { get; set; }
            public Clouds clouds { get; set; }
            public Wind wind { get; set; }
            public Rain rain { get; set; }
            public Sys sys { get; set; }
            public string dt_txt { get; set; }
        }

        public class Coord
        {
            public double lat { get; set; }
            public double lon { get; set; }
        }

        public class City
        {
            public int id { get; set; }
            public string name { get; set; }
            public Coord coord { get; set; }
            public string country { get; set; }
        }

        public class WeatherData
        {
            public string cod { get; set; }
            public double message { get; set; }
            public int cnt { get; set; }
            public List<List> list { get; set; }
            public City city { get; set; }
        }
    }
```

As you can see, there are quite a lot of classes. This maps directly to the response we get from the service.

Adding the app-specific models

In this section, we will create the models that our app will translate the Weather API models into. Let's start by adding the `WeatherData` class (unless you created this manually in the preceding section):

1. Create a new folder called `Models` in the `Weather` project.
2. Add a new file called `WeatherData`.
3. Paste or write the code for the classes based on the JSON. If code other than the properties is generated, ignore it and just use the properties.
4. Rename `MainClass` (this is what quicktype names the root object) `WeatherData`.

Now, we will create models based on the data we are interested in. This will make the rest of the code more loosely coupled to the data source.

Adding the ForecastItem model

The first model we are going to add is `ForecastItem`, which represents a specific forecast for a point in time. We do this as follows:

1. In the `Weather` project and in the `Models` folder, create a new class called `ForecastItem`.
2. Add the following code:

```
using System;
using System.Collections.Generic;

namespace Weather.Models
{
    public class ForecastItem
    {
        public DateTime DateTime { get; set; }
        public string TimeAsString => DateTime.ToShortTimeString();
        public double Temperature { get; set; }
        public double WindSpeed { get; set; }
        public string Description { get; set; }
        public string Icon { get; set; }
    }
}
```

Adding the Forecast model

Next, we'll create a model called `Forecast` that will keep track of a single forecast for a city. `Forecast` keeps a list of multiple `ForeCastItem` objects, each representing a forecast for a specific point in time. Let's set this up:

1. In the `Weather` project, create a new class called `Forecast`.
2. Add the following code:

```
using System;
using System.Collections.Generic;

namespace Weather.Models
{
    public class Forecast
    {
        public string City { get; set; }
        public List<ForecastItem> Items { get; set; }
    }
}
```

Now that we have our models for both the Weather API and the app, we need to fetch data from the Weather API.

Creating a service to fetch the weather data

To make it easier to change the external weather service and to make the code more testable, we will create an interface for the service. Here's how we go about it:

1. In the `Weather` project, create a new folder called `Services`.
2. Create a new `public interface` called `IWeatherService`.
3. Add a method for fetching data based on the location of the user, as shown in the following code. Name the method `GetForecast`:

```
public interface IWeatherService
{
    Task<Forecast> GetForecast(double latitude, double
longitude);
}
```

When we have an interface, we can create an implementation for it, as follows:

1. In the `Services` folder, create a new class called `OpenWeatherMapWeatherService`.
2. Implement the interface and add the `async` keyword to the `GetForecast` method.
3. The code should look as follows:

```
using System;
using System.Globalization;
using System.Linq;
using System.Net.Http;
using System.Threading.Tasks;
using Newtonsoft.Json;
using Weather.Models;

namespace Weather.Services
{
    public class OpenWeatherMapWeatherService : IWeatherService
    {
        public async Task<Forecast> GetForecast(double latitude,
        double longitude)
        {
        }
    }
}
```

Before we call the `OpenWeatherMap` API, we need to build a URI for the call to the Weather API. This will be a GET call, and the latitude and longitude of the position will be added as query parameters. We will also add the API key and the language that we would like the response to be in. Let's set this up:

1. In `WeatherProject`, open the `OpenWeatherMapWeatherService` class.

2. Add the code marked in bold in the following code snippet:

```
public class OpenWeatherMapWeatherService : IWeatherService
{
    public async Task<Forecast> GetForecast(double latitude, double
    longitude)
    {
        var language =
        CultureInfo.CurrentUICulture.TwoLetterISOLanguageName;
        var apiKey = "{AddYourApiKeyHere}";
        var uri =
        $"https://api.openweathermap.org/data/2.5/forecast?
```

```
        lat={latitude}&lon={longitude}&units=metric&lang=
        {language}&appid={apiKey}";
    }
}
```

In order to deserialize the JSON that we will get from the external service, we will use `Json.NET`, the most popular NuGet package for serializing and deserializing JSON in .NET applications. We can install it like so:

1. Open the **NuGet Package Manager**.
2. Install the `Json.NET` package. The ID of the package is `Newtonsoft.Json`.

To make a call to the `Weather` service, we will use the `HttpClient` class and the `GetStringAsync` method, as follows:

1. Create a new instance of the `HttpClient` class.
2. Call `GetStringAsync` and pass the URL as the argument.
3. Use the `JsonConvert` class and the `DeserializeObject` method from `Json.NET` to convert the JSON string into an object.
4. Map the `WeatherData` object to a `Forecast` object.
5. The code for this should look like the bold code shown in the following snippet:

```
public async Task<Forecast> GetForecast(double latitude, double
                                         longitude)
{
    var language =
    CultureInfo.CurrentUICulture.TwoLetterISOLanguageName;
    var apiKey = "{AddYourApiKeyHere}";
    var uri = $"https://api.openweathermap.org/data/2.5/forecast?
    lat={latitude}&lon={longitude}&units=metric&lang=
    {language}&appid={apiKey}";

    var httpClient = new HttpClient();
    var result = await httpClient.GetStringAsync(uri);

    var data = JsonConvert.DeserializeObject<WeatherData>(result);

    var forecast = new Forecast()
    {
        City = data.city.name,
        Items = data.list.Select(x => new ForecastItem()
        {
            DateTime = ToDateTime(x.dt),
            Temperature = x.main.temp,
            WindSpeed = x.wind.speed,
```

```
                Description = x.weather.First().description,
                Icon =
                $"http://openweathermap.org/img/w/{
                        x.weather.First().icon}.png"
        }).ToList()
    };
    return forecast;
}
```

To optimize the performance of the app, we can use `HttpClient` as a singleton and reuse it for all network calls in the application. The following information is from Microsoft's documentation: *HttpClient is intended to be instantiated once and reused throughout the life of an application. Instantiating an HttpClient class for every request will exhaust the number of sockets available under heavy loads. This will result in SocketException errors.* This can be found at `https://docs.microsoft.com/en-gb/dotnet/ api/system.net.http.httpclient?view=netstandard-2.0`.

In the preceding code, we have a call to a `ToDateTime` method, which is a method that we will need to create. This method converts the date from a Unix timestamp into a `DateTime` object, as shown in the following code:

```
private DateTime ToDateTime(double unixTimeStamp)
{
    DateTime dateTime = new DateTime(1970, 1, 1, 0, 0, 0, 0,
    DateTimeKind.Utc);
    dateTime = dateTime.AddSeconds(unixTimeStamp).ToLocalTime();
    return dateTime;
}
```

By default, `HttpClient` uses the Mono implementation of `HttpClient` (iOS and Android). To increase performance, we can use a platform-specific implementation instead. For iOS, use `NSUrlSession`. This can be set in the project settings of the iOS project under the **iOS Build** tab. For Android, use **Android**. This can be set in the project settings of the Android project under **Android Options | Advanced**.

Configuring the applications so they use location services

To be able to use location services, we need to carry out some configurations on each platform. We will use Xamarin.Essentials and the classes it contains. Ensure that you have installed Xamarin.Essentials from NuGet for all the projects in the solution before going through the steps in the following sections.

Configuring the iOS app so that it uses location services

To use location services in an iOS app, we need to add a description to indicate why we want to use the location in the `info.plist` file. In this app, we only need to get the location when we are using the app, so we only need to add a description for this. Let's set this up:

1. Open `info.plist` in `Weather.iOS` with the **XML (Text) Editor**.
2. Add the `NSLocationWhenInUseUsageDescription` key using the following code:

   ```
   <key>NSLocationWhenInUseUsageDescription</key>
   <string>We are using your location to find a forecast for
   you</string>
   ```

Configuring the Android app so that it uses location services

For Android, we need to set up the app so that it requires the following two permissions:

- **ACCESS_COARSE_LOCATION**
- **ACCESS_FINE_LOCATION**

We can set this in the `AndroidManifest.xml` file, which can be found in the `Properties` folder in the `Weather.Android` project. However, we can also set this in the project properties on the **Android Manifest** tab, as shown in the following screenshot:

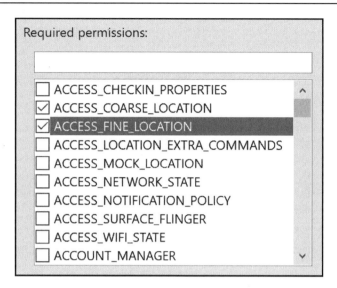

When we request permissions in an Android app, we also need to add the following code to the `MainActivity.cs` file in the Android project:

```
public override void OnRequestPermissionsResult(int requestCode, string[]
permissions,
[GeneratedEnum] Android.Content.PM.Permission[] grantResults)
{
    Xamarin.Essentials.Platform.OnRequestPermissionsResult(requestCode,
permissions, grantResults); base.OnRequestPermissionsResult(requestCode,
permissions, grantResults);
}
```

For Android, we also need to initialize Xamarin.Essentials. We will do this in the `OnCreate` method of `MainActivity`:

```
protected override void OnCreate(Bundle savedInstanceState)
{
    TabLayoutResource = Resource.Layout.Tabbar;
    ToolbarResource = Resource.Layout.Toolbar;

    base.OnCreate(savedInstanceState);
    global::Xamarin.Forms.Forms.Init(this, savedInstanceState);
    Xamarin.Essentials.Platform.Init(this, savedInstanceState);
    LoadApplication(new App());
}
```

Configuring the UWP app so that it uses location services

Since we will be using location services in the UWP app, we need to add the **Location** capability under **Capabilities** in the `Package.appxmanifest` file of the `Weather.UWP` project, as shown in the following screenshot:

Application	Visual Assets	Capabilities	Declarations	Content URIs	Packaging

Use this page to specify system features or devices that your app can use.

Capabilities:

Description:

- [ ] AllJoyn
- [ ] Appointments
- [ ] Background Media Playback
- [ ] Blocked Chat Messages
- [ ] Bluetooth
- [ ] Chat Message Access
- [ ] Code Generation
- [ ] Contacts
- [ ] Enterprise Authentication
- [ ] Internet (Client & Server)
- [x] Internet (Client)
- [x] Location
- [ ] Low Level
- [ ] Low Level Devices
- [ ] Microphone
- [ ] Music Library
- [ ] Objects 3D
- [ ] Offline Maps Management
- [ ] Phone Call

Provides access to the current location, which is obtained from dedicated hardware like a GPS sensor in the PC or derived from available network information.

More information

Creating the ViewModel class

Now that we have a service that's responsible for fetching weather data from the external weather source, it's time to create a `ViewModel`. First, however, we will create a base view model where we can put the code that can be shared between all the `ViewModels` of the app. Let's set this up:

1. Create a new folder called `ViewModels`.
2. Create a new class called `ViewModel`.

3. Make the new class `public` and `abstract`.

4. Add and implement the `INotifiedPropertyChanged` interface. This is necessary because we want to use data bindings.

5. Add a `Set` method. This will make it easier to raise the `PropertyChanged` event from the `INotifiedPropertyChanged` interface. The method will check whether the value has changed. If it has, it will raise the event:

```
public abstract class ViewModel : INotifyPropertyChanged
{
    public event PropertyChangedEventHandler PropertyChanged;
    protected void Set<T>(ref T field, T newValue,
    [CallerMemberName] string propertyName = null)
    {
        if (!EqualityComparer<T>.Default.Equals(field,
        newValue))
        {
            field = newValue;
            PropertyChanged?.Invoke(this, new
            PropertyChangedEventArgs(propertyName));
        }
    }
}
```

The `CallerMemberName` attribute can be used in a method body if you want the name of the method or the property that made the call to the method to be a parameter. Note that we can always override this by simply passing a value to it. The default value of the parameter is required when you are using the `CallerMember` attribute.

We now have a base view model. We can use this for the view model that we are creating now, as well as for all of the other view models that we will add later.

Now, it's time to create `MainViewModel`, which will be the `ViewModel` for our `MainView` in the app. Perform the following steps to do so:

1. In the `ViewModels` folder, create a new class called `MainViewModel`.

2. Add the abstract `ViewModel` class as a base class.

3. Because we are going to use constructor injection, we will add a constructor with the `IWeatherService` interface as a parameter.

4. Create a read-only `private` field. We will use this to store the `IWeatherService` instance:

```
public class MainViewModel : ViewModel
{
    private readonly IWeatherService weatherService;

    public MainViewModel(IWeatherService weatherService)
    {
        this.weatherService = weatherService;
    }
}
```

`MainViewModel` takes any object that implements `IWeatherService` and stores a reference to that service in a field. We will be adding functionality that will fetch weather data in the next section.

Getting the weather data

Now, we will create a new method for loading the data. This will be a three-step process. First, we will get the location of the user. Once we have this, we can fetch data related to that location. The final step is to prepare the data that the views can consume to create a user interface for the user.

To get the location of the user, we will use Xamarin.Essentials, which we installed earlier as a NuGet package, and the `Geolocation` class, which exposes methods that can fetch the location of the user. Perform the following steps:

1. Create a new method called `LoadData`. Make it an asynchronous method that returns a `Task`.
2. Use the `GetLocationAsync` method on the `Geolocation` class to get the location of the user.
3. Pass the latitude and longitude from the result of the `GetLocationAsync` call and pass it to the `GetForecast` method on the object that implements `IWeatherService` using the following code:

```
public async Task LoadData()
{
    var location = await Geolocation.GetLocationAsync();
    var forecast = await weatherService.GetForecast
    (location.Latitude, location.Longitude);
}
```

Grouping the weather data

When we present the weather data, we will group it by day so that all of the forecasts for one day will be under the same header. To do this, we will create a new model called `ForecastGroup`. To make it possible to use this model with the Xamarin.Forms `CollectionView`, it has to have an `IEnumerable` type as the base class. Let's set this up:

1. Create a new class called `ForecastGroup` in the `Models` folder.
2. Add `List<ForecastItem>` as the base class for the new model.
3. Add an empty constructor and a constructor that has a list of `ForecastItem` instances as a parameter.
4. Add a `Date` property.
5. Add a property, `DateAsString`, that returns the `Date` property as a short date string.
6. Add a property, `Items`, that returns the list of `ForecastItem` instances, as shown in the following code:

```
using System;
using System.Collections.Generic;

namespace Weather.Models
{
    public class ForecastGroup : List<ForecastItem>
    {
        public ForecastGroup() { }
        public ForecastGroup(IEnumerable<ForecastItem> items)
        {
            AddRange(items);
        }

        public DateTime Date { get; set; }
        public string DateAsString => Date.ToShortDateString();
        public List<ForecastItem> Items => this;
    }
}
```

When we have done this, we can update `MainViewModel` with two new properties, as follows:

1. Create a property called `City` for the name of the city that we are fetching the weather data for.
2. Create a property called `Days` that will contain the grouped weather data.

3. The `MainViewModel` class should look like the bold code shown in the following snippet:

```
public class MainViewModel : ViewModel
{
    private string city;
    public string City
    {
        get => city;
        set => Set(ref city, value);
    }

    private ObservableCollection<ForecastGroup> days;
    public ObservableCollection<ForecastGroup> Days
    {
        get => days;
        set => Set(ref days, value);
    }

    // Rest of the class is omitted for brevity
}
```

Now, we are ready to group the data. We will do this in the `LoadData` method. We will loop through the data from the service and add items to various groups, as follows:

1. Create an `itemGroups` variable of the `List<ForecastGroup>` type.
2. Create a `foreach` loop that loops through all the items in the `forecast` variable.
3. Add an `if` statement that checks whether the `itemGroups` property is empty. If it is empty, add a new `ForecastGroup` to the variable and continue to the next item in the item list.
4. Use the `SingleOrDefault` method (this is an extension method from `System.Linq`) on the `itemGroups` variable to get a group based on the date of the current `ForecastItem`. Add the result to a new variable, `group`.
5. If the group property is `null`, then there is no group with the current day in the list of groups. If this is the case, a new `ForecastGroup` should be added to the list in the `itemGroups` variable. The code will continue executing until it gets to the next `forecast` item in the `forecast.Items` list. If a group is found, it should be added to the list in the `itemGroups` variable.
6. After the `foreach` loop, set the `Days` property with a new `ObservableCollection<ForecastGroup>` and use the `itemGroups` variable as an argument in the constructor.
7. Set the `City` property to the `City` property of the `forecast` variable.

8. The `LoadData` method should now look as follows:

```
public async Task LoadData()
{
    var itemGroups = new List<ForecastGroup>();

    foreach (var item in forecast.Items)
    {
        if (!itemGroups.Any())
        {
            itemGroups.Add(new ForecastGroup(
                new List<ForecastItem>() { item })
                { Date = item.DateTime.Date});
            continue;
        }

        var group = itemGroups.SingleOrDefault(x => x.Date ==
        item.DateTime.Date);

        if (group == null)
        {
            itemGroups.Add(new ForecastGroup(
                new List<ForecastItem>() { item })
                { Date = item.DateTime.Date });

                        continue;
        }

        group.Items.Add(item);
    }

    Days = new ObservableCollection<ForecastGroup>(itemGroups);
    City = forecast.City;
}
```

Don't use the `Add` method on `ObservableCollection` when you want to add more than a couple of items. It is better to create a new instance of `ObservableCollection` and pass a collection to the constructor. The reason for this is that every time you use the `Add` method, you will have a binding to it from the view, which will cause the view to be rendered. We will get better performance if we avoid using the `Add` method.

Creating a Resolver

Now, we need to create a helper class for **Inversion of Control** (**IoC**). This will help us create types based on a configured IoC container. In this project, we will use Autofac as the IoC library. Let's set this up:

1. Install the **Autofac** NuGet package in the `Weather` project.
2. Create a new class called `Resolver` in the `Weather` project.
3. Add a `private static` field called `container` of the `IContainer` type (from Autofac).
4. Add a `public static` method called `Initialize` with `IContainer` as a parameter. Set the value of the parameter to the `container` field.
5. Add a generic `public static` method called `Resolve<T>`, which will return an instance of an object of the type specified with the `T` parameter. The `Resolve<T>` method will then call the `Resolve<T>` method on the `IContainer` instance that was passed to it during initialization.
6. The code should now look as follows:

```
using Autofac;

namespace Weather
{
    public class Resolver
    {
        private static IContainer container;

        public static void Initialize(IContainer container)
        {
            Resolver.container = container;
        }

        public static T Resolve<T>()
        {
            return container.Resolve<T>();
        }
    }
}
```

Creating a bootstrapper

In this section, we will create a Bootstrapper class. We will use this to set up the common configurations that we need in the startup phase of the app. Usually, there is one part of the bootstrapper for each target platform and one that is shared for all platforms. In this project, we only need the shared part. Let's set this up:

1. In the Weather project, create a new class called Bootstrapper.
2. Add a new public static method called Init.
3. Create a new ContainerBuilder and register the types to container.
4. Create a Container by using the Build method of ContainerBuilder. Create a variable called container that contains the instance of Container.
5. Use the Initialize method on Resolver and pass the container variable as an argument.
6. The Bootstrapper class should now look as follows:

```
using Autofac;
using TinyNavigationHelper.Forms;
using Weather.Services;
using Weather.ViewModels;
using Weather.Views;
using Xamarin.Forms;

namespace Weather
{
    public class Bootstrapper
    {
        public static void Init()
        {
            var containerBuilder = new ContainerBuilder();
            containerBuilder.RegisterType
            <OpenWeatherMapWeatherService>().As
            <IWeatherService>();
            containerBuilder.RegisterType<MainViewModel>();

            var container = containerBuilder.Build();

            Resolver.Initialize(container);
        }
    }
}
```

Call the `Init` method of `Bootstrapper` in the constructor in the `App.xaml.cs` file after the call to the `InitializeComponent` method. Also, set the `MainPage` property to `MainView`, as shown in the following code:

```
public App()
{
    InitializeComponent();
    Bootstrapper.Init();
    MainPage = new NavigationPage(new MainView());
}
```

Creating the view for tablets and desktop computers

The next step is to create the view that we will use when the app is running on a tablet or a desktop computer. Let's set this up:

1. Create a new folder in the `Weather` project called `Views`.
2. Create a new **Content Page** with **XAML** called `MainView`.
3. Use `Resolver` in the constructor of the view to set `BindingContext` to `MainViewModel`, as shown in the following code:

```
public MainView ()
{
    InitializeComponent ();
    BindingContext = Resolver.Resolve<MainViewModel>();
}
```

To trigger the `LoadData` method in `MainViewModel`, call the `LoadData` method by overriding the `OnAppearing` method on the main thread. We need to make sure that the call is executed on the UI thread since it will interact with the user interface.

To do this, perform the following steps:

1. In the `Weather` project, open the `MainView.xaml.cs` file.
2. Create an override of the `OnAppearing` method.

3. Add the code shown in bold in the following snippet:

```
protected override void OnAppearing()
{
    base.OnAppearing();

    if (BindingContext is MainViewModel viewModel)
    {
        MainThread.BeginInvokeOnMainThread(async () =>
        {
            await viewModel.LoadData();
        });
    }
}
```

In the XAML, add a binding for the `Title` property of `ContentPage` to the `City` property in `ViewModel`, as follows:

1. In the `Weather` project, open the `MainView.xaml` file.
2. Add the `Title` binding to the `ContentPage` element, as highlighted in bold in the following code snippet:

```
<ContentPage xmlns="http://xamarin.com/schemas/2014/forms"
    xmlns:x="http://schemas.microsoft.com/winfx/2009/xaml"
    xmlns:controls="clr-namespace:Weather.Controls"
    x:Class="Weather.Views.MainView"
    Title="{Binding City}">
```

Using FlexLayout

In Xamarin.Forms, we can use `CollectionView` or `ListView` if we want to show a collection of data. Using both `CollectionView` and `ListView` works great in most cases, and we will use `CollectionView` later in this chapter, but `ListView` can only show data vertically. In this app, we want to show data in both directions. In the vertical direction, we will have the days (we group forecasts based on days), while in the horizontal direction, we will have the forecasts within a particular day. We also want the forecasts within a day to wrap if there is not enough space for all of them in one row. `CollectionView` can show data in a horizontal direction, but it will not wrap. With `FlexLayout`, we are able to add items in both directions and we can use `BindableLayout` to bind items to it. When we are using `BindableLayout`, we will use `ItemSource` and `ItemsTemplate` as attached properties.

Perform the following steps to build the view:

1. Add a `Grid` as the root view of the page.
2. Add a `ScrollView` to `Grid`. We need this to be able to scroll if the content is higher than the height of the page.
3. Add a `FlexLayout` to `ScrollView` and set the direction to `Column` so that the content will be in a vertical direction.
4. Add a binding to the `Days` property in `MainViewModel` using `BindableLayout.ItemsSource`.
5. Set a `DataTemplate` to the content of `ItemsTemplate`, as shown in the following code:

```
<Grid>
    <ScrollView BackgroundColor="Transparent">
        <FlexLayout BindableLayout.ItemsSource="{Binding Days}"
                Direction="Column">
            <BindableLayout.ItemTemplate>
                <DataTemplate>
                  <!--Content will be added here -->
                </DataTemplate>
            </BindableLayout.ItemTemplate>
        </FlexLayout>
    </ScrollView>
</Grid>
```

The content for each item will be a header with the date and a horizontal `FlexLayout` with the forecasts for the day. Let's set this up:

1. In the `Weather` project, open the `MainView.xaml` file.
2. Add `StackLayout` so that the children we add to it will be placed in a vertical direction.
3. Add `ContentView` to `StackLayout` with `Padding` set to `10` and `BackgroundColor` set to `#9F5010`. This will be the header. The reason we need `ContentView` is that we want to have padding around the text.
4. Add `Label` to `ContentView` with `TextColor` set to `White` and `FontAttributes` set to `Bold`.
5. Add a binding to `DateAsString` for the `Text` property of `Label`.
6. The code should be placed at the `<!-- Content will be added here -->` comment and should look as follows:

```
<StackLayout>
    <ContentView Padding="10" BackgroundColor="#9F5010">
```

```
                    <Label Text="{Binding DateAsString}" TextColor="White"
                        FontAttributes="Bold" />
                </ContentView>
            </StackLayout>
```

Now that we have the date in the user interface, we need to add a FlexLayout that will repeat through any Items in MainViewModel. Perform the following steps to do so:

1. Add a FlexLayout after the </ContentView> tag, but before the </StackLayout> tag.

2. Set JustifyContent to Start to set the Items so that they're added from the left-hand side, without distributing them over the available space.

3. Set AlignItems to Start to set the content to the left of each item in FlexLayout, as shown in the following code:

```
        <FlexLayout BindableLayout.ItemsSource="{Binding Items}"
        Wrap="Wrap"
            JustifyContent="Start" AlignItems="Start">
```

After defining FlexLayout, we need to provide an ItemsTemplate that defines how each item in the list should be rendered. Continue adding the XAML directly under the <FlexLayout> tag you just added. as follows:

1. Set the ItemsTemplate property to DataTemplate.

2. FillDataTemplate with elements, as shown in the following code:

If we want to add formatting to a binding, we can use StringFormat. In this case, we want to add the degree symbol after the temperature. We can do this by using the {Binding Temperature, StringFormat='{0}° C'} phrase. With the StringFormat property of the binding, we can format data with the same arguments that we would use if we were to do this in C#. This is the same as string.Format("{0}° C", Temperature) in C#. We can also use it to format a date; for example, {Binding Date, StringFormat='yyyy'}. In C#, this would look like Date.ToString("yyyy").

```
        <BindableLayout.ItemTemplate>
            <DataTemplate>
                <StackLayout Margin="10" Padding="20" WidthRequest="150"
                    BackgroundColor="#99FFFFFF">
                    <Label FontSize="16" FontAttributes="Bold"
                        Text="{Binding TimeAsString}"
                        HorizontalOptions="Center" />
                    <Image WidthRequest="100" HeightRequest="100"
```

```
        Aspect="AspectFit" HorizontalOptions="Center"
          Source="{Binding Icon}" />
      <Label FontSize="14" FontAttributes="Bold"
        Text="{Binding Temperature, StringFormat='{0}° C'}"
        HorizontalOptions="Center" />
      <Label FontSize="14" FontAttributes="Bold"
        Text="{Binding Description}"
        HorizontalOptions="Center" />
    </StackLayout>
  </DataTemplate>
</BindableLayout.ItemTemplate>
```

The `AspectFill` phrase, as a value of the `Aspect` property for `Image`, means that the whole image will always be visible and that the aspects will not be changed. The `AspectFit` phrase will also keep the aspect of an image, but the image can be zoomed into and out of and cropped so that it fills the whole `Image` element. The last value that `Aspect` can be set to, `Fill`, means that the image can be stretched or compressed to match the `Image` view to ensure that the aspect ratio is kept.

Adding a toolbar item to refresh the weather data

To be able to refresh the data without restarting the app, we will add a **Refresh** button to the toolbar. `MainViewModel` is responsible for handling any logic that we want to perform, and we must expose any action as an `ICommand` that we can bind to.

Let's start by creating the `Refresh` command property on `MainViewModel`:

1. In the `Weather` project, open the `MainViewModel` class.
2. Add an `ICommand` property called `Refresh` and a `get` method that returns a new `Command`.
3. Add an action as an expression to the constructor of the `Command` that calls the `LoadData` method, as shown in the following code:

```
public ICommand Refresh => new Command(async () =>
{
    await LoadData();
});
```

Now that we have defined `Command`, we need to bind it to the user interface so that when the user clicks the toolbar button, the action will be executed.

To do this, perform the following steps:

1. In the `Weather` app, open the `MainView.xaml` file.
2. Add a new `ToolbarItem` with the `Text` property set to `Refresh` to the `ToolbarItems` property of `ContentPage` and set the `Icon` property to `refresh.png` (the icon can be downloaded from GitHub; see `https://github.com/PacktPublishing/Xamarin.Forms-Projects/tree/master/Chapter-5`).
3. Bind the `Command` property to the `Refresh` property in `MainViewModel`, as shown in the following code:

```
<ContentPage.ToolbarItems>
    <ToolbarItem Icon="refresh.png" Text="Refresh"
Command="{Binding
    Refresh}" />
</ContentPage.ToolbarItems>
```

That's all for refreshing the data. Now, we need some kind of indicator that the data is loading.

Adding a loading indicator

When we refresh the data, we want to show a loading indicator so that the user knows that something is happening. To do this, we will add `ActivityIndicator`, which is what this control is called in Xamarin.Forms. Let's set this up:

1. In the `Weather` project, open the `MainViewModel` class.
2. Add a Boolean property called `IsRefreshing` to `MainViewModel`.
3. Set the `IsRefreshing` property to `true` at the beginning of the `LoadData` method.
4. At the end of the `LoadData` method, set the `IsRefreshing` property to `false`, as shown in the following code:

```
private bool isRefreshing;
public bool IsRefreshing
{
    get => isRefreshing;
    set => Set(ref isRefreshing, value);
}

public async Task LoadData()
```

```
        {
            IsRefreshing = true;
            .... // The rest of the code is omitted for brevity
            IsRefreshing = false;
        }
```

Now that we have added some code to `MainViewModel`, we need to bind the `IsRefreshing` property to a user interface element that will be displayed when the `IsRefreshing` property is `true`, as shown in the following code:

1. In `MainView.xaml`, add a `Frame` after `ScrollView` as the last element in `Grid`.
2. Bind the `IsVisible` property to the `IsRefreshing` method that we created in `MainViewModel`.
3. Set `HeightRequest` and `WidthRequest` to 100.
4. Set `VerticalOptions` and `HorizontalOptions` to `Center` so that `Frame` will be in the middle of the view.
5. Set `BackgroundColor` to `#99000000` to set the background to white with a little bit of transparency.
6. Add `ActivityIndicator` to `Frame` with `Color` set to `Black` and `IsRunning` set to `True`, as shown in the following code:

```
<Frame IsVisible="{Binding IsRefreshing}"
       BackgroundColor="#99FFFFFF"
       WidthRequest="100" HeightRequest="100"
       VerticalOptions="Center"
       HorizontalOptions="Center">
    <ActivityIndicator Color="Black" IsRunning="True" />
</Frame>
```

This will create a spinner that will be visible while data is loading, which is a really good practice when creating any user interface. Now, we'll add a background image to make the app look a bit nicer.

Setting a background image

The last thing we will do to this view, for the moment, is add a background image. The image we will be using in this example is a result of a Google search for images that are free to use. Let's set this up:

1. In the `Weather` project, open the `MainView.xaml` file.
2. Set the `Background` property of `ScrollView` to `Transparent`.

3. Add an `Image` element in `Grid` with `UriImageSource` as the value of the `Source` property.

4. Set the `CachingEnabled` property to `true` and `CacheValidity` to 5. This means that the image will be cached in 5 days.

5. The XAML should now look as follows:

```xml
<ContentPage xmlns="http://xamarin.com/schemas/2014/forms"
             xmlns:x="http://schemas.microsoft.com/winfx/2009/xaml"
             xmlns:controls="clr-namespace:Weather.Controls"
             x:Class="Weather.Views.MainView" Title="{Binding
                                               City}">
    <ContentPage.ToolbarItems>
        <ToolbarItem Icon="refresh.png" Text="Refresh" Command="
        {Binding Refresh}" />
    </ContentPage.ToolbarItems>

    <Grid>
        <Image Aspect="AspectFill">
          <Image.Source>
           <UriImageSource
Uri="https://upload.wikimedia.org/wikipedia/commons/7/79/
Solnedg%C3%A5ng_%C3%B6ver_Laholmsbukten_augusti_2011.jpg"
            CachingEnabled="true" CacheValidity="1" />
          </Image.Source>
        </Image>
        <ScrollView BackgroundColor="Transparent">
            <!-- The rest of the code is omitted for brevity -->
```

We can also set the URL directly in the `Source` property by using `<Image Source="https://ourgreatimage.url" />`. However, if we do this, we can't specify caching for the image.

Creating the view for phones

Structuring content on a tablet and on a desktop computer is very similar in many ways. On phones, however, we are much more limited in what we can do. Therefore, in this section, we will create a specific view for this app when it's used on phones. To do so, perform the following steps:

1. Create a new **XAML**-based **Content Page** in the `Views` folder.

2. Call the new view `MainView_Phone`.

3. Use `Resolver` in the constructor of the view to set `BindingContext` to `MainViewModel`, as shown in the following code:

```
public MainView_Phone ()
{
    InitializeComponent ();
    BindingContext = Resolver.Resolve<MainViewModel>();
}
```

To trigger the `LoadData` method in `MainViewModel`, call the `LoadData` method by overriding the `OnAppearing` method on the main thread. To do this, perform the following steps:

1. In the `Weather` project, open the `MainView_Phone.xaml.cs` file.
2. Add the override of the `OnAppearing` method, as shown in the following code:

```
protected override void OnAppearing()
{
    base.OnAppearing();

    if (BindingContext is MainViewModel viewModel)
    {
        MainThread.BeginInvokeOnMainThread(async () =>
        {
            await viewModel.LoadData();
        });
    }
}
```

In the XAML, add a binding for the `Title` property of `ContentPage` to the `City` property in `ViewModel`, as follows:

1. In the `Weather` project, open the `MainView_Phone.xaml` file.
2. Add the `Title` property with a binding to the `City` property of `MainViewModel`, as shown in the following code:

```
<ContentPage xmlns="http://xamarin.com/schemas/2014/forms"
    xmlns:x="http://schemas.microsoft.com/winfx/2009/xaml"
    xmlns:controls="clr-namespace:Weather.Controls"
    x:Class="Weather.Views.MainView_Phone"
    Title="{Binding City}">
```

Using a grouped CollectionView

We could use `FlexLayout` for the phone's view, but because we want our user experience to be as good as possible, we will use `CollectionView` instead. To get the headers for each day, we will use grouping for `CollectionView`. For `FlexLayout`, we had `ScrollView`, but for `CollectionView`, we don't need this because `CollectionView` can handle scrolling by default.

Let's continue creating the user interface for the phone's view:

1. In the `Weather` project, open the `MainView_Phone.xaml` file.
2. Add a `CollectionView` to the root of the page.
3. Set a binding to the `Days` property in `MainViewModel` for the `ItemSource` property.
4. Set `IsGrouped` to `True` to enable grouping in `CollectionView`.
5. Set `BackgroundColor` to `Transparent`, as shown in the following code:

```
<CollectionView ItemsSource="{Binding Days}" IsGrouped="True"
        BackgroundColor="Transparent">
</CollectionView>
```

To format how each header will look, we will create a `DataTemplate`, as follows:

1. Add a `DataTemplate` to the `GroupHeaderTemplate` property of `CollectionView`.
2. Add the content for the row to `DataTemplate`, as shown in the following code:

```
<CollectionView ItemsSource="{Binding Days}" IsGrouped="True"
                BackgroundColor="Transparent">
    <CollectionView.GroupHeaderTemplate>
      <DataTemplate>
            <ContentView Padding="15,5"
            BackgroundColor="#9F5010">
            <Label FontAttributes="Bold" TextColor="White"
            Text="{Binding DateAsString}"
            VerticalOptions="Center"/>
            </ContentView>
      </DataTemplate>
    </CollectionView.GroupHeaderTemplate>
</CollectionView>
```

To format how each forecast will look, we will create a `DataTemplate`, as we did with the group header. Let's set this up:

1. Add a `DataTemplate` to the `ItemTemplate` property of `CollectionView`.

2. In `DataTemplate`, add a `Grid` that contains four columns. Use the `ColumnDefinition` property to specify the width of the columns. The second column should be `50`; the other three will share the rest of the space. We will do this by setting `Width` to `*`.

3. Add the following content to `Grid`:

```
<CollectionView.ItemTemplate>
    <DataTemplate>
            <Grid Padding="15,10" ColumnSpacing="10"
                BackgroundColor="#99FFFFFF">
                <Grid.ColumnDefinitions>
                    <ColumnDefinition Width="*" />
                    <ColumnDefinition Width="50" />
                    <ColumnDefinition Width="*" />
                    <ColumnDefinition Width="*" />
                </Grid.ColumnDefinitions>
                <Label FontAttributes="Bold" Text="{Binding
                  TimeAsString}" VerticalOptions="Center" />
                <Image Grid.Column="1" HeightRequest="50"
                  WidthRequest="50" Source="{Binding Icon}"
                  Aspect="AspectFit" VerticalOptions="Center" />
                <Label Grid.Column="2" Text="{Binding Temperature,
                StringFormat='{0}° C'}"
                 VerticalOptions="Center" />
                <Label Grid.Column="3" Text="{Binding Description}"
                 VerticalOptions="Center" />
            </Grid>
    </DataTemplate>
</CollectionView.ItemTemplate>
```

Adding pull to refresh functionality

For the tablet and desktop versions of the view, we added a button to the toolbar to refresh the weather forecast. In the phone version of the view, however, we will add pull to refresh functionality, which is a common way to refresh content in a list of data. `CollectionView` in Xamarin.Forms has no built-in support for pull to refresh like `ListView` has.

Instead, we can use `RefreshView`. `RefreshView` can be used to add pull to refresh behavior to any control. Let's set this up:

1. Go to `MainView_Phone.xaml`.
2. Wrap `CollectionView` inside `RefreshView`.
3. Bind the `Refresh` property in `MainViewModel` to the `Command` property of `RefreshView` to trigger a refresh when the user performs a pull-to-refresh gesture.
4. To show a loading icon when the refresh is in progress, bind the `IsRefreshing` property in `MainViewModel` to the `IsRefreshing` property of `RefreshView`. When we are setting this up, we will also get a loading indicator when the initial load is running, as shown in the following code:

```
<RefreshView Command="{Binding Refresh}" IsRefreshing="{Binding
IsRefreshing}">
<CollectionView ItemsSource="{Binding Days}" IsGrouped="True"
 BackgroundColor="Transparent">
....
</CollectionView>
</RefreshView>
```

Navigating to different views based on the form factor

We now have two different views that should be loaded in the same place in the app. `MainView` should be loaded if the app is running on a tablet or on a desktop, while `MainView_Phone` should be loaded if the app is running on a phone.

The `Device` class in Xamarin.Forms has a static `Idiom` property that we can use to check which form factor the app is running on. The value of `Idiom` can be `Phone`, `Table`, `Desktop`, `Watch`, or `TV`. Because we only have one view in this app, we could have used an `if` statement when we were setting `MainPage` in `App.xaml.cs` and checked what the `Idiom` value was. Here, however, we are going to build a solution that we can also use for a bigger app.

One solution is to build a navigation service that we can use to navigate to different views based on a key. Which view will be loaded for which key will be configured when we start the app. With this solution, we can configure different views on the same key on different types of devices. An open source navigation service that we can use for this purpose is TinyNavigationHelper, which can be found at https://github.com/TinyStuff/ TinyNavigationHelper. It was created by the authors of this book.

There is also an MVVM library called TinyMvvm that includes TinyNavigationHelper as a dependency. The TinyMvvm library is a library that contains helper classes so that you can get started quickly with MVVM in a Xamarin.Forms app. We created TinyMvvm because we wanted to avoid writing the same code again and again. You can read more about this at https://github.com/TinyStuff/TinyMvvm.

Perform the following steps to add TinyNavigationHelper to the app:

1. Install the TinyNavigationHelper.Forms NuGet package in the Weather project.
2. Go to Bootstrapper.cs.
3. At the start of the Execute method, create a FormsNavigationHelper and pass the current application to the constructor.
4. Add an if statement to check whether Idiom is Phone. If this is true, the MainView_Phone view should be registered for the MainView key.
5. Add an else statement that registers MainView for the MainView key.
6. The Bootstrapper class should now look as follows, with the new code marked in bold:

```
public class Bootstrapper
{
    public static void Init()
    {
        var navigation = new FormsNavigationHelper();

        if (Device.Idiom == TargetIdiom.Phone)
        {
            navigation.RegisterView("MainView",
            typeof(MainView_Phone));
        }
        else
        {
            navigation.RegisterView("MainView", typeof(MainView));
        }
```

```
var containerBuilder = new ContainerBuilder();
containerBuilder.RegisterType<OpenWeatherMapWeatherService>
().As<IWeatherService>();
containerBuilder.RegisterType<MainViewModel>();

var container = containerBuilder.Build();

Resolver.Initialize(container);
    }
}
```

Now, we can use the `NavigationHelper` class to set the root view of the app in the constructor of the `App` class, as follows:

1. In the `Weather` app, open the `App.xaml.cs` file.
2. Locate the constructor of the `App` class.
3. Remove the assignment of the `MainPage` property.
4. Add the code to set the root view via `NavigationHelper`.
5. The constructor should now look like the bold code shown in the following snippet:

```
public App()
{
    InitializeComponent();
    Bootstrapper.Init();
    NavigationHelper.Current.SetRootView("MainView", true);
}
```

If we want to load different views on different operating systems, we can use the static `RuntimePlatform` method on the Xamarin.Forms `Device` class – for example, `if(Device.RuntimePlatform == Device.iOS)`.

Handling states with VisualStateManager

`VisualStateManager` was introduced in Xamarin.Forms 3.0. It is a way to make changes in the UI from the code. We can define states and set values for selected properties to apply for a specific state. `VisualStateManager` can be really useful in cases where we want to use the same view for devices with different screen resolutions. It was first introduced in UWP to make it easier to create Windows 10 applications for multiple platforms. This was because Windows 10 could run on Windows Phone, as well as on desktops and tablets (the OS was called Windows 10 Mobile). However, Windows Phone has now been depreciated. `VisualStateManager` is really interesting for us as Xamarin.Forms developers, especially when both iOS and Android can run on both phones and tablets.

In this project, we will use it to make a forecast item bigger when the app is running in landscape mode on a tablet or on a desktop. We will also make the weather icon bigger. Let's set this up:

1. In the `Weather` project, open the `MainView.xaml` file.
2. In the first `FlexLayout` and in `DataTemplate`, insert a `VisualStateManager.VisualStateGroups` element into the first `StackLayout`:

```
<StackLayout Margin="10" Padding="20" WidthRequest="150"
    BackgroundColor="#99FFFFFF">
    <VisualStateManager.VisualStateGroups>
        <VisualStateGroup>
        </VisualStateGroup>
    </VisualStateManager.VisualStateGroups>
</StackLayout>
```

Regarding `VisualStateGroup`, we should add two states, as follows:

1. Add a new `VisualState` called `Portrait` to `VisualStateGroup`.
2. Create a setter in `VisualState` and set `WidthRequest` to 150.
3. Add another `VisualState` called `Landscape` to `VisualStateGroup`.
4. Create a setter in `VisualState` and set `WidthRequest` to 200, as shown in the following code:

```
<VisualStateGroup>
    <VisualState Name="Portrait">
        <VisualState.Setters>
            <Setter Property="WidthRequest" Value="150" />
        </VisualState.Setters>
    </VisualState>
```

```
<VisualState Name="Landscape">
    <VisualState.Setters>
        <Setter Property="WidthRequest" Value="200" />
    </VisualState.Setters>
</VisualState>
</VisualStateGroup>
```

We also want the icons in a forecast item to be bigger when the item itself is bigger. To do this, we will use `VisualStateManager` again. Let's set this up:

1. Insert a `VisualStateManager.VisualStateGroups` element into the second `FlexLayout` and in the `Image` element in `DataTemplate`.

2. Add `VisualState` for both `Portrait` and `Landscape`.

3. Add setters to the states to set `WidthRequest` and `HeightRequest`. The value should be 1oo in the `Portrait` state and 150 in the `Landscape` state, as shown in the following code:

```
<Image WidthRequest="100" HeightRequest="100" Aspect="AspectFit"
HorizontalOptions="Center" Source="{Binding Icon}">
    <VisualStateManager.VisualStateGroups>
        <VisualStateGroup>
            <VisualState Name="Portrait">
                <VisualState.Setters>
                    <Setter Property="WidthRequest" Value="100" />
                    <Setter Property="HeightRequest" Value="100" />
                </VisualState.Setters>
            </VisualState>
            <VisualState Name="Landscape">
                <VisualState.Setters>
                    <Setter Property="WidthRequest" Value="150" />
                    <Setter Property="HeightRequest" Value="150" />
                </VisualState.Setters>
            </VisualState>
        </VisualStateGroup>
    </VisualStateManager.VisualStateGroups>
</Image>
```

Creating a behavior to set state changes

With `Behavior`, we can add functionality to controls without having to subclass them. With behaviors, we can also create more reusable code than we could if we subclassed a control. The more specific the `Behavior` we create, the more reusable it will be. For example, a `Behavior` that inherits from `Behavior<View>` could be used on all controls, but a `Behavior` that inherits from a `Button` can only be used for buttons. Because of this, we always want to create behaviors with a less specific base class.

When we create a `Behavior`, we need to override two methods: `OnAttached` and `OnDetachingFrom`. It is really important to remove event listeners in the `OnDeattached` method if we have added them to the `OnAttached` method. This will make the app use less memory. It is also important to set values back to the values that they had before the `OnAppearing` method ran; otherwise, we might see some strange behavior, especially if the behavior is in a `CollectionView` or a `ListView` that is reusing cells.

In this app, we will create a `Behavior` for `FlexLayout`. This is because we can't set the state of an item in `FlexLayout` from the code behind. We could have added some code to check whether the app runs in portrait or landscape in `FlexLayout`, but if we use `Behavior` instead, we can separate that code from `FlexLayout` so that it will be more reusable. Perform the following steps to do so:

1. In the `Weather` project, create a new folder called `Behaviors`.
2. Create a new class called `FlexLayoutBehavior`.
3. Add `Behavior<FlexLayoutView>` as a base class.
4. Create a `private` field of the `FlexLayout` type called `view`.
5. The code should look as follows:

```
using System;
using Weather.Controls;
using Xamarin.Essentials;
using Xamarin.Forms;

namespace Weather.Behaviors
{
    public class FlexLayoutBehavior : Behavior<FlexLayout>
    {
        private FlexLayout view;
    }
}
```

`FlexLayout` is a class that inherits from the `Behavior<FlexLayout>` base class. This will give us the ability to override some virtual methods that will be called when we attach and detach the behavior from a `FlexLayout`.

But first, we need to create a method that will handle the change in state. Perform the following steps to do so:

1. In the `Weather` project, open the `FlexlayoutBehavior.cs` file.
2. Create a private method called `SetState`. This method will have a `VisualElement` and a `string` argument.
3. Call `VisualStateManager.GoToState` and pass the parameters to it.
4. If the view is of the `Layout` type, it is possible for there to be child elements that also need to get the new state. To do that, we will loop through all the children of the layout. Instead of just setting the state directly to the children, we will call the `SetState` method, which is the method that we are already inside. The reason for this is that it is possible that some of the children have their own children:

```
private void SetState(VisualElement view, string state)
{
    VisualStateManager.GoToState(view, state);
    if (view is Layout layout)
    {
        foreach (VisualElement child in layout.Children)
        {
            SetState(child, state);
        }
    }
}
```

Now that we have created the `SetState` method, we need to write a method that uses it and also determines what state to set. Perform the following steps to do so:

1. Create a `private` method called `UpdateState`.
2. Run the code on `MainThread` to check whether the app is running in portrait or landscape mode.
3. Create a variable called `page` and set its value to `Application.Current.MainPage`.

4. Check whether `Width` is larger than `Height`. If this is true, set the `VisualState` property on the view variable to `Landscape`. If this is not true, set the `VisualState` property on the view variable to `Portrait`, as shown in the following code:

```
private void UpdateState()
{
    MainThread.BeginInvokeOnMainThread(() =>
    {
        var page = Application.Current.MainPage;

        if (page.Width > page.Height)
        {
            SetState(view, "Landscape");
            return;
        }

        SetState(view, "Portrait");
    });
}
```

With that, the `UpdateState` method has been added. Now, we need to override the `OnAttachedTo` method, which will be called when the behavior is added to `FlexLayout`. When it is, we want to update the state by calling this method and also hook it up to the `SizeChanged` event of `MainPage` so that when the size changes, we will update the state again.

Let's set this up:

1. In the `Weather` project, open the `FlexLayoutBehavior` file.
2. Override the `OnAttachedTo` method from the base class.
3. Set the `view` property to the parameter from the `OnAttachedTo` method.
4. Add an event listener to `Application.Current.MainPage.SizeChanged`. In the event listener, add a call to the `UpdateState` method, as shown in the following code:

```
protected override void OnAttachedTo(FlexLayout view)
{
    this.view = view;

    base.OnAttachedTo(view);

    UpdateState();

    Application.Current.MainPage.SizeChanged +=
```

```
                    MainPage_SizeChanged;
        }

                    void MainPage_SizeChanged(object sender, EventArgs e)
        {
                    UpdateState();
        }
```

When we remove behaviors from a control, it's very important to also remove any event handlers from it in order to avoid memory leaks, and in the worst case, the app crashing. Let's do this:

1. In the `Weather` project, open the `FlexLayoutBehavior.cs` file.
2. Override `OnDetachingFrom` from the base class.
3. Remove the event listener from `Application.Current.MainPage.SizeChanged`.
4. Set the `view` field to `null`, as shown in the following code:

```
protected override void OnDetachingFrom(FlexLayout view)
{
    base.OnDetachingFrom(view);
    Application.Current.MainPage.SizeChanged -=
    MainPage_SizeChanged;
    this.view = null;
}
```

Perform the following steps to add the `behavior` to the view:

1. In the `Weather` project, open the `MainView.xaml` file.
2. Import the `Weather.Behaviors` namespace, as shown in the following code:

```
<ContentPage xmlns="http://xamarin.com/schemas/2014/forms"
xmlns:x="http://schemas.microsoft.com/winfx/2009/xaml"
        xmlns:controls="clr-namespace:Weather.Controls"
        xmlns:behaviors="clr-
        namespace:Weather.Behaviors"
        x:Class="Weather.Views.MainView" Title="{
        Binding City}">
```

The last thing we will do is add `FlexLayoutBehavior` to the second `FlexLayout`, as shown in the following code:

```
<FlexLayout ItemsSource="{Binding Items}" Wrap="Wrap"
JustifyContent="Start" AlignItems="Start">
    <FlexLayout.Behaviors>
    <behaviors:FlexLayoutBehavior />
    </FlexLayout.Behaviors>
    <FlexLayout.ItemsTemplate>
```

Summary

In this chapter, we successfully created an app for three different operating systems – iOS, Android, and Windows – and three different form factors – phones, tablets, and desktop computers. To create a good user experience on all platforms and form factors, we used `FlexLayout` and `VisualStateManager`. We also learned how to handle to use different views for different form factors, as well as how to use `Behaviors`.

The next app we will build will be a chat app with real-time communication. In the next chapter, we will take a look at how we can use the SignalR service in Azure as the backend for the chat app.

8

Setting Up a Backend for a Chat App Using Azure Services

In this chapter, we will set up a backend for a chat app with real-time communication. We will create a backend that can scale up to handle a large number of users but also scale down when the number of users is reduced. To build that backend, we will use a serverless architecture based on services in Microsoft Azure.

The following topics will be covered in this chapter:

- Understanding the different Azure serverless services
- Creating a SignalR service in Microsoft Azure
- Using Azure Functions as an **application programming interface (API)**
- Scheduling jobs with Azure Functions
- Using Azure Blob storage to store photos
- Using Azure Cognitive Services and the Customer Vision API to scan photos for adult content

Technical requirements

To be able to complete this project, you need to have Visual Studio for Mac or PC installed. Refer to `Chapter 1`, *Introduction to Xamarin*, for more details on how to set up your environment.

You also need an Azure account. If you have a Visual Studio subscription, there is a specific amount of Azure credits included each month. To activate your Azure benefits, go to the following link: `https://my.visualstudio.com`

You can also create a free account, whereby you can use selected services for free over 12 months. You will get $200 worth of credit to explore any Azure service for 30 days, and you can also use the free services at any time. Read more at the following link: `https://azure.microsoft.com/en-us/free/`

Understanding the different Azure serverless services

Before we start to build a backend with a serverless architecture, we need to define what *serverless* actually means. In a serverless architecture, of course, the code will run on a server, but we don't need to worry about that; the only thing we need to focus on is building our software. We let someone else handle everything to do with servers. We don't need to think about how much memory or **CPU (Central Processing Unit)** the server needs, or even how many servers we need. When we use services in Azure, Microsoft takes care of this for us.

Azure SignalR Service

Azure SignalR Service is a service in **Microsoft Azure** for real-time communication between a server and clients. The service will push content to the clients without them having to poll the server to get content updates. SignalR can be used for multiple types of applications, including mobile applications, web applications, and desktop applications.

SignalR will use WebSockets if that option is available. If it is not, SignalR will use other techniques for communication, such as **Server-Sent Events (SSE)** or **long polling**. SignalR will detect which transport technology is available and use it without the developer having to think about it at all.

SignalR can be used in the following examples:

- **Chat applications**: Where the application requires updates from the server as soon as new messages are available
- **Collaborative applications**: For example, meeting applications or when users on multiple devices are working with the same document
- **Multiplayer games**: Where all users need live updates about other users
- **Dashboard applications**: Where users need live updates

Azure Functions

Azure Functions is a Microsoft Azure service that allows us to run code in a serverless way. We will deploy small pieces of code called **functions**. Functions are deployed in groups, called **function apps**. When we are creating a function app, we need to select whether we want it to run on a consumption plan or on an App Service plan. We select a consumption plan if we want the application to be completely serverless, while with an App Service plan, we have to specify the requirements of the server. With a consumption plan, we pay for the execution time and for how much memory the function uses. One benefit of an App Service plan is that you can configure it to be **Always-On**, and you won't have any cold starts as long as you don't have to scale up to more instances. The big benefit of a consumption plan is that it will always scale according to which resources are needed at that time.

There are several ways in which a function can be triggered to run. Two examples are `HttpTrigger` and `TimeTrigger`. `HttpTrigger` will trigger the function to run when an HTTP request is calling the function. With `TimeTrigger`, functions will run at an interval that we can specify. There are also triggers for other Azure services. For example, we can configure a function to run when a file is uploaded to Azure Blob storage, when a new message is posted to an event hub or service bus, or when data is changed in an Azure Cosmos DB service.

Azure Blob storage

Azure Blob storage is used for storing unstructured data objects, such as images, videos, audio, and documents. Objects or blobs can be organized into containers. Blob storage can be redundant over multiple data centers in Azure. This is to protect the data from unplanned events, ranging from transient hardware failures to network or power outages, or even massive natural disasters. Blob storage in Azure can have different tiers, depending on how often we want to use the objects that we are storing. These include Archive and Cold tiers, and Hot and Premium tiers, which are used for applications in which we need to access data more often. As well as Blob storage, we can add a **Content Delivery Network** (**CDN**) to make the content in our storage closer to our users. This is important if we have users around the globe. If we can deliver our content from a place that is closer to the user, we can reduce the loading time of content and give users a better experience.

Azure Cognitive Services

The easiest way to describe **Azure Cognitive Services** is that it is **machine learning** as a service. With just a simple API call, we can use machine learning in our applications, without which we have to use complex data science techniques. When we use APIs, we are making predictions against the models that Microsoft has trained for us.

The services in Azure Cognitive Services have been organized into five categories, detailed as follows:

- **Vision**: The vision services are about image processing. These include APIs for face recognition, detection of adult content, image classification, and **Optical Character Recognition** (**OCR**).
- **Knowledge**: An example of a knowledge service is the **Question and Answer** (**QnA**) makers that allow us to train a model with a knowledge base. When we have trained the model, we can use it for getting answers when we are asking questions.
- **Language**: The language services are about understanding text, examples being text analytics, language understanding, and translations.
- **Speech**: Examples of speech APIs include speaker recognition, speech-to-text functionality, and speech translation.
- **Search**: The search services are about using the power of a web search engine to find an answer to your problems. These include knowledge acquisition from images, the autocompletion of search queries, and the identification of similar people.

Project overview

The main aim of this project will be to set up the backend for a chat application. The biggest part of the project will be the configuration that we will carry out in the Azure portal. We will also write some code for the Azure Functions that will handle the SignalR connections. There will be one function to return information about the SignalR connection and one that posts messages to the SignalR service. The function that we will post messages to will also determine whether the message contains an image. If it does, it will be sent to the Vision API in Azure Cognitive Services to analyze whether it contains adult content. If it does, it won't be posted to the SignalR service and the other users will not get it. Because the SignalR Service has a limitation about how big messages can be, we need to store images in Blob storage and just post the **Uniform Resource Locator** (**URL**) of the image to the users. Because we don't save any chat history in this app, we also want to clear the Blob storage at specific intervals. To do this, we will create a function that uses `TimeTrigger`.

The following diagram shows an overview of the architecture of this application:

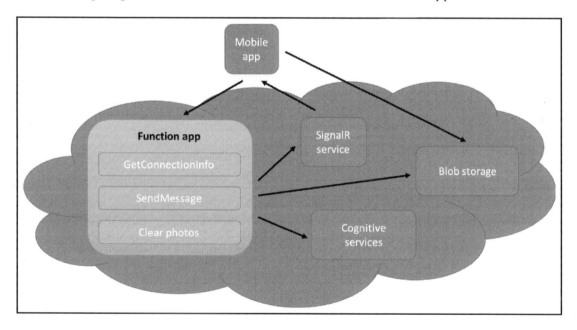

The estimated time to complete this part of the project is about 2 hours.

Building the serverless backend

Let's start setting up the backend based on the services described in the preceding section.

Creating a SignalR service

The first service that we will set up is the one for SignalR. To create such a service, proceed as follows:

1. Go to the Azure portal, at `https://portal.azure.com`.
2. Create a new resource. The **SignalR Service** resource is in the **Web** category.
3. Fill in a name for the resource in the form.
4. Select the subscription you want to use for this project.
5. We recommend that you create a new **Resource group** and use it for all the resources that we will create for this project. The reason that we want one resource group is that it is easier to track which resources are related to this project, and it is also easier to delete all the resources together.
6. Select a location that is close to your users.
7. Select a pricing tier. For this project, we can use the **Free** tier. We can always use the **Free** tier for development, and later scale up to a tier that can handle more connections.
8. Set **ServiceMode** to **Serverless**.
9. Click **Review + create** to review the settings before creating the SignalR Service.
10. Click **Create** to create the storage account.

Refer to the following screenshot to view the preceding information:

This is all we need to do to set up a SignalR Service. We will return to it in the Azure portal later to grab a connection string to it.

Creating a storage account

The next step is to set up a storage account in which we can store the images that are uploaded by the users. To create such an account, proceed as follows:

1. Create a new **Storage Account** resource. **Storage Account** is found under the **Storage** category.
2. Select a subscription and a resource group. We recommend that you use the same as you did for the SignalR Service.
3. Give the storage account a name.

4. Select a location that is close to your users.
5. Select a performance option. If we use **Premium** storage, the data will be stored on **solid-state drive (SSD)** disks. Select **Standard** storage for this project.
6. Use **StorageV2** for the **Account kind** field.
7. In the **Replication** field, we can select how we want our data to be replicated across the data centers.
8. For the **Access tier**, we will use **Hot**, becuse we will need to access the data frequently in this app.
9. Click **Review + create** to review the settings before creating the storage account.
10. Click **Create** to create the storage account.

Refer to the following screenshot to view the preceding information:

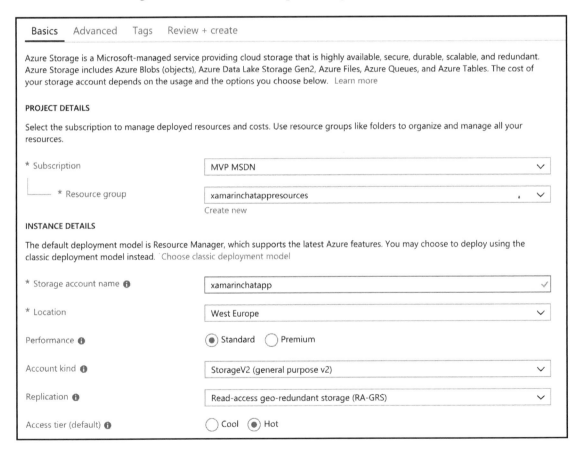

The last step of the configuration of the Blob storage is to go to the resource and create a container for the chat images. To do so, proceed as follows:

1. Go to the resource and select **Containers**.
2. Create a **New container** with the name `chatimages`.
3. Set the **Public access level** to **Blob (anonymous read access for blobs only)**. This means that it will have public read access, but that you have to be authorized to upload content.

Refer to the following screenshot to view the preceding information:

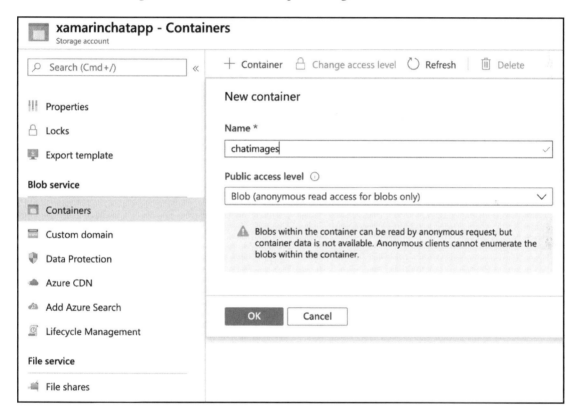

Creating an Azure Cognitive Service

To be able to use Azure **Cognitive Services** to scan images for adult content, we need to create a resource in the Azure portal. This will give us a key that we can use when making calls to the API. Proceed as follows:

1. Create a new **Computer Vision** resource.
2. Give the resource a name and select a subscription.
3. Select a location that is close to your users.
4. Select a pricing tier.
5. Select the same resource groups that you selected for the other resources.
6. Click **OK** to create the new resource.

Refer to the following screenshot to view the preceding information:

We have now finished creating the Cognitive Service. We will come back later to grab a key that we will use for the calls we will make against the API.

Using Azure Functions as an API

All the code we will write in the backend will be in Azure Functions. So, let's begin.

Creating the Azure service for functions

Before we start to write any code, we will create the function app. This will contain the functions in the Azure portal. Proceed as follows:

1. Create a new **Function App** resource. **Function app** is found under the **Compute** category.
2. Give the function app a name. The name will also be the start of the URL of the function.
3. Select a subscription for the function app.
4. Select a resource group for the function app, which should be the same as the other resources we have created in this chapter.
5. Select **.NET Core** as the runtime stack for the functions. It will then run at top of .NET Core 3 runtime.
6. Select a location that is closest to your users.

Refer to the following screenshot to view the preceding information:

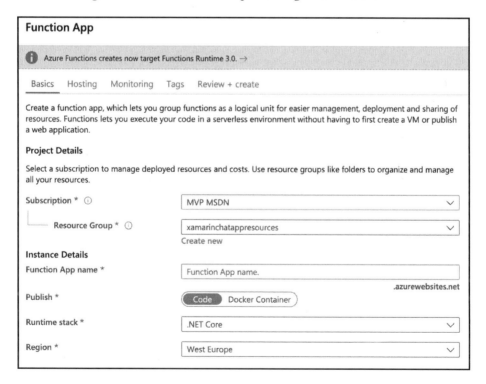

7. Go to the **Hosting** tab.
8. For storage, we can either create a new storage account or use the one we created earlier in this project.
9. We will use the **Consumption** plan as our **Hosting** plan, so we only pay for what we use. The **Function app** will scale both up and down according to our requirements—without us having to think about it at all—if we select a **Consumption** plan.
10. Click **Review + create** to review the settings before creating the function app.
11. Click **Create** to create the function app.

Refer to the following screenshot to view the preceding information:

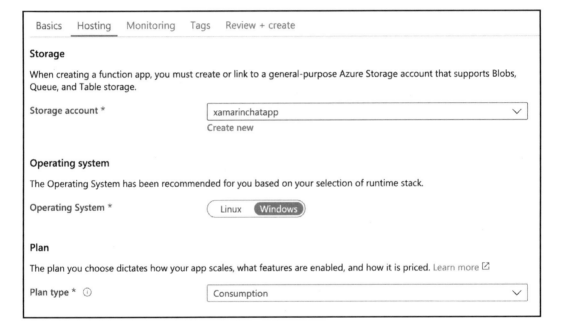

Creating a function to return the connection information for the SignalR service

If you want, you can create functions in the Azure portal. I prefer to use Visual Studio, however, because the code editing experience is much better and you can use source control. Proceed as follows:

1. Create a new project in Visual Studio.
2. Search for `function` in the search field to find the template for Azure Functions.
3. Click the **Azure Functions** template to continue, as illustrated in the following screenshot:

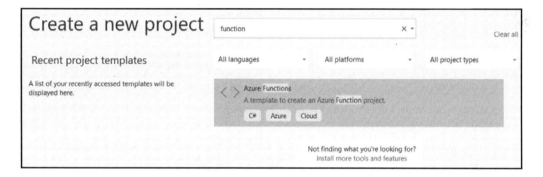

4. Name the project `Chat.Functions`.
5. Name the solution `Chat`, as illustrated in the following screenshot:

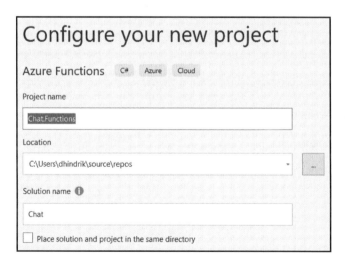

The next step is to create our first function, as follows:

1. Select **Azure Functions v3 (.NET Core)** at the top of the dialog box.
2. Select **Http trigger** as the trigger for our first function.
3. Change the **Authorization level** from **Admin** to **Anonymous**.
4. Click **OK** to continue, and our functions project will be created.

Refer to the following screenshot to view the preceding information:

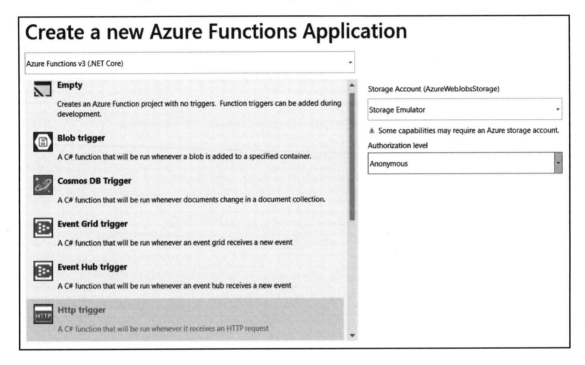

Our first function will return the connection information for the SignalR Service. To do that, we need to connect the function by adding a connection string to the SignalR Service, as follows:

1. Go to the **SignalR Service** resource in the Azure portal.
2. Go to the **Keys** tab and copy the connection string.
3. Go to the **Function App** resource and add the connection string under **Application Settings**. Use `AzureSignalRConnectionString` as the name for the setting.

4. Add the connection string to the `Values` array in the `local.settings.json` file in the Visual Studio project to be able to run the function locally on the development machine, as illustrated in the following code block:

```
{
    "IsEncrypted": false,
    "Values": {
    "AzureWebJobsStorage": "",
    "AzureWebJobsDashboard": ""
    "AzureSignalRConnectionString":
"{EnterTheConnectingStringHere}"
    }
}
```

Now, we can write the code for the function that will return the connection information. Go to Visual Studio and follow these instructions:

1. Install the `Microsoft.Azure.WebJobs.Extensions.SignalRService` NuGet package in the Functions project. The package contains the classes we need to communicate with the SignalR Service. If an error occurs during this and you are not able to install the package, make sure that you have the latest version of all other packages in the project and try again.

2. Rename the function that was created when we created the Functions project as `GetSignalRInfo`.

3. Also, rename the class as `GetSignalRInfo`.

4. To implement the binding to the SignalR Service, we will add a parameter of the `SignalRConnectionInfo` type to the method of the function. The parameter will also have the `SignalRConnectionInfo` attribute, which specifies `HubName`.

5. Return the connection info parameter, as illustrated in the following code block:

```
using Microsoft.AspNetCore.Http;
using Microsoft.Azure.WebJobs;
using Microsoft.Azure.WebJobs.Extensions.Http;
using Microsoft.Azure.WebJobs.Extensions.SignalRService;

    [FunctionName("GetSignalRInfo")]
    public static SignalRConnectionInfo GetSignalRInfo(
    [HttpTrigger(AuthorizationLevel.Anonymous)] HttpRequest req,
    [SignalRConnectionInfo(HubName = "chat")] SignalRConnectionInfo
    connectionInfo)
{
    return connectionInfo;
}
```

Creating a message library

We will now define a couple of message classes that we will use to send chat messages. We will create a base message class that will contain information that is shared between all types of messages. We will also create a separate project for the messages, which will be a .NET Standard library. The reason that we will create it as a separate .NET Standard library is that we can then reuse it in the app we will build in the next chapter. Proceed as follows:

1. Create a new **.NET Standard 2.1** project and name it `Chat.Messages`.
2. Add a reference to `Chat.Messages` in the `Chat.Functions` project.
3. Create a new class in the `Chat.Messages` project and name it `Message`.
4. Add a `TypeInfo` property to the `Message` class. We will need this property later in `Chapter 9`, *Building a Real-Time Chat Application* when we will carry out serialization of the messages.
5. Add a property for `Id`, of the `string` type.
6. Add a property for `Timestamp`, of the `DateTime` type.
7. Add a property for `Username`, of the `string` type.
8. Add an empty constructor.
9. Add a constructor that takes a username as a parameter.
10. Set the values of all properties, as illustrated in the following code block:

```
public class Message
{
    public Type TypeInfo { get; set; }
    public string Id {get;set;}
    public string Username { get; set; }
    public DateTime Timestamp { get; set; }

    public Message(){}
    public Message(string username)
    {
        Id = Guid.NewGuid().ToString();
        TypeInfo = GetType();
        Username = username;
        Timestamp = DateTime.Now;
    }
}
```

When a new client is connecting, a message will be sent to other users to indicate that they have connected. To create such a message, proceed as follows:

1. Create a new class called `UserConnectedMessage`.
2. Set `Message` as the base class.
3. Add an empty constructor.
4. Add a constructor that takes the username as a parameter and sends it to the constructor of the base class, as shown in the following code snippet:

```
public class UserConnectedMessage : Message
{
    public UserConnectedMessage() { }
    public UserConnectedMessage(string username) : base(username) {
}
}
```

When a client is sending a message with text, it will send a `SimpleTextMessage`. To create such a message, proceed as follows:

1. Create a new class called `SimpleTextMessage`.
2. Add `Message` as the base class.
3. Add an empty constructor.
4. Add a constructor that takes the username as a parameter and sends it to the constructor of the base class.
5. Add a `string` property called `Text`. Refer to the following code snippet:

```
public class SimpleTextMessage : Message
{
    public SimpleTextMessage(){}
    public SimpleTextMessage(string username) : base(username){}
    public string Text { get; set; }
}
```

If a user uploads an image, it will be sent to the functions as a `base64` string. To create such a string, proceed as follows:

1. Create a new class called `PhotoMessage`.
2. Add `Message` as the base class.
3. Add an empty constructor.
4. Add a constructor that takes the username as a parameter and sends it to the constructor of the base class.

5. Add a `string` property called `Base64Photo`.

6. Add a `string` property called `FileEnding`, as shown in the following code snippet:

```
public class PhotoMessage : Message
{
    public PhotoMessage() { }
    public PhotoMessage(string username) : base(username) { }

    public string Base64Photo { get; set; }
    public string FileEnding { get; set; }
}
```

The last message we will create is used to send information about a photo to the user. Proceed as follows:

1. Create a new class called `PhotoUrlMessage`.

2. Add `Message` as the base class.

3. Add an empty constructor.

4. Add a constructor that takes the username as a parameter and sends it to the constructor of the base class.

5. Add a `string` property called `Url`. Refer to the following code snippet:

```
public class PhotoUrlMessage : Message
{
    public PhotoUrlMessage() {}
    public PhotoUrlMessage(string username) : base(username){}

    public string Url { get; set; }
}
```

Creating a storage helper

We will create a helper to share some of the code that we will write for Azure Blob storage between the `SendMessages` function and the `ClearPhotos` function that we will create. To use Aure Blob storage locally, we need to add the connection strings to our `local.settings.json` file.

You will find the connection string under **Access keys** if you navigate to the **Storage Account** resource in the Azure portal, as illustrated in the following screenshot:

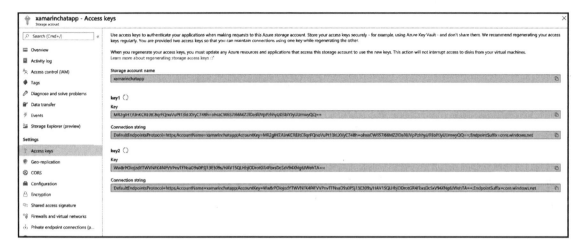

The name for the connection string will be `StorageConnection`. Also, add the same connection string to the `AzureWebJobsStorage` key, as illustrated in the following code block:

```
{
    "IsEncrypted": false,
    "Values": {
        "AzureWebJobsStorage": "{EnterTheConnectingStringHere}",
        "AzureWebJobsDashboard": "",
        "AzureSignalRConnectionString": "{EnterTheConnectingStringHere}"
        "StorageConnection": "{EnterTheConnectingStringHere}"
    }
}
```

You also need to add the keys and values to the function in the Azure portal. Navigate to the **Function App** resource and add them to **Application Settings**.

For the helper, we will create a new static class, as set out in the following steps:

1. Install the `Microsoft.Azure.Storage.Blob` NuGet package in the `Chat.Functions` project. This is to get the classes we need to work with Azure Blob storage.
2. Create a new class called `StorageHelper` in the `Chat.Functions` project.
3. Make the class `static`.
4. Create a new static method called `GetContainer`.

5. Use the static `GetEnvironmentVariable` method on the `Environment` class to read the connection string for storage.

6. Create a `CloudStorageAccount` object of it using the static `Parse` method on the `CloudStorageAccount` class.

7. Create a new `CloudBlobClient` instance using the `CreateCloudBlobClient` method on the `CloudStorageAccount` class.

8. Get the container reference using the `GetContainerReference` method on the `CloudBlobClient` class and pass the name of the container we created earlier in the chapter as an argument.

All of this is illustrated in the following code block:

```
using Microsoft.WindowsAzure.Storage;
using Microsoft.WindowsAzure.Storage.Blob;
using System;
using System.IO;
using System.Threading.Tasks;
using System.Linq;

public static class StorageHelper
{

    private static CloudBlobContainer GetContainer()
    {
        string storageConnectionString =
        Environment.GetEnvironmentVariable("StorageConnection");
        var storageAccount =
        CloudStorageAccount.Parse(storageConnectionString);
        var blobClient = storageAccount.CreateCloudBlobClient();

        var container =
        blobClient.GetContainerReference("chatimages");

        return container;
    }
}
```

To upload files to the Blob storage, we will create a method that has the bytes of the photo and what type of photo it is as parameters. The phototype will be defined by its file ending, Proceed as follows:

1. Create a new `async static` method that returns `Task<string>`.
2. Add a `byte[]` and a `string` parameter to the method. Name the parameters `bytes` and `fileEnding`.
3. Call the `GetContainer` method to get a reference to the container.
4. Define a filename for the new blob and use it as an argument to `GetBlockBlobReference` in the `CloudBlobContainer` class. Use GUID as the filename to make sure that it is unique.
5. Create a `MemoryStream` of the bytes.
6. Use the `UploadFromStreamAsync` method on the `BlockBlobReference` class to upload the photo to the cloud.
7. Return the `AbsoluteUri` of the blob.

All of this is illustrated in the following code block:

```
public static async Task<string> Upload(byte[] bytes, string fileEnding)
{
    var container = GetContainer();
    var blob = container.GetBlockBlobReference($"
{Guid.NewGuid().ToString()}.{fileEnding}");

    var stream = new MemoryStream(bytes);
    await blob.UploadFromStreamAsync(stream);

    return blob.Uri.AbsoluteUri;
}
```

The second public method that we will add to the helper is a method to delete all photos that are older than an hour. Proceed as follows:

1. Create a new `async static` method called `Clear` that returns `Task`.
2. Use the `GetContainer` method to get a reference to the container.
3. Get all blobs in the container by calling the `ListBlobsSegmentedAsync` method with the arguments shown in the code block that follows.
4. Loop through all blobs that are of the `CloudBlob` type.

5. Add an `if` statement to check whether the photos were created more than an hour ago. If so, the blob should be deleted. Refer to the following code block:

```
public static async Task Clear()
{
    var container = GetContainer();
    var blobList = await
    container.ListBlobsSegmentedAsync(string.Empty, false,
    BlobListingDetails.None, int.MaxValue, null, null, null);

    foreach(var blob in blobList.Results.OfType<CloudBlob>())
    {
        if(blob.Properties.Created.Value.AddHours(1) <
          DateTime.Now)
        {
            await blob.DeleteAsync();
        }
    }
}
```

Creating a function for sending messages

To handle messages that are sent by the user, we will create a new function, as follows:

1. Create a function with an `HttpTrigger` and with anonymous access rights.
2. Name the function `Messages`.
3. Add a collection of `SignalRMessages`.
4. Use the `SignalR` attribute to specify the hub name. Refer to the following code snippet:

```
[FunctionName("Messages")]
  public async static Task SendMessages(
    [HttpTrigger(AuthorizationLevel.Anonymous, "post")] object
    message,
    [SignalR(HubName = "chat")] IAsyncCollector<SignalRMessage>
    signalRMessages)
  {
```

The `message` parameter will be the message that the user sent. It will be of the `JObject` type (from `Newtonsoft.Json`). We need to convert it to the `Message` type that we created earlier. To do that, we need to add a reference to the `Chat.Messages` project. However, because the parameter is of an `object` type, we first need to cast it to `JObject`. Once we have done this, we can use the `ToObject` method to get a message, as illustrated in the following code snippet:

```
var jsonObject = (JObject)message;
var msg = jsonObject.ToObject<Message>();
```

If the message is a `PhotoMessage`, we will upload the photo to Blob storage. All other messages will be sent directly to the SignalR Service using the `AddAsync` method on the `signalRmessages` parameter, as illustrated in the following code block:

```
if (msg.TypeInfo.Name == nameof(PhotoMessage))
{
    //ToDo: Upload the photo to blob storage.
}

await signalRMessages.AddAsync(new SignalRMessage
  {
    Target = "newMessage",
    Arguments = new[] { message }
  });
```

Before we upload the photo to Blob storage with the helper we created, we need to convert the `base64` string to a `byte[]`. Proceed as follows:

1. Use the static `FromBase64String` method on the `Converter` class to convert the `base64` string to a `byte[]`.
2. Upload the photo to Blob storage with the static `Upload` method on `StorageHelper`.
3. Create a new `PhotoUrlMessage` class, pass the username to the constructor, and set it as the value for the `msg` variable.
4. Set the `Timestamp` property to the value of the original message, because we are interested in when the message was created by the user.
5. Set the `Id` property to the value of the original message so that it will be handled as the same message on the client.
6. Set the `Url` property to the URL that was returned by `StorageHelper` when we uploaded the photo.

7. Use the `AddAsync` method on the `signalRMessages` variable to send a message to the SignalR Service.

8. Add an empty `return` statement. Refer to the following code block:

```
if (msg.TypeInfo.Name == nameof(PhotoMessage))
{
    var photoMessage = jsonObject.ToObject<PhotoMessage>();
    var bytes = Convert.FromBase64String(photoMessage.Base64Photo);
    var url = await StorageHelper.Upload(bytes,
    photoMessage.FileEnding);
    msg = new PhotoUrlMessage(photoMessage.Username)
    {
        Id = photoMessage.Id,
        Timestamp = photoMessage.Timestamp,
        Url = url
    };

    await signalRMessages.AddAsync(new SignalRMessage
                                    {
                                        Target = "newMessage",
                                        Arguments = new[] { message }
                                    });
    return;
}
```

Using the Computer Vision API to scan photos for adult content

To minimize the risk of offensive photos being shown in our chat app, we will use machine learning to try to find problematic material and prevent it from being posted to the chat. For that, we will use the **Computer Vision API** in Azure, which is part of **Azure Cognitive Services**. To use the API, we need a key. We will add it to the application settings of the function app. Proceed as follows:

1. Go to **Azure Portal**.
2. Go to the resource we created for the **Computer Vision API**.
3. The key can be found under the **Keys and Endpoint** tab. You can use either **KEY 1** or **KEY 2**, as illustrated in the following screenshot:

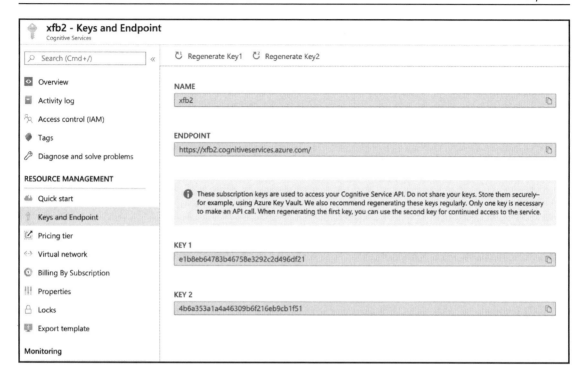

4. Go to the resource for **Function App**.

5. Add the **Key** as an application setting named `ComputerVisionKey`. Also, add the key to `local.settings.json`.

6. Also, add the **ENDPOINT** as an application setting. Use the name `ComputerVisionEndpoint`. The **ENDPOINT** can be found under the **Overview** tab of the **Function App** resource. Also, add the **ENDPOINT** to `local.settings.json`.

7. Install the `Microsoft.Azure.CognitiveServices.Vision.ComputerVision` NuGet package in the `Chat.Functions` project in Visual Studio. This is to get the necessary classes to use the Computer Vision API.

8. The code for the call to the Computer Vision API will be added to the `Message` function. After that, we convert the `base 64` string to a `byte[]`.

9. Create a `MemoryStream` based on the `byte[]`.

10. Create a `ComputerVisonClient`, and send the credentials to the constructor.

11. Create a list of which features we will use when we are analyzing the photo. In this case, we will use the `VisualFeatureTypes.Adult` feature.

12. Use the `AnalyzeImageInStreamAsync` method on `ComputerVisionClient` and pass the stream and feature list to the constructor to analyze the photo.

13. If the result is `IsAdultContent`, stop the execution of the function by using an empty `return` statement, as illustrated in the following code block:

```
var stream = new MemoryStream(bytes);
  var subscriptionKey =
  Environment.GetEnvironmentVariable("ComputerVisionKey");
  var computerVision = new ComputerVisionClient(new
  ApiKeyServiceClientCredentials(subscriptionKey), new
  DelegatingHandler[] { });

  computerVision.Endpoint =
  Environment.GetEnvironmentVariable("ComputerVisionEndpoint");

  var features = new List<VisualFeatureTypes>() {
  VisualFeatureTypes.Adult };

  var result = await
  computerVision.AnalyzeImageInStreamAsync(stream, features);

if (result.Adult.IsAdultContent)
{
    return;
}
```

Creating a scheduled job to clear photos from storage

The last thing we will do is clean the Blob storage at regular intervals and delete photos that are older than 1 hour. We will do that by creating a function that is triggered by `TimeTrigger`. Proceed as follows:

1. To create a new function, right-click the `Chat.Functions` project and click **New Azure Function**, which can be found under the **Add** menu.
2. Name the function `ClearPhotos`.
3. Select the option where the function will use a **Timer trigger** because we want it to run on a time interval.
4. Use a CRON expression to make it run every 60 minutes. Set the **Schedule** to `0 */60 * * * *`, as illustrated in the following screenshot:

 If you want to read more about CRON expressions, you can do so by going to the following URL: https://docs.microsoft.com/en-us/azure/ azure-functions/functions-bindings-timer?tabs=csharp#ncrontab-expressions

The only thing we will do in the `ClearPhotos` function is to call the `Clear` method of the `StorageHelper` class that we created earlier in this chapter and replace `void` with `async Task`, as illustrated in the following code snippet:

```
[FunctionName("ClearPhotos")]
  public static async Task Run(
    [TimerTrigger("0 */60 * * * *")]TimerInfo myTimer, ILogger log)
{
    await StorageHelper.Clear();
}
```

Deploying the functions to Azure

The final step in this chapter is to deploy the functions to Azure. You can do that as a part of a **Continous Integration/Continuous Deployment (CI/CD)** pipeline—for example, with Azure DevOps. But the easiest way to deploy the functions, in this case, is to do it directly from Visual Studio. Perform the following steps to deploy the functions:

1. Right-click on the `Chat.Functions` project and select **Publish**.
2. Select the **Select existing** option. Also, check the `Run from package` file option.
3. Click the **Create profile** button.
4. Sign in to the same Microsoft account that we used in the Azure portal when we were creating the **Function App** resource.
5. Select the subscription that contains the function app. All function apps we have in the subscription will now be loaded.
6. Select the function app and click **OK**.
7. When the profile is created, click the **Publish** button.

The following screenshot shows the last step. After that, the publishing profile is created:

Summary

In this chapter, we have learned how to set up a serverless backend for real-time communication with Azure Functions and the Azure SignalR Service. We have also learned how to use Azure Blob storage and machine learning with Azure Cognitive Services to scan for adult content in photos.

In the next chapter, we will build a chat app that will use the backend we have built in this project.

Building a Real-Time Chat Application

9

In this chapter, we will build a chat app with real-time communication. In the app, you will be able to send and receive messages and photos to and from other users, which will appear without a manual refresh. We will look at how we can use SignalR to implement a real-time connection with the server.

The following topics will be covered in this chapter:

- How to use SignalR in a Xamarin.Forms app
- How to use template selectors for a CollectionView
- How to use CSS styling in a Xamarin.Forms app

Let's get started.

Technical requirements

Before you can build the app for this project, you need to build the backend that we detailed in Chapter 8, *Setting Up a Backend for a Chat App Using Azure Services*. You will also need to have Visual Studio for Mac or PC installed, as well as the Xamarin components. See Chapter 1, *Introduction to Xamarin*, for more details on how to set up your environment. The source code for this chapter is available in this book's GitHub repository: https://github.com/PacktPublishing/Xamarin.Forms-4-Projects.

Project overview

When building a chat app, it is really important to have real-time communication because the user expects messages to arrive more or less immediately. To achieve this, we will use SignalR, which is a library for real-time communication. SignalR will use WebSockets if they are available and, if not, it will have several fallback options it can use instead. In the app, a user will be able to send text, and photos from the photo library on the device.

The build time for this project is about 180 minutes.

Getting started

We can use either Visual Studio 2019 on a PC or Visual Studio for Mac to complete this project. To build an iOS app using Visual Studio for PC, you have to have a Mac connected. If you don't have access to a Mac at all, you can choose to just build the Android part of the app.

Building the chat app

It's time to start building the app. We recommend that you use the same solution we used in Chapter 8, *Setting Up a Backend for a Chat App Using Azure Services*, because this will make code sharing easier. In that solution, we created a **Mobile App (Xamarin.Forms)** called Chat:

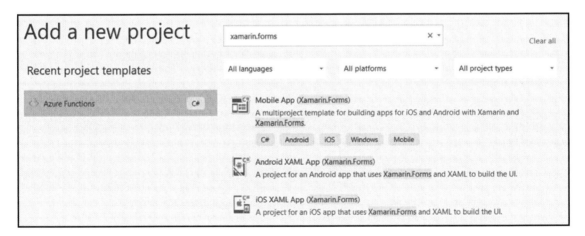

Select the **Blank** template and **iOS** and **Android** as the platforms. Now that we have created the project, we will update all NuGet packages to the latest versions because the project templates are not updated as often as the packages that are used inside the templates are:

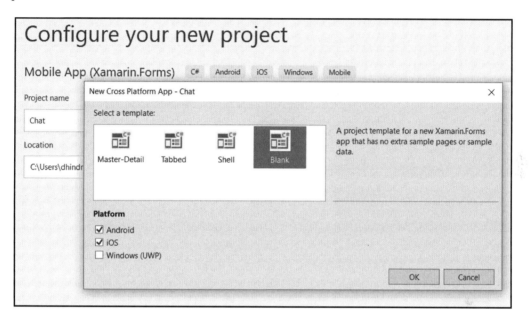

Creating the chat service

The first thing we will do is create a chat service that will be used by both the iOS and Android applications. To make the code more testable and to make it easier to replace the chat service if we want to use another provider in the future, we need to perform the following steps:

1. In the Chat project, add a reference to the Chat.Messages project.
2. Create a new folder in the Chat project called Services.
3. Create a new interface called IChatService in the Services folder.
4. Create a bool property called IsConnected.
5. Create a method called SendMessage that takes Message as an argument and returns Task.

6. Create a method called `CreateConnection` that returns `Task`. This method will create and start a connection to the SignalR service.

7. Create a method called `Dispose` that returns `Task`. This method will be used when the app goes to sleep to ensure that the connection to the SignalR service has been closed properly:

```
using Chat.Events;
using Chat.Messages;
using System;
using System.Threading.Tasks;

namespace Chat.Services
{
    public interface IChatService
    {
        bool IsConnected { get; }

        Task CreateConnection();
        Task SendMessage(Message message);
        Task Dispose();
    }
}
```

The interface will also contain an event, but before we add the event to the interface, we will create an `EventArgs` class that the event will use. Perform the following steps:

1. In the `Chat` project, create a new folder called `Events`.
2. Create a new class called `NewMessageEventArgs` in the `Events` folder.
3. Add `EventArgs` as a base class.
4. Create a property called `Message` of the `Message` type with a public getter and a private setter.
5. Create an empty constructor.
6. Create a constructor with `Message` as a parameter.
7. Set the parameter of the constructor to the `Message` property.

The following code is the result of completing these steps:

```
using Chat.Messages;
using System;
namespace Chat.Events
{
    public class NewMessageEventArgs : EventArgs
    {
        public Message Message { get; private set; }
```

```
        public NewMessageEventArgs(Message message)
        {
            Message = message;
        }
    }
}
```

Now that we have created a new `EventArgs` class, we can use it and add an event to the interface. We will name the event `NewMessage`:

```
public interface IChatService
{
    event EventHandler<NewMessageEventArgs> NewMessage;

    bool IsConnected { get; }

    Task CreateConnection();
    Task SendMessage(Message message);
    Task Dispose();
}
```

The first thing we will do in the service is make a call to the `GetSignalRInfo` service that we created in `Chapter 8`, *Setting Up a Backend for a Chat App Using Azure Services*, to obtain information about how to connect to the SignalR service. To serialize that information, we will create a new class, as follows:

1. In the `Chat` project, create a new folder called `Models`.
2. Create a new class called `ConnectionInfo`.
3. Add a string property called `Url` for our `string`.
4. Add a string property called `AccessToken` for our `string`:

    ```
    public class ConnectionInfo
    {
        public string Url { get; set; }
        public string AccessToken { get; set; }
    }
    ```

Now that we have the interface and a model to obtain the connection information, it is time to create an implementation of the `IChatService` interface. To use SignalR, we need to add a package for NuGet that will give us the necessary classes. Perform the following steps:

1. In the `Chat` project, install the `Microsoft.AspNetCore.SignalR.Client` and `Newtonsoft.Json` NuGet packages.
2. In the `Services` folder, create a new class called `ChatService`.

3. Add the `IChatService` interface to `ChatService` and implement it.

4. Add a private field for `HttpClient` called `httpClient`.

5. Add a private field for `HubConnection` called `hub`.

6. Add a private field for `SemaphoreSlim` called `semaphoreSlim` and create a new instance with an initial and maximum count of 1 in the constructor:

```
using Chat.Events;
using Chat.Messages;
using Microsoft.AspNetCore.SignalR.Client;
using Newtonsoft.Json;
using System;
using System.Net.Http;
using System.Text;
using System.Threading;
using System.Threading.Tasks;

public class ChatService : IChatService
{
    private HttpClient httpClient;
    private HubConnection hub;
    private readonly SemaphoreSlim semaphoreSlim =
        new SemaphoreSlim(1, 1);

    public event EventHandler<NewMessageEventArgs> NewMessage;
    public bool IsConnected { get; set; }

    public async Task CreateConnection()
    {
    }

    public async Task SendMessage(Message message)
    {
    }
    public async Task Dispose()
    {
    }
}
```

We will start with `CreateConnection`, which will call the `GetSignalRInfo` function. We will then use the information in the response to connect to the SignalR service and start listening for messages. To do this, carry out the following steps:

1. Add a call to the `WaitAsync` method of `SemaphoreSlim` to make sure that only one thread can use the method at any time.

2. Check whether `httpClient` is `null`. If it is, create a new instance. We will reuse the `httpClient` instance because this is better from a performance perspective.

3. Make a call to `GetSignalRInfo` and serialize the result to a `ConnectionInfo` object:

```
public async Task CreateConnection()
{
    await semaphoreSlim.WaitAsync();

    if(httpClient == null)
    {
        httpClient = new HttpClient();
    }

    var result = await
httpClient.GetStringAsync("https://{theNameOfTheFunctionApp}.azurew
ebsites.net/api/GetSignalRInfo");

    var info = JsonConvert.DeserializeObject<Models.ConnectionInfo>
    (result);
}
```

When we have the necessary information about how to connect to the SignalR service, we can use `HubConnectionBuilder` to create a connection. Then, we can start listening for messages:

1. Create a new `HubConnectionBuilder`.

2. Use the `WithUrl` method to specify the URL to the SignalR service as the first argument. The second argument is an `Action` of the `HttpConnectionObject` type. This means that you will get an object of the `HttpConnectionObject` type as a parameter.

3. In the action, set `AccessTokenProvider` to a `Func` that returns the value of the `AccessToken` property on the `ConnectionInfo` object.

4. Use the `Build` method of `HubConnectionBuilder` to create a connection object.

5. Add an `Action` that will run when new messages arrive using the `On<object>` method on the `HubConnection` object. The action will be specified as the second argument. For the first argument, we will specify the name of the target (we specified the target in Chapter 8, *Setting Up a Backend for a Chat App Using Azure Services*, when we sent the message), which is `newMessage`.

6. In `Action`, convert the incoming message into a string using the `ToString` method and deserialize it to a `Message` object so we can read its `TypeInfo` property. To do this, use the `JsonConvert` class and the `DeserializeObject<Message>` method.

> The reason we have to deserialize the object twice is that we only get the value of properties in the `Message` class the first time we use it. When we know which subclass of `Message` we've received, we can use this to deserialize that information for that class. We are casting it to `Message` so that we can pass it to the `NewMessageEventArgs` object. In this case, we will not lose the properties of the subclass. To access the properties, we just cast the class back to the subclass.

7. When we know what type the message is, we can use this to deserialize the object to the actual type. Use the `DeserializeObject` method of `JsonConvert`, pass the JSON string and `TypeInfo` to it, and then cast it to `Message`.

8. Invoke the `NewMessage` event and pass the current instance of `ChatService` and a new `NewMessageEventArgs` object to it. Pass the `Message` object to the constructor of `NewMessageEventArgs`.

9. Once we have a connection object and we have configured what will happen when a message arrives, we can start listening to messages with the `StartAsync` method of `HubConnection`.

10. Set the `IsConnected` property to `true`.

11. Use the `Release` method of `SemaphoreSlim` to let other threads go to the `CreateConnection` method:

```
var connectionBuilder = new HubConnectionBuilder();
connectionBuilder.WithUrl(info.Url,
(Microsoft.AspNetCore.Http.Connections.Client.HttpConnectionOptions
obj) =>
    {
        obj.AccessTokenProvider = () => Task.Run(() =>
        info.AccessToken);
    });

hub = connectionBuilder.Build();
hub.On<object>("newMessage", (message) =>
{
        var json = message.ToString();
        var obj = JsonConvert.DeserializeObject<Message>(json);
        var msg = (Message)JsonConvert.DeserializeObject(json,
```

```
obj.TypeInfo);
        NewMessage?.Invoke(this, new NewMessageEventArgs(msg));
});

await hub.StartAsync();

IsConnected = true;
semaphoreSlim.Release();
```

The next method we need to implement is `SendMessage`. This will send a message to an Azure function, which will add the message to the SignalR service:

1. Use the `Serialize` method on the `JsonConvert` class to serialize the `Message` object to JSON.
2. Create a `StringContent` object and pass the JSON string as the first argument, `Encoding.UTF8` as the second argument, and the `application/json` content-type as the last argument to the constructor.
3. Create a new instance of `HttpClient` if the `httpClient` variable is `null`.
4. Use the `PostAsync` method on the `HttpClient` object with the URL as the first argument and the `StringContent` object as the second argument in order to post the message to the function:

```
public async Task SendMessage(Message message)
{
    var json = JsonConvert.SerializeObject(message);

    var content = new StringContent(json, Encoding.UTF8,
    "application/json");

    if (httpClient == null)
    {
        httpClient = new HttpClient();
    }

    await
    httpClient.PostAsync
("https://{TheNameOfTheFunctionApp}.azurewebsites.net/api/messages"
, content);
}
```

The last method we need to implement is `Dispose`. This will close the connection when the app enters its background state, for example, when a user hits the home button or switches apps:

1. Use the `WaitAsync` method to ensure that there are no threads trying to create a connection or dispose of a connection when we are running the method.
2. Add an `if` statement to ensure that the hub field isn't `null`.
3. If it isn't `null`, call the `StopAsync` and `DisposeAsync` methods of `HubConnection`.
4. Set the `httpClient` field to `null`.
5. Set `IsConnected` to `false`.
6. Release `SemaphoreSlim` with the `Release` method:

```
public async Task Dispose()
{
    await semaphoreSlim.WaitAsync();

    if(hub != null)
    {
        await hub.StopAsync();
        await hub.DisposeAsync();
    }

    httpClient = null;

    IsConnected = false;

    semaphoreSlim.Release();
}
```

Initializing the app

Now, we are ready to write the initialization code for the app. We will set up **Inversion-of-Control (IoC)** and carry out the necessary configuration.

Creating a resolver

We need to create a helper class that will ease the process of resolving object graphs through `Autofac`. This will help us create types based on a configured IoC container.

In this project, we will use `Autofac` as the IoC library:

1. Install the `Autofac` NuGet package in the `Chat` project.
2. Create a new class called `Resolver` in the `Chat` project.
3. Add a `private static` field called `container` of the `IContainer` type (from `Autofac`).
4. Add a public static method called `Initialize` with `IContainer` as a parameter. Set the value of the parameter to the `container` field.
5. Add a generic static public method called `Resolve`, which will return an instance that is based on the argument type, with the `Resolve` method of `IContainer`:

```
using Autofac;

public class Resolver
{
    private static IContainer container;

    public static void Initialize(IContainer container)
    {
        Resolver.container = container;
    }

    public static T Resolve<T>()
    {
        return container.Resolve<T>();
    }
}
```

Creating a Bootstrapper

Here, we will create a `Bootstrapper` class so that we can set up the common configurations that we need in the startup phase of the app. Usually, there is one part of the `Bootstrapper` class for each target platform and one that is shared for all platforms. In this project, we only need the shared part:

1. Create a new class called `Bootstrapper` in the `Chat` project.
2. Add a new public static method called `Init`.
3. Create a new `ContainerBuilder` and register the types to `container`.

4. Create a `Container` using the `Build` method of `ContainerBuilder`. Create a variable called `container` that contains the `Container` instance.

5. Use the `Initialize` method on `Resolver` and pass the `container` variable as an argument, as shown in the following code:

```
using Autofac;
using Chat.Chat;
using System;
using System.Reflection;

public class Bootstrapper
{
    public static void Init()
    {
        var builder = new ContainerBuilder();

        builder.RegisterType<ChatService>().As<IChatService>
        ().SingleInstance();

        var currentAssembly = Assembly.GetExecutingAssembly();

        builder.RegisterAssemblyTypes(currentAssembly)
                .Where(x => x.Name.EndsWith("View",
                StringComparison.Ordinal));

        builder.RegisterAssemblyTypes(currentAssembly)
                .Where(x => x.Name.EndsWith("ViewModel",
                StringComparison.Ordinal));

        var container = builder.Build();

        Resolver.Initialize(container);
    }
}
```

Call the `Init` method of `Bootstrapper` in the constructor in the `App.xaml.cs` file, after the call to `InitializeComponents`:

```
public App()
{
    InitializeComponent();
    Bootstrapper.Init();
    MainPage = new MainPage();
}
```

Creating a base ViewModel

We now have a service that is responsible for handling communication with the backend. Now, it's time to create a `ViewModel`. First, however, we will create a base view model, where we can put the code that will be shared between all the view models of the app:

1. Create a new folder called `ViewModels`.
2. Create a new class called `ViewModel`.
3. Make the new class public and abstract.
4. Add a static field called `Navigation` of the `INavigation` type. This will be used to store a reference to the navigation services provided by Xamarin.Forms.
5. Add a static field called `User` of the `string` type. The field will be used when connecting to the chat service so that messages you send will be displayed with your name attached.
6. Add and implement the `INotifiedPropertyChanged` interface. This is necessary because we want to use data bindings.
7. Add a `Set` method. This will make it easier for us to raise the `PropertyChanged` event from the `INotifiedPropertyChanged` interface. This method will check if the value has changed. If it has, it will raise the event:

```
using System.Collections.Generic;
using System.ComponentModel;
using System.Runtime.CompilerServices;
using Xamarin.Forms;

public abstract class ViewModel : INotifyPropertyChanged
{
    public static INavigation Navigation { get; set; }
    public static string User { get; set; }

    public event PropertyChangedEventHandler PropertyChanged;
    protected void Set<T>(ref T field, T newValue,
                    [CallerMemberName] string propertyName =
                    null)
    {
        if (!EqualityComparer<T>.Default.Equals(field, newValue))
        {
            field = newValue;
            PropertyChanged?.Invoke(this, new
            PropertyChangedEventArgs(propertyName));
        }
    }
}
```

Creating the main view

Now that we have our `ViewModel` base class set up, as well as all of the code for receiving and sending messages, it's time to create the two views. These will act as the user interface of the app.

We are going to start by creating the main view. This is the view that will be displayed when the user starts the app. We will add an entry control (an input text box) so that the user can enter a username and add a command to navigate to the chat view.

The main view will be composed of the following:

- A `ViewModel` file called `MainViewModel.cs`
- A XAML file called `MainView.xaml`, which contains the layout
- A code-behind file called `MainView.xaml.cs`, which will carry out the data binding process

Let's start by creating the `ViewModel` for `MainView`.

Creating MainViewModel

The `MainViewModel` that we are about to create will hold a username that the user will enter into the UI. It will also contain a `Command` property called `Start`. This will be bound to a `Button` that the user will click after entering their username:

1. In the `ViewModel` folder, create a class called `MainViewModel.cs`.
2. Inherit the class from `ViewModel`.
3. Make the class `public`.
4. Add a property called `Username` of the `string` type.
5. Add a property called `Start` of the `ICommand` type and implement it, as shown in the following code. The `Start` command will assign `Username` from the `Username` property and assign it to the static `User` property in the base `ViewModel`. Then, it will create a new instance of `ChatView` by using `Resolver` and pushing it onto the navigation stack.

`MainViewModel` should now look as follows:

```
using System.Windows.Input;
using Chat.Views;
using Xamarin.Forms;
 namespace Chat.ViewModels
```

```
{
    public class MainViewModel : ViewModel
    {
        public string Username { get; set; }

        public ICommand Start => new Command(() =>
        {
            User = Username;

            var chatView = Resolver.Resolve<ChatView>();
            Navigation.PushAsync(chatView);
        });
    }
}
```

Now that we have `MainViewModel`, we need a view to go with it. It's time to create `MainView`.

Creating MainView

`MainView` will display a user interface that allows the user to enter a name before starting the chat. This section will be about creating the `MainView` XAML file and the code behind that view.

We will start by removing the template-generated `MainPage` and replacing it with an MVVM-friendly `MainView`.

Replacing MainPage

When we created the app, the template generated a page called `MainPage`. Since we are using MVVM as a pattern, we need to remove this page and replace it with a view called `MainView` instead:

1. In the root of the `Chat` project, delete the page called `MainPage`.
2. Create a new folder called `Views`.
3. Add a new XAML page called `MainView` in the `Views` folder.

Editing the XAML

Now, it's time to add some content to the newly created `MainView.xaml` file. The icons mentioned here can be found in the same folder that they have been added to (you can check this by looking at the project on GitHub – the GitHub URL can be found at the beginning of this chapter). There is a lot going on here, so make sure to check what you write against the code:

1. Add the `chat.png` icon to the `Drawable` folder that is inside the `Resources` folder in the Android project.
2. Add the `chat@2x.png` icon to the `Resources` folder in the iOS project.
3. Open the `MainView.xaml` file.
4. Add a `Title` property to the `ContentPage` node. This is the title that will be displayed in the navigation bar of the app.
5. Add a `Grid` and define two rows in it. The first one should have a height of `"*"`, while the second one should have a height of `"2*"`. This will partition the space in two rows, of which the first will take up 1/3 of the space and the second will take up 2/3 of the space.
6. Add an `Image` with `Source` set to `"chat.png"` and its `VerticalOptions` and `HorizontalOptions` set to `"Center"`.
7. Add `StackLayout` with `Grid.Row` set to `"1"`, `Padding` set to `"10"`, and `Spacing` set to `"20"`. The `Grid.Row` property positions `StackLayout` in the second row. `Padding` adds 10 units of space around `StackLayout`, while `Spacing` defines the amount of space between each element added in `StackLayout`.
8. In `StackLayout`, add an `Entry` node that has its `Text` property set to `"{Binding UserName}"` and the `Placeholder` property set to `"Enter a username"`. Binding the `Text` node will make sure that when the user enters a value in the `Entry` control, it's updated in `ViewModel`.
9. In `StackLayout`, add a `Button` control that will have the `Text` property set to `"Start"` and its `Command` property set to `"{Binding Start}"`. The `Command` property binding will execute when the user taps the button. It will run the code that we defined in the `MainViewModel` class.

When finished, the code should look as follows (shown in bold):

```xml
<?xml version="1.0" encoding="UTF-8"?>
<ContentPage xmlns="http://xamarin.com/schemas/2014/forms"
             xmlns:x="http://schemas.microsoft.com/winfx/2009/xaml"
             x:Class="Chat.Views.MainView" Title="Welcome">
```

```
<Grid>
    <Grid.RowDefinitions>
        <RowDefinition Height="*" />
        <RowDefinition Height="2*" />
    </Grid.RowDefinitions>
    <Image Source="chat.png" VerticalOptions="Center"
                             HorizontalOptions="Center" />
    <StackLayout Grid.Row="1" Padding="10" Spacing="20">
        <Entry Text="{Binding Username}"
        Placeholder="Enter a username" />
        <Button Text="Start" Command="{Binding Start}" />
    </StackLayout>
</Grid>
</ContentPage>
```

The layout is complete. Now, we need to turn our attention to the code behind this view so that we can wire up some loose ends.

Fixing the code behind the view

As with all views, when using MVVM, we need to pass our view of `ViewModel`. Since we are using dependency injection in this project, we will pass it through the constructor and then assign it to the view's `BindingContext`. We will also make sure that we enable safe areas to avoid controls being partially hidden behind the iPhone X notch at the top:

1. Open the `MainView.xaml.cs` file.
2. Add a parameter called `viewModel` of the `MainViewModel` type in the constructor of the `MainView` class. The argument for this parameter will be injected by `Autofac` at runtime.
3. Add a `platform-specific` statement that instructs the application to use safe areas on iOS. A safe area makes sure that the app does not use the space on the side of the notch at the top of the screen on an iPhone X.
4. Assign the `viewModel` argument to the `BindingContext` property of the view.

The changes that need to be made have been marked in bold in the following code:

```
using Chat.ViewModels;
using Xamarin.Forms;
using Xamarin.Forms.PlatformConfiguration.iOSSpecific;

using Xamarin.Forms.Xaml;

public partial class MainView : ContentPage
{
```

```
public MainView(MainViewModel viewModel)
{
    InitializeComponent();

    On<Xamarin.Forms.PlatformConfiguration.iOS>
    ().SetUseSafeArea(true);

    BindingContext = viewModel;
}
}
```

Now, our `MainView` is complete, but we still need to tell the application to use it as the entry point view.

Setting the main view

The entry point view, also referred to as the application's `MainPage`, is set during the initialization of a Xamarin.Forms app. Usually, it is set in the constructor of the `App` class. We will be creating `MainView` through the resolver we created earlier and wrapping it in `NavigationPage` to enable platform-specific navigation on the device that the app runs on. We could have used Shell as well, but in this case, there are no reasons to use it:

1. Open the `App.xaml.cs` file.
2. Resolve an instance to a `MainView` class by using `Resolver` and storing it in a variable called `mainView`.
3. Create a new instance of `NavigationPage` by passing the `mainView` variable as a constructor argument and assigning it to a variable called `navigationPage`.
4. Assign the `navigationPage.Navigation` property to the static `Navigation` property, which is of the `ViewModel` type. This property will be used when navigating between pages later on.
5. Assign the `navigationPage` variable to the `MainPage` property of the `App` class. This sets the starting view of our application:

```
public App()
{
    InitializeComponent();
    Boostrapper.Init();

    var mainView = Resolver.Resolve<MainView>();
    var navigationPage = new NavigationPage(mainView);
    ViewModel.Navigation = navigationPage.Navigation;
    MainPage = navigationPage;
}
```

That's it for `MainView`; nice and easy. Now, let's move on to something more interesting: `ChatView`. This will be used to send and receive messages.

Creating ChatView

`ChatView` is a standard chat client. It will have an area for displaying incoming and outgoing messages, as well as a text field at the bottom that the user can type a message into. It will also have a button for taking a photo and a button for sending messages if the user doesn't hit *return* on the on-screen keyboard.

We will start by creating `ChatViewModel`, which contains all of the necessary logic by acting as the glue between the view and the model. Our model, in this case, is represented by our `ChatService`.

After that, we will create `ChatView`, which handles how the **Graphical User Interface (GUI)** is rendered.

Creating ChatViewModel

As we mentioned previously, `ChatViewModel` is the glue between the visual representation (`View`) and the model (which is basically our `ChatService`). `ChatViewModel` will store messages and any communication that's made with `ChatService` by hooking up the necessary functionality for sending and receiving messages.

Creating the class

`ChatViewModel` is a simple class that inherits from the `ViewModel` base class we created earlier. In the first code exercise, we will create the class, adding relevant `using` statements and a property called `Messages`, which we will use to store the messages that we have received. The view will use the `Message` collection to display the messages in a `ListView`.

Since this is a large block of code, we recommend that you write it first and then go over the numbered list to get to grips with what has been added to the class:

1. Create a new class called `ChatViewModel` in the `ViewModels` folder of the `Chat` project.

2. Make the class `public` and inherit it from the `ViewModel` base class to gain the common base functionality from the base class.

3. Add a `readonly` property called `chatService` of the `IChatService` type. This will store a reference to an object that implements `IChatService` and make the concrete implementation of `ChatService` replaceable. It's good practice to expose any service as an interface.

4. Add a public property called `Messages` of the `public` `ObservableCollection<Message>` type with a private setter. This collection will hold all messages. The private setter makes the property inaccessible from outside this class. This maintains the integrity of the collection by ensuring messages are not inserted anywhere except inside the class.

5. Add a constructor parameter called `chatService` of the `IChatService` type. When we use dependency injection, this is where `Autofac` will inject an object that implements `IChatService`.

6. In the constructor, assign the `chatService` parameter to the `chatService` property. This will store the reference to `ChatService` so that we can use it during the lifetime of `ChatViewModel`.

7. In the constructor, instantiate the `Messages` property to a new `ObservableCollection<Message>`.

8. In the constructor, create a `Task.Run` statement that will call the `chatService.CreateConnection()` method if the `chatService.IsConnected` property is `false`. The reason we're using `Task.Run` is because we want the code to run asynchronously, even if this is done from the constructor. End the `Task.Run` statement by sending a new `UserConnected` message:

```
using System;
using System.Collections.ObjectModel;
using System.IO;
using System.Linq;
using System.Threading.Tasks;
using System.Windows.Input;
using Acr.UserDialogs;
using Chat.Messages;
using Chat.Services;
using Plugin.Media;
```

```
using Plugin.Media.Abstractions;
using Xamarin.Forms;

namespace Chat.ViewModels
{
    public class ChatViewModel : ViewModel
    {
        private readonly IChatService chatService;
        public ObservableCollection<Message> Messages { get;
        private set; }

        public ChatViewModel(IChatService chatService)
        {
            this.chatService = chatService;

            Messages = new ObservableCollection<Message>();

            Task.Run(async() =>
            {
                if(!chatService.IsConnected)
                {
                    await chatService.CreateConnection();
                }

                await chatService.SendMessage(new
                UserConnectedMessage(User));
            });
        }
    }
}
```

Now that we have instantiated our ChatViewModel, it's time to add a property that will hold whatever the user is typing at that moment.

Adding the text property

At the bottom of the GUI, there will be a text field (an entry control) that will allow the user to enter a message. This entry will be data-bound to a property that we will call `Text` in `ChatViewModel`. Whenever the user changes the text, this property will be set. This is a classic case of data-binding:

1. Add a new private field called `text` of the `string` type.
2. Add a public property called `Text` that returns the private text field in the getter and makes a call to the `Set()` method of the base class in the setter. The `Set` method is defined in the `ViewModel` base class and will raise an event back to the view if the property changes in `ChatViewModel`, effectively keeping them in sync:

```
private string text;
public string Text
{
    get => text;
    set => Set(ref text, value);
}
```

Now, we have a property that we can use for data binding. Let's look at the code we will use to receive messages from `ChatService`.

Receiving messages

When a message is sent from the server, over SignalR, `ChatService` will parse this message and transform it into a `Message` object. Then, it will raise an event called `NewMessage`, which is defined in `ChatService`.

In this section, we will implement an event handler to handle these events and add them to the `Messages` collection, unless a message with the same ID already exists.

Again, perform the following steps and look at the code to get to grips with it:

1. In `ChatViewModel`, create a method called `ChatService_NewMessage`, which will be a standard event handler. This has two parameters: `sender`, which is of the `object` type, and `e`, which is of the `Events.NewMessageEventArgs` type.
2. Wrap the code in this method in `Device.BeginInvokeOnMainThread()`. We're doing this since we are going to add messages to the `Message` collection. Items that are added to this collection will modify the view, and any code that modifies the view must be run on the UI thread.

3. In `Device.BeginInvokeOnMainThread`, add the incoming message from `e.Message` to the `Messages` collection if a message with that specific `Message.Id` isn't already present. This is to avoid message duplication.

The method should look as follows:

```
private void ChatService_NewMessage(object sender,
Events.NewMessageEventArgs e)
{
    Device.BeginInvokeOnMainThread(() =>
    {
        if (!Messages.Any(x => x.Id == e.Message.Id))
        {
            Messages.Add(e.Message);
        }
    });
}
```

Now that the event handler has been defined, we need to hook it up in the constructor:

1. Locate the constructor of the `ChatViewModel` class.
2. Wire up a `chatService.NewMessage` event to the `ChatService_NewMessage` handler we just created. A good place to do this is under the instantiation of the `Messages` collection.

The code marked in bold is what we should add to the `ChatViewModel` class:

```
public ChatViewModel(IChatService chatService)
{
    this.chatService = chatService;

    Messages = new ObservableCollection<Message>();

    chatService.NewMessage += ChatService_NewMessage;

    Task.Run(async() =>
    {
        if(!chatService.IsConnected)
        {
            await chatService.CreateConnection();
        }

        await chatService.SendMessage(new UserConnectedMessage(User));
    });
}
```

The app will now be able to receive messages. How about sending them? Well, stay tuned!

Creating the LocalSimpleTextMessage class

To make it easier to recognize whether a message is coming from the server or whether it is being sent by the user of the device that the code is executing on, we will create a `LocalSimpleTextMessage`:

1. Create a new class called `LocalSimpleTextMessage` in the `Chat.Messages` project.

2. Add `SimpleTextMessage` as the base class.

3. Create a constructor with `SimpleTextMessage` as the parameter.

4. Set the value to all of the base properties with the value from the parameter, as shown in the following code:

```
public class LocalSimpleTextMessage : SimpleTextMessage
{
    public LocalSimpleTextMessage(SimpleTextMessage message)
    {
        Id = message.Id;
        Text = message.Text;
        Timestamp = message.Timestamp;
        Username = message.Username;
        TypeInfo = message.TypeInfo;
    }
}
```

Sending text messages

Sending text messages is also very straightforward. We need to create a command that we can bind for the GUI. The command will be executed either when the user hits *return* or when the user clicks the send button. When a user does either of these two things, the command will create a new `SimpleTextMessage` and pass in the current user to identify the message for other users. We will use the text from the `ChatViewModel` text property, which, in turn, is bound to the `Entry` control.

We will then add the message to the `Messages` collection, triggering `ListView`, which will be handling messages that need to be updated. After that, we will pass the message to `ChatService` and clear the `ChatViewModel` text property. By doing this, we notify the GUI that it has changed and let the data binding magic clear the field.

Refer to the following steps and look at the code to get to grips with it:

1. Create a new property called `Send` of the `ICommand` type.
2. Assign it a new `Command` instance.
3. Create a new instance of the `SimpleTextMessage` class by passing the `User` property of the base class as an argument. Assign the instance to a variable called `message`.
4. Set the `Text` property of the message variable to the `Text` property of the `ChatViewModel` class. This copies the current text in the chat entry defined by the GUI later on.
5. Create a `LocalSimpleTextMessage` object and pass in the message variable as a constructor argument. `LocalSimpleTextMessage` is a `SimpleTextMessage` and makes it possible for the view to recognize it as a message that the user of the app sent, effectively rendering it on the right-hand side of the chat area. Add the `LocalSimpleTextMessage` instance to the `Messages` collection. This will display the message in the view.
6. Make a call to the `chatService.SendMessage()` method and pass the message variable as an argument.
7. Empty the `Text` property of `ChatViewModel` to clear the entry control in the GUI:

```
public ICommand Send => new Command(async()=>
{
    var message = new SimpleTextMessage(User)
    {
        Text = this.Text
    };

    Messages.Add(new LocalSimpleTextMessage(message));

    await chatService.SendMessage(message);

    Text = string.Empty;
});
```

What good is a chat app if we can't send photos? We'll implement this in the next section.

Installing the Acr.UserDialogs plugin

`Acr.UserDialogs` is a plugin that makes it possible to use several standard user dialogs from code that are shared between platforms. To install and configure it, there are a few steps we need to follow:

1. Install the `Acr.UserDialogs` NuGet package for the `Chat-`, `Chat.iOS`, and `Chat.Android` projects.

2. In the `MainActivity.cs` file, add `UserDialogs.Init(this)` to the `OnCreate` method:

```
protected override void OnCreate(Bundle savedInstanceState)
{
    TabLayoutResource = Resource.Layout.Tabbar;
    ToolbarResource = Resource.Layout.Toolbar;
    base.OnCreate(savedInstanceState);
    UserDialogs.Init(this);

    global::Xamarin.Forms.Forms.Init(this, savedInstanceState);
    LoadApplication(new App());
}
```

Installing the Media plugin

We will use the `Xam.Plugin.Media` NuGet package to access the photo library of the device. We need to install this package for the `Chat-`, `Chat.iOS`, and `Chat.Android` projects in the solution. Before we can use the package, however, we need to do some configuration for each platform. We will start with Android:

1. The plugin needs the `WRITE_EXTERNAL_STORAGE` and `READ_EXTERNAL_STORAGE` permissions. The plugin will add these for us, but we need to override `OnRequestPermissionResult` in `MainActivity.cs` first.

2. Call the `OnRequestPermissionsResult` method.

3. Add `CrossCurrentActivity.Current.Init(this, savedInstanceState)` after initializing Xamarin.Forms in the `OnCreate` method in the `MainActivity.cs` file, as shown in the following code:

```
public override void OnRequestPermissionsResult(int requestCode,
string[] permissions, Android.Content.PM.Permission[] grantResults)
{
Xamarin.Essentials.Platform.OnRequestPermissionsResult(requestCode,
permissions, grantResults);
}
```

We also need to add some configuration for the file paths that the users will be able to pick photos from:

1. Add a folder called xml to the Resources folder in the Android project.
2. Create a new XML file called file_paths.xml in the new folder.
3. Add the following code to file_paths.xml:

```
<?xml version="1.0" encoding="utf-8"?>
<paths xmlns:android="http://schemas.android.com/apk/res/android">
    <external-files-path name="my_images" path="Pictures" />
    <external-files-path name="my_movies" path="Movies" />
</paths>
```

The last thing we need to do to set up the plugin for the Android project is add the following code to the AndroidManifest.xml field, inside the application element:

```
<manifest xmlns:android="http://schemas.android.com/apk/res/android"
android:versionCode="1" android:versionName="1.0" package="xfb.Chat">
<uses-sdk android:minSdkVersion="21" android:targetSdkVersion="27" />
    <application android:label="Chat.Android">
    <provider
    android:name="android.support.v4.content.FileProvider"
    android:authorities="${applicationId}.fileprovider"
    android:exported="false" android:grantUriPermissions="true">
    <meta-data android:name="android.support.FILE_PROVIDER_PATHS"
    android:resource="@xml/file_paths"></meta-data>
    </provider>
    </application>
</manifest>
```

For the iOS project, the only thing we need to do is add the following four usage descriptions to info.plist:

```
<key>NSPhotoLibraryUsageDescription</key>
<string>This app needs access to photos.</string>
<key>NSPhotoLibraryAddUsageDescription</key>
<string>This app needs access to the photo gallery.</string>
```

Sending photos

To be able to send photos, we will have to use a source of photos. In our case, we will be using the phone's camera as the source. The camera will return the photo as a stream after it has been taken. We need to convert that stream into a byte array and then Base64 encode it into a string that is easy to send over SignalR.

The method that we are about to create, called `ReadFully()`, takes a stream and turns it into a byte array, which is a step toward achieving the Base64-encoded string. This is a standard piece of code that creates a buffer that will be used when we are reading the `Stream` parameter and writing it to `MemoryStream` in chunks until we have read the full stream, hence the name of the method.

Perform the following steps and check out the code to get to grips with it:

1. Create a method called `ReadFully` that takes a `stream` called `input` as a parameter and returns a `byte` array.

2. Inside a `using` statement, create a new `MemoryStream` called `ms`.

3. Copy the input `Stream` to the memory stream.

4. Return `MemoryStream` as an array using the `ToArray` method:

```
private byte[] ReadFully(Stream input)
{
    using (MemoryStream ms = new MemoryStream())
    {
        ms.CopyTo(input);
        return ms.ToArray();
    }
}
```

After doing this, we're left with a large chunk of code. This code exposes a command that will be executed when the user clicks the photo button in the app. It starts by configuring `CrossMedia` (a media plugin), which indicates the quality the photo should be, and then it starts the photo picker. When the photo picker returns from the `async` call to `PickPhotoAsync()`, we start uploading the photo. To notify the user, we use `UserDialogs.Instance.ShowLoading` to create a loading overlay with a message to indicate that we are uploading the photo.

Then, we will get the stream of the photo, convert it into a byte array using the `ReadFully()` method, and Base64 encode it into a string. The string will be wrapped in a `PhotoMessage` instance, added to the local `Message` collection of the `ChatViewModel`, and then sent to the server.

Perform the following steps and study the code to get to grips with it:

1. Create a new property called `Photo` of the `ICommand` type. Assign it a new `Command` instance.

2. Create an anonymous `async` method (a lambda expression) and add the code defined in the upcoming steps to it. You can see the full code for this method in the code snippet that follows.

3. Create a new instance of the `PickMediaOptions` class and set the `CompressionQuality` property to 50.

4. Call `CrossMedia.Current.PickPhotoAsync` with an `async` method call and save the result to a local variable called `photo`.

5. Install the NuGet package.

6. Show a message dialog by calling `UserDialogs.Instance.ShowLoading()` with the text `"Uploading photo"`.

7. Get the photostream by calling the `GetStream()` method of the photo variable and save it as a variable called `stream`.

8. Convert the stream into a byte array by calling the `ReadFully()` method.

9. Convert the byte array into a Base64-encoded string using the `Convert.ToBase64String()` method. Save the string as a variable called `base64photo`.

10. Create a new `PhotoMessage` instance and pass `User` as the constructor argument. Set the `Base64Photo` property to the `base64photo` variable and the `FileEnding` property to the file ending of the `photo.Path` string using the `Split` function of the string object. Store the new `PhotoMessage` instance in a variable called `message`.

11. Add the message object to the `Messages` collection.

12. Send the message to the server by calling the async `chatService.SendMessage()` method.

13. Hide the loading dialog by calling `UserDialogs.Instance.HideLoading()`.

The code that follows shows how this can be implemented:

```
public ICommand Photo => new Command(async () =>
{
    var options = new PickMediaOptions();
    options.CompressionQuality = 50;

    var photo = await CrossMedia.Current.PickPhotoAsync();

    UserDialogs.Instance.ShowLoading("Uploading photo");

    var stream = photo.GetStream();
    var bytes = ReadFully(stream);

    var base64photo = Convert.ToBase64String(bytes);

    var message = new PhotoMessage(User)
```

```
        {
            Base64Photo = base64photo,
            FileEnding = photo.Path.Split('.').Last()
        };

        Messages.Add(message);
        await chatService.SendMessage(message);

        UserDialogs.Instance.HideLoading();
    });
```

The `ChatViewModel` is complete. Now, it's time to create our GUI.

Creating the ChatView

`ChatView` is responsible for creating the user interface that the user will interact with. It will display local and remote messages, both text and photos, and also notify a user when another user has joined the chat. We'll start by creating a converter that will convert photos represented as Base64-encoded strings into an `ImageSource` that can be used as the source of the image control process in XAML.

Creating Base64ToImageConverter

When we take a picture using the phone's camera, it will be handed to us as a byte array. To send this to the server, we will convert it into a Base64-encoded string. To display that message locally, we will need to convert it back into a byte array and then pass that byte array to a helper method of the `ImageSource` class to create an instance of the `ImageSource` object. This object will make sense to the `Image` control and an image will be displayed.

Since there is a lot of code here, we suggest that you perform the following steps and look at each line of code in detail as you follow them:

1. Create a folder called `Converters` in the `Chat` project.
2. Create a new class called `Base64ImageConverter` in the `Converters` folder; ensure the class implements the `IValueConverter` interface.
3. In the `Convert()` method of the class, cast the `value` object parameter to a string called `base64String`.
4. Convert `base64String` into a byte array using the `System.Convert.FromBase64String()` method. Save the result in a variable called `bytes`.

5. Create a new `MemoryStream` by passing the byte array into its constructor. Save the stream in a variable called `stream`.

6. Call the `ImageSource.FromStream()` method and pass the stream as a lambda expression that returns the stream variable. Return the `ImageSource` object that's created by doing this.

7. The `ConvertBack()` method doesn't need to be implemented since we will never convert an image back into a Base64-encoded string via data binding. We will just let it throw a `NotImplementedException`:

```
using System;
using System.Globalization;
using Xamarin.Forms;
using System.IO;

namespace Chat.Converters
{
    public class Base64ToImageConverter : IValueConverter
    {
        public object Convert(object value, Type targetType,
                              object parameter, CultureInfo
                              culture)
        {
            var base64string = (string)value;
            var bytes =
            System.Convert.FromBase64String(base64string);
            var stream = new MemoryStream(bytes);
            return ImageSource.FromStream(() => stream);
        }

        public object ConvertBack(object value, Type targetType,
                                  object parameter, CultureInfo
                                  culture)
        {
            throw new NotImplementedException();
        }
    }
}
```

Now, it's time to start adding some actual XAML code to the view. We will start by creating the main layout skeleton, which we will then gradually build on until we have the finished view.

Creating the skeleton ChatView

This XAML file will contain the view that lists the messages we have sent and the messages we have received. It's quite a large file to create, so for this part, I suggest that you copy the XAML and study every step carefully:

1. Create a new XAML `ContentPage` in the `Views` folder called `ChatView`.
2. Add XML namespaces for `Chat.Selectors` and `Chat.Converters` and call them `selectors` and `converters`.
3. Add a `ContentPage.Resources` node. This will contain the resources for this view.
4. Add `ScrollView` as the page content. `ScrollView` should only be able to scroll on iOS to handle when the onscreen keyboard is visible. On Android, this isn't necessary and causes some other problems. Use `OnPlatform` to set `Orientation` to `Neither` for Android and `Vertical` for iOS.
5. Add `Grid` as the only child of `ScrollView` and name it `MainGrid` by setting the `x:Name` property to `MainGrid`.

6. Create a `RowDefinitions` element that contains three rows. The first should have a height of `*`, the second a height of `1`, and the third a platform-specific height based on the platform by using an `OnPlatform` element.
7. Save some space for the `CollectionView` that will be inserted later on.
8. Add a `BoxView`. This will act as a visual divider by setting the `HeightRequest` property to `1`, the `BackgroundColor` property to `#33000000`, and the `Grid.Row` property to `1`. This will position `BoxView` in the one-unit-high row of the grid, effectively drawing a single line across the screen.
9. Add another `Grid`. This will use the space of the third row by setting the `Grid.Row` property to `2`. Also, add some padding by setting the `Padding` property to `10`. Define three rows in the grid with heights of `30`, `*`, and `30`:

```xml
<?xml version="1.0" encoding="UTF-8"?>
<ContentPage xmlns="http://xamarin.com/schemas/2014/forms"
             xmlns:x="http://schemas.microsoft.com/winfx/2009/xaml"
             xmlns:selectors="clr-namespace:Chat.Selectors"
             xmlns:converters="clr-namespace:Chat.Converters"
             x:Class="Chat.Views.ChatView">
    <ContentPage.Resources>
        <!-- TODO Add resources -->
    </ContentPage.Resources>
    <ScrollView>
        <ScrollView.Orientation>
            <OnPlatform x:TypeArguments="ScrollOrientation">
```

```
                    <On Platform="iOS" Value="Vertical" />
                    <On Platform="Android" Value="Neither" />
                </OnPlatform>
        </ScrollView.Orientation>
          <Grid x:Name="MainGrid">
            <Grid.RowDefinitions>
                <RowDefinition Height="*" />
                <RowDefinition Height="1" />
                <RowDefinition>
                    <RowDefinition.Height>
                        <OnPlatform x:TypeArguments="GridLength">
                            <On Platform="iOS" Value="50" />
                            <On Platform="Android" Value="100" />
                        </OnPlatform>
                    </RowDefinition.Height>
                </RowDefinition>
            </Grid.RowDefinitions>

            <!-- TODO Add CollectionView -->
            <BoxView Grid.Row="1" HeightRequest="1"
            BackgroundColor="#33000000" />
            <Grid Grid.Row="2" Padding="10">
                <Grid.ColumnDefinitions>
                    <ColumnDefinition Width="30" />
                    <ColumnDefinition Width="*" />
                    <ColumnDefinition Width="30" />
                </Grid.ColumnDefinitions>
                <!-- TODO Add buttons and entry controls -->
            </Grid>
        </Grid>
    </ScrollView>
</ContentPage>
```

Now that we have completed the main skeleton of our page, we need to start adding some specific content. First, we will add ResourceDictionary to create a DataTemplate selector. This will select the correct layouts for different chat messages. Then, we need to put Base64ToImageConverter to use. To do that, we need to define it in the view.

Adding ResourceDictionary

Now, it's time to add some resources to the view. In this case, we will be adding a template selector, which we will create later on, and `Base64ToImageConverter`, which we created earlier. The template selector will look at each row that we will bind to `ListView`. This will be presenting messages and selecting the best layout template that suits that message:

1. Locate the `<!-- TODO Add resources -->` comment inside the `ContentPage.Resources` element.

2. Add the XAML to the sample as follows, right underneath the comment mentioned in *step 1*:

```
<ResourceDictionary>
    <selectors:ChatMessageSelector
    x:Key="SelectMessageTemplate" />
    <converters:Base64ToImageConverter x:Key="ToImage" />
</ResourceDictionary>
```

This will create one instance of each resource that we've defined and make them accessible to the rest of the view.

Adding CollectionView

We will be using a `CollectionView` to display the messages in the chat app. Again, perform the following steps and take a look at the code to make sure you understand each step:

1. Locate the `<!-- TODO Add CollectionView -->` comment in the `ChatView.xaml` file.

2. Add a `CollectionView` and set the `x:Name` property to `MessageList`.

3. Data-bind `CollectionView` by setting the `ItemsSource` property to `{Binding Messages}`. This will make `CollectionView` aware of any changes that are made in `ObservableCollection<Message>`, which is exposed through the `Messages` property. Any time a message is added or removed, `ListView` will update to reflect this change.

4. Add the `SelectMessageTemplate` resource we defined in the previous section to the `ItemTemplate` property. This will run some code each time an item is added to make sure that we programmatically select the correct visual template for a specific message. Don't worry about this right now – we will write the code for this soon.

5. Now, need to define a placeholder where we will add resources. The resources we will be adding are the different *DataTemplates* that will be used to render different types of messages.

The XAML should look as follows:

```
<CollectionView x:Name="MessageList" ItemsSource="{Binding Messages}"
  ItemTemplate="{StaticResource SelectMessageTemplate}">
    <CollectionView.Resources>
      <ResourceDictionary>
        <!-- Resources go here later on -->
      </ResourceDictionary>
    </CollectionView.Resources>
</CollectionView>
```

Adding templates

Now, we will add five different templates, each corresponding to a specific message type that the app either sends or receives. Each of these templates goes under the `<!-- Resources go here later on -->` comment from the code snippet in the previous section.

We won't be explaining each of these templates step by step since the XAML that they contain should be starting to feel familiar to you at this point.

Each template starts the same way: the root element is a `DataTemplate` with a name. The name is important because we will be referencing it in our code very soon. The content that follows after this element is the actual content that the row will be constructed from.

The bindings inside `DataTemplate` will also be local to each item or row that `CollectionView` renders. In this case, it will be an instance of a `Message` class since we are data binding `CollectionView` to a collection of `Message` objects. You will see some `StyleClass` properties in the code. These will be used when we finalize the styling for the app using **Cascading Style Sheets (CSS)**.

Our task here is to write each of these templates under the `<!-- Resources go here later on -->` comment.

`SimpleText` is the `DataTemplate` that is selected when `Message` is a remote message. It will be rendered on the left-hand side of the list view, just as you might expect. It displays a `username` and a `text` message:

```
<DataTemplate x:Key="SimpleText">
    <Grid Padding="10">
        <Grid.ColumnDefinitions>
            <ColumnDefinition Width="*" />
            <ColumnDefinition Width="*" />
        </Grid.ColumnDefinitions>
        <Frame StyleClass="remoteMessage" HasShadow="false">
            <StackLayout>
             <Label Text="{Binding Username}"
              StyleClass="chatHeader" />
             <Label Text="{Binding Text}" StyleClass="chatText" />
            </StackLayout>
        </Frame>
    </Grid>
</DataTemplate>
```

The `LocalSimpleText` template is the same as the `SimpleText` data template, except that it renders on the right-hand side of `CollectionView` by setting the `Grid.Column` property to `1`, effectively using the right column:

```
<DataTemplate x:Key="LocalSimpleText">
    <Grid Padding="10">
        <Grid.ColumnDefinitions>
            <ColumnDefinition Width="*" />
            <ColumnDefinition Width="*" />
        </Grid.ColumnDefinitions>
        <Frame Grid.Column="1" StyleClass="localMessage"
        HasShadow="false">
            <StackLayout>
              <Label Text="{Binding Username}"
              StyleClass="chatHeader" />
              <Label Text="{Binding Text}" StyleClass="chatText" />
            </StackLayout>
```

```
                </Frame>
            </Grid>
    </DataTemplate>
```

`DataTemplate` is used when a user connects to the chat:

```
<DataTemplate x:Key="UserConnected">
        <StackLayout Padding="10" BackgroundColor="#33000000"
        Orientation="Horizontal">
            <Label Text="{Binding Username}" StyleClass="chatHeader"
            VerticalOptions="Center" />
            <Label Text="connected" StyleClass="chatText"
            VerticalOptions="Center" />
        </StackLayout>
</DataTemplate>
```

A photo that is uploaded to the server is accessible via a URL. This `DataTemplate` displays an image based on a URL and is used for remote images:

```
<DataTemplate x:Key="Photo">
        <Grid Padding="10">
            <Grid.ColumnDefinitions>
                <ColumnDefinition Width="*" />
                <ColumnDefinition Width="*" />
            </Grid.ColumnDefinitions>
            <StackLayout>
                <Label Text="{Binding Username}"
                 StyleClass="chatHeader" />
                <Image Source="{Binding Url}" Aspect="AspectFill"
                HeightRequest="150" HorizontalOptions="Fill" />
            </StackLayout>
        </Grid>
</DataTemplate>
```

A message that contains a photo is sent by the user and rendered directly based on the Base64-encoded image that we generate from the camera. Since we don't want to wait for the image to upload, we use this `DataTemplate`, which utilizes the `Base64ImageConverter` that we wrote earlier to transform the string into an `ImageSource` that can be displayed by the `Image` control:

```
<DataTemplate x:Key="LocalPhoto">
        <Grid Padding="10">
            <Grid.ColumnDefinitions>
                <ColumnDefinition Width="*" />
                <ColumnDefinition Width="*" />
            </Grid.ColumnDefinitions>
            <StackLayout Grid.Column="1">
```

```
                    <Label Text="{Binding Username}"
                    StyleClass="chatHeader" />
                    <Image Source="{Binding Base64Photo, Converter=
                    {StaticResource ToImage}}"
                    Aspect="AspectFill" HeightRequest="150"
                    HorizontalOptions="Fill" />
                </StackLayout>
            </Grid>
        </DataTemplate>
```

These are all of the templates we need. Now, it's time to add some code to make sure we select the right template for the message to display.

Creating a template selector

Using a template selector is a powerful way of injecting different layouts based on the items that are being data-bound. In this case, we will look at each message that we want to display and select the best `DataTemplate` for them. The code is somewhat repetitive, so we will be using the same approach that we used for the XAML – simply adding the code and letting you study it yourself:

1. Create a folder called `Selectors` in the `Chat` project.

2. Create a new class called `ChatMessageSelector` in the `Selectors` folder and inherit it from `DataTemplateSelector`.

3. Add the following code, which will look at each object that is data-bound and pull the correct `DataTemplate` from the resources we just added:

```
using Chat.Messages;
using Xamarin.Forms;

namespace Chat.Selectors
{
    public class ChatMessageSelector : DataTemplateSelector
    {
        protected override DataTemplate OnSelectTemplate(object
        item, BindableObject container)
        {
            var list = (CollectionView)container;

            if(item is LocalSimpleTextMessage)
            {
                return
                (DataTemplate)list.Resources["LocalSimpleText"];
```

```
        }
        else if(item is SimpleTextMessage)
        {
            return (DataTemplate)list.Resources["SimpleText"];
        }
        else if(item is UserConnectedMessage)
        {
            return
(DataTemplate)list.Resources["UserConnected"];
        }
        else if(item is PhotoUrlMessage)
        {
            return (DataTemplate)list.Resources["Photo"];
        }
        else if (item is PhotoMessage)
        {
            return (DataTemplate)list.Resources["LocalPhoto"];
        }

        return null;
    }
  }
}
```

Adding the buttons and entry control

Now, we will add the buttons and the entry that the user will use to write chat messages. The icons that we will be using can be found in the GitHub repository for this chapter. For Android, the icons will be placed in the `Drawable` folder inside the `Resource` folder and for iOS, they will be in the `Resource` folder. The icons are in the same folder on GitHub:

1. Locate the `<!-- TODO Add buttons and entry controls -->` comment in the `ChatView.xaml` file.
2. Add an `Image`. `Source` should be set to `photo.png` and `VerticalOptions` and `HorizontalOptions` should be set to `Center`. `Source` will be used to display an image, while `HorizontalOptions` and `VerticalOptions` will be used to center the image in the middle of the control.
3. Add a `TapGestureRecognizer` object to the `GestureRecognizers` property of `Image`. `Command` will be executed when a user taps the image. Bind the `Command` property of `Image` to the `Photo` property on `ViewModel`.

4. Add an `Entry` control to allow the user to enter a message to be sent. The `Text` property should be set to `{Binding Text}`. Set the `Grid.Column` property to 1 and `ReturnCommand` to `{Binding Send}` in order to execute the `send` command in `ChatViewModel` when a user hits *Enter*.

5. Add an `Image` with the `Grid.Column` property set to 2, `Source` set to `send.png`, and `Command` set to `{Binding Send}` (the same as the `return` command). Center it horizontally and vertically.

6. Add a `TapGestureRecognizer` to the `GestureRecognizers` property of `Image`. `Command` will be executed when a user taps the image. Bind the `Command` property of `Image` to the `Send` property on `ViewModel`:

```
<Image Source="photo.png" VerticalOptions="Center"
HorizontalOptions="Center">
    <Image.GestureRecognizers>
        <TapGestureRecognizer Command="{Binding Photo}" />
    </Image.GestureRecognizers>
</Image>
<Entry Text="{Binding Text}" Grid.Column="1"
            ReturnCommand="{Binding Send}" />
<Image Grid.Column="2" Source="send.png" VerticalOptions="Center"
HorizontalOptions="Center">
    <Image.GestureRecognizers>
        <TapGestureRecognizer Command="{Binding Photo}" />
    </Image.GestureRecognizers>
</Image>
```

Fixing the code behind

Now that the XAML is complete, we have some work to do in the code behind. We'll start by adding some `using` statements:

1. Open the `ChatView.xaml.cs` file.
2. Add `using` statements for `Chat.ViewModels`, `Xamarin.Forms`, and `Xamarin.Forms.PlatformConfiguration.iOSSpecific`.
3. Add a `private` field called `viewModel` of the `ChatViewModel` type, which will hold a local reference to `ChatViewModel`.

The class should now look as follows. The code in bold indicates what should have changed:

```
using System.Linq;
using Chat.ViewModels;
using Xamarin.Forms;
```

```
using Xamarin.Forms.PlatformConfiguration.iOSSpecific;

namespace Chat.Views
{
    public partial class ChatView : ContentPage
    {
        private ChatViewModel viewModel;
        public ChatView()
        {
            InitializeComponent();
        }
    }
}
```

When a new message arrives, this will be added to the `Messages` collection in `ChatViewModel`. To make sure that `CollectionView` scrolls appropriately so that the new message is visible, we need to write some additional code:

1. Create a new method called `Messages_CollectionChanged` that takes an object as the first parameter and `NotifyCollectionChangedEventArgs` as the second parameter.
2. Add a call to the `MessageList.ScrollTo()` method and pass the last `Message` in the `viewModel.Messages` collection by calling `viewModel.Messages.Last()`. Pass `null` as the second argument. The third argument should be set to `ScrollPosition.End`, indicating that we want to make the entire messages' `CollectionView` row visible. The last argument should be set to `true` to enable animations.

The method should now look as follows:

```
private void Messages_CollectionChanged(object sender,
        System.Collections.Specialized.NotifyCollectionChangedEventArgs e)
{
    MessageList.ScrollTo(viewModel.Messages.Last(), null,
    ScrollToPosition.End, true);
}
```

Now, it's time to extend the constructor so that it takes `ChatViewModel` as a parameter and sets `BindingContext` in the way that we are used to. The constructor will also make sure that we use the safe area when rendering controls and that we hook up to the events that will handle changes in the `Messages` collection of `ChatViewModel`:

1. Modify the constructor in the `ChatView` class so that it takes a `ChatViewModel` as the only parameter. Name it `viewModel`.

2. Assign the `viewModel` parameter from the constructor to the local `viewModel` field in the class.

3. Then, call the `InitializeComponent()` method. Add a platform-specific call to the `SetUseSafeArea(true)` method to ensure that the app will be visually safe to use on an iPhone X and not partially hidden behind the notch at the top:

```
public ChatView(ChatViewModel viewModel)
{
    this.viewModel = viewModel;

    InitializeComponent();
    On<Xamarin.Forms.PlatformConfiguration.iOS>
    ().SetUseSafeArea(true);

    viewModel.Messages.CollectionChanged +=
    Messages_CollectionChanged;
    BindingContext = viewModel;
}
```

Every time a view appears, the `OnAppearing()` method is called. This method is virtual and can be overridden. We will use this feature to make sure that we have the correct height on `MainGrid`. This is because we have to wrap everything in a `ScrollView` because the view has to be able to scroll when the keyboard appears. If we don't calculate the width of `MainGrid`, it could be bigger than the screen because `ScrollView` allows it to expand:

1. Override the `OnAppearing()` method.

2. Calculate the safe area to use by calling the platform-specific `On<Xamarin.Forms.PlatformConfiguration.iOS>().SafeAreaInsets()` method. This will return a `Xamarin.Forms.Thickness` object that contains the inset information we need in order to calculate the height of `MainGrid`. Assign the `Thickness` object to a variable called `safeArea`.

3. Set the `MainGrid.HeightRequest` property to the height of the view (`this.Height`) and then subtract the `Top` and `Bottom` properties of `safeArea`:

```
protected override void OnAppearing()
{
    base.OnAppearing();
    var safeArea = On<Xamarin.Forms.PlatformConfiguration.iOS>
    ().SafeAreaInsets();
    MainGrid.HeightRequest = this.Height - safeArea.Top -
    safeArea.Bottom;
}
```

Styling

Styling is an important part of an app. Just like we can with HTML, we can style by setting properties on each control directly, or by setting `Style` elements in the application's resource dictionary. Recently, however, a new way of styling has emerged in Xamarin.Forms, which is using Cascading Style Sheets, better known as CSS.

Since CSS doesn't cover all cases, we will fall back to standard application resource dictionary styling as well.

Styling with CSS

Xamarin.Forms supports styling via CSS files. For web developers, it can be more intuitive to use compared to XAML styling. It provides a subset of the functionalities you would expect from normal CSS, but support is getting better with each version. We are going to use two different selectors to apply the styling we need.

First, let's create the style sheet. We'll discuss the content of it afterward:

1. Create a folder called `Css` in the `Chat` project.
2. Create a new text file in the `Css` folder called `Styles.css`.
3. Copy the style sheet into that file, as follows:

```
button {
 background-color: #A4243B;
 color: white;
}

.chatHeader {
 color: white;
 font-style: bold;
 font-size: small;
```

```
        }

        .chatText {
         color: white;
         font-size: small;
        }

        .remoteMessage {
         background-color: #F04D6A;
         padding: 10;
        }

        .localMessage {
         background-color: #24A43B;
         padding: 10;
        }
```

The first selector, button, applies to every button control in the entire application. It sets the background color to #A4243B and the foreground color to white. You can do this for almost every type of control in Xamarin.Forms.

The second kind of selectors we will be using are class selectors, which are the ones beginning with a period, such as .chatHeader. These selectors are used in XAML with the StyleClass property. Take a look at the ChatView.xaml file we created earlier – you'll find these in the template resources.

Each property in the CSS is mapped to a property on the control itself. There are also some Xamarin.Forms-specific properties that can be used, but those are out of the scope of this book. If you search for Xamarin.Forms and CSS on the internet, you'll find all of the information you'll need to dive deeper into this.

Applying the style sheet

A style sheet is no good on its own. We need to apply it to our application. We also need to set some styling on NavigationPage here as well, since we can't gain access to it from the CSS directly.

We will be adding some resources and a reference to the style sheet. Copy the code that follows and refer to these steps to study what each line does:

1. Open the App.xaml file in the Chat project.
2. In the Application.Resources node, add a <StyleSheet Source="/Css/Styles.css" /> node to reference the style sheet.

3. The next node we need to work on is the `StyleSheet` node. Add a `Style` node with `TargetType` set to `"NavigationPage"`. Create a setter for the `BarBackgroundColor` property with a value of `"#273E47"` and a setter for the `BarTextColor` property with a value of `"White"`.

The `App.xaml` file should now look as follows:

```xml
<?xml version="1.0" encoding="utf-8"?>
<Application xmlns="http://xamarin.com/schemas/2014/forms"
            xmlns:x="http://schemas.microsoft.com/winfx/2009/xaml"
            x:Class="Chat.App">
    <Application.Resources>
        <StyleSheet Source="/Css/Styles.css" />
        <ResourceDictionary>
            <Style TargetType="NavigationPage">
                <Setter Property="BarBackgroundColor" Value="#273E47" />
                <Setter Property="BarTextColor" Value="White" />
            </Style>
        </ResourceDictionary>
    </Application.Resources>
</Application>
```

Handling life cycle events

Finally, we need to add some life cycle events that will take care of our SignalR connection in case the app goes to sleep or when it wakes up again:

1. Open the `App.xaml.cs` file.
2. Add the following code somewhere inside the `App` class:

```csharp
protected override void OnSleep()
{
    var chatService = Resolver.Resolve<IChatService>();
    chatService.Dispose();
}
protected override void OnResume()
{
    Task.Run(async() =>
    {
        var chatService = Resolver.Resolve<IChatService>();

        if (!chatService.IsConnected)
        {
            await chatService.CreateConnection();
        }
```

```
        });

        Page view = null;

        if(ViewModel.User != null)
        {
            view = Resolver.Resolve<ChatView>();
        }
        else
        {
            view = Resolver.Resolve<MainView>();
        }

        var navigationPage = new NavigationPage(view);
        MainPage = navigationPage;
    }
```

The `OnSleep()` method will be called when the user minimizes the app. It will dispose of any active `chatService` that is running by closing the active connections. The `OnResume()` method does a little bit more than this. It will recreate the connection if there isn't one already active and, depending on whether the user is set or not, it will resolve to the correct view. If a user isn't present, it will display `MainView`; otherwise, it will display `ChatView`. Finally, it sets the selected view, wrapped in a navigation page.

Summary

That's that – good work! In this chapter, we created a chat app that connects to our backend. We have learned how to work with SignalR, how to style an app with CSS, how to use template selectors in a `CollectionView`, and how to use a value converter to convert a `byte[]` into a Xamarin.Forms `ImageSource`.

In the next chapter, we will dive into an augmented world! We will create an AR game for iOS and Android using UrhoSharp, along with ARKit (iOS) and ARCore (Android).

Creating an Augmented Reality Game

10

In this chapter, we will be exploring **augmented reality** (**AR**) using Xamarin.Forms. We will be using custom renderers to inject platform-specific code, **UrhoSharp** to render the scene and handle input, and `MessagingCenter` to pass internal messages around in the app.

The following topics will be covered in this chapter:

- Overview of the project
- Setting up the project
- Using ARKit
- Using ARCore
- Learning how to use UrhoSharp to render graphics and handle input
- Using custom renderers to inject platform-specific code
- Using `MessagingCenter` to send messages

Technical requirements

To be able to complete this project, you will need to have Visual Studio for Mac or PC installed, as well as the Xamarin components. See `Chapter 1`, *Introduction to Xamarin*, for more details on how to set up your environment.

You cannot run AR on an emulator. To run AR, you need a physical device, along with the following software:

- On iOS, you need iOS 11 or higher, and a device that has an A9 processor or above.
- On Android, you need Android 9, and a device that supports ARCore.

Essential theory

This section will describe how AR works. The implementation differs slightly between platforms. Google's implementation is called **ARCore,** and Apple's implementation is called **ARKit**.

AR is all about superimposing computer graphics on top of a camera feed. This sounds like a simple thing to do, except that you have to track the camera position with great accuracy. Both Google and Apple have written some great **application programming interfaces (APIs)** to do this magic for you, with the help of motion sensors in your phone and data from the camera. The computer graphics that we add on top of the camera feed are synced to be in the same coordinate space as the surrounding real-life objects, making them appear as if they are part of the image you see on your phone.

An overview of the project

In this chapter, we are going to create a game that explores the fundamentals of AR. We are also going to learn how to integrate AR control in Xamarin.Forms. Android and iOS implement AR differently, so we will need to unify the platforms along the way. We will do this using UrhoSharp, an open source 3D game engine, which will do the rendering for us. This is simply made up of bindings to the **Urho3D** engine, which allows us to use Urho3D with .NET and C#.

The game will render boxes in AR that the user needs to tap to make disappear. You can then extend the game yourself by learning about the Urho3D engine.

The estimated build time for this project is 90 minutes.

Setting up the project

It's time to start coding! First, however, make sure you have your development environment set up, as described in Chapter 1, *Introduction to Xamarin*.

This chapter will be a classic **File | New | Project** chapter, guiding you step by step through the process of creating the app. There will be no downloads required whatsoever.

Creating the project

Follow these few steps in order to create the project:

1. Open Visual Studio and click on **File** | **New** | **Project**, as shown in the following screenshot:

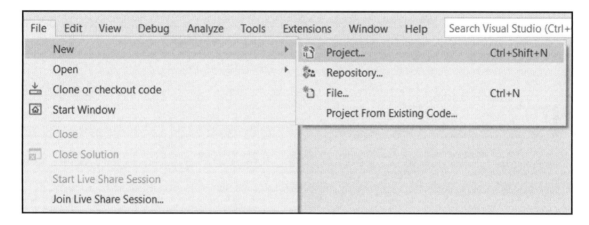

This will open up the **Create a new project** wizard.

2. Enter `xamarin forms` in the search field and select the **Mobile App (Xamarin.Forms)** template, as shown in the following screenshot, and click **Next**:

3. We will be calling our application `WhackABox` in this project, so let's enter that into the **Project name** field, as shown in the following screenshot, and click **Create**:

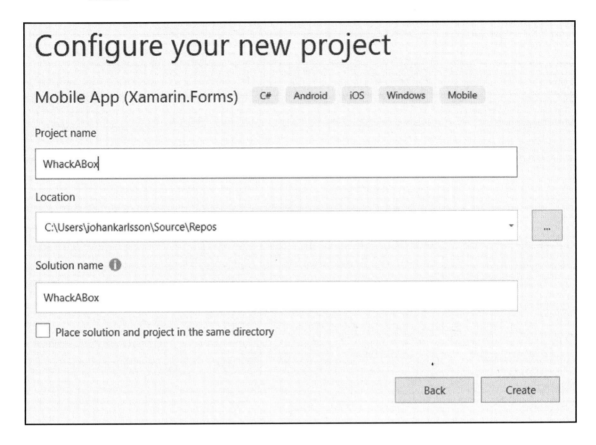

4. Next, we select a project template. Select the **Blank** template option to create a bare minimum Xamarin.Forms app.

5. Uncheck the **Windows (UWP)** checkbox under the **Platform** heading, since this app will only be supporting **iOS** and **Android**.

6. Finish the setup wizard by clicking **OK**, and let Visual Studio scaffold the project for you. This might take a couple of minutes. You can see the aforementioned fields and options that you need to select in the following screenshot:

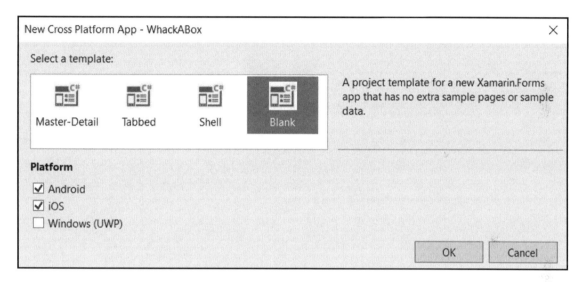

Just like that, the app has been created. Let's move on to updating Xamarin.Forms to the latest version.

Updating the Xamarin.Forms NuGet packages

Currently, the Xamarin.Forms version that your project has been created with is most likely a bit old. To rectify this, we need to update the NuGet packages. Please note that you should only update the Xamarin.Forms packages and not the Android packages; updating the Android packages might cause your packages to get out of sync with each other, resulting in the app not building at all. To update the NuGet packages, go through the following steps:

1. Right-click on our **solution** in the **Solution Explorer**.
2. Click **Manage NuGet Packages for Solution...**, as shown in the following screenshot:

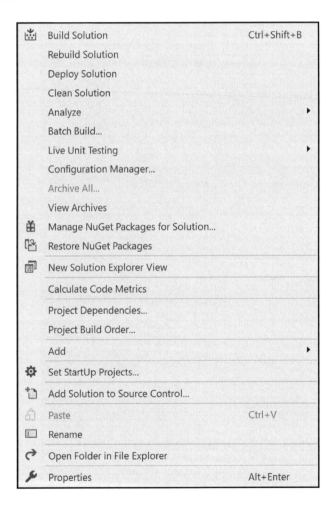

🗒	Build Solution	Ctrl+Shift+B
	Rebuild Solution	
	Deploy Solution	
	Clean Solution	
	Analyze	▶
	Batch Build...	
	Live Unit Testing	▶
	Configuration Manager...	
	Archive All...	
	View Archives	
🎁	Manage NuGet Packages for Solution...	
🗒	Restore NuGet Packages	
📄	New Solution Explorer View	
	Calculate Code Metrics	
	Project Dependencies...	
	Project Build Order...	
	Add	▶
⚙	Set StartUp Projects...	
🗂	Add Solution to Source Control...	
📋	Paste	Ctrl+V
🔳	Rename	
↪	Open Folder in File Explorer	
🔧	Properties	Alt+Enter

This will open the **NuGet Package Manager** in Visual Studio, as shown in the following screenshot:

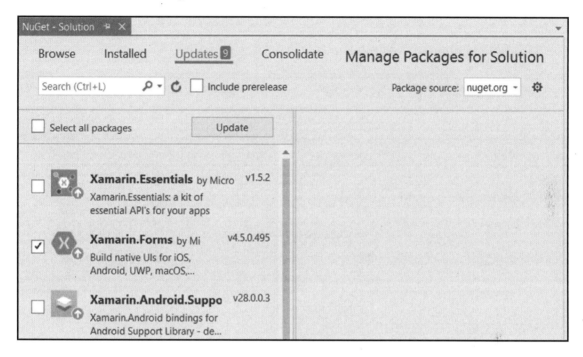

To update Xamarin.Forms to the latest version, go through the following steps:

1. Click the **Updates** tab.
2. Check the **Xamarin.Forms** checkbox and click **Update**.
3. Accept any license agreements.

The update takes, at most, a few minutes. Look at the output pane to find information about the update. At this point, we can run the app to make sure it works. We should see the text **Welcome to Xamarin.Forms!** in the middle of the screen.

Setting the Android target framework version to 9.0

ARCore is available from Android version 9.0 and later. We will, therefore, verify the **Target Framework** version for the Android project by going through the following steps:

1. In the **Solution Explorer,** double-click on the **Properties** node under the Android project.
2. Verify that the **Target Framework** version is at least **Android 9.0 (Pie)**, as shown in the following screenshot:

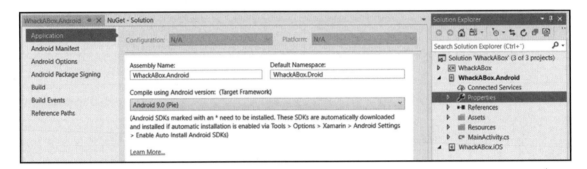

If there is an asterisk next to the **Target Framework** name, then you will need to install that **software development kit** (**SDK**) by going through the following steps:

1. Locate the **Android SDK Manager** in the toolbar. You can also find it in **Tools | Android | Android SDK Manager** in the menu.
2. Click the highlighted button to open the **Android SDK Manager**, as shown in the following screenshot:

This is the control center for all SDK versions of Android that are installed on the system.

3. Expand the SDK version you want to install. In our case, this should be at least **Android 9.0 - Pie**.

4. Select the **Android SDK Platform <version number>** node. You can also select which emulator images will be used by the emulator to run the selected version of Android.

5. Click **Apply Changes**, as shown in the following screenshot:

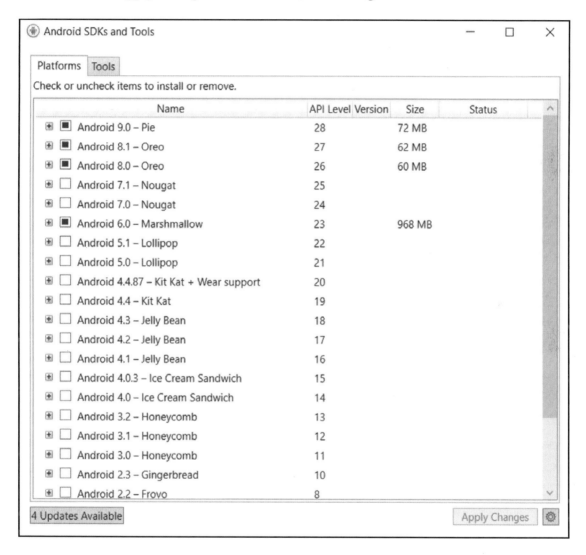

Android SDKs and Tools

Platforms Tools

Check or uncheck items to install or remove.

Name	API Level	Version	Size	Status
Android 9.0 – Pie	28		72 MB	
Android 8.1 – Oreo	27		62 MB	
Android 8.0 – Oreo	26		60 MB	
Android 7.1 – Nougat	25			
Android 7.0 – Nougat	24			
Android 6.0 – Marshmallow	23		968 MB	
Android 5.1 – Lollipop	22			
Android 5.0 – Lollipop	21			
Android 4.4.87 – Kit Kat + Wear support	20			
Android 4.4 – Kit Kat	19			
Android 4.3 – Jelly Bean	18			
Android 4.2 – Jelly Bean	17			
Android 4.1 – Jelly Bean	16			
Android 4.0.3 – Ice Cream Sandwich	15			
Android 4.0 – Ice Cream Sandwich	14			
Android 3.2 – Honeycomb	13			
Android 3.1 – Honeycomb	12			
Android 3.0 – Honeycomb	11			
Android 2.3 – Gingerbread	10			
Android 2.2 – Froyo	8			

4 Updates Available   Apply Changes

Adding the camera permission to Android

In order to get access to the camera in Android, we must add the required permission to the Android manifest. This can be done by following these steps:

1. In the **Solution Explorer**, open up the Android project node.
2. Double-click the **Properties** node to open the properties for Android.
3. Click the **Android Manifest** tab on the left, and scroll down until you see the **Required permissions:** section.
4. Locate the **CAMERA** permission and check the box.
5. Save the file by pressing *Ctrl + S* or **File**, and then **Save**. You can see the aforementioned fields and options that you need to select in the following screenshot:

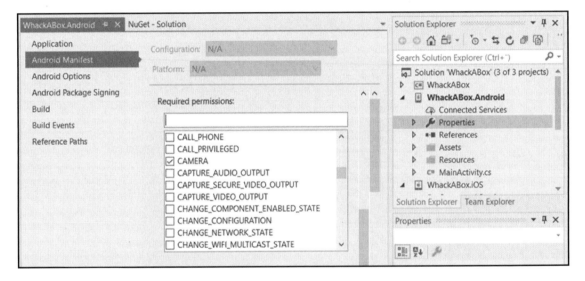

Now that we have configured Android, we only have one small change to make on iOS before we are ready to write some code.

Adding a camera usage description for iOS

In iOS, you need to specify why you need access to the camera. The way to do this is to add an entry to the `Info.plist` file in the root folder of the iOS project. The `Info.plist` file is an **Extensible Markup Language** (**XML**) file that you can edit in any text editor. A simpler way to do this, however, is by using the **Generic PList Editor** provided by Visual Studio.

Add the required **Camera Usage Description** using the **Generic PList Editor**, as follows:

1. Locate the `WhackABox.iOS` project.
2. Right-click on `Info.plist` and click **Open With...**, as shown in the following screenshot:

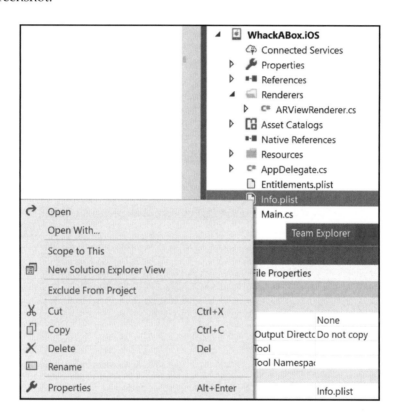

3. Select **Generic PList Editor** and click **OK**, as shown in the following screenshot:

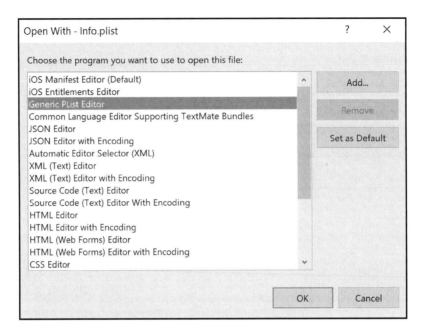

4. Locate the plus (+) icon at the bottom of the property list.
5. Click the plus (+) icon to add a new key. Make sure that the key is in the root of the document and not under another property, as shown in the following screenshot:

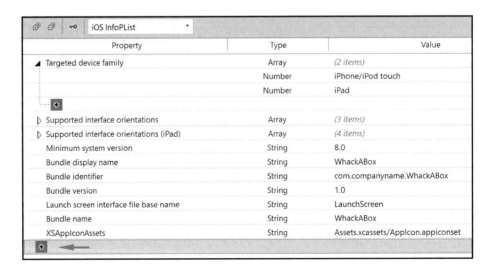

The **Generic PList Editor** helps you to find the right property by giving it a more user-friendly name. Let's add the value we need to describe why we want to use the camera, as follows:

1. Open the drop-down menu on the newly created row.
2. Select **Privacy - Camera Usage Description**.
3. Write a good reason in the values field to the right, as shown in the following screenshot. The field for the reason is a free-text field, so use plain English to describe why your app needs access to the camera:

Minimum system version	String	8.0
Bundle display name	String	WhackABox
Bundle identifier	String	com.companyname.WhackABox
Bundle version	String	1.0
Launch screen interface file base name	String	LaunchScreen
Bundle name	String	WhackABox
XSAppIconAssets	String	Assets.xcassets/AppIcon.appiconset
Privacy - Camera Usage Description ▼	String	For augmented-reality!
⊕ Privacy - Camera Usage Description ▲		
Privacy - Contacts Usage Description		
Privacy - Health Share Usage Description		
Privacy - Health Update Usage Description		

That's it. The setup of both Android and iOS is complete, and we can now focus on the fun part—writing code!

> You can also open the `Info.plist` file in any text editor, since it's an XML file. The key's name is `NSCameraUsageDescription`, and it must be added as a direct child of the root node.

Defining the user interface

We are going to start off by defining the **user interface** (**UI**) that will wrap the AR components. First, we will define a custom control that we will use as a placeholder for injecting an `UrhoSurface` that will contain the AR components. Then, we will add this control in a grid that will contain some statistics about how many planes we have found and how many boxes are active in the world. The goal of the game is to find boxes in AR using your phone and tap on them to make them disappear.

Let's start by defining the custom `ARView` control.

Creating the ARView control

The `ARView` control belongs in the .NET Standard project since it will be a part of both applications. It's a standard Xamarin.Forms control that inherits directly from `Xamarin.Forms.View`. It will not load any **Extensible Application Markup Language (XAML)** (so it will simply be a single class), nor will it contain any functionality other than simply being defined, so we can add it to the main grid.

Go over to Visual Studio and go through the following three steps to create an `ARView` control:

1. In the `WhackABox` project, add a folder called `Controls`.
2. In the `Controls` folder, create a new class called `ARView`.
3. Add the following code to the `ARView` class:

```
using Xamarin.Forms;

namespace WhackABox.Controls
{
    public class ARView : View
    {
    }
}
```

What we have created here is a simple class, without implementation, that inherits from `Xamarin.Forms.View`. The point of this is to make use of custom renderers for each platform, allowing us to specify platform-specific code to be inserted at the place in the XAML code where we put this control. Your project should now look as follows:

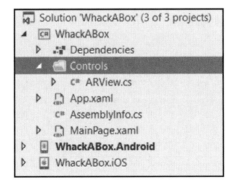

The `ARView` control is no good just sitting there. We need to add it to the `MainPage` XAML code.

Modifying the MainPage

We will be replacing the entire contents of the `MainPage` and adding a reference to the `WhackABox.Controls` namespace so that we can use the `ARView` control. Let's set this up by going through the following steps:

1. In the `WhackABox` project, open the `MainPage.xaml` file.

2. Edit the XAML code to look like the following code. The XAML in bold represents the new elements that must be added:

```xml
<?xml version="1.0" encoding="utf-8"?>
<ContentPage xmlns="http://xamarin.com/schemas/2014/forms"
xmlns:x="http://schemas.microsoft.com/winfx/2009/xaml"
            xmlns:local="clr-namespace:WhackABox"
            xmlns:controls="clr-namespace:WhackABox.Controls"
            x:Class="WhackABox.MainPage">
<Grid>
  <Grid.ColumnDefinitions>
    <ColumnDefinition Width="*" />
    <ColumnDefinition Width="*" />
  </Grid.ColumnDefinitions>

  <Grid.RowDefinitions>
    <RowDefinition Height="100" />
    <RowDefinition Height="*" />
  </Grid.RowDefinitions>

  <StackLayout Grid.Row="0" Padding="10">
    <Label Text="Plane count" />
    <Label Text="0" FontSize="Large"
           x:Name="planeCountLabel" />
  </StackLayout>

  <StackLayout Grid.Row="0" Grid.Column="1" Padding="10">
    <Label Text="Box count" />
    <Label Text="0" FontSize="Large"
           x:Name="boxCountLabel"/>
  </StackLayout>

  <controls:ARView Grid.Row="1" Grid.ColumnSpan="2" />
</Grid>
</ContentPage>
```

Now that we have the code, let's go through it step by step, as follows:

- First, we define a `controls` namespace that points to the `WhackABox.Controls` namespace in code. This namespace is used at the end of the XAML to locate the `ARView` control.
- We then define the content element by setting it to a `Grid`. A page can only have one child, which, in this case, is a `Grid`. The `Grid` defines two columns and two rows. The columns split the `Grid` into two equal parts, where we have one row that is `100` units high at the top and one row that takes up all the available space below it.
- We use the top two cells to add instances of `StackLayout` that contain information about the number of planes and the number of boxes in the game. The location of those instances of `StackLayout` in the grid is defined by the `Grid.Row=".."` and `Grid.Column=".."` attributes. Remember that the rows and columns are zero-based. You don't actually have to add attributes for the row or column `0` but it can sometimes be a good practice, to improve code readability.
- Finally, we have the `ARView` control, which resides in row `1` but spans both columns by specifying `Grid.ColumnSpan="2"`.

The next step is to install UrhoSharp, which will be our library for rendering graphics to represent the augmented part of our reality.

Adding UrhoSharp

Urho is an open source 3D game engine. UrhoSharp is a package that contains bindings to iOS and Android binaries, enabling us to use Urho in .NET. It is a very competent piece of software, and we will only be using a very small part of it to do the heavy lifting when it comes to rendering planes and boxes in the app. We urge you to find out more about UrhoSharp to add your own cool features to the app. One great place to start is at `https://github.com/xamarin/urho`.

All you have to do to install UrhoSharp is download a NuGet package for each platform. The iOS platform uses the UrhoSharp NuGet package, and Android uses the UrhoSharp.ARCore package. Also, in Android, we need to add some code to wire up life cycle events, but we will get to that later. Basically, we will set up an `UrhoSurface` on each platform. We will access this to add nodes to the node tree. These nodes will then be rendered based on their type and properties.

First, however, we need to install the packages.

Installing the UrhoSharp NuGet package for iOS and the .NET Standard project

For the `WhackABox` and the `WhackABox.iOS` project, we need to add the UrhoSharp NuGet package. This contains everything we need for our AR app. You can add the package as follows:

1. Right-click on the `WhackABox` solution.
2. Click **Manage NuGet Packages for Solution...**, as shown in the following screenshot:

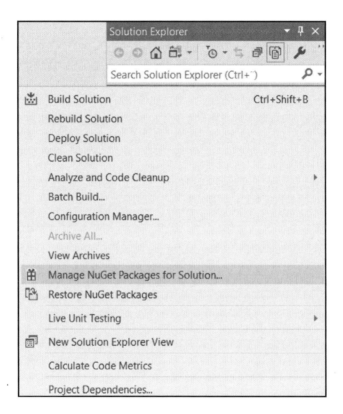

3. This opens the **NuGet Package Manager** window. Click the **Browse** link on the top left of the window.

4. Enter `Urhosharp` in the search box, and hit *Enter*.

5. Select the **UrhoSharp** package, check the `WhackABox` project and the `WhackABox.iOS` project, and click **Install** on the right side of the window, as shown in the following screenshot:

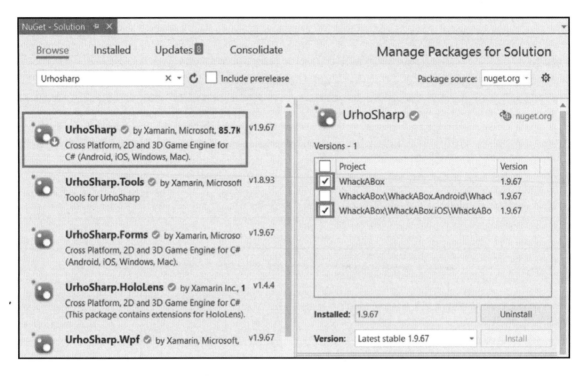

That's it for the `WhackABox` and the `WhackABox.iOS` projects. Android is a little bit trickier to set up, since it needs a special UrhoSharp package and some code to be written to wire everything up.

Installing the UrhoSharp.ARCore NuGet package for Android

For Android, we will be adding the UrhoSharp.ARCore package, which contains extensions for ARCore. It has a dependency on UrhoSharp, so we don't have to add that package specifically. You can add the UrhoSharp.ARCore package as follows:

1. Right-click on the `WhackABox.Android` project.
2. Click **Manage NuGet Packages...**, as shown in the following screenshot:

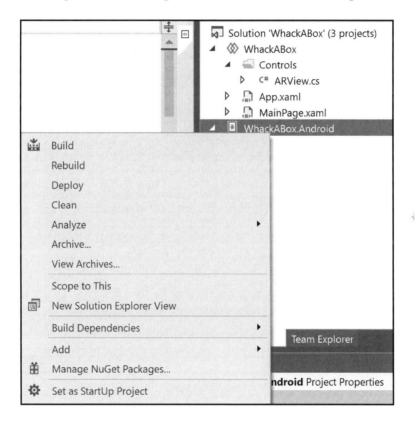

3. This opens the **NuGet Package Manager** window. Click the **Browse** link on the top left of the window.
4. Enter `UrhoSharp.ARCore` in the search box, and hit *Enter*.

5. Select the **UrhoSharp.ARCore** package and click **Install** on the right side of the window, as shown in the following screenshot:

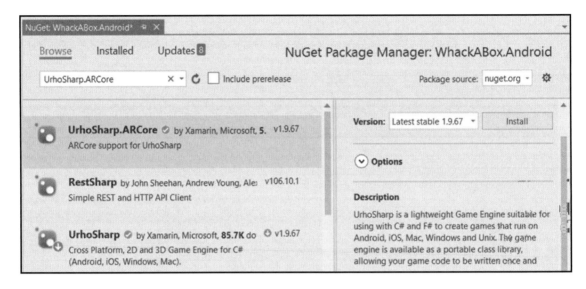

That's it—all your dependencies on UrhoSharp have been installed in the project. We now have to wire up some life cycle events.

Adding the Android life cycle events

In Android, **Urho** needs to know about some specific events and be able to respond to them accordingly. We also need to add an internal message using `MessagingCenter` so that we can react to the `OnResume` event later on in the app. We will get to that when we add the code to initialize ARCore. But for now, add the five required overrides for Android events, as follows:

1. In the Android project, open `MainActivity.cs`.
2. Add the five overrides from the following code anywhere in the `MainActivity` class and the unresolved references by adding `using` statements for `Urho.Droid` and `Xamarin.Forms`, as shown in the following code block:

```
protected override void OnResume()
{
    base.OnResume();
    UrhoSurface.OnResume();

    MessagingCenter.Send(this, "OnResume");
```

```
    }

    protected override void OnPause()
    {
        UrhoSurface.OnPause();
        base.OnPause();
    }

    protected override void OnDestroy()
    {
        UrhoSurface.OnDestroy();
        base.OnDestroy();
    }

    public override void OnBackPressed()
    {
        UrhoSurface.OnDestroy();
        Finish();
    }

    public override void OnLowMemory()
    {
        UrhoSurface.OnLowMemory();
        base.OnLowMemory();
    }
```

The events map one-on-one to internal UrhoSharp events, except for `OnBackPressed`, which calls `UrhoSharp.OnDestroy()`. The reason for this is for memory management so that UrhoSharp knows when to clean up.

 The `MessagingCenter` library is a built-in Xamarin.Forms pub/sub library for passing internal messages in an app. It has a dependency on Xamarin.Forms. We have created a library of our own called `TinyPubSub` that breaks this dependency and has a slightly easier API (as well as some additional features). You can check it out on GitHub at `https://github.com/TinyStuff/TinyPubSub`.

Defining the PlaneNode class

In `Urho`, you work with scenes that contain a tree of nodes. A node can be just about anything in the game, such as a renderer, a sound player, or simply a placeholder for subnodes.

As we talked about earlier when discussing AR fundamentals, planes are a common entity that is shared between the platforms. We need to create a common ground that represents a plane, which we can do by extending an `Urho` node. The position and the rotation will be tracked by the node itself, but we need to add a property to track the origin and the size of the plane, expressed by ARKit and ARCore as the extent of the plane.

We will add this class now and put it to use when we implement the AR-related code on each platform. The code to do this is straightforward, and can be set up by going through the following steps:

1. In the `WhackABox` project root, create a new file called `PlaneNode.cs`.
2. Add the following implementation of the class:

```
using Urho;

namespace WhackABox
{
    public class PlaneNode :Node
    {
        public string PlaneId { get; set; }
        public float ExtentX { get; set; }
        public float ExtentZ { get; set; }
    }
}
```

The `PlaneId` property will be an identifier that allows us to track which platform-specific plane this node represents. In iOS, this will be a string, while in Android, it will be the hashcode of the plane object that is converted to a string. The `ExtentY` and `ExtentZ` properties represent the size of the plane in meters. We are now ready to start creating the game logic and hooking up our application to the AR SDKs.

Adding custom renderers for the ARView control

Custom renderers are a very smart way of extending platform-specific behaviors to custom controls. They can also be used to override behaviors on controls that are already defined. In fact, all of the controls in Xamarin.Forms use renderers to translate the Xamarin.Forms control into a platform-specific control.

We are going to create two renderers, one for iOS and one for Android, that initialize the `UrhoSurface` on which we are going to render. The instantiation of the `UrhoSurface` differs on each platform, which is why we need two different implementations.

For iOS

A custom renderer is a class that inherits from another renderer. It allows us to add custom code for important events, such as when an element in XAML is created when the XAML file is parsed. Since the ARView control inherits from the View, we will be using ViewRenderer as a base class. Let's create the ARViewRenderer class by going through the following steps:

1. In the WhackABox.iOS project, create a folder called Renderers.
2. In that folder, add a new class called ARViewRenderer.
3. Add the following code to the class:

```
using System.Threading.Tasks;
using Urho.iOS;
using WhackABox.Controls;
using WhackABox.iOS.Renderers;using Xamarin.Forms;
using Xamarin.Forms.Platform.iOS;

[assembly: ExportRenderer(typeof(ARView), typeof(ARViewRenderer))]
namespace WhackABox.iOS.Renderers
{
    public class ARViewRenderer : ViewRenderer<ARView, UrhoSurface>
    {
        protected async override void
        OnElementChanged(ElementChangedEventArgs<ARView> e)
        {
            base.OnElementChanged(e);

            if (Control == null)
            {
                await Initialize();
            }
        }

        private async Task Initialize()
        {
            var surface = new UrhoSurface();
            SetNativeControl(surface);
            await surface.Show<Game>();
        }
    }
}
```

The `ExportRenderer` attribute registers this renderer to Xamarin.Forms so that it knows that when it parses (or compiles) an `ARView` element, it should render it using this specific renderer. It takes two arguments: the first is the control that we want to register a renderer to, and the second is the type of the renderer. This attribute must be placed outside the namespace declarations.

The `ARViewRenderer` class inherits `ViewRenderer<ARView, UrhoSurface>`. This specifies which control this renderer is created for and which native control it should render. In this case, the `ARView` element will be natively replaced by a `UrhoSurface` control that in itself is an iOS-specific `UIView`.

We override the `OnElementChanged()` method that is called every time the `ARView` element changes, either when it is created or when it is replaced. We can then check whether the `Control` property is set. The control is of the `UrhoSurface` type since we declared that in the class definition. If it's `null`, then we make a call to `Initialize()` to create it.

The creation is straightforward. We simply create a new `UrhoSurface` control and set the native control to this newly created object. We then call the `Show<Game>()` method to start the game by specifying which class represents our `Urho` game. Note that the `Game` class is not defined yet, but it will be very soon, right after we create the custom renderer for Android.

For Android

The custom renderer for Android does the same thing as it does for iOS, but with the additional step of checking permissions. Let's create the `ARViewRenderer` class for Android by going through the following steps:

1. In the `WhackABox.Droid` project, create a folder called `Renderers`.
2. In that folder, add a new class called `ARViewRenderer`.
3. Add the following code to the class:

```
using System.Threading.Tasks;
using Android;
using Android.App;
using Android.Content;
using Android.Content.PM;
using Android.Support.V4.App;
using Android.Support.V4.Content;
using WhackABox.Droid.Renderers;
using WhackABox;
using WhackABox.Controls;
```

```
using WhackABox.Droid;
using Urho.Droid;
using Xamarin.Forms;
using Xamarin.Forms.Platform.Android;

[assembly: ExportRenderer(typeof(ARView),
typeof(ARViewRenderer))]
namespace WhackABox.Droid.Renderers
{
    public class ARViewRenderer : ViewRenderer<ARView,
    Android.Views.View>
    {
        private UrhoSurfacePlaceholder surface;
        public ARViewRenderer(Context context) : base(context)
        {
            MessagingCenter.Subscribe<MainActivity>(this,
            "OnResume", async (sender) =>
            {
                await Initialize();
            });
        }

        protected async override void
        OnElementChanged(ElementChangedEventArgs<ARView> e)
        {
            base.OnElementChanged(e);

            if (Control == null)
            {
                await Initialize();
            }
        }

        private async Task Initialize()
        {
            if (ContextCompat.CheckSelfPermission(Context,
                Manifest.Permission.Camera) != Permission.Granted)
            {
                ActivityCompat.RequestPermissions(Context as
                Activity, new[] { Manifest.Permission.Camera },
                42);
                return;
            }

            if (surface != null)
                return;

            surface = UrhoSurface.CreateSurface(Context as
```

```
                    Activity);
                SetNativeControl(surface);
                await surface.Show<Game>();
            }
        }
    }
```

This custom renderer also inherits from `ViewRenderer<T1, T2>`, where the first type is the type of the renderer itself and the second is the native control that the renderer will produce. In this case, the native control will be a control that inherits from `Android.Views.View`. The renderer creates a `UrhoSurfacePlaceholder` instance, which it assigns as the native control. `UrhoSurfacePlaceholder` is a class that wraps some functionality of the **Simple DirectMedia Layer** (**SDL**) library that `Urho` uses on Android to access media functionality. The last thing it does is to start the game based on the soon-to-exist `Game` class. We will define this in the next section of this chapter.

Creating the game

To write an application that uses `Urho`, we need to create a class that inherits from `Urho.Application`. This class defines some virtual methods that we can use to set up the scene. The method we will use is `Start()`. Before that, however, we need to create the class. We will create it as an abstract class in the `WhackABox` project that will be used as a base class in each of the platform projects.

Adding the shared abstract Game class

We start by creating the `Game.cs` file that will contain shared code. Let's set this up by going through the following steps:

1. In the `WhackABox` project, create a new file called `Game.cs` in the root of the project.
2. Add the following code to the class:

```csharp
using System;
using System.Linq;
using Urho;
using Urho.Shapes;

namespace WhackABox
{
    public abstract class Game : Application
    {
```

```
        protected Scene scene;

        public Game(ApplicationOptions options) : base(options)
        {
        }
    }
}
```

The `Game` inherits from `Urho.Application`, which will do most of the work regarding the game itself. We define a property called `scene`, of the `Scene` type. A `Scene` in `Urho` represents one screen of the game (we could have different scenes for different parts of a game or for a menu, for example). In this game, we will only be defining one scene, which will be initialized later. A `scene` maintains a hierarchy of nodes that compose it, and each node can have any number of children and any number of components. It's the components that do the work. Later on, for example, we will be rendering boxes, which will be represented by a node that will have a `Box` component attached.

The `Game` class itself is instantiated from the custom renderers that we defined in the earlier section, and it takes an `ApplicationOptions` instance as a parameter in the constructor. This needs to be passed to the base class. We now need to write some methods that will be AR-specific and used by the code we will write later on.

InitializeAR

We need a common entry point for iOS and Android to hook up to. Since the initialization of ARKit and ARCore is platform-specific, we will simply define an abstract method that each platform can override. You can do this by following these steps:

1. In the `WhackABox` project, open the `Game.cs` class.
2. Add the following `InitializeAR()` method to the class:

```
        protected abstract void InitializeAR();
```

Since the class is itself abstract, we can also define methods as abstract. This means that this method must be implemented by any class that inherits from the `Game` class.

CreateSubPlane

The next method is the `CreateSubPlane()` method. When the application finds a plane on which we can place objects, it will create a node. We will write that code specifically for each platform soon. This node also defines a subplane that will position a box, representing the position and size of that plane. We have already defined the `PlaneNode` class earlier in this chapter.

Let's add the code by going through the following steps:

1. In the `WhackABox` project, open the `Game.cs` class.
2. Add the following `CreateSubPlane()` method to the class:

```
protected void CreateSubPlane(PlaneNode planeNode)
{
    var node = planeNode.CreateChild("subplane");
    node.Position = new Vector3(0, 0.05f, 0);

    var box = node.CreateComponent<Box>();
    box.Color = Color.FromHex("#22ff0000");
}
```

Any class inheriting from `Urho.Node`, such as `PlaneNode`, has the `CreateChild()` method. This allows us to create a child node and specify a name for that node. That name will be used later on to find specific children to perform operations on. We position the node at the same position as the parent node, except that we raise it `0.05` meters (5 cm) above the plane.

To see the plane, we add a `box` component with a semi-transparent red color. The `box` is a component that is created with a call to `CreateComponent()` on our node. The color is defined using the AARRGGBB pattern, where AA is the alpha component (the transparency) and RRGGBB is the standard red-green-blue format. We use the hexadecimal representation of the colors.

UpdateSubPlane

Both ARKit and ARCore update planes continuously. What we are interested in are changes in the position of a subplane and the extent of it. By extension, we are referring to the size of the plane. Let's set this up by going through the following steps:

1. In the `WhackABox` project, open the `Game.cs` class.
2. Add the `UpdateSubPlane()` method in the code anywhere in the `Game.cs` class, as shown in the following code snippet:

```
protected void UpdateSubPlane(PlaneNode planeNode, Vector3
position)
{
    var subPlaneNode = planeNode.GetChild("subplane");
    subPlaneNode.Scale = new Vector3(planeNode.ExtentX, 0.05f,
    planeNode.ExtentZ);
    subPlaneNode.Position = position;
}
```

The method takes the `PlaneNode` instance that we want to update, along with a new position for it. We locate the subplane by querying the current node for any node called `"subplane"`. Remember that we named the subplane in the `AddSubPlane()` method. We can now easily access the node by name. We update the scale of the subplane node by taking the `ExtentX` and `ExtentZ` properties from the `PlaneNode`. The `PlaneNode` instance will be updated by some platform-specific code before we call `UpdateSubPlane()`. Finally, we set the position of the subplane to the passed `position` parameter.

FindNodeByPlaneId

We need a method to quickly find nodes. Both ARKit and ARCore keep an internal track of their planes, and to map those internal representations of planes to our `PlaneNode`, we have to assign a custom ID to a plane when it's created. This will be done in the platform-specific code, but we can still write the function to query the scene for `PlaneNode`.

The `planeId` argument is a `string`, since ARKit defines the plane ID in a form that resembles a **Globally Unique Identifier** (**GUID**). A GUID is a structured sequence of hexadecimal numbers that can be represented in a `string` format. Let's add a method that will find the node that we are looking for by using this ID, as follows:

1. In the `WhackABox` project, open the `Game.cs` class.
2. Add the `FindNodeByPlaneId()` method in the code anywhere in the `Game.cs` class, as shown in the following code snippet:

```
protected PlaneNode FindNodeByPlaneId(string planeId)
{
    return scene.Children.OfType<PlaneNode>().FirstOrDefault(e =>
    e.PlaneId == planeId);
}
```

The method queries the scene by using `Linq`, and looks for the first child with the plane ID that it was given. If it can't find one, it returns `null`, since `null` is the default value of a reference type object.

These are all of the methods that we need in the shared code before dropping down into ARKit and ARCore.

Adding platform-specific classes

It's now time to add platform-specific code. We will create two classes, one for iOS and one for Android, which will inherit from the abstract `Game` class.

In this section, we will simply set up the skeleton code for these files.

Adding the iOS-specific class

Let's start by creating the class for Game on iOS, as follows:

1. In the WhackABox.iOS project root, add a new file called Game.cs.
2. Add the code to the class, as shown in the following snippet:

```
using Urho;

namespace WhackABox.iOS
{
    public class Game : WhackABox.Game
    {
        public Game(ApplicationOptions options) : base(options)
        {
        }
    }
}
```

Since the abstract base class requires a constructor to be called, we need to extend that constructor into our platform-specific class. Now, let's do the same thing for Android.

Adding the Android-specific class

The same goes for Android: only the namespace changes. Let's set this up by going through the following steps:

1. In the WhackABox.Android project, add a new file called Game.cs.
2. Add the code as shown in the following snippet:

```
using Urho;

namespace WhackABox.Droid
{
    public class Game : WhackABox.Game
    {
        public Game(ApplicationOptions options) : base(options)
        {
        }
    }
}
```

As you see, it's identical compared to the iOS code except for the namespace. Let's now start adding some platform-specific code.

Writing the ARKit-specific code

In this section, we will write the platform-specific code for iOS that will initialize ARKit, find planes, and create nodes for UrhoSharp to render on the screen. We will be taking advantage of an Urho component that wraps ARKit in iOS. We will also be writing all the functions that will position, add, and remove nodes. ARKit uses anchors, which act as virtual points that glue the overlaid graphics to the real world. We are specifically looking for ARPlaneAnchor, which represents a plane in the AR world. There are other types of anchors available, but for this app, we only need to find horizontal planes.

Let's start off by defining the ARKitComponent field so that we can use it later.

Defining the ARKitComponent

We start by adding a private field to an ARKitComponent that will be initialized later on. Let's set this up by going through the following steps:

1. In the WhackABox.iOS project, open Game.cs.
2. Add a private field that holds an ARKitComponent, as shown in bold in the following code block:

```
using System.Linq;
using ARKit;
using Urho;
using Urho.iOS;

namespace WhackABox.iOS
{
    public class Game : WhackABox.Game
    {
        protected ARKitComponent arkitComponent;

        public Game(ApplicationOptions options) : base(options)
        {
        }
    }
}
```

Make sure that you add all the `using` statements to ensure that all the code we later use resolves the correct types.

Writing handlers for adding and updating anchors

We will now add the necessary code that will add and update anchors. We will also add some methods to help set the orientation of the nodes after ARKit updates the anchors.

SetPositionAndRotation

The `SetPositionAndRotation()` method will be used by both the Add and Update anchors, so we need to define it before creating the handlers for the events that will be raised by ARKit. Let's set this up by going through the following steps:

1. In the `WhackABox.iOS` project, open the `Game.cs` file.
2. Add the `SetPositionAndRotation()` method to the class, as shown in the following code block:

```
private void SetPositionAndRotation(ARPlaneAnchor anchor, PlaneNode
                                    node)
{
    arkitComponent.ApplyOpenTkTransform(node, anchor.Transform,
                                        true);

    node.ExtentX = anchor.Extent.X;
    node.ExtentZ = anchor.Extent.Z;

    var position = new Vector3(anchor.Center.X, anchor.Center.Y, -
                              anchor.Center.Z);
    UpdateSubPlane(node, position);
}
```

The method takes two parameters. The first is an `ARPlaneAnchor` object defined by ARKit, and the second is the `PlaneNode` instance that we have in the scene. The purpose of the method is to make sure that the `PlaneNode` is in sync with the `ARPlaneAnchor` object passed by ARKit. The `arkitComponent` object has a helper method called `ApplyOpenTkTransform()` to translate the position and rotation of the `ARPlaneAnchor` object into the position and rotation objects used by `Urho`. We then update the `Extent` (size) of the plane to the `PlaneNode` and get the `anchor` center position from the `ARPlaneAnchor`. Finally, we call a method that we defined earlier to update the subplane node that holds the `Box` component that will do the actual rendering of the plane as a semi-transparent red box.

We need one more method to handle the update and add functionality.

UpdateOrAddPlaneNode

The UpdateOrAddPlaneNode() method does exactly what the name implies: it takes an ARPlaneAnchor as an argument and either updates or adds a new PlaneNode instance to the scene. Let's set this up by going through the following steps:

1. In the WhackABox.iOS project, open the Game.cs file.
2. Add the UpdateOrAddPlaneNode() method, as shown in the following code block:

```
private void UpdateOrAddPlaneNode(ARPlaneAnchor anchor)
{
    var node = FindNodeByPlaneId(anchor.Identifier.ToString());

    if (node == null)
    {
        node = new PlaneNode()
        {
            PlaneId = anchor.Identifier.ToString(),
            Name = $"plane{anchor.GetHashCode()}"
        };

        CreateSubPlane(node);
        scene.AddChild(node);
    }

    SetPositionAndRotation(anchor, node);
}
```

A node is either already present in the scene or it needs to be added. The first line of code calls the FindNodeByPlaneId() method to query the scene for an object with the given PlaneId. For iOS, we use the anchor.Identifier property to track planes defined by iOS. If this call returns null, it means that the plane is not present in the scene and we need to create it. To do this, we instantiate a new PlaneNode instance, giving it a PlaneId and a user-friendly name for debugging purposes. We then create the subplane to visualize the plane itself by calling CreateSubPlane() (which we defined earlier) and add the node to the scene. Lastly, we update the position and rotation. We do this for every call to the UpdateOrAddPlaneNode() method since it's the same for both new and existing nodes. It's now time to write the handlers that we will eventually hook up to ARKit directly.

OnAddAnchor

Let's add some code. The `OnAddAnchor()` method will be called each time ARKit updates its collection of anchors that describe points that we will use to relate to within our virtual world. We are specifically looking for anchors of the `ARPlaneAnchor` type.

Add the `OnAddAnchor()` (method to the `Game.cs` class by going through the following two steps:

1. In the `WhackABox.iOS` project, open the `Game.cs` file.
2. Add the `OnAddAnchor()` method anywhere in the class, as shown in the following code snippet:

```
private void OnAddAnchor(ARAnchor[] anchors)
{
    foreach (var anchor in anchors.OfType<ARPlaneAnchor>())
    {
        UpdateOrAddPlaneNode(anchor);
    }
}
```

The method takes an array of `ARAnchors` as a parameter. We filter out the anchors that are of the `ARPlaneAnchor` type and iterate through the list. For each `ARPlaneAnchor` object, we call the `UpdateOrAddPlaneNode()` method that we created earlier to add a node to the scene. Let's now do the same for when ARKit wants to update anchors.

OnUpdateAnchors

Each time ARKit receives new information about an anchor, it will call this method. We do the same as we did with the previous code and iterate through the list to update the extent and position of the `anchor` object in the scene, as follows:

1. In the `WhackABox.iOS` project, open the `Game.cs` file.
2. Add the `OnUpdateAnchors()` method anywhere in the class, as shown in the following code snippet:

```
private void OnUpdateAnchors(ARAnchor[] anchors)
{
    foreach (var anchor in anchors.OfType<ARPlaneAnchor>())
    {
        UpdateOrAddPlaneNode(anchor);
    }
}
```

The code is a copy of the `OnAddAnchors()` method. It updates all nodes in the scene based on the information provided by ARKit.

We also need to write some code to remove the anchors that ARKit has removed.

Writing a handler for removing anchors

When ARKit decides that an anchor is invalid, it will remove it from the scene. This does not happen very often, but it's a good practice to handle this call anyway.

OnRemoveAnchors

Let's add a method to handle the removal of an `ARPlaneAnchor` object by going through the following steps:

1. In the `WhackABox.iOS` project, open the `Game.cs` file.
2. Add the `OnRemoveAnchors()` method anywhere in the class, as shown in the following code snippet:

```
private void OnRemoveAnchors(ARAnchor[] anchors)
{
  foreach (var anchor in anchors.OfType<ARPlaneAnchor>())
  {
  FindNodeByPlaneId(anchor.Identifier.ToString())?.Remove();
  }
}
```

As with the `Add` and `Remove` functions, this method accepts an array of `ARAnchor`. We iterate through this array, looking for anchors of the `ARPlaneAnchor` type. We then look for a node that represents this plane by calling the `FindNodeByPlaneId()` method. If it's not `null`, then we call for that node to be removed. Note the null-check operator before the `Remove()` call.

Initializing ARKit

We've now come to the last part of the iOS-specific code, which is where we initialize ARKit. This method is called `InitializeAR()` and takes no parameters. It's defined as an abstract method in the `Game` base class and must be implemented by the `Game` class defined in the iOS project.

The code to initialize ARKit is straightforward, and the `ARKitComponent` class does a lot of work for us. Let's set it up by going through the following steps:

1. In the `WhackABox.iOS` project, open the `Game.cs` file.
2. Add the `InitializeAR()` method anywhere in the class, as shown in the following code block:

```
protected override void InitializeAR()
{
    arkitComponent = scene.CreateComponent<ARKitComponent>();
    arkitComponent.Orientation =
    UIKit.UIInterfaceOrientation.Portrait;
    arkitComponent.ARConfiguration = new
    ARWorldTrackingConfiguration
    {
        PlaneDetection = ARPlaneDetection.Horizontal
    };
    arkitComponent.DidAddAnchors += OnAddAnchor;
    arkitComponent.DidUpdateAnchors += OnUpdateAnchors;
    arkitComponent.DidRemoveAnchors += OnRemoveAnchors;
    arkitComponent.RunEngineFramesInARKitCallbakcs =
    Options.DelayedStart;
    arkitComponent.Run();
}
```

The code starts by creating an `ARKitComponent` class. We then set the allowed orientation and create an `ARWorldTrackingConfiguration` class that states that we are only interested in horizontal planes. To respond to the addition, updating, and removal of planes, we attach the event handlers we created earlier.

We instruct the `ARKitComponent` to delay calling the callbacks to allow ARKit to initialize properly. Note the spelling error in the `RunEngineFramesInARKitCallbakcs` property. This is a good example of why you need to carry out a review of your code since it will be hard to change this name without breaking backward compatibility. Naming is hard.

The last thing is to tell ARKit to start running. We do this by calling the `arkitComponent.Run()` method.

Writing the ARCore-specific code

It's now time to do the same for Android with ARCore. Just as with iOS, we are going to put all Android-specific code in a file of its own. This is the `Game.cs` file in the Android project that we created earlier.

Defining the ARCoreComponent

First, we are going to add a field that stores a reference to the ARCoreComponent instance. This wraps up most of the interaction with ARCore. The ARCoreComponent is defined in the UrhoSharp.ARCore NuGet package that we installed at the beginning of the chapter.

Let's add some using statements and the arCore private field by going through the following steps:

1. In the WhackABox.Droid project, open the Game.cs file.
2. Add the arCore private field, and also make sure that you add the using statements marked in bold in the following code block:

```
using Com.Google.AR.Core;
using Urho;
using Urho.Droid;

namespace WhackABox.Droid
{
    public class Game : WhackABox.Game
    {
        public Game(ApplicationOptions options) : base(options)
        {
        }

        private ARCoreComponent arCore;
    }
}
```

The using statements will allow us to resolve the types that we need in this file, and the arCore property will be a shorthand when we want to access ARCore functions.

We'll continue by adding some methods to this class.

SetPositionAndRotation

We need to add or update a `PlaneNode` whenever a plane is detected or updated. The `SetPositionAndRotation()` method updates the passed `PlaneNode` and sets properties on that node based on the content of the `AR.Core.Plane` object. Let's set this up by going through the following steps:

1. In the `WhackABox.Droid` project, open the `Game.cs` file.
2. Add the `SetPositionAndRotation()` method to the class, as shown in the following code block:

```
private void SetPositionAndRotation(Com.Google.AR.Core.Plane plane,
                                    PlaneNode node)
{
    node.ExtentX = plane.ExtentX;
    node.ExtentZ = plane.ExtentZ;
    node.Rotation = new Quaternion(plane.CenterPose.Qx(),
                                   plane.CenterPose.Qy(),
                                   plane.CenterPose.Qz(),
                                   -plane.CenterPose.Qw());

    node.Position = new Vector3(plane.CenterPose.Tx(),
                                plane.CenterPose.Ty(),
                                -plane.CenterPose.Tz());
}
```

The previous code updates the extent of the plane for the node and creates a rotation, `Quaternion`. Don't worry if you don't know what a `Quaternion` rotation is—few people do—but they seem to magically hold the rotation information of the model in a very flexible way. The `plane.CenterPose` property is a matrix that holds the position and orientation of the plane. Finally, we update the position of the node from the `CenterPose` property.

The next step is to create a method that handles frame updates from ARCore.

Writing a handler for ARFrame updates

Android handles updates from ARCore a little bit differently than ARKit, which exposes three different events for added, updated, and removed nodes. When using ARCore, these events get called whenever any changes occur, and the handler that will take care of this is the one we are about to add.

Let's add the method by going through the following steps:

1. In the `WhackABox.Droid` project, open the `Game.cs` file.
2. Add the `OnARFrameUpdated()` method anywhere in the class, as shown in the following code block:

```
private void OnARFrameUpdated(Frame arFrame)
{
    var all = arCore.Session.GetAllTrackables(
                Java.Lang.Class.FromType(
                typeof(Com.Google.AR.Core.Plane)));

    foreach (Com.Google.AR.Core.Plane plane in all)
    {
        var node =
        FindNodeByPlaneId(plane.GetHashCode().ToString());

        if (node == null)
        {
            node = new PlaneNode
            {
                PlaneId = plane.GetHashCode().ToString(),
                Name = $"plane{plane.GetHashCode()}"
            };

            CreateSubPlane(node);
            scene.AddChild(node);
        }

        SetPositionAndRotation(plane, node);
        UpdateSubPlane(node, Vector3.Zero);
    }
}
```

We start by querying the `arCore` component for all the planes that it keeps track of. We then iterate through this list and see whether we have any nodes in the scene by calling the `FindNodeByPlaneId()` method, using the hash code of the plane as the identifier. If we can't find any, we create a new `PlaneNode` and assign the hash code as the `PlaneId`. We then create a subplane that contains the `Box` component to visualize the plane, and, finally, we add it to the scene. We then update the position and the rotation of the plane and make a call to update the subplane as well. Now that we have the handler written, we need to hook it up.

Initializing ARCore

To initialize ARCore, we will add two methods. The first one is a method that will take care of the configuration of ARCore, called OnConfigRequested(). The second one is the InitializeAR() method that will be called from the shared Game class later on.

OnConfigRequested

ARCore needs to know a few things, just as with iOS. In Android, this is done by defining a method that the ARCore component will call upon initialization. To create the method, go through the following steps:

1. In the WhackABox.Droid project, open the Game.cs file.
2. Add the OnConfigRequested() method anywhere in the class, as shown in the following code snippet:

```
private void OnConfigRequested(Config config)
{
    config.SetPlaneFindingMode(Config.PlaneFindingMode.Horizontal);
    config.SetLightEstimationMode(Config.LightEstimationMode.AmbientInt
ensity);
    config.SetUpdateMode(Config.UpdateMode.LatestCameraImage);
}
```

The method takes a Config object, which will store any configuration you make in this method. First, we set which type of plane we want to find. We are interested in Horizontal planes for this game. We define the kind of light-estimation mode we want to use, and, finally, we select which update mode we want. In this case, we want to use the latest camera image available. You can do a lot of fine-tuning during configuration, but this is out of the scope of this book. Be sure to check out the documentation for ARCore to learn more about its awesome power.

We now have all the code we need to initialize ARCore.

InitializeAR

As mentioned previously, the `InitializeAR()` method is defined in the abstract base class. We will now implement it for Android by overriding it, as follows:

1. In the `WhackABox.Droid` project, open the `Game.cs` file.
2. Add the `InitializeAR()` method anywhere in the class, as shown in the following code snippet:

```
protected override void InitializeAR()
{
    arCore = scene.CreateComponent<ARCoreComponent>();
    arCore.ARFrameUpdated += OnARFrameUpdated;
    arCore.ConfigRequested += OnConfigRequested;
    arCore.Run();
}
```

The first step is to create the `ARCoreComponent` provided by UrhoSharp. This component wraps the initialization of the native ARCore classes. We then add two event handlers: one for taking care of frame updates, and one that will be called during initialization. The last thing we do is call the `Run()` method on the `ARCoreComponent` to start tracking the world.

Now that we have both ARKit and ARCore configured and ready to go, it's time to write the actual game.

Writing the game

In this section, we will initialize `Urho` by setting up the camera, lighting, and a renderer. All the remaining code will now be written in the abstract `Game` class in the `WhackABox` project (the .NET Standard library project). The camera is the object that determines where objects will be rendered. The AR components take care of updating the position of the camera to virtually track your phone so that any object we render will be in the same coordinate space as what you are looking at. First, we need a camera that will be the viewing point of the scene.

Adding a camera

Adding a camera is a straightforward process, as shown in the following steps:

1. In the `WhackABox` project, open the `Game.cs` file.
2. Add the `camera` property to the class, as shown in the following code snippet. A good practice is to place it right after the declaration of the class.

3. Add the `InitializeCamera()` method anywhere in the class, as shown in the following code snippet:

```
private Camera camera;

private void InitializeCamera()
{
    var cameraNode = scene.CreateChild("Camera");
    camera = cameraNode.CreateComponent<Camera>();
}
```

In UrhoSharp, everything is a node, just as everything is a `GameObject` in Unity, including the `camera` object. We create a new node, which we call `camera`, and then we create a `Camera` component on that node and keep the reference to it for later use.

Configuring a renderer

UrhoSharp needs to render the scene to a `viewport`. A game can have multiple viewports, based on multiple cameras. Think of a game where you drive a car. The main `viewport` will be the game from the perspective of the driver. Another `viewport` might be the rear-view mirrors, which would actually be cameras themselves that render what they see onto the main `viewport`. Let's set this up by going through the following steps:

1. In the `WhackABox` project, open the `Game.cs` file.
2. Add the `viewport` property to the class, as shown in the following code snippet. A good practice is to place it right after the declaration of the class itself, but placing it anywhere within the class will work.
3. Add the `InitializeRenderer()` method anywhere in the class, as shown in the following code snippet:

```
private Viewport viewport;

private void InitializeRenderer()
{
    viewport = new Viewport(Context, scene, camera, null);
    Renderer.SetViewport(0, viewport);
}
```

The `viewport` property will hold a reference to the `viewport` for later use. The `viewport` is created by instantiating a new `Viewport` class. The constructor of that class needs a `Context` provided by the base class, the `scene` that we will create while initializing the game, a camera to know which point in space to render from, and a render path, which we default to `null`. A render path allows for postprocessing of the frame created while rendering. This is also outside the scope of this book, but it is worth checking out as well.

Now, let there be light.

Adding lights

To make objects visible, we need to define some lighting. We do this by creating a method that defines the type of lighting we want in the game. Let's set this up by going through the following steps:

1. In the `WhackABox` project, open the `Game.cs` file.
2. Add the `InitializeLights()` method anywhere in the class, as shown in the following code block:

```
private void InitializeLights()
{
    var lightNode = camera.Node.CreateChild();
    lightNode.SetDirection(new Vector3(1f, -1.0f, 1f));
    var light = lightNode.CreateComponent<Light>();
    light.Range = 10;
    light.LightType = LightType.Directional;
    light.CastShadows = true;
    Renderer.ShadowMapSize *= 4;
}
```

Again, everything in UrhoSharp is a node, and lights are no exception to that rule. We create a generic node on the camera node by accessing the stored camera component and accessing the node it belongs to. We then set the direction of that node and create a `Light` component to define a light. The range of the light will be `10` units in length. The type is directional, meaning that it will shine from the position of the node in its defined direction. It will also cast shadows. We set the `ShadowMapSize` to four times the default value to give the shadow map some more resolution.

At this point, we have all we need to initialize UrhoSharp and the AR components.

Implementing the game startup

The base class of the Game class provides some virtual methods that we can override. One of these is Start(), which will be called shortly after the custom renderer has set up the UrhoSurface.

Add the method by going through the following steps:

1. In the WhackABox project, open the Game.cs file.
2. Add the Start() method anywhere in the class, as shown in the following code snippet:

```
protected override void Start()
{
    scene = new Scene(Context);
    var octree = scene.CreateComponent<Octree>();

    InitializeCamera();
    InitializeLights();
    InitializeRenderer();

    InitializeAR();
}
```

The scene that we have been talking about is created here in the first line of the method. This is the scene that we look at when UrhoSharp is running. It keeps track of all nodes that we add to it. All 3D games in UrhoSharp need an Octree, which is a component that implements spatial partitioning. It is used by the 3D engine to quickly find objects in a 3D space without having to query every single one in each frame. The second line of the method creates this component directly on the scene.

Following this, we have the four methods that initialize the camera, the lights, and the renderer, and which make a call to one of the two InitializeAR() methods, based on which platform we are compiling for. If you start the app at this point, you should see that it finds planes and renders them, but that nothing more happens. It's time to add something to interact with.

Adding boxes

We are now going to focus on adding virtual boxes to our augmented world. We are going to write two methods. The first one is the AddBox() method, which will add a new box at a random position on a plane. The second is an override of the OnUpdate() method that UrhoSharp calls with each frame to perform game logic.

AddBox()

To add boxes to a plane, we need to add a method to do so. This method is called AddBox(). Let's set this up by going through the following steps:

1. In the WhackABox project, open the Game.cs file.
2. Add the random property to the class (preferably at the top, but anywhere in the class will work).
3. Add the AddBox() method anywhere in the class, as shown in the following code block:

```
private static Random random = new Random();

private void AddBox(PlaneNode planeNode)
{
    var subPlaneNode = planeNode.GetChild("subplane");

    var boxNode = planeNode.CreateChild("Box");
    boxNode.SetScale(0.1f);

    var x = planeNode.ExtentX * (float)(random.NextDouble() -
        0.5f);
    var z = planeNode.ExtentZ * (float)(random.NextDouble() -
        0.5f);

    boxNode.Position = new Vector3(x, 0.1f, z) +
    subPlaneNode.Position;

    var box = boxNode.CreateComponent<Box>();
    box.Color = Color.Blue;
}
```

The static `random` object that we create will be used for randomizing the location of a box on a plane. We want to use a static `Random` instance since we don't want to risk creating multiple instances that may be seeded with the same value and therefore return the exact same sequence of random numbers. The method starts by finding the subplane child of the `PlaneNode` instance that we pass in by calling `planeNode.GetChild("subplane")`. We then create a node that will render the box. To make the box fit the world, we need to set the scale to `0.1`, which will make it 10 cm in size.

We then randomize the position of the box using the `ExtentX` and `ExtentZ` properties, multiplied by a new random value between `0` and `1` that we first subtract `0.5` from. This is to center the position since the position of the parent node is the center of the plane. Then, we set the position of the box node at the randomized position and `0.1` units above the plane. We also need to add the subplane's position, since it might be a little bit offset from the parent node. Finally, we add the actual box to be rendered and set the color to blue.

Let's now add code to call the `AddBox()` method, based on some game logic.

OnUpdate()

Many games use a game loop. This calls an `Update()` method, which takes an input and calculates the state of the game. UrhoSharp is no exception. The base class of our game has a virtual `OnUpdate()` method that we can override so that we can write code that will be executed with each frame. This method is called frequently, usually about 50 times per second.

We will now override the `Update()` method to add game logic that adds a new box every other second. Let's set this up by going through the following steps:

1. In the `WhackABox` project, open the `Game.cs` file.
2. Add the `newBoxTtl` field and the `newBoxIntervalInSeconds` field to the class at the beginning of the code as shown.
3. Add the `OnUpdate()` method anywhere in the class, as shown in the following code block:

```
private float newBoxTtl;
private readonly float newBoxIntervalInSeconds = 2;

protected override void OnUpdate(float timeStep)
{
    base.OnUpdate(timeStep);

    newBoxTtl -= timeStep;
```

```
if (newBoxTtl < 0)
{
    foreach (var node in scene.Children.OfType<PlaneNode>())
    {
        AddBox(node);
    }

    newBoxTtl += newBoxIntervalInSeconds;
}
}
```

The first field, `newBoxTtl`—where `Ttl` is **time to live (TTL)**—is an internal counter that will be reduced by the number of milliseconds that have passed since the last frame. When it falls below 0, we will add a new box to each plane of the scene. We find all instances of `PlaneNode` by querying the `Children` collection of the scene and returning only the children of the `PlaneNode` type. The second field, `newBoxIntervalInSeconds`, indicates how many seconds we will add to the `newBoxTtl` once it reaches 0. To know how much time has passed since the last frame, we use the `timeStep` parameter that is passed into the `OnUpdate()` method by UrhoSharp. The value of this parameter is the number of seconds since the last frame. It's usually a small value, which will be something such as 0.016 if the update loop runs at 50 frames per second. It could vary, though, which is why you will want to use this value to carry out the subtraction from `newBoxTtl`.

If you run the game now, you will see that boxes appear on the detected planes. We still cannot interact with them, however, and they look pretty boring. Let's continue by making them rotate.

Making boxes rotate

You can add your own components to UrhoSharp by creating a class that inherits from `Urho.Component`. We will be creating a component that will make the boxes spin around all three axes.

Creating the rotate component

As we mentioned, a component is a class that inherits from `Urho.Component`. This base class defines a virtual method called `OnUpdate()` that behaves in the same way as the `Update()` method on the `Game` class itself. This allows us to add logic to the component so that it can modify the state of the node it belongs to.

Let's create the `rotate` component by going through the following steps:

1. In the `WhackABox` project root, create a new class called `Rotator.cs`.
2. Add the following code:

```
using Urho;

namespace WhackABox
{
    public class Rotator : Component
    {
        public Vector3 RotationSpeed { get; set; }

        public Rotator()
        {
            ReceiveSceneUpdates = true;
        }

        protected override void OnUpdate(float timeStep)
        {
            Node.Rotate(new Quaternion(
                RotationSpeed.X * timeStep,
                RotationSpeed.Y * timeStep,
                RotationSpeed.Z * timeStep),
                TransformSpace.Local);
        }
    }
}
```

The `RotationSpeed` property will be used to determine the speed of rotation around any specific axis. It will be set when we assign the component to the `box` node in the next step. To enable the component to receive calls to the `OnUpdate()` method on each frame, we need to set the `ReceiveSceneUpdates` property to `true`. If we don't do this, the component will not be called by UrhoSharp at each update. It's set to `false` by default, for performance reasons.

All the fun happens in the `override` of the `OnUpdate()` method. We create a new quaternion to represent a new rotation state. Again, we don't need to know how this works in detail, only that quaternions belong to the mystical world of advanced mathematics. We multiply each axis in the `RotationSpeed` vector by the `timeStep` parameter to generate a new value. The `timeStep` parameter is the number of seconds that have passed since the last frame. We also define the rotation as being around the local coordinate space of this box.

Now that the component is created, we need to add it to the boxes.

Assigning the Rotator component

Adding the `Rotator` component is as simple as adding any other component. Let's set this up by going through the following steps:

1. In the `WhackABox` project, open the `Game.cs` file.
2. Update the `AddBox()` method by adding the code marked in bold in the following code block:

```
private void AddBox(PlaneNode planeNode)
{
    var subPlaneNode = planeNode.GetChild("subplane");

    var boxNode = planeNode.CreateChild("Box");
    boxNode.SetScale(0.1f);

    var x = planeNode.ExtentX * (float)(random.NextDouble() -
        0.5f);
    var z = planeNode.ExtentZ * (float)(random.NextDouble() -
        0.5f);

    boxNode.Position = new Vector3(x, 0.1f, z) +
    subPlaneNode.Position;

    var box = boxNode.CreateComponent<Box>();
    box.Color = Color.Blue;

    var rotationSpeed = new Vector3(10.0f, 20.0f, 30.0f);
    var rotator = new Rotator() { RotationSpeed = rotationSpeed };
    boxNode.AddComponent(rotator);
}
```

We begin by defining how we want the box to rotate by creating a new `Vector3` struct and assigning it to a new variable called `rotationSpeed`. In this case, we want it to rotate 10 units around the *x* axis, 20 units around the *y* axis, and 30 units around the *z* axis. We use the `rotationSpeed` variable to set the `RotationSpeed` property of the `Rotator` component that we instantiate in the second row of the code we added.

Finally, we add the component to the `box` node. The boxes should now rotate in an interesting way.

Adding a box hit-test

We now have rotating boxes that keep piling up. We need to add a way to remove boxes. The simplest thing would be to add a feature that removes boxes when we touch them, but we are going to make it a little fancier than that: whenever we touch a box, we want it to shrink and disappear before we remove it from the scene. To do this, we are going to use our newly acquired knowledge of components, and then add some code to determine whether we are touching a box.

Adding a death animation

The `Death` component that we are about to add has the same template as the `Rotator` component that we created in the last section. Let's add it by going through the following steps and taking a look at the code:

1. In the `WhackABox` project root, create a new class called `Death.cs`.
2. Replace the code in the class with the following code:

```
using Urho;
using System;

namespace WhackABox
{
    public class Death : Component
    {
        private float deathTtl = 1f;
        private float initialScale = 1;

        public Action OnDeath { get; set; }

        public Death()
        {
            ReceiveSceneUpdates = true;
        }

        public override void OnAttachedToNode(Node node)
        {
            initialScale = node.Scale.X;
        }

        protected override void OnUpdate(float timeStep)
        {
            Node.SetScale(deathTtl * initialScale);

            if (deathTtl < 0)
            {
```

```
            Node.Remove();
        }

        deathTtl -= timeStep;
    }
  }
}
```

We first define two fields. The `deathTtl` field determines how long the animation will be, in seconds. The `initialScale` field keeps track of the scale of the node when the component is attached to the node. To receive updates, we need to set `ReceiveSceneUpdates` to `true` in the constructor. The overridden `OnAttachedToNode()` method is called when the component is attached to a node. We use this method to set the `initialScale` field. After the component is attached, we start getting calls on each frame to `OnUpdate()`. On each call, we set a new scale of the node based on the `deathTtl` field multiplied by the `initialScale` field. When the `deathTtl` field reaches 0, we remove the node from the scene. If we don't reach zero, then we subtract the amount of time since the last frame was called, which is given to us by the `timeStep` parameter. All we need to do now is figure out when to add the `Death` component to a box.

DetermineHit()

We need a method that can interpret a touch on the 2D surface of the screen and figure out which boxes we are hitting using an imaginary ray traveling from the camera toward the scene we are looking at. This method is called `DetermineHit()`. Let's set this up by going through the following steps:

1. In the `WhackABox` project, open the `Game.cs` file.
2. Add the `DetermineHit()` method anywhere in the class, as shown in the following code block:

```
private void DetermineHit(float x, float y)
{
    var cameraRay = camera.GetScreenRay(x, y);
    var result = scene.GetComponent<Octree>
    ().RaycastSingle(cameraRay);

    if (result?.Node?.Name?.StartsWith("Box") == true)
    {
        var node = result?.Node;

        if (node.Components.OfType<Death>().Any())
        {
            return;
```

```
                    }

              node.CreateComponent<Death>();
        }
    }
```

The x and y parameters that are passed into the method range from 0 to 1, where 0 represents the left edge or top edge of the screen, and 1 represents the right edge or bottom edge of the screen. The exact center of the screen would be x=0.5 and y=0.5. Since we want to get a ray from the camera, we can use a method called GetScreenRay() directly on the camera component. This returns a ray from the camera in the scene in the same direction that the camera is set to. We use this ray and pass it to the Octree component's RaycastSingle() method, which returns a result that will contain a single node if one is hit.

We examine the results, perform multiple null checks, and—finally—check whether the name of the node starts with Box. If this is true, we check to see whether the box we hit is already doomed by examining whether there is a Death component attached. If there is, we return. If there isn't, we create a Death component and leave the box to die.

This all looks good so far. We now need something to call the DetermineHit() method.

OnTouchBegin()

Touches are handled as events in UrhoSharp, and this means that they require event handlers. Let's create a handler for the TouchBegin event by going through the following steps:

1. In the WhackABox project, open the Game.cs file.
2. Add the OnTouchBegin() method anywhere in the code, as shown in the following code snippet:

```
private void OnTouchBegin(TouchBeginEventArgs e)
{
    var x = (float)e.X / Graphics.Width;
    var y = (float)e.Y / Graphics.Height;

    DetermineHit(x, y);
}
```

When a touch is registered, this method will be called, and information about that touch event will be sent as a parameter. This parameter has an X and a Y property that represent the point on the screen that we have touched. Since the DetermineHit() method wants the values in the range of 0 to 1, we need to divide the X and Y coordinates by the width and height of the screen.

Once that is done, we call the DetermineHit() method. To complete this section, we just have to wire up the event.

Wiring up input

All that's left now is to wire up the event to the Input subsystem of UrhoSharp. This is done by adding a single line of code to the Start() method, as shown in the following steps:

1. In the WhackABox project, open the Game.cs file.
2. In the Start() method, add the code highlighted in bold in the following code block:

```
protected override void Start()
{
  scene = new Scene(Context);
  var octree = scene.CreateComponent<Octree>();

  InitializeCamera();
  InitializeLights();
  InitializeRenderer();

  Input.TouchBegin += OnTouchBegin;

  InitializeAR();
}
```

This wires up the TouchBegin event to our OnTouchBegin event handler.

If you run the game now, the boxes should animate and disappear when you tap on them. What we need now is some kind of statistic that shows how many planes there are and how many boxes are still alive.

Updating statistics

At the beginning of the chapter, we added some controls to the XAML that displayed the number of planes and boxes that were present in the game. It's now time to add some code to update those numbers. We will be using internal messaging to decouple the game from the Xamarin.Forms page that we use to display this information.

The game will send a message to the main page that will contain a class with all the information we need. The main page will receive this message and update the labels.

Defining a statistics class

We are going to use `MessagingCenter` in Xamarin.Forms, which allows us to send an object along with the message. We need to create a class that can carry the information we want to pass. Let's set this up by going through the following steps:

1. In the `WhackABox` project root, create a new class called `GameStats.cs`.
2. Add the following code to the class:

```
public class GameStats
{
    public int NumberOfPlanes { get; set; }
    public int NumberOfBoxes { get; set; }
}
```

The class will be a simple data carrier that indicates how many planes and boxes we have.

Sending updates via MessagingCenter

When a node is created or removed, we need to send statistics to anything that is listening. To do this, we need a new method that will go through the scene and count how many planes and boxes we have and then send a message. Let's set this up by going through the following steps:

1. In the `WhackABox` project, open the `Game.cs` file.
2. Add a method called `SendStats()` anywhere in the class, as shown in the following code block:

```
private void SendStats()
{
    var planes = scene.Children.OfType<PlaneNode>();
    var boxCount = 0;
```

```
foreach (var plane in planes)
{
    boxCount += plane.Children.Count(e => e.Name == "Box");
}

var stats = new GameStats()
{
    NumberOfBoxes = boxCount,
    NumberOfPlanes = planes.Count()
};

Xamarin.Forms.Device.BeginInvokeOnMainThread(() =>
{
    Xamarin.Forms.MessagingCenter.Send(this, "stats_updated",
    stats);
});
}
```

The method checks all children of the `scene` object to find nodes of the `PlaneNode` type. We iterate through all of these nodes and count how many of the node's children have the name `Box`, and then indicate this number in a variable called `boxCount`. When we have this information, we create a `GameStats` object and initialize it with the box count and the plane count.

The last step is to send the message. We have to make sure that we are using the UI thread (the `MainThread`) since we are going to update the **graphical user interface (GUI)**. Only the UI thread is allowed to touch the GUI. This is done by wrapping the `MessagingCenter.Send()` call in `BeginInvokeOnMainThread()`.

The message that is sent is `stats_updated`. It contains the stats information as an argument. Let's now make use of the `SendStats()` method.

Wiring up events

The scene has a lot of events that we can wire up. We will hook up to `NodeAdded` and `NodeRemoved` to determine when we need to send statistics information. Let's set this up by going through the following steps:

1. In the `WhackABox` project, open the `Game.cs` file.
2. In the `Start()` method, add the code that is highlighted in bold in the following code block:

    ```
    protected override void Start()
    {
    ```

```
scene = new Scene(Context);
scene.NodeAdded += (e) => SendStats();
scene.NodeRemoved += (e) => SendStats();
var octree = scene.CreateComponent<Octree>();

InitializeCamera();
InitializeLights();
InitializeRenderer();

Input.TouchEnd += OnTouchEnd;

InitializeAR();
}
```

Each time a node is either added or removed, a new message will be sent to the GUI.

Updating the GUI

This will be the last method we add to the game. It handles the information updates and also updates the labels in the GUI. Let's add it by going through the following steps:

1. In the WhackABox project, open the MainPage.xaml.cs file.
2. Add a method called StatsUpdated() anywhere in the code, as shown in the following code snippet:

```
private void StatsUpdated(Game sender, GameStats stats)
{
    boxCountLabel.Text = stats.NumberOfBoxes.ToString();
    planeCountLabel.Text = stats.NumberOfPlanes.ToString();
}
```

The method receives the GameStats object that we sent and updates the two labels in the GUI.

Subscribing to the updates in the MainPage class

The last line of code to add will wire up the `StatsUpdated` handler to an incoming message. Let's set this up by going through the following steps:

1. In the `WhackABox` project, open the `MainPage.xaml.cs` file.
2. In the constructor, add the line of code that is highlighted in bold in the following code snippet:

```
public MainPage()
{
    InitializeComponent();
    MessagingCenter.Subscribe<Game, GameStats>(this,
    "stats_updated", StatsUpdated);
}
```

This line of code hooks up an incoming message with the content `stats_updated` to the `StatsUpdated` method. Now, run the game and go out into the world to hunt down those boxes!

The completed app looks something like the following screenshot, with spinning boxes popping up at random locations:

Summary

In this chapter, we learned how to integrate AR into Xamarin.Forms by using custom renderers. We took advantage of UrhoSharp to use cross-platform rendering, components, and input management to interact with the world. We also learned a bit about `MessagingCenter`, which can be used to send internal in-process messages between different parts of an application to reduce coupling.

Next up, we are going to dive into machine learning and create an app that can recognize a hotdog in an image.

11
Hot Dog or Not Hot Dog Using Machine Learning

In this chapter, we will learn how to use machine learning to create a model that we can use for image classification. We will export the model as a TensorFlow model that we can use on Android devices and as a Core ML model that we can use on iOS devices. In order to train and export models, we will use Azure Cognitive Services and the Custom Vision service.

Once we have exported the models, we will learn how to use them for Android and iOS apps.

The following topics will be covered in this chapter:

- Training a model with Azure Cognitive Services and the Custom Vision service
- Using TensorFlow models for image classification on an Android device
- Using Core ML models for image classification on an iOS device

Technical requirements

To be able to complete this project, you need to have Visual Studio for Mac or PC installed, as well as the Xamarin components. See Chapter 1, *Introduction to Xamarin,* for more details on how to set up your environment. You also need an Azure account. If you have a Visual Studio subscription, there are a specific amount of Azure credits included each month. To activate your Azure benefits, go to https://my.visualstudio.com.

You can also create a free account, where you can use selected services for free over 12 months. You will get $200 worth of credit to explore any Azure service for 30 days, and you can also use the free services at any time. Read more at https://azure.microsoft.com/en-us/free/.

The source code for this chapter is available at the GitHub repository for the book at, `https://github.com/PacktPublishing/Xamarin.Forms-4-Projects/tree/master/Chapter11`.

Machine learning

The term **machine learning** was coined in 1959 by Arthur Samuel, an American pioneer in **artificial intelligence** (**AI**). Tom M. Mitchell, an American computer scientist, provided the following more formal definition of machine learning later:

> *"A computer program is said to learn from experience E with respect to some class of tasks T and performance measure P if its performance at tasks in T, as measured by P, improves with experience E."*

> *– Tom M. Mitchell*

In simpler terms, this quote describes a computer program that has the ability to learn without being explicitly programmed. In machine learning, algorithms are used to build a mathematical model of sample data or training data. The models are used for computer programs to make predictions and decisions without being explicitly programmed for the task in question.

Azure Cognitive Services – Custom Vision

Custom Vision is a tool or service that can be used for training models for image classification and for detecting objects in images. With Custom Vision, we are able to upload our own images and tag them so that they can be trained for image classification. If we train a model for object detection, we can also tag specific areas of an image. Because models are already pre-trained for basic image recognition, we don't need a large amount of data to get a great result. The recommendation is to have at least 30 images per tag.

When we have trained a model, we can use it with an **application programming interface** (**API**) that is part of the Custom Vision service. We can also export models for Core ML (iOS), TensorFlow (Android), the **Open Neural Network Exchange** (**ONNX**) (Windows), and to a Dockerfile (Azure IoT Edge, Azure Functions, and Azure ML). These models can be used to carry out classification or object detection without having a connection to the Custom Vision service.

You will need an Azure subscription to use it—go to `https://azure.com/free` to create a free subscription, which should be enough to complete this project.

Core ML

Core ML is a framework that was introduced in iOS 11. Core ML makes it possible to integrate machine learning models into iOS apps. On top of Core ML, we have three high-level APIs, as follows:

- Vision APIs for image analysis
- Natural language APIs for natural language processing
- GameplayKit for evaluating learned decision trees

 More information about Core ML can be found in the official documentation from Apple at `https://developer.apple.com/documentation/coreml`.

TensorFlow

TensorFlow is an open-source machine learning framework. But TensorFlow can be used for more than simply running models on mobile devices—it can also be used for training models. For running it on mobile devices, we have TensorFlow Lite. The models that are exported from Azure Cognitive Services are for TensorFlow Lite. There are also Xamarin bindings for TensorFlow Lite that are available as a NuGet package.

 More information about TensorFlow can be found in the official documentation at `https://www.tensorflow.org/`.

Project overview

If you have seen the TV series *Silicon Valley*, you have probably heard of the *Not Hotdog* application. In this chapter, we will learn how to build that app. The first part of this chapter will involve collecting the data that we will use for creating a machine learning model that can detect whether or not a photo contains a hot dog.

In the second part of the chapter, we will build an app for iOS and an app for Android, whereby the user can pick a photo in the photo library in order to analyze it to see whether it contains a hot dog. The estimated time for completing this project is 120 minutes.

Getting started

We can use either Visual Studio 2019 on a PC or Visual Studio for Mac to do this project. To build an iOS app using Visual Studio for PC, you must have a Mac connected. If you don't have access to a Mac at all, you can choose to just do the Android parts of this project. Similarly, if you only have a Mac, you can choose to just do the iOS or Android parts of this project.

Building the Hot Dog or Not Hot Dog application using machine learning

Let's get started! We will first train a model for image classification that we can use later in the chapter to decide whether a photo contains a hot dog.

Training a model

To train a model for image classification, we need to collect photos of hot dogs and photos that aren't of hot dogs. Because most items in the world are not hot dogs, we need more photos that don't contain hot dogs. It's better if the photos of hot dogs cover a lot of different hot-dog scenarios—with bread, with ketchup, or with mustard. This is so the model will be able to recognize hot dogs in different situations. When we are collecting photos that aren't of hot dogs, we also need to have a big variety of photos that are both of items that are similar to hot dogs and that are completely different from hot dogs.

The model that is in the solution on GitHub was trained with 240 photos, 60 of which were of hot dogs, and 180 of which were not.

Once we have collected all the photos, we will be ready to start training the model by going through the following steps:

1. Go to `https://customvision.ai`.
2. Log in and create a new project.
3. Give the project a name—in our case, `HotDogOrNot`.

4. Select a resource or create a new one by clicking **create new**. Fill in the dialog box and select **CustomVision.Training** in the **Kind** dropdown.

5. The project type should be **Classification**, and the classification type should be **Multiclass (Single tag per image)**.

6. Select **General (compact)** as the domain. We use a compact domain if we want to export models and run them on a mobile device.

7. Click **Create project** to continue, as shown in the following screenshot:

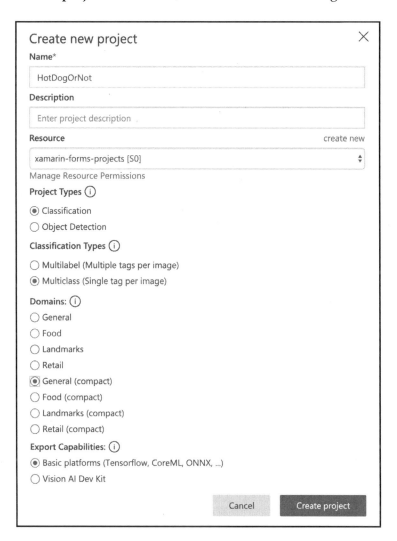

Tagging images

Once we have created a project, we can start to upload images and tag them. The easiest way to get images is to go to Google and search for them. We will start by adding photos of hot dogs by going through the following steps:

1. Click **Add images**.
2. Select the photos of hot dogs that should be uploaded.
3. Tag the photos with `hotdog`, as shown in the following screenshot:

Once we have uploaded all the photos of hot dogs, it's time to upload photos that aren't of hot dogs by going through the following steps. For best results, we should also include photos of objects that look similar to hot dogs but are not. Proceed as follows:

1. Click **Add images**.
2. Select the photos that aren't of hot dogs.
3. Tag the photos with **Negative**. A negative tag is used for photos that don't contain any objects that we have created other tags for. In this case, none of the photos we will upload contain hot dogs, as can be seen in the following screenshot:

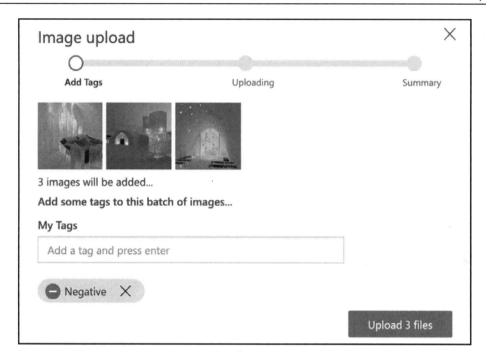

Training a model

Once we have uploaded the photos, it's time to train a model. Not all the photos that we are uploading will be used for training; some will be used for verification, to give us a score about how good the model is. If we upload photos in chunks and train the model after each chunk, we will be able to see our scores improving. To train a model, click the green **Train** button at the top of the page, as illustrated in the following screenshot:

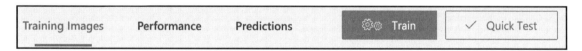

The following screenshot shows the result of a training iteration where the precision of the model is **91.7%**:

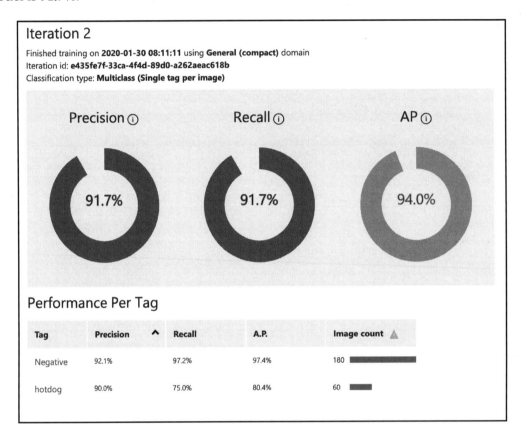

Exporting a model

Once we have trained a model, we will be able to export it so that it can be used on a device. We can use the APIs if we want to, but to make fast classifications and to be able to do this offline, we will add the models to the app packages. Export and download the **CoreML** model and the **TensorFlow** model, as shown in the following screenshot:

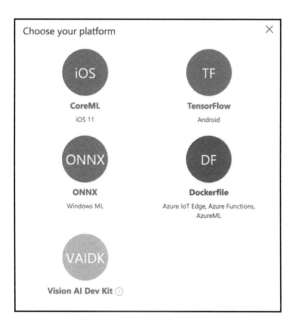

For **TensorFlow**, we can use a different type of model. For this project, we will use **TensorFlow Lite**, as illustrated in the following screenshot:

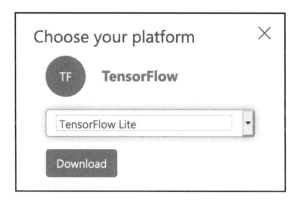

Building the app

Once we have one Core ML model and one TensorFlow model, it's time to build the app. Our app will use the trained models to classify photos according to whether they are photos of hot dogs. The Core ML model that we exported from the Custom Vision service will be used for iOS and the TensorFlow model will be used for Android.

Create a new project with the template for a blank Xamarin.Forms app. Use `HotDotOrNot` as the name of the project.

Before doing anything else, we will update the Xamarin.Forms NuGet package to make sure that we have the latest version of it.

Classifying images with machine learning

The code that we will use for image classification cannot be shared between the iOS and Android projects. However, to be able to carry out classifications from shared code (the `HotDogOrNot` project), we will create an interface. First, however, we will create a class for the `EventArgs` that we will use in the interface, by going through the following steps:

1. In the `HotDogOrNot` project, create a new class called `ClassificationEventArgs`.

2. Add `EventArgs` as a base class, as shown in the following code block:

```
using System;
using System.Collections.Generic;

public class ClassificationEventArgs : EventArgs
{
    public Dictionary<string, float> Classifications { get; private
    set; }

    public ClassificationEventArgs(Dictionary<string, float>
    classifications)
    {
        Classifications = classifications;
    }
}
```

Now that we have created the `ClassificationEventArgs` class, we can create the interface by going through the following steps:

1. In the `HotDogOrNot` project, create a new interface called `IClassifier`.
2. Add a method called `Classify` that doesn't return anything but takes a `byte[]` as an argument.
3. Add an event that uses the `ClassificationEventArgs` class, and call it `ClassificationCompleted`, as shown in the following code block:

```
using System;
using System.Collections.Generic;

public interface IClassifier
{
    void Classify(byte[] bytes);
    event EventHandler<ClassificationEventArgs>
    ClassificationCompleted;
}
```

Using Core ML for image classification

The first thing we will do is add the Core ML model to the `HotDogOrNot.iOS` project, by going through the following steps:

1. Extract the `.zip` file that we got from the Custom Vision service.
2. Find the `.mlmodel` file and rename it as `hotdog-or-not.mlmodel`.
3. Add it to the `Resources` folder in the iOS project.
4. Make sure that the build action is `BundleResource`. If you are using Visual Studio on a Mac, a `.cs` file will be created. Remove this file, because it will be easier to use the model without the code.

When we have added the file to the iOS project, we will be ready to create the iOS implementation of the `IClassifier` interface by going through the following steps:

1. Create a new class called `CoreMLClassifier` in the `HotDogOrNotDog.iOS` project.
2. Add the `IClassifier` interface.
3. Implement the `ClassificationCompleted` event and the `Classify` method from the interface, as shown in the following code block:

```
using System;
using System.Linq;
```

```
using CoreML;
using Foundation;
using ImageIO;
using Vision;
using System.Collections.Generic;

namespace HotDogOrNot.iOS
{
    public class CoreMLClassifier : IClassifier
    {
        public event EventHandler<ClassificationEventArgs>
        ClassificationCompleted;
        public void Classify(byte[] bytes)
        {
            //Code will be added here
        }
    }
}
```

The first thing we will do in the `Classify` method is to compile the Core ML model by going through the following steps:

1. Get the path of the model with the `NSBundle.MainBundle.GetUrlForResource` method.
2. Compile the model with the `MLModel.CompileModel` method. Pass the model's **Uniform Resource Locator (URL)** and an error object that will indicate whether one or more errors occurred during the compilation of the model.
3. Use the URL from the `CompileModel` method and pass it to `MLModel.Create` to create a model object that we can work with, as shown in the following code snippet:

```
var modelUrl = NSBundle.MainBundle.GetUrlForResource("hotdog-or-
not", "mlmodel");
var compiledUrl = MLModel.CompileModel(modelUrl, out var error);
var compiledModel = MLModel.Create(compiledUrl, out error);
```

Because we are going to use a photo for the Core ML model, we can use the Vision APIs that are built on top of the Core ML APIs. To do this, we will use `VNCoreMLRequest`. Before creating the request, however, we will create a callback that will handle when the request is completed, by going through the following steps:

1. Open the `CoreMLClassifier.cs` file.
2. Create a new private method called `HandleVNRequest` with two parameters, one of the `VNRequst` type and one of the `NSError` type.

3. If the error is `null`, invoke the `ClassificationCompleted` event with `ClassificationEventArgs`, which contains an empty `Dictionary`.

4. If the error is not null, get the result with the `GetResults` method on the `VNRequest` object.

5. Order the classifications by `Confidence` so that the classification with the highest confidence is first.

6. Convert the result to a `Dictionary`, using the `ToDictionary` method.

7. Invoke the `ClassificationCompleted` event with `ClassificationEventArgs`, which contains the sorted dictionary. This is shown in the following code block:

```
private void HandleVNRequest(VNRequest request, NSError error)
{
    if (error != null)
    {
    ClassificationCompleted?.Invoke(this, new
    ClassificationEventArgs(new Dictionary<string, float>()));
    }

    var result = request.GetResults<VNClassificationObservation>();
    var classifications = result.OrderByDescending(x =>
    x.Confidence).ToDictionary(x => x.Identifier, x =>
    x.Confidence);

    ClassificationCompleted?.Invoke(this, new
    ClassificationEventArgs(classifications));
}
```

Once we have created the callback, we will go back to the `Classify` method and perform the classification by going through the following steps:

1. Convert the model to a `VNCoreMLModel` object, because we need this to use the Vision APIs. Use the `VNCoreMLModel.FromMLModel` method to convert the model.

2. Create a new `VNCoreMLRequest` object, and pass the `VNCoreMLModel` and the callback we created as arguments to the constructor.

3. Convert the input data to an `NSData` object, using the `NSData.FromArray` method.

4. Create a new `VNImageRequestHandler` object and pass the `CGImagePropertyOrientation.Up` data object and a new `VNImageOptions` object to the constructor.

5. Use the `Perform` method on the `VNImageRequestHandler` object, and pass the `VNCoreMLRequest` object in an array and an error object as an argument, as shown in the following code block:

```
public void Classify(byte[] bytes)
{
    var modelUrl = NSBundle.MainBundle.GetUrlForResource("hotdog-
    or-not", "mlmodel");
    var compiledUrl = MLModel.CompileModel(modelUrl, out
     var error);
    var compiledModel = MLModel.Create(compiledUrl, out error);

    var vnCoreModel = VNCoreMLModel.FromMLModel(compiledModel, out
    error);

    var classificationRequest = new VNCoreMLRequest(vnCoreModel,
    HandleVNRequest);

    var data = NSData.FromArray(bytes);
    var handler = new VNImageRequestHandler(data,
    CGImagePropertyOrientation.Up, new VNImageOptions());

    handler.Perform(new[] { classificationRequest }, out error);
}
```

We have now written the code in iOS to recognize hot dogs.

Using TensorFlow for image classification

It's now time to write the code for Android. The first thing to do is to add the files we exported from the Custom Vision service to the Android project. For TensorFlow, the actual model and the labels (the tags) are separated into two files. Let's set this up by going through the following steps:

1. Extract the `.zip` file that we got from the Custom Vision service.
2. Find the `model.tflite` file and rename it as `hotdog-or-not-model.tflite`.
3. Find the `labels.txt` file and rename it as `hotdog-or-not-labels.txt`.
4. Import the files to the `Assets` folder in the Android project. Make sure that the build action is `AndroidAsset`.

When we have imported the files into the Android project, we can start to write code. To get the libraries we need for TensorFlow, we also need to install a NuGet package by going through the following steps:

1. In the `HotDogOrNotDog.Android` project, install the `Xamarin.Tensorflow.Lite` NuGet package.

2. Then, create a new class called `TensorflowClassifier` in the `HotDogOrNotDog.Android` project.

3. Add the `IClassifier` interface to the `TensorflowClassifier` class.

4. Implement the `ClassificationCompleted` event and the `Classify` method from the interface, as shown in the following code block:

```
using System;
using System.Collections.Generic;
using System.IO;
using System.Linq;
using Android.App;
using Android.Graphics;

public class TensorflowClassifier : IClassifier
{
        public event EventHandler<ClassificationEventArgs>
        ClassificationCompleted;

        public void Classify(byte[] bytes)
        {
            //Code will be added here
        }
}
```

The first thing we will do is to import the TensorFlow Lite model from the **assets** folder and convert it to a `MappedByteBuffer` object. Follow these next steps to create a method that does that:

1. Create a new private method that returns a `MappedByteBuffer` with the name `GetModelAsMappedByteBuffer`.

2. Create an `AssetFileDescriptor` object to a variable with the name `assetDescriptor` using the `Application.Context.Assets.OpenFd` method, and pass the filename of the model as the argument.

3. Create a new `FileInputStream` object and pass `assetDescriptor.FileDescriptor` as an argument to it into a variable with the name `inputStream`.

4. Create a `MappedByteByffer` object into a variable with the name `mappedByteBuffer`, using the `Map` method of the `Channel` property on the `inputStream` variable. Pass `FileChannel.MapMode.ReadOnly`, the value of the `StartOffset` property of the `fileDescriptor` variable, and the value of the `DeclaredLength` property of the `fileDescriptor` variable.

5. Return the `mappedByteBuffer` variable, as illustrated in the following code block:

```
private MappedByteBuffer GetModelAsMappedByteBuffer()
{
    var assetDescriptor =
Application.Context.Assets.OpenFd("hotdog-or-not-model.tflite");
    var inputStream = new
FileInputStream(assetDescriptor.FileDescriptor);

    var mappedByteBuffer =
inputStream.Channel.Map(FileChannel.MapMode.ReadOnly,
assetDescriptor.StartOffset, assetDescriptor.DeclaredLength);

    return mappedByteBuffer;
}
```

Now, when we have the `MappedByteBuffer`, we can create a `Xamarin.TensorFlow.Lite.Interpreter` object that we will use for predictions. But before we can do predictions, we need to determine the size of the images we send to the model. Follow these steps:

1. Use the `GetModelAsMappedByteBuffer` object to create a `MappedByteBuffer` in a variable with the name `mappedByteBuffer`.

2. Create a new `Xamarin.TensorFlow.Lite.Interpreter` and pass the `mappedByteBuffer` variable to it.

3. Get the input tensor by using the `GetInputTensor` method of the `Interpreter`. Pass `0` as an argument to it. Save it in a variable with the name `tensor`.

4. Get the shape from the tensor using the `Shape` method. Save it in a variable with the name `shape`.

5. Create a variable for width and one for height. `width` is at index 1 in the `shape` array, and `height` is at index 2, as illustrated in the following code block:

```
public void Classify(byte[])
{
    var mappedByteBuffer = GetModelAsMappedByteBuffer();
    var interpreter = new
Xamarin.TensorFlow.Lite.Interpreter(mappedByteBuffer);
```

```
var tensor = interpreter.GetInputTensor(0);
var shape = tensor.Shape();

var width = shape[1];
var height = shape[2];
}
```

Now, we will create a private method that converts the input photo to a `ByteBuffer` object so that we can pass it to the `Interpreter` to do predictions. But first, we will add two constants to the class—`FloatSize` with the value 4, because a float value is 4 bytes large, and `PixelSize` with the value 3, because a pixel has the **Red-Green-Blue** (**RGB**) color channels, as illustrated in the following code snippet:

```
public const int FloatSize = 4;
public const int PixelSize = 3;
```

Now, we can continue with the method, as follows:

1. Create a new method that returns a `ByteBuffer` with the name `GetPhotoAsByteBuffer` that has the following parameters: `bytes` (the photo as a byte array), `width` (the width to resize the photo to), and `height` (the height to resize the photo to).
2. First, we need to create a bitmap of the byte array so that we can resize it. We will do it with the `DecodeByteArray` static method of the `BitmapFactory` class.
3. Use the `Bitmap.CreateScaledBitmap` method to resize the image, pass the bitmap from the previous step, and pass the `width` to resize to, the `height` to resize to, and `true` as the last argument.
4. Calculate the size of the `ByteBuffer`, `FontSize` * `height` * `width` * `PixelSize`, and save it in a variable with the name `modelInputSize`.
5. Create the `ByteBuffer` object in a variable with the name `byteBuffer`. Use the `ByteBuffer.AllocateDirect` method and pass the `modelInputSize` variable to do that.
6. Set the order of the `ByteBuffer` to be `NativeOrder`, using the `Order` method of the `ByteBuffer`, and pass `ByteBuffer.NativeOrder()` to it.
7. Next, we will loop through all pixels of the photo to add it to the `ByteBuffer`. First, we will create an `int` array with all pixels of the photo, create a variable with the name `pixels`, and create an `int` array with the size that is equal to the number of pixels in the photo (width * height).
8. Loop through the pixels and pass the pixel values into the `ByteBuffer`, as shown in the code marked in bold in the code block that follows.

9. Recycle the bitmap to free up memory.
10. Return the `byteBuffer` variable.

All of this is illustrated in the following code block:

```
private ByteBuffer GetPhotoAsByteBuffer(byte[] bytes, int width, int
height)
{
    var bitmap = BitmapFactory.DecodeByteArray(bytes, 0, bytes.Length);
    var resizedBitmap = Bitmap.CreateScaledBitmap(bitmap, width, height,
     true);

    var modelInputSize = FloatSize * height * width * PixelSize;

    var byteBuffer = ByteBuffer.AllocateDirect(modelInputSize);
    byteBuffer.Order(ByteOrder.NativeOrder());

    var pixels = new int[width * height];
    resizedBitmap.GetPixels(pixels, 0, resizedBitmap.Width, 0, 0,
     resizedBitmap.Width, resizedBitmap.Height);

    var pixel = 0;

    for (var i = 0; i < width; i++)
    {
        for (var j = 0; j < height; j++)
        {
            var pixelVal = pixels[pixel++];
            byteBuffer.PutFloat(pixelVal'>> 16 & 0xFF);
            byteBuffer.PutFloat(pixelVal >> 8 & 0xFF);
            byteBuffer.PutFloat(pixelVal & 0xFF);
        }
    }

    bitmap.Recycle();

    return byteBuffer;
}
```

Now, when we have prepared the model and the photo, the last thing to prepare is the output object. The input should be a two-dimensional array of floats. The size of the output object will be based on the labels that we exported from the Custom Vision service. Follow these next steps to create an output object:

1. Go to the end of the `Classify` method.
2. Read the labels from the `hotdog-or-not-labels.txt` file with the `StreamReader` class. Use the `Application.Context.Assets.Open` method to open the file and pass it to the constructor of a `StreamReader` object.
3. Read the file to the end with the `ReadToEnd` method, and create a list of labels from it (`List<string>`). Split the text from the file based on new rows, and use `Linq` to filter it from empty values and convert it to a `List<string>` object. Don't forget to trim each item.
4. Create the two-dimensional float array, as in the first bold row in the code block that follows.
5. Because the `Interpreter` requires the output object to be a `Java.Lang.Object` object, we need to convert it to that type. We will do this with the `Java.Lang.Object.FromArray` method, as illustrated in the following code block:

```
var sr = new StreamReader(Application.Context.Assets.Open("hotdog-
or-not-labels.txt"));
var labels = sr.ReadToEnd().Split('\n').Select(s =>
s.Trim()).Where(s => !string.IsNullOrEmpty(s)).ToList();

var outputLocations = new float[1][] { new float[labels.Count] };
var outputs = Java.Lang.Object.FromArray(outputLocations);
```

Now, everything is ready to run the prediction with the `Interpreter`. Follow these next steps to run the prediction and handle the result:

1. Get the photo as a `ByteBuffer` using the `GetPhotoAsByteBuffer` method that we created earlier. Save it in a variable with the name `byteBuffer`.
2. Run the prediction with the `Run` method of the `Interpreter`, passing the `byteBuffer` and `output` variables to it.
3. Now, we have the result in the `output` variable. To use it, convert it back to a two-dimensional float array, using the `ToArray` method.
4. Create a new `Dictionary<string, float>` for the result, and name the variable `result`.

5. Loop through the `labels` list and map the result to a label, as shown in bold in the code block that follows.

6. Invoke the `ClassificationCompleted` method and pass the pass the instance of the `TensorFlowClassifier` using the `this` keyword, and a new `ClassificationEventArgs` object to it. Pass the `result` variable to the constructor of the `ClassificationEventArgs` class, as illustrated in the following code block:

```
var byteBuffer = GetPhotoAsByteBuffer(bytes, width, height);

interpreter.Run(byteBuffer, outputs);

var predictionResult = outputs.ToArray<float[]>();

var result = new Dictionary<string, float>();

for (var i = 0; i < labels.Count; i++)
{
    var label = labels[i];
    result.Add(label, predictionResult[0][i]);
}

ClassificationCompleted?.Invoke(this, new
ClassificationEventArgs(result));
```

Creating a base ViewModel class

Before we initialize the app, we will create a base `ViewModel` class so that we can use it when we are registering the other `ViewModel` instances. In this, we will put the code that can be shared between all the `ViewModel` instances of the app. Let's set this up by going through the following steps:

1. In the `HotDogOrNot` project, create a new folder called `ViewModels`.

2. Create a new class called `ViewModel` in the `ViewModels` folder we created.

3. Make the class public and abstract.

4. Add and implement the `INotifiedPropertyChanged` interface. This is necessary because we want to use data bindings.

5. Add a `Set` method that will make it easier for us to raise the `PropertyChanged` event from the `INotifiedPropertyChanged` interface. The method will check whether the value has changed. If it has, it will raise the event.

6. Add a static property of the `INavigation` type called `Navigation`, as shown in the following code block:

```
using System;
using System.Collections.Generic;
using System.ComponentModel;
using System.Runtime.CompilerServices;
using Xamarin.Forms;

namespace HotDogOrNot
{
    public abstract class ViewModel : INotifyPropertyChanged
    {
        public event PropertyChangedEventHandler PropertyChanged;
        protected void Set<T>(ref T field, T newValue,
        [CallerMemberName] string propertyName = null)
        {
            if (!EqualityComparer<T>.Default.Equals(field,
                newValue))
            {
                field = newValue;
                PropertyChanged?.Invoke(this, new
                PropertyChangedEventArgs(propertyName));
            }
        }

        public static INavigation Navigation { get; set; }
    }
}
```

Initializing the app

We are now ready to write the initialization code for the app. We will set up **inversion of control (IoC)**, creating a `Resolver` class and a bootstrapper that will be used to handle the initial configuration of the app.

Creating a Resolver class

We will now create a helper class that will ease the process of resolving object graphs through Autofac. This will help us to create types based on a configured IoC container. In this project, we will use Autofac as the IoC library by going through the following steps:

1. In the HotDogOrNot project, install the Autofac NuGet package to the HotDogOrNot project.

2. Create a new class called Resolver in the root.

3. Add a private static field of the IContainer type called container (from Autofac).

4. Add a public static method called Initialize with IContainer as a parameter. Set the value of the parameter to the container field.

5. Add a generic public static method called Resolve, which will return an instance that is based on the type argument with the Resolve method of IContainer, as shown in the following code block:

```
using System;
using Autofac;

namespace HotDogOrNot
{
    public class Resolver
    {
        private static IContainer container;

        public static void Initialize(IContainer container)
        {
            Resolver.container = container;
        }

        public static T Resolve<T>()
        {
            return container.Resolve<T>();
        }
    }
}
```

Creating a bootstrapper

To configure the dependency injection and initialize the `Resolver` class, we will create a bootstrapper. We will have one shared bootstrapper and one bootstrapper for each platform, to match their specific configurations. We will have different implementations of the `IClassifier` object in iOS and Android. To create a bootstrapper, go through the following steps:

1. Create a new class in the `HotDogOrNot` project and name it `Bootstrapper`.
2. Write the following code in the new class:

```
using System.Linq;
using System.Reflection;
using Autofac;
using HotdogOrNot.ViewModels;
using Xamarin.Forms;
namespace HotDogOrNot
{
    public class Bootstrapper
    {
        protected ContainerBuilder ContainerBuilder { get; private
        set; }

        public Bootstrapper()
        {
            Initialize();
            FinishInitialization();
        }

        protected virtual void Initialize()
        {
            ContainerBuilder = new ContainerBuilder();

            var currentAssembly = Assembly.GetExecutingAssembly();

            foreach (var type in
            currentAssembly.DefinedTypes.Where(e =>
            e.IsSubclassOf(typeof(Page))))
            {
                ContainerBuilder.RegisterType(type.AsType());
            }

            foreach (var type in
            currentAssembly.DefinedTypes.Where(e =>
            e.IsSubclassOf(typeof(ViewModel))))
            {
                ContainerBuilder.RegisterType(type.AsType());
```

```
                }
            }

            private void FinishInitialization()
            {
                var container = ContainerBuilder.Build();

                Resolver.Initialize(container);
            }
        }
    }
```

Creating the iOS bootstrapper

In the iOS bootstrapper, we will have configurations that are specific to the iOS app. To create an iOS app, we will go through the following steps:

1. In the `HotDogOrNot.iOS` project, create a new class and name it `Bootstrapper`.

2. Make the new class inherit from `HotDogOrNot.Bootstrapper`.

3. Write the following code and resolve all the references:

```
using System;
using Autofac;

public class Bootstrapper : HotdogOrNot.Bootstrapper
{
    public static void Init()
    {
        var instance = new Bootstrapper();
    }

    protected override void Initialize()
    {
        base.Initialize();

        ContainerBuilder.RegisterType<CoreMLClassifier>
        ().As<IClassifier>();
    }
}
```

4. Go to `AppDelegate.cs` in the iOS project.

5. Before the call to `LoadApplication`, in the `FinishedLaunching` method, call the `Init` method of the platform-specific bootstrapper, as shown in the following code block:

```
public override bool FinishedLaunching(UIApplication app,
NSDictionary options)
{
        global::Xamarin.Forms.Forms.Init();
        Bootstrapper.Init();

        LoadApplication(new App());

        return base.FinishedLaunching(app, options);
}
```

Creating the Android bootstrapper

In the Android bootstrapper, we will have configurations that are specific to the Android app. To create a bootstrapper in Android, we will go through the following steps:

1. In the Android project, create a new class and name it `Bootstrapper`.
2. Make the new class inherit from `HotDogOrNot.Bootstrapper`.
3. Write the following code and resolve all the references:

```
using System;
using Autofac;

public class Bootstrapper : HotDogOrNot.Bootstrapper
{
        public static void Init()
        {
            var instance = new Bootstrapper();
        }

        protected override void Initialize()
        {
            base.Initialize();

            ContainerBuilder.RegisterType<TensorflowClassifier>
            ().As<IClassifier>().SingleInstance();
        }
}
```

4. Go to the `MainActivity.cs` file in the Android project.

5. Before the call to `LoadApplication`, in the `OnCreate` method, call the `Execute` method of the platform-specific bootstrapper, as shown in the following code block:

```
protected override void OnCreate(Bundle savedInstanceState)
{
        TabLayoutResource = Resource.Layout.Tabbar;
        ToolbarResource = Resource.Layout.Toolbar;

        base.OnCreate(savedInstanceState);
        global::Xamarin.Forms.Forms.Init(this, savedInstanceState);

        Bootstrapper.Init();

        LoadApplication(new App());
}
```

Building the first view

The first view in this app will be a simple view with two buttons. One button will be for starting the camera so that the users can take a photo of something to determine whether it is a hot dog. The other button will be for picking a photo from the photo library of the device.

Building the ViewModel class

We will start by creating the `ViewModel` class, which will handle what will happen when a user taps one of the buttons. Let's set this up by going through the following steps:

1. Create a new class called `MainViewModel` in the `ViewModels` folder.
2. Add `ViewModel` as a base class for `MainViewModel`.
3. Create a private field of the `IClassifier` type and call it `classifier`.
4. Create a constructor that has the `IClassifier` as a parameter.
5. Set the value of the `classifier` field to the value of the parameter in the constructor, as shown in the following code block:

```
using System.IO;
using System.Linq;
using System.Windows.Input;
using HotdogOrNot.Models;
using HotdogOrNot.Views;
using Xamarin.Forms;
```

```
public class MainViewModel : ViewModel
{
    private IClassifier classifier;

    public MainViewModel(IClassifier classifier)
    {
        this.classifier = classifier;
    }
}
```

We will use the `Xam.Plugin.Media` NuGet package for taking the photo and accessing the photo library of the device. We need to install the package for all projects in the solution by using the NuGet package manager. Before we can use the package, however, we need to do some configuration for each platform. We will start with Android. Let's set this up by going through the following steps:

1. The plugin needs the `WRITE_EXTERNAL_STORAGE` and `READ_EXTERNAL_STORAGE` permissions. The plugin will add these for us, but we need to override the `OnRequestPermissionResult` method in the `MainActivity.cs` class.
2. Call the `OnRequestPermissionsResult` method, as shown in the code block that follows.
3. Add `CrossCurrentActivity.Current.Init(this, savedInstanceState)` after initializing Xamarin.Forms in the `OnCreate` method in the `MainActivity.cs` file, as shown in the following code block:

```
public override void OnRequestPermissionsResult(int requestCode,
string[] permissions, Android.Content.PM.Permission[] grantResults)
{
Xamarin.Essentials.Platform.OnRequestPermissionsResult(requestCode,
permissions, grantResults);
}
```

We also need to add some configuration about the file paths from which users can pick photos. This is because the user needs to grant permission for us to use them. Let's set this up by going through the following steps:

1. In the `HotDogOrNot.Android` project, add a folder called `xml` to the `Resources` folder.
2. Create a new **Extensible Markup Language (XML)** file called `file_paths.xml` in the new folder.

3. Add the following code to `file_paths.xml`:

```xml
<?xml version="1.0" encoding="utf-8"?>
<paths xmlns:android="http://schemas.android.com/apk/res/android">
    <external-files-path name="my_images" path="Pictures" />
    <external-files-path name="my_movies" path="Movies" />
</paths>
```

The last thing we need to do to set up the plugin for the Android project is to add the code in the `AndroidManifest.xml` file (this can be found in the `Properties` folder of the Android project) inside the application element, as follows:

```xml
<manifest xmlns:android="http://schemas.android.com/apk/res/android"
  android:versionCode="1" android:versionName="1.0"
  package="xfb.HotdogOrNot">
    <uses-sdk android:minSdkVersion="21" android:targetSdkVersion="27"
    />
    <application android:label="HotdogOrNot.Android">
    <provider android:name="android.support.v4.content.FileProvider"
    android:authorities="${applicationId}.fileprovider"
    android:exported="false" android:grantUriPermissions="true">
    <meta-data android:name="android.support.FILE_PROVIDER_PATHS"
    android:resource="@xml/file_paths"></meta-data>
    </provider>
    </application>
</manifest>
```

For the iOS project, the only thing we need to do is add the following four usage descriptions to the `info.plist` file:

```xml
<key>NSCameraUsageDescription</key>
<string>This app needs access to the camera to take photos.</string>
<key>NSPhotoLibraryUsageDescription</key>
<string>This app needs access to photos.</string>
<key>NSMicrophoneUsageDescription</key>
<string>This app needs access to microphone.</string>
<key>NSPhotoLibraryAddUsageDescription</key>
<string>This app needs access to the photo gallery.</string>
```

Once we have finished with the configuration for the plugin, we can start using it. We will start by creating a method that will handle the media file that we will get both when the user is taking a photo and when the user is picking a photo.

Let's set this up by going through the following steps:

1. Open the `MainViewModel.cs` file.
2. Create a private method called `HandlePhoto` that has a parameter of the `MediaFile` type.
3. Add an `if` statement to check whether the `MediaFile` parameter is `null`. If so, perform an empty return.
4. Get the stream of the photo using the `GetStream` method of the `MediaFile` class.
5. Add a private field of the `byte []` type called `bytes`.
6. Convert the stream into a byte array with the `ReadFully` method that we will create in the next step.
7. Add an event handler to the `ClassificationCompleted` event of the classifier. We will create the event handler later in this chapter.
8. Finally, add a call to the `Classify` method of the classifier and use the byte array as the argument, as shown in the following code block:

```
private void HandlePhoto(MediaFile photo)
{
    if(photo == null)
    {
        return;
    }

    var stream = photo.GetStream();
    bytes = ReadFully(stream);

    classifier.ClassificationCompleted +=
    Classifier_ClassificationCompleted;
    classifier.Classify(bytes);
}
```

We will now create the `ReadFully` method that we called in the preceding code. We will use this to read the full stream into a byte array. The code will look like this:

```
private byte[] ReadFully(Stream input)
{
    using (MemoryStream memoryStream = new MemoryStream())
    {
        using (MemoryStream memoryStream = new MemoryStream())
        {
            input.CopyTo(memoryStream);

            return memoryStream.ToArray();
```

```
            }
        }

    }
```

Before we create the event handler, we will create a model that we will use inside the event handler by going through the following steps:

1. In the `HotDogOrNot` project, create a new folder called `Models`.
2. Create a new class called `Result` in the `Models` folder.
3. Add a property of the `bool` type, called `IsHotdog`.
4. Add a property of the `float` type, called `Confidence`.
5. Add a property of the `byte[]` type, called `PhotoBytes`, as shown in the following code block:

```
public class Result
{
    public bool IsHotdog { get; set; }
    public float Confidence { get; set; }
    public byte[] PhotoBytes { get; set; }
}
```

We can now add an event handler to the `ViewModel` class by going through the following steps:

1. Create a method called `Classifier_ClassificationCompleted` that has an `object` parameter and a `ClassificationEventArgs` parameter.
2. Remove the event handler from the classifier so that we don't allocate unnecessary memory.
3. Check whether the `Classifications` dictionary contains any items. If it does, order the dictionary so that the classifications with the highest confidence values will be first.
4. Create a new `Result` object and set the properties, as shown in the following code block:

```
void Classifier_ClassificationCompleted(object sender,
ClassificationEventArgs e)
{
    classifier.ClassificationCompleted -=
    Classifier_ClassificationCompleted;

    Result result = null;

    if (e.Classifications.Any())
```

```
{
    var classificationResult =
    e.Classifications.OrderByDescending(x => x.Value).First();

    result = new Result()
    {
        IsHotdog = classificationResult.Key == "hotdog",
        Confidence = classificationResult.Value,
        PhotoBytes = bytes
    };
}
else
{
    result = new Result()
    {
        IsHotDog = false,
        Confidence = 1.0f,
        PhotoBytes = bytes
    };
}
}
```

When we have created the result view, we will go back to the event handler to add the navigation to this view. The last thing we will do in this `ViewModel` class is to create a `Command` property for the buttons that we have in the view to handle what should happen when the user taps them. Let's start by setting up the **Take photo** button, by going through the following steps:

1. Create a new property of the `ICommand` type, called `TakePhoto`, in the `MainViewModel.cs` file.
2. Use an expression to return a new `Command`.
3. Pass an `Action` as an expression to the constructor of the `Command`.
4. In the `Action`, use the `CrossMedia.Current.TakePhotoAsync` method and pass a `StoreCameraMediaOptions` object to it.
5. In `StoreCameraMediaOptions`, set the default camera as the rear camera, using the `DefaultCamera` property.
6. Pass the result of the call to the `TakePhotoAsync` method to the `HandlePhoto` method, as shown in the following code block:

```
public ICommand TakePhoto => new Command(async() =>
{
    var photo = await CrossMedia.Current.TakePhotoAsync(new
    StoreCameraMediaOptions()
    {
```

```
            DefaultCamera = CameraDevice.Rear
        });

    HandlePhoto(photo);
});
```

The final thing we will do in the `MainViewModel` for now is to handle what happens when the **pick photo from library** button is tapped. Let's set this up by going through the following steps:

1. Create a new property of the `ICommand` type, called `PickPhoto`.
2. Use an expression to return a new `Command`.
3. Pass an `Action` as an expression to the constructor of the `Command`.
4. In the `Action`, use the `CrossMedia.Current.PickPhotoAsync` method to open the default photo picker of the operating system.
5. Pass the result of the call to the `TakePhotoAsync` method of the `HandlePhoto` method, as shown in the following code block:

```
public ICommand PickPhoto => new Command(async () =>
{
    var photo = await CrossMedia.Current.PickPhotoAsync();

    HandlePhoto(photo);
});
```

Building the view

Now, once we have created the `ViewModel` class, it is time to create the code for the **graphical user interface (GUI)**. Go through the following steps to create the GUI for the `MainView` view:

1. Create a new folder called `Views` in the `HotDogOrNot` project.
2. Add a new **XAML ContentPage** called `MainView`.
3. Set the `Title` property of the `ContentPage` to `Hotdog or Not hotdog`.
4. Add a `StackLayout` to the page, and set its `VerticalOptions` property to `Center`.
5. Add a `Button` to the `StackLayout`, with the text `Take Photo`. For the `Command` property, add a binding to the `TakePhoto` property in the `ViewModel` class.

6. Add a `Button` to the `StackLayout`, with the text `Pick Photo`. For the `Command` property, add a binding to the `Pick Photo` property in the `ViewModel` class, as shown in the following code block:

```
<ContentPage xmlns="http://xamarin.com/schemas/2014/forms"
             xmlns:x="http://schemas.microsoft.com/winfx/2009/xaml"
             x:Class="HotDogOrNot.Views.MainView"
             Title="Hot dog or Not hot dog">
    <ContentPage.Content>
        <StackLayout VerticalOptions="Center">
            <Button Text="Take Photo" Command="{Binding TakePhoto}" />
            <Button Text="Pick Photo" Command="{Binding PickPhoto}" />
        </StackLayout>
    </ContentPage.Content>
</ContentPage>
```

In the code-behind, `MainView.xaml.cs` file, we will set the binding context of the view by going through the following steps:

1. Add `MainViewModel` as a parameter of the constructor.
2. After the `InitialComponent` method call, set the `BindingContext` property of the view to the `MainViewModel` parameter.
3. Use the `SetBackButtonTitle` static method on the `NavigationPage` class so that an arrow for navigation back to this view will be shown in the navigation bar on the result view, as shown in the following code block:

```
public MainView(MainViewModel viewModel)
{
    InitializeComponent();

    BindingContext = viewModel;
    NavigationPage.SetBackButtonTitle(this, string.Empty);
}
```

Now, we can go to `App.xaml.cs` and set the `MainPage` to `MainView` by going through the following steps:

1. In the `HotDogOrNot` project, go to `App.xaml.cs`.
2. Create an instance of `MainView` using the `Resolve` method on the `Resolver` class.
3. Create a `NavigationPage` object and pass the `MainView` to the constructor.
4. Set the static `Navigation` property on the `ViewModel` to the value of the `Navigation` property on the `NavigationPage`.

5. Set the `MainPage` property to the instance of the `NavigationPage` that we created in *Step 3*.

6. Delete `MainPage.xaml` because we no longer need it. You should be left with the following code:

```
public App()
{
    InitializeComponent();

    var mainView = Resolver.Resolve<MainView>();
    var navigationPage = new NavigationPage(mainView);

    ViewModel.Navigation = navigationPage.Navigation;

    MainPage = navigationPage;
}
```

Building the result view

The last thing we need to do in this project is to create the result view. This view will show the input photo, and whether or not it is a hot dog.

Building the ViewModel class

Before we create the view, we will create a `ViewModel` class that will handle all the logic for the view, by going through the following steps:

1. Create a class called `ResultViewModel` in the `ViewModels` folder in the `HotdogOrNot` project.

2. Add `ViewModel` as a base class to the `ResultViewModel` class.

3. Create a property of the `string` type, called `Title`. Add a private field for the property.

4. Create a property of the `string` type, called `Description`. Add a private field for the property.

5. Create a property of the `byte[]` type, called `PhotoBytes`. Add a private field for the property, as shown in the following code block:

```
using HotdogOrNot.Models;

namespace HotDogOrNot.ViewModels
{
    public class ResultViewModel : ViewModel
```

```
    {
        private string title;
        public string Title
        {
            get => title;
            set => Set(ref title, value);
        }

        private string description;
        public string Description
        {
            get => description;
            set => Set(ref description, value);
        }

        private byte[] photoBytes;
        public byte[] PhotoBytes
        {
            get => photoBytes;
            set => Set(ref photoBytes, value);
        }
    }
}
```

The final thing we will do in the ViewModel is to create an Initialize method that will have the result as a parameter. Let's set this up by going through the following steps:

1. In the Initialize method, set the PhotoBytes property to the value of the PhotoBytes property of the result parameter.

2. Add an if statement that checks whether the IsHotDog property of the result parameter is true and whether the Confidence is higher than 90%. If this is the case, set the Title to "Hot dog" and the Description to "This is for sure a hotdog".

3. Add an else if statement to check whether the IsHotdog property of the result parameter is true. If this is the case, set the Title to "Maybe" and the Description to "This is maybe a hotdog".

4. Add an else statement that sets the Title to "Not a hot dog" and the Description to "This is not a hot dog", as shown in the following code block:

```
public void Initialize(Result result)
{
    PhotoBytes = result.PhotoBytes;

    if (result.IsHotdog && result.Confidence > 0.9)
```

```
    {
        Title = "Hot dog";
        Description = "This is for sure a hot dog";
    }
    else if (result.IsHotdog)
    {
        Title = "Maybe";
        Description = "This is maybe a hot dog";
    }
    else
    {
        Title = "Not a hot dog";
        Description = "This is not a hot dog";
    }
}
```

Building the view

Because we want to show the input photo in the input view, we need to convert it from `byte[]` to `Xamarin.Forms.ImageSource`. We will do this in a value converter that we can use together with the binding in the **XAML** by going through the following steps:

1. Create a new folder called `Converters` in the `HotDogOrNot` project.

2. Create a new class called `BytesToImageConverter`.

3. Add and implement the `IValueConverter` interface, as shown in the following code block:

```
using System;
using System.Globalization;
using System.IO;
using Xamarin.Forms;
public class BytesToImageConverter : IValueConverter
{
    public object Convert(object value, Type targetType, object
    parameter, CultureInfo culture)
    {
        throw new NotImplementedException();
    }

    public object ConvertBack(object value, Type targetType, object
    parameter, CultureInfo culture)
    {
        throw new NotImplementedException();
    }
}
```

The `Convert` method will be used when a `ViewModel` updates a view. The `ConvertBack` method will be used in two-way bindings when the `View` updates the `ViewModel`. In this case, we only need to write code for the `Convert` method by going through the following steps:

1. First, check whether the `value` parameter is `null`. If so, we should return `null`.
2. If the value is not `null`, cast it as `byte[]`.
3. Create a `MemoryStream` object from the byte array.
4. Return the result of the `ImageSource.FromStream` method to which we will pass the stream, as shown in the following code block:

```
public object Convert(object value, Type targetType, object
parameter, CultureInfo culture)
{
    if(value == null)
    {
        return null;
    }
    var bytes = (byte[])value;
    var stream = new MemoryStream(bytes);

    return ImageSource.FromStream(() => stream);
}
```

The view will contain the photo, which will take up two thirds of the screen. Under the photo, we will add a description of the result. Let's set this up by going through the following steps:

1. In the `Views` folder, create a new **XAML ContentPage** and name it `ResultView`.
2. Import the namespace for the converter.
3. Add the `BytesToImageConverter` to the `Resources` for the page and give it the `"ToImage"` key.
4. Bind the `Title` property of the `ContentPage` to the `Title` property of the `ViewModel`.
5. Add a `Grid` to the page with two rows. The `Height` value for the first `RowDefinition` should be `2*`. The height of the second row should be `*`. These are relative values that mean that the first row will take up two thirds of the `Grid`, while the second row will take up one third of the `Grid`.
6. Add an `Image` to the `Grid` and bind the `Source` property to the `PhotoBytes` property in the `ViewModel`. Use the converter to convert the bytes to an `ImageSource` object and set the `Source` property.

7. Add a `Label` and bind the `Text` property to the `Description` property of the `ViewModel`, as shown in the following code block:

```
<ContentPage xmlns="http://xamarin.com/schemas/2014/forms"
             xmlns:x="http://schemas.microsoft.com/winfx/2009/xaml"
             xmlns:converters="clr-
namespace:HotdogOrNot.Converters"
             x:Class="HotdogOrNot.Views.ResultView"
             Title="{Binding Title}">
<ContentPage.Resources>
        <converters:BytesToImageConverter x:Key="ToImage" />
</ContentPage.Resources>
    <Grid>
        <Grid.RowDefinitions>
            <RowDefinition Height="2*" />
            <RowDefinition Height="*" />
        </Grid.RowDefinitions>

        <Image Source="{Binding PhotoBytes, Converter=
{StaticResource ToImage}}" Aspect="AspectFill" />
        <Label Grid.Row="1" HorizontalOptions="Center"
        FontAttributes="Bold" Margin="10" Text="{Binding
        Description}" />
    </Grid>
</ContentPage>
```

We also need to set the `BindingContext` of the view. We will do this in the same way as we did in the `MainView`—in the code-behind file (`ResultView.xaml.cs`), as shown in the following code snippet:

```
public ResultView (ResultViewModel viewModel)
{
    InitializeComponent ();
    BindingContext = viewModel;
}
```

The very last thing we need to do is add navigation from the `MainView` to the `ResultView`. We will do this by adding the following code at the end of the `Classifier_ClassificationCompleted` method in the `MainViewModel`:

```
var view = Resolver.Resolve<ResultView>();
((ResultViewModel)view.BindingContext).Initialize(result);

Navigation.PushAsync(view);
```

Now, we are ready to run the app. If we use the simulator/emulator, we can just drag and drop photos to it if we need photos to test with. When the app has started, we can now pick a photo and run it against the model. The following screenshot shows how the app will look if we upload a photo of a hot dog:

 Note: The prediction result for Android is not as accurate as compared to iOS and the web portal, `https://github.com/Azure-Samples/cognitive-services-android-customvision-sample/issues/12`. As it is not accurate for exported model and we recommend to use the rest apis to get a better result.

You can also check out my other app with same code as an exercise: `https://github.com/dhindrik/MushroomDetector`

Summary

In this chapter, we built an app that can recognize whether or not a photo contains a hot dog. We accomplished this by training a machine learning model for image classification using Azure Cognitive Services and the Custom Vision service.

We exported models for Core ML and TensorFlow, and we learned how to use them in apps for both iOS and Android. In these apps, a user can take a photo or pick a photo from their photo library. This photo will be sent to the model to be classified, and we will get a result that tells us whether or not the photo is of a hot dog.

Now, we can continue to build other apps and use what we have learned in this chapter regarding machine learning, both on-device and in the cloud using Azure Cognitive Services. Even if we are building other apps, the concept will be the same.

Now, we have completed all chapters in this book. We have learned the following:

- What Xamarin is and how we can get started building apps
- How to use the basic layouts and controls of Xamarin.Forms
- How to work with navigation
- How to make the user experience better with animations
- How to use sensors such as the **Global Positioning System** (**GPS**) in the background
- How to build apps for multiple form factors
- How to build real-time apps powered by Azure
- How to build an **augmented reality** (**AR**) app using Xamarin
- How to make apps smarter with machine learning

The next step is to start to build your own apps. To stay up to date and learn more about Xamarin, our recommendation is to read the official Microsoft dev blogs, watch live streams on Twitch, and YouTube videos from the Xamarin team.

Thank you for reading the book!

Other Books You May Enjoy

If you enjoyed this book, you may be interested in these other books by Packt:

Mastering Xamarin.Forms - Third Edition
Ed Snider

ISBN: 978-1-83921-338-0

- Find out how, when, and why to use architecture patterns and best practices with Xamarin.Forms
- Implement the Model-View-ViewModel (MVVM) pattern and data binding in Xamarin.Forms mobile apps
- Incorporate client-side validation in Xamarin.Forms mobile apps
- Extend the Xamarin.Forms navigation API with a custom ViewModel-centric navigation service
- Leverage the inversion of control and dependency injection patterns in Xamarin.Forms mobile apps
- Work with online and offline data in Xamarin.Forms mobile apps
- Use platform-specific APIs to build rich custom user interfaces in Xamarin.Forms mobile apps
- Explore how to monitor mobile app quality using Visual Studio App Center

Hands-On Mobile Development with .NET Core
Can Bilgin

ISBN: 978-1-78953-851-9

- Implement native applications for multiple mobile and desktop platforms
- Understand and use various Azure Services with .NET Core
- Make use of architectural patterns designed for mobile and web applications
- Understand the basic Cosmos DB concepts
- Understand how different app models can be used to create an app service
- Explore the Xamarin and Xamarin.Forms UI suite with .NET Core for building mobile applications

Leave a review - let other readers know what you think

Please share your thoughts on this book with others by leaving a review on the site that you bought it from. If you purchased the book from Amazon, please leave us an honest review on this book's Amazon page. This is vital so that other potential readers can see and use your unbiased opinion to make purchasing decisions, we can understand what our customers think about our products, and our authors can see your feedback on the title that they have worked with Packt to create. It will only take a few minutes of your time, but is valuable to other potential customers, our authors, and Packt. Thank you!

Index

X

Printed in Great Britain
by Amazon